DRUGS IN
AMERICAN SOCIETY

Drugs in American Society

THIRD EDITION

Erich Goode
State University of New York,
Stony Brook

ALFRED A. KNOPF New York

For Si

This is a Borzoi Book published by Alfred A. Knopf, Inc.

Third Edition
987654321
Copyright © 1972, 1984, 1989 by Alfred A. Knopf, Inc.

Library of Congress Cataloging in Publication Data

Goode, Erich.
  Drugs in American society.

  Bibliography: p.
  Includes index.
  1. Drug abuse—United States. 2. Drugs—United
States. I. Title.
HV5825.G63 1988   362.2′9   88–13594
ISBN 0–394–38294–3

Cover design: Karin Batten

Manufactured in the United States of America

ACKNOWLEDGMENTS: The accounts that appear at the end of Chapters 5, 6, 7, 8, 9, and 10 are published with the permission of their contributors. The author would like to express gratitude for their permission to publish this material.

PREFACE

The changes that have taken place in the world of drug use since the publication of the previous edition of this book (1984) have been massive, perhaps even more so than for the period between the first (1972) and the second editions. Consequently, I found that a thorough revision and updating of *Drugs in American Society* was necessary. As with the second edition, more of this edition's pages are completely new than were carried over from the previous edition, even in rewritten form. The drug world has changed, public attitudes toward drug use have changed, I have changed, and far more information now exists concerning drug use.

A number of subjects that were barely in evidence in the early 1980s (when the previous revision was undertaken) or did not seem crucial enough to merit a discussion, now seem to me to be so important that they cannot be ignored. They include: the connection between intravenous drug use and acquired immunity deficiency syndrome (AIDS); the use of "crack"; mandatory drug testing; the failure of the British system of maintaining addicts on narcotics; the decline in new recruits to narcotic use and addiction in the United States; the growing internationalization of drug smuggling into the United States; the appearance of and growth in the use of "designer" drugs, including "ecstasy" (MDMA) and fentanyl, a narcotic; the divergence of lower- and middle-class patterns of drug use; the irrelevance of the distinction between physical addiction and psychological and behavioral dependence; the massive rise in cocaine abuse and dependence; the growing awareness in the study of drug use of controlled narcotics use; and the growing "hard line" toward illegal drug use ("zero tolerance"). In short, the world of drug use has changed drastically in the past half-dozen or so years.

Perhaps the most momentous of these changes has been the emergence of a "moral panic" in the United States about illicit drugs: the dramatic rise of public concern about the danger of drug use and what to do about it. The number of articles published in newspapers and popular magazines more than tripled between the middle and the late 1980s. Television news stories about drug arrests, seizures, and drug-related homicides have multiplied many times over. TV and newspaper propaganda advising the public not to take drugs appear with daily regularity. Organizations designed to combat drug abuse—usually with mere words—have cropped up like mushrooms after a spring rain. The position of drug abuse on the American public's list of "most serious" social problems has marched steadily upward during the past half-dozen years. In 1988, a New York Times/CBS poll reported that 16 percent of the respondents questioned said that drugs was the most important issue facing the nation today—and no other concern was ranked as highly. The subject of drug abuse and what to do about it has assumed major importance in the speeches of politicians and other notables. In 1988, President Ronald Reagan stated at the graduating ceremony of the Coast Guard Academy that drugs are "the foremost concern in our country." In a recent poll, the American public was asked whether the "most important international problem" was stopping drugs or stopping communism. More than six respondents in ten (63 percent) said stopping drugs, while only one-fifth (21 percent) said stopping communism. According to Senator Christopher Dodd (D-Conn.), in the late 1980s, politicians engaged in a "feeding frenzy" to assure their constituents that they are concerned with the drug issue. "Things are getting a little crazy out there," added Dodd. In short, from the point of view of public concern, drug use has become a social problem of the highest magnitude—indeed, perhaps *the* social problem of central importance for the 1980s and the 1990s as well. That all of this has taken place in a period during which the actual use of drugs has declined is remarkable.

It is a central thesis of this book that conventional anti-drug thinking cannot hope to understand the reality of the drug world. Once you build an argument on the simple "drugs are bad, don't use drugs" message, you are forced to bend and twist evidence to fit that simplistic point of view. Moralistic thinking assumes that there is something that is unique and completely different about illegal drug use that is not shared by phenomena in the conventional world. Illegal drugs possess no magical intrinsic quality that is not also shared by legal drugs—indeed, by many ordinary, everyday entities, phenomena, substances, and activities as well. "Drugs can kill" says the anti-drug propagandist—a true but obvious statement. And so can alcohol, a drug, and tobacco, which contains at least one major drug. So can cars, boats, motorcycles, boxing, sky-diving, scuba diving, and shoveling the snow from one's driveway in the wintertime. They all kill—some people, some of the time, under certain conditions. Like a number of other activities, taking illicit drugs to get high entails a certain risk.

The 1980s will be remembered for some of the silliest utterances ever made on the subject of drug use. A number of them originated with the First Lady, Nancy Reagan. In 1986, Mrs. Reagan was quoted as saying: "Drug use is a repudiation of everything America is." Within months of this statement, the American Tobacco Institute issued a lavish, expensively produced pamphlet on tobacco, a substance which, the title of the pamphlet declared, is "deeply rooted in America's heritage." And, as we see in this volume, alcohol has a distinguished history in America: The Indians made alcoholic beverages before Columbus arrived on these shores, and the Puritans brought more beer to this continent than drinking water. Even if we pretend that alcohol and tobacco are not drugs, it is clear that the American government has supported regimes abroad that have been involved, directly or indirectly, in the drug trade. The major source of income of the Afghan rebels has been the cultivation and sale of opium, and the U.S.-supported "contra" rebels have been involved in the sale of marijuana and cocaine for several years. Nearly 20 million Americans use marijuana regularly; cocaine attracts nearly six million users. To paraphrase a saying, "psychoactive drug use is as American as apple pie." It is not going to disappear from the landscape by issuing silly, misinformed statements.

In 1988, Nancy Reagan asserted that the casual drug user is an "accomplice to murder," presumably a reference to the fact that all drug users, casual and more intensely committed, support an industry which sells a product that kills some users. The fact that cigarettes kill far more users than illegal drugs do seems to have escaped Mrs. Reagan; are cigarette manufacturers and executives "accomplices to murder"? (The same year that Mrs. Reagan issued this absurd statement, author Larry White published a book on the cigarette industry with the title *Merchants of Death.*) While no one seriously doubts the dangers of illicit drug use, it is crucial to understand the place of drugs in the context of the many other problems that American society faces.

Most people who take illegal mood-altering drugs are not harmed by that use. A minority (perhaps on the order of one in ten) of the users of a number of illicit drugs end up taking their drug of choice so frequently and in such a quantity that they threaten or destroy what they previously valued— school, an education, a job, a career, relations with loved ones, monetary savings, property, a house, a car, their self-respect, their health. What is becoming clear is that the causal mechanism here lies less in the substance in question—the particular drug they use—and more in the characteristics of the user. Many individuals, in all likelihood a majority, can use illegal drugs, possibly any and all illegal drugs currently in use, regularly, in a controlled fashion, without becoming dependent on them. A minority cannot, and ruin their lives and the lives of others in the process. To claim that most or all recreational drug users live a life of horror and misery is dishonest or self-deceptive. Such a statement calls for a close look at the evidence—which I've attempted to do in this book.

In the past few years, the call for some form of legalization of currently illegal drugs has become bolder, more assertive. In 1988, Kurt Schmoke, Mayor of Baltimore, shocked the United States Conference of Mayors by calling for the decriminalization of narcotics. Such a move would, he said, "take the profit" out of drug sales. In my view, this position is not only naive; such a move would be catastrophic. Level of profit in the drug trade is only partly dependent on the legal status of drugs. The fact is, a number of drugs are *highly* pleasurable or reinforcing; the current criminal sanctions against the possession and sale of these drugs deter the curious, the timid, the conventional. If decriminalized or legalized, the drugs that are now illegal would be used by *many* more times the number of individuals currently using them. Alcohol Prohibition (1919–1933) is often cited as an example of the failure of applying criminal sanctions to the possession, use, or sale of a drug, but this turns out to be not only a cliché but a poor example as well: In fact, alcohol consumption did decline significantly during Prohibition, as we'll see in this book.

The fact is, the criminalization of certain drugs has a range of effects, some good, some bad. It fails to deter all use, it does deter some use, and it has some consequences that all would agree are bad. Criminalization increases the price of drugs, makes money-making criminal activity among drug users much more likely, strengthens the criminal underworld and the drug-using subculture as well, and makes illicit drug use and sale a more dangerous activity in a number of ways than would otherwise be the case. On the other hand, criminalization does keep drugs out of the hands of a certain proportion of the public. Cocaine, for instance, is a *far* more pleasurable drug than alcohol, and yet, there are sixty million regular alcohol users and only six million regular users of cocaine. Is it not reasonable to assume that if legal sanctions were removed from cocaine possession and use, the number of users of that highly reinforcing drug would increase—possibly to the level of alcohol use? The either–or thinking that most observers of the drug scene bring to the problem makes the assumption that one solution will have mostly positives while another, mostly negatives. In fact, any solution will be a mixture of positive and negative; it is our job to pick out the one that will be least disastrous.

I would like to express my gratitude to several friends, colleagues, and others who have assisted me in the preparation of this edition of *Drugs in American Society.* They include: Paul Attewell, Nachman Ben-Yehuda, Lester Grinspoon, James Inciardi, Eric Jensen, Paula Holzman Kleinman, William McAuliffe, Stephen Chappel, Jennifer Brown, Lisa Castelluzzo Dolan, and Gina Bisagni.

CONTENTS

DRUGS IN
AMERICAN SOCIETY

Prologue

Landing on a hidden airstrip in two helicopters and a light plane, forty police officers assaulted and took the jungle compound in a hail of gunfire. Dubbed Tranquilandia, the "land of tranquillity," the complex was devoted entirely to the production of cocaine. Set deep in the Colombian Amazon basin, far from a town of any size, it included a dormitory large enough to sleep eighty; a Betamax video recorder; a dining area equipped with a refrigerator, microwave oven, and dishwasher; and bathrooms furnished with showers and flush toilets made of Italian ceramic. Fresh supplies of pigs and chickens were flown in daily. Some 1,000 employees—including cooks, waiters, and plumbers—were on the settlement's payroll. Just outside the compound, there were nineteen separate laboratories for processing and refining cocaine.

Before the raid, Colombia's total annual cocaine production was officially estimated at 50 tons per year. Tranquilandia alone was capable of producing 300 tons a year. In the raid, the police arrested 40 workers and seized 14 tons of the drug. They poured the confiscated cocaine, valued at $1.2 billion, into the nearby Yari River, which ran white with the powder (Iyer et al., 1986).

James, 62, is surrounded by his daughter and several friends. His is wearing a bathrobe and isn't feeling well. He says his problem is medical; everyone else knows better. He has recently lost his architectural firm; his telephone has been disconnected for nonpayment of bills; a woman who loves him has decided to marry another man; a chess partner says James has begun cheating; a former business partner says his once-brilliant mind has become "addled into dull predictability." His daughter, holding her 9-month-old baby, speaks up: "Daddy, we are here because we love you." James says he understands her concern; he says he has the flu and has been getting daily shots from his doctor. His daughter replies that she checked with his doctor, and he hasn't seen him for two years. Finally she tells him, "We think your problem is alcoholism." James protests, "That's preposterous! My problems have nothing to do with alcohol. Look, can't you understand? I'm sick, yes; depressed, yes; getting old, yes. But that's all."

After fourteen hours along these lines, James, exasperated, admits, "Geez, if I couldn't go down to the pub for a few, I think I'd go nuts!" His daughter places her baby on his knee. "Look at your granddaughter," she says. "This is your immortality, Daddy, and she needs you. Please don't die. Please choose life, for us." James puts his head in his hands. No one speaks.

Looking up, his face the color of gravel, he agrees to go to a local hospital. The tests reveal extensive liver damage, an almost certain sign of alcoholism. Still, James protests. "It could be my lousy diet," he says. Finally, after more arguments, he decides to check into a treatment center. Halfway through the program, James begrudgingly concedes that the treatment saved his life. "A person I haven't known for years is taking the place of alcohol. I like and respect him, and I never want to lose him, or my family, again" (Franks, 1985).

After hearing an antidrug lecture by a deputy sheriff at her church, Deanna Young, 13, decided to act. She went home and filled a plastic garbage bag with pills, cocaine, and marijuana and took it to her local police precinct. She explained that her parents, Bobby Dale Young, 49, a bartender, and Judith Ann Young, 37, a court clerk, were drug users. The Youngs were arrested, then released on their own recognizance; Deanna was taken to a county shelter for abused and abandoned children. She turned her parents in, she explained, to protect them, to get them off drugs—because they couldn't stop on their own. It was, she said, "for their own good." A few months later, a social service petition charging that Bobby and Judith Ann are unfit parents was dismissed by a local judge (Johnson, 1986). Deanna is now living with her parents again. Said Judith Ann, "We're just very happy to be all back together and have this all behind us" (*The New York Times*, September 10, 1986, p. A18).

Lorraine Mitchell has been a cigarette smoker for twenty-two years. In August 1984, Suffolk County, where she lives and works, passed a law requiring companies with more than fifty employees to ban smoking in rest rooms, conference rooms, hallways, and elevators. In November, the firm for which Lorraine works, going considerably beyond the county law, banned smoking in all of its work areas. To smoke during work hours, Lorraine, who smokes a pack and a half per day, must leave her desk and step outside. "I understand why they're doing it," she commented. "But it's a pain in the neck in the winter." Seven of the firm's employees smoke, and during the day they can be seen in the parking lot, filling the "butt bucket" that stands by the president's parking space. In the winter, Lorraine joins another employee for a smoke in her car during breaks and lunch hours. Members of the firm were given the option of staying with the firm or leaving because of the new rule. Said a vice-president, "Nobody left." Commenting on the law, the county Commissioner of Health Services said, "The air has never been cleaner in Suffolk County. . . . Common sense has won out" (Ketcham, 1986).

David is 35; both of his parents are lawyers. He has a bachelor's degree from an Ivy League university and several years of graduate education; he works as an advertising executive. He is successful and extremely well paid, but he lives modestly because he supports three ex-wives, each with two children.

David is charming, articulate, and clearly intelligent. He smokes marijuana every day, usually at night, after work; he indulges only occasionally during the day. He has taken LSD more than a dozen times, but only in a protective environment, with close friends nearby and no obligations facing him. He also uses opium when he can obtain it, the usual array of uppers and downers, usually for instrumental purposes—such as being alert in order to work harder, or getting to sleep at night—and a fair quantity of cocaine. As I interview him, he is smoking a marijuana joint.

"I use marijuana to relax," David explains, "to contemplate, and to enjoy myself." He draws deeply on his joint, exhales languidly, and speaks slowly, deliberately, from the back of his throat. "It makes me feel good, and I get a lot of insight from it. My dimensions of thinking shift, especially with other people. . . . I'm more able to get away from my own private perceptions and observations, and more able to perceive who the other person is, and suspend all of life's petty 'games.' " David takes another deep drag on his joint and stares into space for a minute or two. "Anyway, I feel good when I'm stoned. That's why I do it. That's why I do it *regularly.* I mean, in the last year, I've smoked pot on 365 days. It's fun. Food tastes better, sex is more expressive and enjoyable—yes, pot is an aphrodisiac, at least it is for me—I enjoy music more, I use my imagination more listening to music." He pauses, then adds, "When someone asks me, why do I smoke dope, I answer, why not? There are no negatives, only positives. Really. Why not?"

Ginny is 29. She's a college graduate and works as a dress designer in New York City. She is divorced, and she has one child. Until three or four months ago, she smoked marijuana once or twice a week; when she met her current boyfriend, she began smoking every day. Her use of the drug is totally dependent on her social environment, usually the man she is dating at the time. She doesn't buy marijuana but uses it only if it is offered to her; she never smokes it alone. She has experimented with other drugs—she took opium once, LSD three times, and amyl nitrite several times—but cannot imagine using any of them regularly. She used to be a fairly heavy drinker, but has given up alcohol entirely.

"When I smoke grass," she explains, "I'm much more relaxed. I'm *very* relaxed. It slows my movements down. It makes me tired. Heavy. Motions are more effort. It's harder to do things; you forget what you're doing. I couldn't cut or sew a dress high. Like, with reading or writing, you have to concentrate more—you can't keep your mind on what you're doing." Ginny pauses and looks out the window. "For me, marijuana isn't a serious drug; it is always a happy drug. If I'm depressed to the point that I want to cry, I feel better if I'm high, as if I don't have to cry. I become funnier—people laugh at what I say." She pulls a tobacco cigarette out of a pack, lights up, and puffs contemplatively. "My senses are more receptive. With sex, my sensitivity level is higher. Through grass, I learned to control my orgasms. Sex is better—it's different. But I have a lot of interest in sex anyway, so my interest in sex doesn't increase. It makes me calmer, though. More relaxed.

Those lousy late-night movies you could never watch straight, you can watch when you're high. You can enjoy something unrelated to the structure or the plot of the movie. And you don't evaluate or judge so much. You just get into things more—some things anyway." Ginny is staring out of the window again. I ask her why she smokes marijuana—an almost redundant question at this point. She doesn't seem surprised by the question. "Why do I smoke grass? I enjoy it. It's part of my life. It's part of the lives of the people around me, it's part of what I do. It makes my life more fun. It's good, it's mellow, it's, uh. . . . Well, it's *me*, you know? *Why the hell not?"*

In Afghanistan, the fields burst with red, purple, and white poppies. When the petals fall from the plants, farmers take a knife and slit open the golf-ball–size green pods, out of which a thick, blackish gum—opium—oozes. Reapers walk through the fields of the 3-to-4-foot plants, scraping the gum from the pods with small serrated blades and placing them in tin cans tied around their necks. Although Islam forbids smoking opium, it says nothing about growing it. "How else can we get money?" said Mohammed, a teacher, whose brother Nazim is a powerful rebel commander. "We must grow and sell opium to fight our holy war against the Russian nonbelievers."

Opium can be sold directly from the fields for $40 to $50 a pound. "That's 100 times more than I can get from another crop on the same land," said Ali, a young rebel commander whose family grows and harvests the poppy. "If one of our soldiers is sick or wounded, we must send money to his family. . . . We must also feed them and give them money for shoes and clothes. Where else can we get money?" Growing opium can make the difference between remaining on your land and living a precarious existence in a refugee camp, crowded into mud huts. Unlike nearly all other crops, opium has a ready market, poses no storage problems, is easy to transport, and commands a high price. Moreover, opium is harvested in the spring, which means that after harvesting it, farmers are free to grow other crops.

Kandahar, a provincial capital, has been largely destroyed in the fighting between Russian troops and Afghan rebels. On the outskirts of town, Mussa, a rebel commander, shows a visitor the ruins of his family's property. Drug cultivation, he explains, is above all a weapon for the rebels. "With the money they get from opium," he said, "Afghans can fight until all the Russians get out from our country" (Bonner, 1986).

Carl is 26, single, and a graduate student. He was born in South Africa. He was two when his father died; eighteen months later, his mother married a physician with two children. Carl's parents are moderate social drinkers who serve wine or beer at meals. At 12, he tried tobacco; at 19, he smoked a pack and a half a day, as he does today. At 16, he tried marijuana and settled into a pattern of smoking two to three times a week, but only in the late evening. Between the ages of 16 and 18, Carl used amphetamine sporadically on social occasions; now he uses it extremely rarely. When he was 17, he and a friend, whose father was also a physician, stole some morphine and syringes from the friend's father's office and injected one another with the drug. They both found the experience extremely pleasurable.

Carl moved to the United States at age 18 and entered college. He became friendly with a group who used psychedelics, and for the next year, he used these substances two or three times a month; today, he very rarely "trips." At 20, Carl's curiosity about heroin became piqued, he tracked down a source, and he began using the drug once a month. He has continued this practice, more or less, for the past six years. During a vacation to the wide-open city of Amsterdam, Carl used heroin almost every day, but he resumed his once-a-month pattern upon returning to the States. He always uses the drug in a group, almost always snorts or injects intramuscularly, and, if he injects, always sterilizes the needle. Carl purchases the drug from a close friend; if his friend left town, he admits, he wouldn't know where to obtain it.

Neither Carl's best friend nor his roommate knows about his use of heroin. "I don't want to be deceptive," he explains, "but some people have an exaggerated fear of heroin and make a big fuss about it. . . . It's nobody's business what I like, and I don't want to be judged for it." Carl controls the amount he takes. "The trick," he says, "is to get high with the least amount possible." If he takes too much, there are not only side effects but also the danger of escalating the quantity he uses—and, of course, the risk of physical dependence. If he takes too little, he doesn't get high. Carl hopes to be able to continue at his current level of use for the foreseeable future (Zinberg, 1984, pp. 1–3).

John grew up in a religious, middle-class family in Harlem; his father is a New York Police Department sergeant. "My father used to drive me around and point out junkies nodding out on the street. . . . I thought I could never become an addict." He experimented with marijuana, then cocaine, in the Catholic high school he attended. At Howard University, John's use of cocaine escalated to the point where he felt forced to invent lies to his parents to get more money to pay for his drug habit. Doing poorly academically, he dropped out of Howard after his sophomore year. At this point, he still regarded drug use as a peripheral part of his life.

In his early twenties, John decided to become a police officer. A month before taking his medical entrance exam, he abstained from cocaine and stayed drug-free for a year thereafter, through his stint in the police academy and during his first few months on the force. But the lure of cocaine became too great for him to resist. For nearly a year, his life revolved around freebasing, that is, smoking a potent crystalline form of cocaine. Toward the end of that year, he was spending nearly his entire paycheck on cocaine. After repeatedly showing up for work late and calling in sick a half-dozen times, he was ordered off active duty and asked to see a departmental psychologist. Fearful that he would be dismissed if he admitted his drug problem, he was evasive in his sessions with his counselor; moreover, he often missed appointments with him. After being out three more days of work and skipping too many sessions with the psychologist, John was or-dered to take a urine test, which he failed. He resigned the same day, even before the test results came in. Alienated from his friends and thousands of dollars in debt, he managed to get admitted to Phoenix House, a drug treatment center in Manhattan.

Just before entering the program, John talked about his drug problem. "I see my life divided," he explained. "On one side I see suffering, lying, cheating, and dereliction. On the other side I see responsibility. I'm scared and nervous. But I know it's now or never" (Kerr, 1986a).

Jane, a 30-year-old nurse, began the heavy recreational use of drugs as a teenager, and became addicted to amphetamines. By age 17, she began experimenting with opiates; at 19, she was addicted. Jane became a drug dealer, then a prostitute; she was arrested for selling narcotics and was placed on probation. She continued to use opiates mainly on weekends, enrolled in a community college, achieved high grades, and entered nursing school. Jane's use of heroin increased throughout nursing school, and her grades declined.

Jane became a registered nurse and began stealing vials of opiates on the job, replacing them with vials filled with saline solution. Occasionally she bought narcotics on the street from friends. One day, injecting a very large dose of Demerol, Jane overdosed, passed out, and sustained a head injury when she fell. She subsequently lost her job, although her supervisor did not report her drug problem to the authorities. For a while, Jane relied on street drugs exclusively. She was admitted to a methadone program and worked for five years as a nurse while on methadone, only rarely resorting to street narcotics. Jane recently detoxified from methadone, but she soon returned to the use of street and stolen opiates. She's now back on the methadone program (McAuliffe, 1983, pp. 358–360).

The subject of this book is drugs. Used in every nation on earth, drugs have become a major problem worldwide. The impact of drug use has been debated in all complex urban societies: is it good, bad, or neutral?

Some believe that no one can handle drugs, that drugs have harmful effects regardless of the characteristics of the user and the context of use. They oppose consumption of alcohol, coffee, tobacco, and even drugs used in medicine.

Most people have a somewhat more moderate position. They make an exception for legal drugs—such as alcohol—and argue that societies are wise enough to prohibit the bad and permit the more-or-less good. They further believe that if used strictly in a healing capacity, some drugs can have a positive effect. But, they hold, illegal drugs taken for the purpose of getting high can have only disastrous consequences.

A very tiny number of people maintain that certain drugs have magical properties and make people better, smarter, wiser, and more in tune with themselves and the world.

The view presented in this book differs somewhat from these three positions. Drugs are not magical substances whose effects emerge under any and all conditions. Drugs do have pharmacological properties. Biochemical reactions do take place in the body when drugs are ingested. There are limits as to what drugs can and cannot do. At the same time, those limits are vast—not limitless, but vast. Exactly how drugs are used—who uses them, for what reasons, under what circumstances, at what dosage levels, in combination with what other drugs or activities, how frequently, and so on—is not dictated by the biochemical or pharmacological properties of drugs alone. The precise effects of a drug depends in large part on the social circumstances surrounding use because how drugs are used is influenced by a host of social and psychological factors.

This does not mean that if you think you've just taken a dose of LSD and you've really taken heroin, you'll have an experience identical to the one you would have had on LSD. When I say that the effects of a drug are partly dependent on the context of use, I am saying something a great deal more complicated than this. I mean that the effects of drug use, both immediate and long-range, are a consequence of an *interplay* among the substance that is taken, the individual who takes it, and both the immediate drug-taking setting and the broader sociocultural context of use. The effects that drugs have are contingent on many factors; the intrinsic properties of the drug make up only one of them. Drugs do not "do" things to people in the abstract until people "do" things to drugs—that is, take them in a certain way. Taken one way, drugs will have one set of effects; taken another way, they may have a different set of effects.

Often, the effects of drug use are studied in a laboratory or a clinical setting. Standard doses of a drug are given to subjects, the effects are observed, and the results of the experiment are published, everyone assuming that the effects observed in that setting at that dosage level will occur everywhere among all users. While such studies are valuable, we must always realize that, in real life, drugs may not be taken under conditions like the ones studied. Drugs have a certain *potential* to bring about a wide range of effects, some of which will often manifest themselves under actual circumstances of use, while others will rarely, if ever, appear. To assume that a drug and it alone determines what will happen to someone who takes it—always and under all circumstances—is fallacious. It is a perfect example of what the great philosopher Alfred North Whitehead called the *fallacy of misplaced concreteness* (1948, pp. 52ff.) and what Karl Marx called *fetishism* (1906, pp. 81ff.; Himmelstein, 1979). It does not belong in any thinking person's approach to reality.

Likewise, countless experiments have been conducted on the effects of drugs on laboratory animals. Such experiments, once again, provide a *clue* to understanding the impact that the substances will have in contexts of real-life human consumption. These studies show us the drugs' *potential*. It would be foolish to discount the findings of animal experiments as entirely irrelevant to the human situation. It would be equally foolish to argue that these findings can be extrapolated to humans on a point-for-point basis. They are suggestive, not definitive. We do not know from an animal experiment what the norms surrounding use will be in human societies—what is regarded as an acceptable dose, the proper frequency of use, what social occasions are seen as acceptable times to use the drug, what other drugs may or may not be taken in conjunction with the ones studied, who may or may not use the drug, and so on. In short, we cannot determine how a drug will be used in real life from artificial experiments. If every animal in every species tested dropped dead after ingesting minute doses of a given drug, or if every animal became totally addicted to the drug, we would be wise to assume that the drug's effects will not be benign on humans. On the other hand, these dramatic results occur with very few drugs; with most, human reactions are highly variable because psychological, individual, and social factors—different for different people—are highly influential.

Beginning in the mid-1980s, a resurgence of antidrug propaganda erupted in the United States. The slogan for today has become "Just say no to drugs." "Don't even try it," we are warned. "If you're going to die for something," a spokesperson for an antidrug campaign says, "this [meaning drugs] sure as hell ain't it." One ad suggests that taking drugs—any drug? at any dosage? at every level of frequency?—has the same effect on one's brain as frying does on an egg. Celebrities such as Nancy Reagan and Bob Hope have joined forces in "speaking out against drugs," as if mere words could possibly take the place of meaningful, valid prevention and treatment programs. Pamphlets, books, newsletters, and videotapes are offered for sale to concerned parents who want to put a stop to drug abuse in their communities. Such organizations as College Challenge, World Youth Against Drug Abuse, the Just Say No Club, PRIDE, STOPP, Responsible Adolescents Can Help, and Youth to Youth have sprung up to denounce the drug menace. They warn of a nation of glassy-eyed zombies high on marijuana, of cocaine sprinkled in the popcorn at teen parties, of junkies nodding out on every street corner in America. Every drug user "is a scourge and a bum," a police officer declares (Williams, 1986), and a chorus of concerned citizens nods in approval. This is a view that does not have much confidence in human wisdom; it is one that holds that once drugs take hold of you, you become a slave to a demonic, compulsive force.

This book represents something of an alternative to these hysterical views. Am I saying that drugs are harmless, that drugs never hurt anyone? Of course not. I am, however, saying the following.

Evidence counts. Thousands—indeed, hundreds of thousands—of good, solid, valid studies have been conducted on drug use and its impact. These studies are based on *systematic* data, not on scattered, silly anecdotes, whether true or fictitious like the cocaine in the popcorn. It is to these studies that we must look—the *full range* of these studies, not just those few that support our personal opinions.

Myths about drugs and drug use abound. It should come as no surprise that much of what we read or hear about drugs is false. Most of us are impatient with ambiguity and complexity; we want to hear a clear-cut story, simple and unadorned. We believe that there are answers to questions like "Is marijuana dangerous or not?" "Which is the most dangerous drug known?" "Is alcohol safer than marijuana?" As we'll see in this book, these questions have no easy answers because we have to set up meaningful criteria in advance to evaluate information relevant to answering them. We believe simplistic formulas, such as, for heroin, "One shot and you're hooked for life," or, for cocaine, "For the thrill that can kill." Real life is a great deal more complicated than these slogans suggest. It is time to set aside such myths and face the reality of drugs squarely, bravely, factually.

Numbers count. If we want to understand the impact of drug use, we must see how many people are affected. The Surgeon General of the United States estimates that cigarette smoking is responsible for 300,000 premature deaths in the United States each year. Estimates of the number of alcoholics in America hover in the range of 10 million or so. Surely the use of tobacco and alcohol must be counted as more serious problems than the use of illegal drugs, whose users and victims account for a fraction of these figures.

Proportions count. It makes a great deal of difference if a drug is used by one American in two, one in ten, or one in 100. It makes a great deal of difference if one user in two eventually becomes dependent on a drug, as opposed to one in ten or one in a hundred. It makes a great deal of difference if a drug kills one in 100 users each year, one in 1,000, or one in 100,000. We simply cannot be taken seriously if we dig up a few examples of dependency or harm and then claim that a given drug "produces" dependency or "is" harmful. We must always keep in mind the proportions in which specific outcomes occur. Otherwise, we are talking nonsense.

Frequency of use counts. When we refer to a specific individual, or to average levels of use for users as a whole, it makes a great deal of difference if we are talking about occasional use or compulsive, several-times-a-day use. It makes no sense to equate these patterns of use, any more than we can equate someone who drinks the occasional wine or beer at dinner with someone who is an alcoholic. Effects take place at the upper reaches of frequency of use that are practically nonexistent at occasional levels. To fail to distinguish among these levels of use is to disqualify oneself automatically from attempting to talk sense in the area of drug use.

The "slippery slope" argument is fallacious. Some people believe that once you start dabbling in something that's a little bad, a little harmful, you end up getting totally and completely involved with very bad, very harmful activities. You cannot be moderate about something like illegal recreational drug use, they claim, because, well, you just can't. This "slippery slope" argument is false as a general rule; people everywhere draw the line on what they do, and drug use is no different from any other activity in this respect. Empirical evidence shows that most people who use drugs to get high are moderate in their use and do not progress to more dangerous levels. Only a minority of users of most drugs become involved to the point where their lives and values are threatened by their drug use.

The user makes a difference. Drugs do not have identical effects on different people. People use drugs in different ways. The characteristics of the user has an impact on how a drug is used and the impact it has on the user. For instance, a 16-year-old will typically smoke marijuana less wisely than a 30-year-old. Most countries recognize this and place age restrictions on the use of legal drugs. Some individuals can "handle" certain drugs, including alcohol, and use them sensibly and moderately; others cannot, and, for them, use becomes dependency extremely quickly.

Drug use is a risk-taking activity. No substance or activity is completely safe. Some are riskier than others. To each, we can assign a likelihood of specific kinds of risk. As substances and activities go, drugs and drug use are fairly risky. They have a great deal in common with racing cars, skydiving, flying an ultralight, exploring caves, scuba diving, and—especially these days—having sex with strangers. Drug use is not a completely risk-free activity. There is the possibility of dependency—using a drug so often and so compulsively that our health and what we value, including school, our job, and relations with loved ones, are threatened. There is the possibility that we become so involved with a drug that we must resort to crime to pay for it. There is the possibility of an overdose, even death. And there is the possibility of arrest for obtaining and possessing the drug. These are very real hazards. They are a bit different from the risks that other risky activities entail, but they are not *qualitatively* different from these other risks.

Some risks—including drug use—are run simply as a result of hanging out with the kind of crowd that engages in a certain activity. Drug users are not the same as nonusers; they are less conventional, less law-abiding, less achievement-oriented. Just by using drugs, one is more likely to associate with a drug-using social circle and to find one's values and behavior moving in a less conventional, less law-abiding, less achievement-oriented direction. A risk? Certainly. But again, one not qualitatively or markedly different from listening to punk-rock music, associating with "bikers," or becoming involved with a group whose members worship Elvis, make predictions with tarot cards, believe in astrology, believe that UFOs are visiting this planet, or attend wrestling matches religiously.

The legal-illegal boundary is artificial. Societies are not always wise in outlawing dangerous drugs and tolerating relatively safe ones. If they were, we'd find drug laws to be the same everywhere throughout history, But they aren't. Alcohol is illegal in orthodox Islamic countries. Marijuana has been legal in Nepal and in certain states in India. Even within the United States, the possession of small quantities of marijuana has been decriminalized in some states but remains completely illegal in others. Statistics show that the number of deaths from tobacco, alcohol, and legal prescription drugs outstrips that from illegal drugs by more than ten to one. Societies, including our own, are not always particularly wise in their passage or nonpassage of laws, and the fact that one substance or activity is legal or illegal says little or nothing about its inherent safety or danger. Polluting our air and water is one of the more deadly of current human activities, but the laws passed against it are feeble, ineffective, and, for the most part, unenforced. Such harmful activities are tolerated to this day, and relatively benign ones outlawed. The fact that one drug is legal (tobacco, say, or alcohol) and another is not is no argument in favor of validating the inherent safety of the former or the harm of the latter.

Media attention to drugs and the extent of drug use bear an extremely loose relation to one another. Newspaper and television campaigns focused on drug use and abuse come and go; their connection with level of use is practically nonexistent. Between 1963 and 1966, for example, media attention on LSD peaked—at a time when the actual use of this drug was considerably lower than it became in the 1970s, when media attention was extremely low. Similarly, in the early 1980s, media coverage of drugs was fairly low and actual use was high; by the mid- and late 1980s, however, media attention to drugs intensified—whereas the use of most drugs was actually dropping.

The relationship between objective harm and public concern is also extremely loose. The public does not become concerned about a condition or phenomenon solely because of its actual impact on society. In fact, most people have an extremely imprecise estimate of the size or extent of most problems. In one survey, when asked if asthma or botulism is a more common cause of death, only a slight majority said asthma, in spite of the fact that death from asthma is 900 times more common than death from botulism. Homicides were judged to be about five times as numerous as suicide; in real life, suicide is 30 percent more common (Slovic, Fischoff, and Lichtenstein, 1980, p. 44). Radon contamination kills tens of thousands of Americans each year (Eckholm, 1986b), yet most people have never heard of radon and have no idea what it is. What the public thinks of as a problem is extremely remotely related to the actual danger posed by a given condition.

Not all of the accompaniments of use are a direct result of drugs themselves. We compare marijuana users with nonusers. We find that users are more likely to be underachievers in school than are nonusers. Can we say that marijuana is a direct cause of underachievement? This inference is unwarranted unless we have more information. It is entirely possible that users belong to a social circle or subculture in which academic achievement is not highly valued—regardless of the effects of the drug. Heroin users, abusers, and addicts are vastly more likely to commit money-making crimes than are nonusers. Does heroin directly cause the commission of money-making crimes? Again, such an inference is improper. Heroin is illegal, therefore expensive, and few addicts earn enough money to pay for their habit by working at a legal job.

Often, the accompaniments of use result not so much from the direct effects of drugs themselves as from the circumstances of use. Only the ignorant would ask, "What difference does it make?" since the contexts of use often change and result in different accompaniments. Focusing on causes and effects that stem as much from the conditions of use as from use itself, we will always find ourselves barking up the wrong tree. Unless we track down the causal connections entailed in drug use, we will never be able to make a dent in controlling this problem. When we are more concerned with denouncing and eliminating something than understanding it, we may very well contribute to its continuation. Above all, the issue of drug use and abuse requires *understanding,* and it is understanding that seems to me to be in markedly short supply nowadays.

Almost everything in the world of drug use is a matter of odds. Not all smokers get lung cancer. Not all junkies die of an overdose. Not all alcoholics have automobile accidents. To each episode of drug use and to each drug user there is a certain statistical likelihood that specific consequences of use will take place. This likelihood is never 100 percent; it is never *absolutely* greater than it is for nonuse or nonusers. Some bad things will happen when someone is not using drugs, or to nonusers; bad things will not necessarily happen when someone uses drugs or to some users. If very bad things always happened when drugs are used, or happened to all users, it is likely that use would be much lower than it is.

Most people who use drugs experience no harm whatsoever with a given episode of use. And: *Most users are not seriously harmed by drug use.* If drug use became the horror show that anti-drug propagandists claim, hardly anyone would indulge. The horrors are there, but not for most users. While most users report some discomfort or problems with their use upon occasion, they are hardly ever as horrific or as frequent as most nonusers assume.

Almost everything in the world of drug use is a matter of degree. The consequences of drug abuse are usually a matter of degree; they are rarely an all-or-nothing affair. One person uses a given drug once a week; another, several times a week; a third, every day. One person feels slight headaches from time to time from his or her drug use; a second feels painful stomach cramps; a third passed out several times; a fourth died of an overdose. With drugs, there is pleasure and death—and everything in between. The consequences form a spectrum, a continuum, infinite shades of gray. Anyone peddling an all-or-nothing view of drugs is deluded or lying.

Most people who use drugs weigh pleasure against pain—and usually, pleasure comes out on top. The reason why people use drugs is that they experience pleasure from their experiences. Anyone painting a horrific view of drug use has to answer one extremely vexing question: *Why do they do it?* There must be certain appeals to the activity for so many people to indulge in it. Some use drugs to "escape," some because they want to go along with the crowd, and still others, after an extended period of use, out of compulsive motives. But most people who use drugs do so because it is pleasurable to them. In order to understand drug use, we must assess the experience from the perspective of the user. I hope that this book makes a contribution to an understanding of this complex phenomenon.

CHAPTER 1

Looking at Drugs

Humans have ingested drugs for at least 10,000 years. Alcohol was discovered and drunk during the Stone Age; its use predates the fashioning of metal instruments (Ray and Ksir, 1987, p. 139). Dozens of plants containing chemicals with mind-altering properties have been smoked, chewed, swallowed, and sniffed by members of societies all over the world (Efron, 1967; Harner, 1973; Furst, 1976; Schultes and Hofmann, 1979). Coca leaves, containing about 1 percent cocaine, have been chewed by South American Indians for thousands of years, beginning even before Incan rule; statues dating from 300 B.C. display puffed-out cheeks, indicating a wad of coca in the mouth (Grinspoon and Bakalar, 1976, pp. 9–10), and a grave in Peru dating from A.D. 500 reveals a record of the use of coca leaves (Ray and Ksir, 1987, p. 113). Smoking or inhaling the smoke of the marijuana plant is mentioned in texts from ancient India, China, Greece, Assyria, and Thebes (Schultes, 1969, p. 247). Indians living in Mexico have been chewing hallucinogenic mushrooms, containing psilocybin, in religious ceremonies since the time of the pre-Columbian Aztecs (Schultes and Hofmann, 1979, pp. 147–153). The peyote cactus, containing the psychedelic drug mescaline, is eaten by members of a number of North American Indian tribes to achieve ecstatic visions (Slotkin, 1956); the practice has been incorporated into the Native American Church, which claims a quarter of a million members. In the thousands of tribes, cultures, societies, and nations around the world and throughout history, only a tiny handful of peoples have not routinely taken drugs to experience their effects. Drug-taking comes close to being a cultural universal.

Surely a phenomenon as common as drug use must be understood. Humans are biological, psychological, and social beings. Each aspect or dimension of our existence is approached and studied by a specific discipline or field. Just as the biochemist and the pharmacologist can tell us a great deal about drug use by studying it in a laboratory, the sociologist can likewise describe and explain drug-taking in more naturalistic, real-life social settings. Each perspective has a slightly different story to tell; each focuses on a different facet of the drug phenomenon. By piecing together the perspectives from the various disciplines that study drug use, we may be able to assemble an accurate overall view. It is to this goal that this book is dedicated.

Drugs are used today on a massive scale. In the United States, nearly 1.5 billion prescriptions for pharmaceutical substances are written each year (*Pharmacy Times,* April 1987). Over-the-counter preparations account for billion a year in retail sales in this country. Roughly six adult Americans in ten drink alcoholic beverages more or less regularly; a third of the American population smokes cigarettes on a steady basis. Marijuana, the most popular illegal drug in this country, has been used by more than 60 million Americans; some 18 million smoked it once or more during the last month (NIDA, 1986). More than half of all high-school seniors in the nation have tried marijuana, and roughly half of this figure uses the drug regularly (Johnston, O'Malley, and Bachman, 1987, pp. 47, 49). Estimates of the value of the illegal drug trade at the retail level range well over $100 billion a year. If the illicit drug business were a single industry, it would rank very near the top of all corporations in the *Fortune* 500.

SOCIAL CONTEXT AND HUMAN MEANING

If there is anything distinctive about the sociological perspective, it is its emphasis on *social context.* It might appear that this concept seeped into the public consciousness long ago, that it is a banality. But if this were so, the blunders committed every day by commentators on the drug scene would not occur. If the concept really were understood, a large part of the drug problem would also be understood. Social context refers to the setting in which drug use takes place. In a religious or ceremonial setting (as with eating the peyote cactus among members of the Native American Church), a drug will have certain effects, and the user will have certain subjective experiences under the influence of the drug. Taking that same drug to get high—for recreational, not religious, reasons—will induce quite different effects and experiences in the user. Being administered a drug in a laboratory or a hospital by researchers or technicians will yield behavioral, pharmacological, and subjective changes that may not be matched under different conditions—say, taking the same drug with friends in the comfort of one's living room. The *social context* within which drug use occurs is a powerful determinant of what the drug is and does to the user. To extrapolate from drug use in one setting to that in another is a risky enterprise, and often altogether invalid.

The social context of use influences or determines at least four central aspects of the drug reality, aspects that traditionally have been presumed to grow directly out of the chemical and pharmacological properties of the drugs themselves. These four aspects are *drug definitions, drug effects, drug-related behavior,* and the *drug experience.* Whether a given drug is defined as good or bad, socially acceptable or undesirable, conventional or "deviant," is not a simple outgrowth of the properties or objective characteristics of the drug itself, but is in no small measure a result of the history of its use, what social strata of society use it, for what purposes, the publicity surrounding its use, and so on. In short, how a drug is regarded—by the public, the law, its users, and even the medical profession—depends as much on irrational cultural factors as on its objective properties. Likewise, what a drug does to the human mind and body, what people do subsequent to ingesting it, and what subjective experiences they have under its influence, are all at least in part a function of how, under what circumstances, and for what purposes it is taken. Generally, the more "objective" the effects in question are, the less prominent the role played by social context; the more "subjective" the effects are, the more influential this factor is. However, even "objective" effects, such as heartbeat rate, pupillary dilation, blood sugar level, and so on, can be influenced by sociological factors, as we will see throughout this book. And the "subjective" effects of drugs, the drug experience itself—whether the effects are experienced as pleasurable *(euphoric)* or unpleasant *(dysphoric),* weak or intense, hedonistic or depressing, hallucinatory or mundane, serene or exciting—are *largely* a function of sociological factors. We must turn our attention away from a simple examination of the drug itself to just how that drug is taken to understand the phenomenon of drug use.

The sociological perspective stands in direct opposition to what might be called the *chemicalistic fallacy,* what I called earlier fetishism or the fallacy of misplaced concreteness—the view that drug A automatically and inevitably causes effects X through Z, that what we see as behavior and effects associated with a given drug are solely, or even mainly, a function of the biochemical and pharmacological properties of that drug. Drug effects and drug-associated behavior are enormously complicated, highly variable, and contingent on many things, one of which is social and contextual in nature. Humans are infinitely more intelligent and difficult to study than animals, which makes automatic translations from the effects a drug has on animals in cages to those it has on humans in their natural settings suspect. This is why social context is so important.

One of the central dimensions of all human experience is *meaning.* No object or event has meaning in the abstract, in a natural state. Rather, meaning is imposed, socially fabricated—in short, symbolic. Meaning has two features: it is both internal and external. Meaning is assigned externally to objects or behavior in the process of human collaboration or interaction. But it also resides within the individual: it is arrived at as a result of a private act of choosing on the individual's part. In order for an observer to grasp that internal meaning, he must view the world from the subject's perspective, which inevitably involves empathy.

The same behavior, the same phenomenon, the same material reality, can mean completely different things to different people or to the same person in different contexts. Meaning is an ascription. It is superimposed on a phenomenon, a reality. It does not arise naturally. Anything may have multiple meanings, depending on one's point of view. Human action is suffused with meaning—just about everything we do is evaluated, thought about, mulled over, judged, interpreted.

Take anything—an object, an act, a thought. Put into two different settings, it will mean radically different things to us—perhaps contradictory things—simply because of our variability in interpretations. It is not the thing, the act, the thought, we are reacting to. The same thing quite simply "means" different things; the thing does not generate the meaning—we put it there. Consider two scenes: one the boudoir, husband and wife alone, engaging in foreplay; the other the examining room of a gynecologist's office, the physician, a man, examining a patient for breast cancer. In both cases, a woman's breasts are being felt. But in one, the behavior is linked with a "script" we refer to as lovemaking. In the second, it is linked with a different script: a medical examination (Gagnon and Simon, 1973, pp. 22–23). Though the specific acts involved are almost identical in a sheerly physical sense, they "mean" radically different things, and the participants act and react, think and feel, differently as a consequence. Thus they are in fact totally different acts, not because they differ externally but because different interpretations have been brought to them.

A large proportion of all assertions about social reality are ideologically imperialistic in nature—that is, an external meaning is imposed on a reality that should be investigated from an internal perspective. For example, many people equate long hair on men with feminization, without first asking what long hair actually means to the person growing it. Their point of view is that of an external observer who thinks that long hair should mean something definite and unvarying. A few generations ago anthropologists, armed with psychoanalytic insights, invaded non-Western civilizations and imposed their interpretations on what they saw. Snakes were interpreted as phallic symbols, regardless of what snakes actually meant to the particular cultures involved. Nakedness was given a sexual meaning, though in some societies nakedness has the overwhelming meaning of poverty, and not at all of sexuality. Today many of these biases have been eliminated from most analyses of other civilizations, but they are depressingly routine when it comes to our own.

And drugs. How do social definitions, interpretations, and meaning impinge on drugs, drug effects, and drug-related behavior? Are the same drug realities defined and interpreted in vastly different ways? How do contextual features change the relevant characteristics of drug use? For example, peyote taken by American Indians in a ceremony participated in by adherents of the Native American Church is legal and legitimate—even holy. Yet the same substance, taken by college students—even for the same purposes—is suddenly, magically, labeled a dangerous drug, debilitating and damaging to the user and a threat to society—and quite illegal. Another example: heroin and morphine. These two drugs are not very different pharmacologically and biochemically, except that pure heroin is several times more potent than morphine. (In fact, the morphine administered for therapeutic purposes in hospitals is stronger than the heroin sold on the street, since black-market heroin is considerably diluted.) An experienced drug addict would probably not be able to discern the difference between comparable doses of heroin and morphine, and a pharmacologist would have to look very, very closely to distinguish the laboratory effects of the two drugs. In short, by "objective" standards they are very nearly the same drug; they do more or less the same things to the tissues of the body. Nonetheless,

heroin is declared to have no medical uses whatsoever. It is
menace, a killer. Morphine, on the other hand, is regarded
humankind. It has the stamp of approval from the medical f
a valuable therapeutic tool. And yet the role and medical functions ᴏ.
two drugs, and hence their social meanings, could easily be reversed. It is
not the characteristics of drugs themselves, their pharmacological actions,
that generate such contrasting interpretations; rather it is the meanings that
have been more or less arbitrarily assigned to them.

The sociologist's view of drugs and drug use goes a good deal farther
than merely recognizing that there are variable interpretations of similar
drug realities and drug-related situations. It also emphasizes that the drug
experience and drug effects will vary when different meanings are brought
into the drug-taking situation. The one-dimensional, chemicalistic view of
drug-taking is that humans are basically passive receptors for drug actions,
and that when a certain drug is administered, a certain effect, or standard
set of effects, takes place. This view has been discredited as a general model,
but the comments of many drug experts indicate that it is still operative. It
is not uncommon to encounter analyses that utilize such concepts as the
"complete marihuana intoxication syndrome" (Wikler, 1970, p. 324), as if
the effects of marijuana were a clinical entity with distinct configurations
analogous to an H_2O molecule or a cumulus cloud; or the notion that drug
users are part of "an abnormal subculture" (Willis, 1969, p. 34), as if this
could be determined by means of objective, scientific examination.

Naturally, some drug effects will be fairly distinct and will not vary a great
deal, and there will be widespread agreement on their occurrence. In almost
every case the whites of a person's eyes will become bloodshot after he or
she has smoked a sizable quantity of marijuana. A person with a .2-percent
blood-alcohol concentration in his or her bloodstream will not be able to
operate a complex piece of machinery as well as he or she could when sober.
Nearly everyone will go through some sort of withdrawal distress after
long-term administration of a gram a day of barbiturates. But drug effects
with such narrow variability are themselves limited in number; drug effects
that are highly sensitive to external conditions and about which interpretations vary enormously are far more common, as well as far more important
and interesting to most observers.

It is crucial to distinguish between drug effects and the drug *experience*.
What happens in one's mind subsequent to taking a given drug is the
outcome of many different factors, not solely a function of specific biochemical reactions. A number of changes take place in the body when a chemical
is ingested, and not all these changes are automatically noticed and classified. The subject must be attuned to certain drug effects to be able to
interpret and categorize them and thus place them within his or her experiential and conceptual realms. Otherwise, the effect of a drug may simply be
sensed as a vague, unsettling, dizzyish sort of experience. A drug effect has
to be interpreted and categorized in order to "happen" internally, in order
to be part of one's experiencing of it. Out of many potential "effects" of

drugs individuals and drug subcultures (as well as the general society) select several to pay special attention to. Very few hospital patients who are administered morphine experience it as euphoric or pleasurable, yet the illegal street user of morphine experiences euphoria and pleasure from it. Psychedelic drugs taken for religious purposes, after spiritual preparation and training, are typically felt as having a religious impact, yet people who take hallucinogenic drugs simply to get high do not usually report anything like a religious or a mystical experience. Drugs only *potentiate* certain experiences; they make them possible, but they do not produce them outright. It is the situation, the social definition surrounding use—not simply the drug's "objective" biochemical properties—that determines the experiential dimension.

Societies define not only the meaning of drugs but also the meaning of the drug experience; these definitions differ radically among different societies and among subgroups and subcultures within the same society. Social groups and cultures define what kind of drug-taking is appropriate. They define which drugs are acceptable and which are not. They define who takes drugs and why. They decide what amounts of each drug are socially acceptable. They spell out which social situations are approved for drug use and which are not. They define what drugs do, what their actions and effects on people will be. Right or wrong, *each of these social definitions and descriptions will have some degree of impact on actual people in actual drug-taking situations.* Each will exert a powerful influence on what drugs actually do. That a fantastic power to enslave is attributed to heroin actually helps to give heroin the power to enslave; the "effect" does not rest completely within the biochemical properties of the drug (Young, 1971, p. 43). The effective role of placebos in medical therapy has been underscored in numerous discussions and research. (As one psychopharmacologist wryly remarked: "The lethal dosage of placebo is unknown" [Claridge, 1970, p. 26].) That marijuana tends to have a negative and inhibitory effort on the sexual activity of caged rats and a positive and disinhibitory impact on sex in humans indicates the overwhelming role played by social expectations and definitions.

THE POLITICS OF REALITY

The word "politics" has become attached to a variety of phenomena that were previously thought to be unrelated to the arena of politics—the "politics of experience," "the politics of consciousness expansion," "the politics of therapy." Implied in any such term is the notion that what becomes taken for granted in any society is, in fact, arbitrary and problematic. We think that, for example, the psychiatrist-patient relationship and interaction is a technical and medical matter *in toto,* whereas recent thinking in this area has come to the conclusion that ideological, moral, and political considerations are densely woven into the therapeutic process. In a sense, psychiatry becomes a means of upholding one particular ideological view and repressing others, rather than simply helping to make a patient healthy. Likewise, with scientific definitions of reality we can look at science as an institution that has as its task the verification of a special world-view. The rules of science can be looked at as forensic strategies, facts wielded as ideological weapons. This view holds that science is deeply involved with ideology, and that the classical view of scientific "objectivity" is completely mythical.

This concept of "the politics of reality" is especially important in areas of controversy. An extremely naive and outmoded "rationalist" position on facts is that human beings are essentially reasonable, and that the truth will win simply because it is the truth. This point of view assumes that reality has a kind of brute hardness to it. The sociological position is that what is true (whatever this might mean) is less important than what is thought to be true. One of the more fascinating processes to be observed in society is *the way in which certain assertions come to be regarded as true.* Obviously, different individuals and social groups have different stakes, both ideological and material, in certain definitions of what is true. Thus gaining acceptance of one's own view of reality, of what is true, is an ideological and political victory. Science has become the basic arbiter of reality. Almost no one aside from the scientist—and even then usually only the specialist within a given field—has any direct contact with the empirical phenomena scientists describe. The fact that the earth revolves about the sun "makes sense" only when interpreted through specialists; almost no one who believes it has ever tested it for himself or herself. In this sense, scientific truth is not very different from religious truth: We accept it as an act of faith.

In any dispute, we not only want to be morally right, whatever that might entail; we also want to be empirically and scientifically correct. Nothing has greater discrediting power than the assertion that a certain statement has been "scientifically disproven." Generally we search about for evidence to "prove" our value judgments. If we believe marijuana use to be morally reprehensible, we want to back up our position with "objective" facts to show that we are also empirically correct—hence the claim that marijuana is physically or psychologically damaging. Almost no one who believes that marijuana use is immoral also believes that it is harmless; most who view marijuana use with moral indifference do not regard marijuana as damaging (though many feign moral indifference, simply to make their empirical view more credible). We shop around for evidence in much the same way that we trundle through a supermarket, selecting here and there. Facts are manipulated, wielded as bludgeons, employed as rhetorical devices. Presenting facts in the drug area is more like *making a case* than searching objectively for evidence.

Any phenomenon is far more complicated than it appears at first blush. We have been taught to perceive only a small portion of the almost infinite number of possible experiences. Philosophers call this process of selective perception *attending.* We attend to certain kinds of facts and ignore others. "Seeing" is also "not seeing." Whenever a certain observation is made, a sociologically relevant question would be not only "Is it true?" but also

"Why stress this observation rather than another equally valid one?" Thus almost any conceivable discussion of the harmfulness or relative harmlessness of marijuana could be presented validly, with extensive documentation, simply by attending to one segment of the marijuana reality and ignoring others. In medical terms marijuana *is* harmful—damaging and dangerous—to some people under certain circumstances, according to some definitions of harm, at certain dosage levels, in some moods and psychological states. But marijuana is also relatively harmless medically—for most people, most of the time, at the potency levels generally available, and so on.

There is enormous leeway, then, in presenting different views of a phenomenon, especially one as controversial as drug use. We are ultimately interested not in highly concrete facts but in generalizations from the facts. ("Is marijuana harmful?" "Does marijuana use lead to heroin dependency?" "Does marijuana debilitate driving skills?") Since so many different things can and do happen to so many different individuals, the gates are open to pick and choose those facts that are compatible with our own views. One of the central concerns of this book will be an exploration of the politics of reality in the area of drug use.

WHAT IS A DRUG?

The question "What is a drug?" might seem absurdly easy to answer; "everybody knows" what a drug is. The fact is, things are not quite so simple or straightforward. Any adequate definition has to group together all the things that share a given trait and set them apart from those things that do not share that trait. What is the defining trait that all drugs share and that separates them from those phenomena that we cannot call drugs? Most of us assume that the term "drug" refers to a set of substances with clearly identifiable chemical properties or biological effects. It is a common belief that the category "drug" is based on a natural pharmacological reality—that drugs must *be* something or *do* something that makes them part of a natural chemical entity. In short, people generally believe that specific characteristics are *intrinsic* or *dwell within* the substances that are called drugs. This could be called the "objectivistic" definition of what a drug is. One commonly cited definition of a drug is "any substance, other than food, that by its chemical or physical nature alters structure or function in the living organism." However, a moment's reflection tells us that this definition, although widely used, is far too broad and all-encompassing to be of much use; a cup of coffee would qualify, as would vitamin C, penicillin, perfume, ammonia, beer, automobile exhaust fumes, a cold shower, even a bullet fired from a gun.

In fact, no formal, objective property of chemical agents will satisfy the criteria of inclusion and exclusion simultaneously. There is no effect that is common to all "drugs" that at the same time is not shared by "nondrugs." Some drugs are powerful psychoactive agents—they influence how the mind works; others have little or no impact on mental processes. Some drugs have medicinal properties; others have no medical value at all. Some drugs are toxic—they require very small amounts to kill living beings; the toxicity of other drugs is extremely low. Some drugs build tolerance very rapidly—increasingly higher doses are required to achieve a constant effect; others do so slowly or not at all. Some drugs are "addicting"—they produce a physical dependence; others are not. There is no conceivable characteristic that applies to all substances considered drugs.

A sociologist would argue that any accurate and valid definition of drugs must include the social and cultural dimension. The concept "drug" is a cultural artifact, a social fabrication. *A drug is something that has been arbitrarily defined by certain segments of society as a drug.* Although all substances called drugs do not share certain pharmacological traits that set them apart from other, nondrug substances, they do share the trait of being *labeled* drugs by members of society. What this means is that the effects of different drugs have relatively little to do with the way they are conceptualized, defined, and classified. The classification is an artificial one; it resides in the mind, not in the substances themselves. But it is no less real because it is arbitrary. Society defines what a drug is, and this social definition shapes our attitudes toward the class of substances so described. The statement "He uses drugs" calls to mind only certain kinds of drugs. If what is meant by that statement is "He smokes cigarettes and drinks beer," we are chagrined, since cigarettes and beer are not part of our stereotype of what a drug is, even though nicotine and alcohol are certainly drugs by at least one criterion—they are both psychoactive.

Thus there is a popular conception of drugs (mainly illegal drugs) and a psychopharmacological definition (psychoactive drugs) that are somewhat independent of one another. A given chemical substance may be a drug within one definition or sphere of interest but not another. Substances such as primaquine, primadone, prinadol, priodox, priscoline, and privine have important medical uses and are described in reference to works on therapeutics. Yet it would not occur to the man or woman on the street that any of these substances were drugs. Other substances such as peyote, kava-kava, coca leaves, and *Amanita muscaria* are used by certain tribal peoples, but they would not appear anywhere in a work on therapeutic medicine. Penicillin has been one of the most valuable drugs in medical therapy in human history, but it is not used illicitly on the street. Alcohol is a drug in a psychoactive sense, but not if we adopt conventional society's definition: A man who drinks liquor does not think of himself as a drug user, and he would rarely be so defined even by nondrinkers. Nothing is a drug according to some abstract formal definition, but only within certain behavioral and social contexts. Which substances we elect to examine in any discussion of drugs is always arbitrary and depends entirely on our purposes.

Thus, rather than seeking an intrinsic or an objectivistic definition of what a drug is, we must instead use a *subjective* definition. This does *not* mean that the effects of drugs are imaginary or all in the mind—in other words, in the "subjective" realm. It does *not* mean that drugs do not have objective effects. What it *does* mean is that whether a substance is or is not a drug depends on which of its many characteristics or effects are relevant to a given definition. There are many different and equally valid definitions of drugs. Each is created or activated by emphasizing a different facet or *dimension* of the substances in question. Is alcohol a drug? Yes, if we examine its effects: it influences the workings of the mind and body. But no, if we ask the man or woman in the street; most people do not regard alcohol as a drug. Is penicillin a drug? Yes, in that it is used by physicians in medical therapy; no, in that it is not used for its effects on the mind—it is not used to get high. Substances can be drugs in one way, according to one dimension, but not another.

Here are a few of the most important aspects or dimensions of what chemicals are, do, how they are seen, or how they tend to be used, that qualify them for the title "drug."

1. *Medical utility:* substances currently accepted and used in conjunction with healing the body or the mind by physicians (examples: penicillin, aspirin, Thorazine).
2. *Psychoactivity:* substances that have a direct and significant impact on the processes of the mind, that influence emotion, thinking, perception, feeling (LSD, alcohol, amphetamines).
3. *Recreational use:* substances that are used for their subjective effects, to get high (alcohol, marijuana, cocaine).
4. *Illegality:* substances whose possession, use, or sale are against the law for the general public (heroin, LSD, cocaine).
5. *Public definition:* substances that most people think of when they are asked to provide examples of what a drug is (heroin, cocaine, barbiturates).

Clearly, then, some substances can be drugs according to one definition but not another. And equally clearly, each of these dimensions entails a judgment by an actual group of people—the first by the medical profession, the second and third by the people who use or take them or by those who watch or study those who take them, the fourth by the police, the courts, and lawmakers, and the fifth by the general public. Calling a substance a drug entails choosing one or another dimension as important.

Sociologically, all of these dimensions are relevant. Sociologists of medicine and mental illness study the therapeutic use of drugs; sociologists interested in deviant behavior study the recreational use of psychoactive drugs and how public definitions and conceptions of what a drug is influences the social and cultural climate of drug-taking; and criminologists examine the use of substances whose possession and sale are against the law.

In short, when we speak or write of drugs, we are referring to a social and linguistic category of phenomena, not to a natural, objective, or pharmacological category. In other words, "Nothing is a drug but naming it makes it so" (Barber, 1967, p. 166). This does not mean that drug effects are imaginary, that people just think that they occur when they really don't, that there is no such thing as objective or "real" drug effects. The effects are real; we just have to consider them important enough to pay attention to.

When the term "drug" is used in this book, it will refer primarily to *psychoactive* substances, chemicals that influence the workings of the human mind. The term will include marijuana, hallucinogens (such as LSD), cocaine, amphetamines, sedatives and tranquilizers, alcohol, narcotics like heroin, and, interestingly, the nicotine found in ordinary tobacco cigarettes. The possession of several of these substances is more or less completely outlawed; some others it is legal to possess; two (alcohol and tobacco) are legal for everyone above a certain age; and some are pharmaceuticals, legal if taken with a physician's prescription, illegal if not. Almost all of them are used recreationally, to achieve a certain effect, a certain psychic state, to get high, if you will. Nearly all are socially and publicly *defined* as drugs, but a few are not. And several are used therapeutically. But in this book, what is meant by a drug is a psychoactive substance. It is this dimension that all of the substances discussed in this book have in common.

DRUG ABUSE

Physicians commonly apply the term "abuse" to refer to the use of a drug outside a medical context; this the official definition of drug abuse given by the American Medical Association. The term, however, conveys a moral rather than a scientific judgment. Since "abuse" clearly connotes something negative or bad, to employ the term is to discredit and stigmatize drug use rather than to understand or describe it. Those who use the term declare that nonmedical drug use is invariably harmful, without first investigating whether it is in fact so or what constitutes harm in the first place. The concept of "abuse" suggests that only physicians should be permitted to administer drugs. But since the term "drug" is a social and not a medical concept, such strictly medical claims are inconsistent. One never hears of "medically unsupervised" use (and therefore, automatically, "abuse") of alcohol, even though alcohol has effects similar in many ways to those of substances that physicians feel they ought to control or veto. Alcohol use is considered abuse only if it is excessive. On the other hand, by the AMA definition, *any* use of marijuana, regardless of its medical consequences, constitutes abuse, since the drug is not approved for medical purposes by most, and by the most credible, physicians. Purposes such as euphoria, pleasure, relaxation, or mind transformation are considered illegitimate.

As "abuse" is used in context, however, it conveys the distinct impression that something quite measurable is being referred to, something very much like a disease, a medical pathology, a sickness in need of a cure. Thus the term simultaneously serves two functions: it claims clinical objectivity, and it discredits the phenomenon it categorizes. "Abuse" announces to the world that the nonmedical taking of drugs—actually, only *certain types* of drugs, since legal drugs such as alcohol are magically exempt from the definition (and thus the medical definition is a passive and curious reflection of the legal situation)—is undesirable, that the benefits obtained from illegal drugs are counterfeit, and that they are in any case outweighed by the hard rock of medical damage. But since the weighing of values is a moral and not a scientific process, we are able to see the ideological assumptions built into the term. Furthermore, the linguistic category *demands verification.* When labeling anything "abuse," it is necessary to prove that the label is valid. The term so structures our perceptions of the phenomenon that it is possible to see only "abusive" aspects in it. Therefore data must be collected to "demonstrate" the damages of nonmedical drug use. In such ways do science and medicine become the handmaidens of morality and politics.

SOCIAL PROBLEMS, DRUG LEGISLATION, AND MORAL PANICS

Social problems have two aspects or features—objective and subjective. Some observers have stressed the objective features of social problems— that is, concrete conditions that can be readily measured, such as the damage, death, and disease certain conditions cause (Manis, 1974, 1976). Some observers emphasize the subjective features—that is, the degree of public concern that certain issues or conditions generate (Spector and Kitsuse, 1977; Schneider, 1985). The subjective aspect of social problems is related to another concept: the *moral panic* (Cohen, 1980; Ben-Yehuda, 1986). A "moral panic" is a widespread feeling on the part of the public that something is terribly wrong in their society because of the moral failure of a specific group of individuals, a subpopulation defined as the enemy. In short, a category of people has been *deviantized* (Schur, 1980).

As I mentioned in the Prologue, public concern and moral panic surrounding a given issue or condition are only remotely related to the objective consequences or harm of that issue or condition. Extremely damaging conditions or issues often generate little public concern or panic, while conditions or issues that are relatively benign, and have few objective consequences, may generate a firestorm of popular concern and controversy. There is nothing inherent in a concrete phenomenon or condition that makes it a subjectively felt social problem or crisis (Reasons, 1974). It is not solely the objective consequences of conditions that makes them a problem to much of the public; other factors are at work here.

Why do certain conditions become thought of as social problems while others do not? Why are certain conditions looked upon as problems at one point in time, and considered neutral or benign in their impact at another? Why was alcohol accepted as a little more than wholesome beverage (the "good creature of God") in the United States at the turn of the eighteenth century, when consumption was quite high, while by the turn of the nineteenth century, when consumption had declined considerably, sizable segments of the American population defined alcohol an unmixed evil, a scourge—"demon rum" itself (Lender and Martin, 1987)?

Why is the teaching of evolution a problem in one community and banning the teaching of evolution a problem in another? How did the use of psychiatry to silence political dissidence come to be regarded as a problem to the members of the American Psychiatric Association (Spector and Kitsuse, 1977, pp. 97–129)? Why were trailer camps thought of as a problem in some American communities in the 1930s (Fuller and Myers, 1941)? Why does homosexuality float on and off a prominent ranking of the public's hierarchy of social problems? Why was crime against the elderly thought to be of major concern at a time when the elderly were, and still are, the least victimized segment of the population (Yin, 1980; Fishman, 1978)? Why is radon contamination, a cause of 5,000 to 20,000 deaths in the United States each year from lung cancer alone (Eckholm, 1986b), an issue of little public concern or even awareness, while the absurd rumor that the former Procter & Gamble logo was a symbol of Satanism—it showed the face of the man in the moon on a field of thirteen stars—provoked some 6,000 calls a month to the company, which finally had to drop the logo from its packages (Anonymous, 1985)? Why, in short, is there such a loose relationship between the objective impact of a phenomenon and the subjective concern it touches off in the public?

Moral panics are generated as a result of a variety of forces, including the protection, maintenance, or aggrandizement of the interests of a specific class or organization, and the moral "nerve" that issues touch off in the general public (Ben-Yehuda, 1986). While subjectively perceived social crises do not rise and fall randomly or magically, there is nonetheless a great deal of leeway with which issues loom large in the public consciousness as social problems. The process is far from inevitable.

Few people have even a rough idea of the size or extent of many of the harmful—or not-so-harmful—conditions that exist in a given society, as I said in the Prologue. Which causes more deaths—accident or disease? In one survey, they were judged to be equally frequent, in spite of the fact that disease takes about fifteen times as many lives as accidents (Slovic, Fischhoff, and Lichtenstein, 1980). Events that are dramatic and easy to recall are judged to be more common, other things being equal, than those that are less dramatic and more difficult to remember. The media play a role in this process; more dramatic events are more newsworthy, more likely to be reported in the media, more likely to be recalled by readers and viewers, and therefore more likely to be thought of by the public as frequent. Though disease takes 100 times as many lives as homicide, newspapers contain three times as many articles on death from homicide as death from disease (Slovic, Fischhoff, and Lichtenstein, 1980). One study found that the public perception of the extent of crime in a community correlated not at all with the actual crime rate, but very strongly with the amount of news about crime in the media (Davis, 1952).

The subjective dimension of a given social problem is composed of a number of strands. The first is public opinion: the extent to which a significant proportion of the public regards a given condition as a serious social problem (Blumer, 1971). Several times a year, the Gallup Poll asks a sample of the American public what it regards as "the most serious problems facing this country today." The second is the emergence of a social movement designed to deal with the condition (Mauss, 1975): If a segment of the public is sufficiently aroused about a given condition to mobilize, organize, and work together to correct it, it becomes a social problem to a certain extent. And the third is the passage of legislation to correct or eliminate the supposedly undesirable condition (Spector and Kitsuse, 1977, pp. 165–166). Whenever legislation is proposed and passed to correct or eliminate a given condition, we know that a segment of the public—even if it is primarily a small elite that profits from the legislation—regards it as a social problem.

Issues do not become social problems unless there is some reason. Public concern and action about a certain issue rise and fall in part for political, ideological, and moral reasons. There is, in other words, a "politics of social problems." The public may be stirred up as a result of the efforts of a "moral entrepreneur"—an individual who feels that "something ought to be done" about supposed wrongdoing, and takes steps to make sure that certain rules are enforced (Becker, 1963, pp. 147–163). Sometimes, issues emerge as social problems because a social class, an industry, a professional group, or a segment of the public will profit—or lose—as a result of certain changes in the society. Clearly, the tobacco industry's attempt to define legal restrictions on public smoking as violations of the public's constitutional rights falls into this category. Politicians may make speeches about a particular issue and generate concern among the public that a problem exists where none was previously suspected. Events may take place in the lives of celebrities that publicize a condition and galvanize public sentiment toward seeing it as a serious problem; clearly, the death of Rock Hudson from AIDS is a dramatic example. While one or another of these various factors has been emphasized by different observers, they all play a role in generating subjectively perceived crises at different times and in different places.

As we'll see in more detail in later chapters, much of the drug legislation passed in this century was motivated by political and moral reasons rather than by a genuine concern for the health and welfare of vulnerable members of the society. At the very least, political considerations play a significant role in the process by which an objective condition becomes subjectively transformed into a social problem. For example, a major reason for the passage of a series of extremely harsh laws in Canada in the 1920s designed to eradicate the use and sale of opium was prejudice against Chinese immigrants (Cook, 1970).

The criminalization of cocaine possession and sale in forty-six states—at a time when only twenty-nine outlawed opiates such as heroin and morphine—and by the federal Harrison Act of 1914 was spurred by the fear that Blacks were especially heavy cocaine users and did nasty things to whites under the drug's influence (Ashley, 1975, pp. 66–78). More than 2,000

Blacks in Georgia were admitted to hospital in 1914, but only two patients were reported cocaine users (Musto, 1973, p. 8). This fact suggests that the fear that Blacks were especially heavy users of cocaine was not only fanciful, but probably politically and ideologically based.

Perhaps the most powerful factor in the passage of antimarijuana legislation in the 1930s, especially in the western states, was hostility toward and fear of Mexican immigrants. Mexican-Americans were thought to be major consumers of the drug and, it was suspected, acted in a dangerous fashion under its influence. In addition, they were presumed to menace the white community by spreading the use of marijuana. And, moreover, they took jobs away from native-born whites. Because of these political and ideological considerations, antimarijuana legislation appealed to much of the public and to a majority of legislators (Musto, 1973, pp. 221–233; Bonnie and Whitebread, 1970, pp. 1035–1037; 1974, pp. 34–37).

The motivation behind the 1930s marijuana laws leads us to consider another political feature of some social problems: The reason why the public should be concerned about a specific issue often shifts from one era to another. In the 1930s, marijuana use was opposed because it was presumed to cause violence and sexual "excess." None of the antimarijuana tracts of the day failed to mention these two supposed effects, and no other ill effect was stressed as prominently. In contrast, in the 1970s and 1980s, these effects are conspicuously absent even in the most virulent antimarijuana diatribes (Eastland, 1974; Nahas, 1975, 1976; Jones and Jones, 1977; Mann, 1985). In short: "The Killer Weed image virtually disappeared from public discussion in the middle and late 1960s" (Himmelstein, 1983, p. 27).

The Volstead Act, passed in 1918, banning the sale of alcohol in the United States, represented the triumph of rural, white, middle-class native-born Protestants of native-born parentage over urban, working-class ethnics, predominantly Catholic, who were either immigrants or the children of immigrants. The failure of Prohibition represented not only the growing power of the latter group, but a sign that abstinence was no longer a requirement for respectability. Furthermore, the struggle over Prohibition represented a struggle not simply over the consumption of alcohol, but over the relative prestige of two competing groups in American society (Gusfield, 1963).

In short, with alcohol specifically and drugs generally:

> The most passionate support for legal prohibition of narcotics has been associated with fear of a given drug's effect on a specific minority. Certain drugs were dreaded because they seemed to undermine essential social restrictions which kept these groups under control: cocaine was supposed to enable blacks to withstand bullets which would kill normal persons and to stimulate sexual assault. Fear that smoking opium facilitated sexual contact between Chinese and white Americans was also a factor in its total prohibition. Chicanos in the Southwest were believed to be incited to violence by smoking marijuana. Heroin was linked in the 1920s with a turbulent age-group: adolescents in reckless and promiscuous urban gangs. Alcohol was associated with immigrants crowding

into large and corrupt cities. In each instance, use of a particular drug was attributed to an identifiable and threatening minority group (Musto, 1973, pp. 244–245).

The motivation underlying the passage of drug legislation need not be the irrational fear on the part of the white, middle-class majority of a supposedly dangerous or corrupt minority group. At the same time, a form of behavior is unlikely to be regarded as a problem to the society as long as it is more strongly associated with "decent and respectable" classes, segments, or groups. When the public views "unrespectable elements as the primary indulgers," the behavior is more likely to be regarded as deviant, immoral, damaging, and dangerous, and a problem to society—a problem about which something ought to be done (Duster, 1970, pp. 247–248). On the other hand, when the reverse is true—that is, when drug users are perceived to be members of the majority—a more compassionate approach toward legislation is likely to be adopted. While drug use will still be seen as a problem, the nature of the problem will be quite different, and the laws that are passed and enforced to deal with the problem will also differ.

Nevada has one of the harshest set of marijuana laws in the United States. In fact, it is the only state in which first-offense possession of even a minuscule quantity of marijuana is a felony, punishable by up to six years in prison. Interestingly, Nevada is one of only a small handful of states to permit casino gambling, and it is the only state in which prostitution is legal. It is a state with an extremely high rate of transiency, and perhaps the highest ratio of tourists to local residents. Therefore, although most marijuana arrests are of locals—often children of high-status residents—the drug problem is blamed on tourists and transients. The harsh marijuana penalties are rarely invoked; there are very few arrests or convictions under the state statutes. In fact, the actual punishment of marijuana offenders is not too different from that of states with more lenient penalties. The harsh marijuana penalties serve as an announcement to both Nevadans and conservative tourists that Nevada is a state "not totally without moral standards." The law thus is both symbolic and instrumental: It protects the gambling industry, encourages tourists to keep coming, reminds them to stay in line, and warns locals of the consequences of drug violations—and yet does not deal with offenders harshly. Nevada's marijuana law is a perfect political device (Galliher and Cross, 1982, 1983).

In contrast, Utah's marijuana laws, passed in 1971, reduced the penalty for first-offense possession to a misdemeanor. Such legislation may seem odd, given Utah's population, which is extremely conservative and heavily Mormon. Why were these liberal laws passed in such a conservative state? Did Utah's legislators perceive no problem or threat from drugs and drug use? Compared with the population of nearly every state in the nation, and in stark contrast to Nevada's, Utah's population is notably homogeneous and stable. Utah has the lowest rate of alcohol consumption in the nation, the largest families, and the highest per capita level of education. A strong feeling existed in the state that "our kids" should be protected not only from drug use but also from unnecessarily harsh legislation and penalties. Drug use was not perceived (as it has been in other locales) as an external threat from an alien minority, but as an activity in which the sons and daughters of local residents engaged. "If tough laws were to be passed and enforced, they would be used not against some threatening racial or ethnic minority, since few minorities live in Utah, nor against a specific economic class, but against 'our kids.' " Ironically, after the new bill was passed, the number of arrests in the state increased significantly; with more lenient sentences and more discretion given to judges in handing down penalties to offenders, the police were more willing to arrest local youth, knowing that they would not be dealt with harshly (Galliher and Basilick, 1979).

The drug "panic" or "crisis" of the mid- and late 1980s illustrates the notion of the politics of social problems very nicely. The drug issue, although building throughout the 1980s, exploded late in 1985 and early in 1986—a time, ironically, when the use of most drugs was actually declining. How do we know that a drug crisis took place at this time? How did this panic or crisis manifest itself? In what ways was drug use regarded as more of a problem in 1986 than it had been previously?

One concrete measure of how certain phenomena or conditions are perceived as burning issues at a particular time is the number of articles published on those subjects in magazines and newspapers. *The Reader's Guide to Periodical Literature* indexes all the articles published each year in a large number of magazines around the country. In 1979–1980 (March to February), only 15 articles were published nationally on the subjects of "Drug Abuse," "Drugs and Youth," "Drugs and Sports," "Drugs and Employment," "Drugs and Celebrities," "Drugs and Musicians," and "Drug Education." (I did not count cross-listed articles in this tally.) In 1980–1981, the tally was 37; in 1981–1982, 29; in 1982–1983, 38; in 1983–1984, 48; and in 1984–1985, 76. In 1985, the *Reader's Guide* changed the period included in the count to coincide with the calendar year; in that year, there were 103 articles on drug-related topics. In 1986, there were a total of 280 articles on these subjects—more than a twofold increase in only a year, and a sixfold increase in less than three years. Interestingly, according to another count, by December 1986, the number of articles on drugs had begun to drop off from the monthly totals for June through November, suggesting that the crisis had run its course (Jensen, Gerber, and Babcock, 1987).

Another indication of the degree of felt concern about an issue is the legislation proposed to deal with a given issue or problem—both seriously and rhetorically—by politicians and lawmakers. In June 1986, Ed Koch, mayor of the City of New York, urged the death penalty for any drug dealer caught with at least a kilo (2.2 pounds) of either cocaine or heroin. Two months later, Mario Cuomo, governor of New York state and a more temperate politician than Koch, called for a life sentence for anyone caught selling three vials of crack—$50 worth of the drug. In September, during the debates over a new federal drug bill, Claude Pepper, a representative from Florida, said cynically: "Right now, you could put an amendment through to hang, draw, and quarter" drug dealers. "That's what happens when you get on an emotional issue like this," he added (Kerr, 1986c, p. B6). In a series of speeches between June and September, President Ronald Reagan called for a "nationwide crusade against drugs, a sustained, relentless effort to rid America of this scourge." His proposed legislation first added (then, strangely, partly rescinded) $2 billion in federal monies to fight the problem, including $56 million for drug testing for federal employees. In September 1986, the House of Representatives approved, by the overwhelming vote of 393 to 16, a package of drug enforcement, stiffer federal sentences, increased spending for education, treatment programs, and penalties against drug-producing countries that would not cooperate in eradication programs. Approved by the Senate in October, the drug bill, costing $1.7 billion, was signed into law by President Reagan. In short, the drug question preoccupied numerous politicians and lawmakers at the municipal, state, and federal levels, all "scrambling to put their imprint on the issue." For all, "politics have become as important as the substance" (Fuerbringer, 1986).

Social problems or crises are also identified by the public's rankings of the "most important problem facing this country" in opinion polls. Although conditions rarely fluctuate as much in terms of objective seriousness, the feeling on the part of the public that certain conditions are more of a problem than others does vary significantly from year to year. Between 1981 and 1984, drug abuse was not listed among the most important problems named by the public in Gallup polls, indicating a comparatively and consistently low level of concern about it. Throughout 1985 and into January 1986, between 2 and 3 percent of the American public named it as the nation's most important problem. By July 1986, this figure had risen to 8 percent, which placed drug abuse as fourth among major American social problems. In a set of polls conducted by *The New York Times* and CBS in April 1986, 2 percent named drug abuse as the nation's number-one problem; by August, this figure had increased to 13 percent (Clymer, 1986; Jensen, Gerber, and Babcock, 1987). Another Gallup poll, focused specifically on the schools, found that the proportion of respondents who believed that drug use by students was the most important problem facing the public schools increased from 15 percent in 1981 to 20 percent in 1982 and 1983 to 30 percent in 1986 (A. M. Gallup, 1986; Jensen, Gerber, and Babcock, 1987).

Clearly, then, by the middle of 1986, drug abuse was a social problem—in the subjective sense of the word—to the American public. Something of a "moral panic" was taking place, a felt sense of crisis; as Nachman Ben-Yehuda says, the *timing* of moral panics is every bit as important as their focus (1986, pp. 498–499). However, surveys indicated not a rise but an actual decline in drug use between the early and mid-1980s (NIDA, 1986; Johnston, O'Malley, and Bachman, 1987).

Why, then, the increase in concern over the drug issue at this particular time? Several key reasons have been isolated and discussed (Kerr, 1986c; Jensen, Gerber, and Babcock, 1987). As we might expect, they represent a mixture of objective and subjective factors.

The explosion of crack use. At the beginning of 1985, crack, a potent crystalline form of cocaine, was practically an unknown—and unused—drug in the United States. By late 1985, the drug was beginning to be used extensively in urban areas, and the press gave prominent coverage to it. Its previous obscurity, the seeming suddenness of its widespread use—although it had been used on a smaller scale since the early 1980s—and the degree to which it caught on in some neighborhoods made the crack story newsworthy, and gave the public the impression that a major drug crisis had erupted practically overnight. Actually, the drug is heavily used only in some urban areas and, in those, only in certain neighborhoods. The 1986 national high school survey (see Chapter 4 for a description) asked a question about crack use for the first time; about 4 percent of all high-school seniors in a nationwide study said that they had used crack at least once (Johnston, O'Malley, and Bachman, 1987, pp. 16–17, 45).

The death of athletes from cocaine abuse. In June 1986, barely a week apart, two popular young athletes died of a cocaine overdose—on June 19, University of Maryland basketball forward Len Bias, and on June 27, Cleveland Browns defensive back Don Rogers. Bias's death was felt to be especially devastating, to some degree because of the proximity of Maryland's campus to the nation's capital. Said one member of the House of Representatives, "Congress is predominantly male and very sports-oriented." With Bias's death, he said, "you were hit with a devastating blow" (Kerr, 1986c, p. B6).

The role of the media. The drug-related events or developments mentioned above, which would have received a great deal of media attention in any case, were even more nationally prominent because they occurred in close proximity to major media centers—Bias's death in the Washington area, and the emergence of crack specifically in neighborhoods in New York and Los Angeles, "only blocks from the offices of major national news organizations" (Kerr, 1986c, p. B6).

The social class factor. Cocaine has been thought of by the public as an affluent person's drug since the 1920s; this reputation, while not entirely deserved, is to some degree accurate. In terms of the cost per period of time one is intoxicated, cocaine is several times more expensive than heroin. While the cost of powdered cocaine has been dropping throughout the 1980s because of its increased availability, and while the cost of cocaine in the form of crack is far lower than that of powdered cocaine, the public still associates cocaine with a glittery, affluent lifestyle. (To a certain degree, crack is perceived as a separate drug from powdered cocaine.) In contrast, heroin—again, with some justification—is viewed as a drug used by the poor, especially by members of racial minorities. Cocaine happens to be practically the only drug whose use has been increasing during the 1980s, while heroin use and addiction may have actually decreased during the mid- and late 1980s. It is an unfortunate fact that individuals of higher socioeconomic status receive more media and public attention than those ranking lower on the class ladder; bad things that happen to individuals with less education, money, and occupational status are less likely to be written about and less likely to capture the public interest. To some extent, then, a drug crisis was perceived between late 1985 and early 1986 because the only drug (with the exception of crack) whose use was growing was a drug that was associated with the upper reaches of the social hierarchy, especially the rich and famous.

The general political climate. Although not specific to 1986, one factor that helped to highlight the drug issue as a major social problem was the generally conservative political climate of the 1980s. Whether a cause or a consequence of this climate, the election of Ronald Reagan as president of the United States in 1980 set the tone for much of what was to follow throughout the decade, especially in the areas of sex, family, abortion, pornography, homosexuality, civil rights and civil liberties, and, of course, drugs. The marijuana-decriminalization movement, which led to the removal of criminal penalties for small-quantity marijuana possession in eleven states during the 1970s, came to a total standstill in the 1980s. The AIDS scare—which affected attitudes toward both homosexuality and intravenous drug use— received widespread attention for the first time in 1983, but then touched off hundreds of articles in national magazines and probably generated a more conservative sexual lifestyle among a sizable proportion of the American population. A number of states raised their legal drinking age to 21, and drunk driving emerged as a major organizational and political issue. Drugs in the workplace came to be thought of as a major social problem, and mandatory drug testing for workers in a number of occupations came to be an acceptable means of controlling abuse. A "get tough" policy toward drug use was instituted in the military, with automatic discharge for officers and mandatory treatment for the first-offense enlisted; public perception holds that this policy has drastically reduced what had previously been seen as a serious problem. In short, "It was in this general setting of conservatism that drugs could emerge as the leading social problem" facing the country today (Jensen, Gerber, and Babcock, 1987, p. 17).

The lag factor. It has been suggested that one of the reasons for the emergence of strong public concern about drug use and abuse in the mid-1980s was the delayed awareness of the existence of a problem that had been building for some time—that is, the *time lag factor.* The irony that heightened awareness came at precisely the time when the use of most drugs was actually declining is of no particular import, according to this view. It simply takes a while for the awareness of the seriousness of a problem to seep in. This is especially the case with a problem such as drug use, where the manifestations of abuse and addiction may take a number of years to appear. "Societies tend to react against drugs slowly, and the reaction usually comes just after the popularity of drugs has peaked," says David Musto, a drug historian. "Societies," Musto argues, "typically pass through three stages in a cycle of drug use: an initial stage of euphoria as a small elite experiments with drugs and reports few negative effects; a middle period as drug use disperses to a wider population and examples of ill effects grow; and finally a period of rejection as the popular image of drugs becomes negative" (Kerr, 1986c, p. B6).

The 1986 Congressional elections. The 1986 elections cannot be discounted as a source of heightened concern about the drug issue (Kerr, 1986c; Jensen, Gerber, and Babcock, 1987). There is something of a *dialectical,* or give-and-take relationship between public concern and attention by politicians to a given issue. On the one hand, we see a "bandwagon" effect here: politicians sense that public concern about and interest in a given topic are growing and they exploit this—in other words, "Congress smells an issue" (Kerr, 1986c, p. B6). "When the media started talking about it, it lit a fire," said one political aide. "Senators, once they started talking, realized they were all hearing similar things from their local officials" (Kerr, 1986c, p. B6). On the other hand, while politicians took advantage of an issue that was in the incipient problem stage, once they got on the drug bandwagon, public concern escalated even further (Jensen, Gerber, and Babcock, 1987, p. 23). We need not accuse politicians of being scheming Machiavellians on the drug issue; it is their job to get elected, and they do it the best way they know how. Moreover, they would say, it is also their job to answer the needs and concerns of their constituency, and dealing with the drug issue, if only with words, was one way of doing just that.

The role of prominent spokespersons. Soon after Ronald Reagan took office in 1981, his wife, Nancy, began making public speeches stressing the anti-drug theme. It was from her office that the "Just say no" slogan emerged. Some observers have suggested (Beck, 1981) that Mrs. Reagan chose the issue in part out of public relations considerations. She had initially been portrayed by the media as a "cold and insensitive person, whose chief concern seemed to be her wardrobe" (Jensen, Gerber, and Babcock, 1987, p. 16). Her choice of the drug issue could very well have been made to boost her public image, to suggest that she is compassionate and concerned. Regardless of its initial motivation, her campaign, while, again, little more than words, bore fruit some five years after it was launched. The drug crisis of the mid-1980s has to be set within the context of Mrs. Reagan's immensely publicized campaign. It was she who took the first steps toward galvanizing public concern and media attention. While other spokespersons have "spoken out against drugs," she, more than any single individual, is responsible for the success of the drug panic.

APPENDIX: THE COMPREHENSIVE DRUG ABUSE PREVENTION AND CONTROL ACT

The federal Comprehensive Drug Abuse Prevention and Control Act (see Table 1.1) distinguished five categories, or "schedules," of drugs on the basis of their "abuse potential" and their medical utility. Schedule I drugs

Table 1.1   Comprehensive Drug Abuse Prevention and Control Act

SCHEDULE I	Great abuse potential; no accepted medical use. (Research use only, separate records, vault storage.) Examples: heroin, LSD, mescaline, marijuana (marijuana's medical status has been amended by 25 state laws).
SCHEDULE II	Great abuse potential; accepted medical use. (Written prescription, no refills, separate records, vault storage.) Examples: codeine, morphine, cocaine, methadone, amphetamines, methaqualone, short-acting barbiturates.
SCHEDULE III	Abuse potential lesser; accepted medical use. (Written or oral prescription, refill if authorized 5 times in 6 months.) Examples: long-acting barbiturates, certain narcotic solutions (such as paregoric, or a tincture of opium in alcohol) or mixtures (such as 1.8% codeine).
SCHEDULE IV	Abuse potential low; accepted medical use. (Prescription requirements same as Schedule III.) Examples: minor tranquilizers, including Valium, Librium, Miltown, and Equanil.
SCHEDULE V	Minimum abuse potential; minimum controls. Examples: antitussives, antidiarrheals.

supposedly have a "high potential for abuse" and "no currently accepted medical use." They include heroin, LSD and the other hallucinogens (peyote, mescaline, psilocybin), methedrine, and marijuana. Use may take place legally on a research basis only. (States have modeled their laws on this act, but have amended it in many cases; for instance, marijuana is approved, on an experimental basis, for medical purposes in twenty-five states.) Schedule II drugs are also regarded as having "great abuse potential," but they do have accepted medical use. Prescriptions, for which there can be no refills, must be written by physicians; these prescriptions must be filled out in triplicate and a record of them kept in three locations—Washington, the capital of the state in which they were written, and the physician's files. In addition, the drugs themselves must be stored in a vault. Schedule II drugs include morphine, cocaine, methaqualone, the short-acting barbiturates, and the amphetamines. Schedule III drugs supposedly have a "lesser" abuse potential than those in Schedules I and II, and they have medical utility. These drugs "may lead to low physical dependence or high psychological dependence." Prescriptions may be filled five times in six months, copies are not required, and the drugs do not have to be stored in a vault. Schedule III drugs include long-acting barbiturates, some non-narcotic painkillers, and some narcotic solutions or mixtures. Schedule IV drugs are those whose abuse potential is considered extremely low; procedures are similar to those for Schedule III drugs. Representative drugs include the minor tranquilizers. The controls on Schedule V drugs are minimal.

As a general rule, there is a direct relationship between a drug's classification and the likelihood that a physician will prescribe it to patients. The greater the restrictions on prescribing it, the less likely it is to be prescribed. Upgrading a drug's schedule (say, from III to II) is a signal to the medical profession of its "abuse potential"; in addition, upgrading a drug entails going through more detailed, even burdensome, procedures to prescribe it. Such upgrading always results in a sharp reduction in the number of prescriptions written for a given drug, and consequently a drop in its sales. It must be said that the Comprehensive Drug Abuse Prevention and Control Act is responsible for a certain proportion of the drop in drug prescriptions for a number of pharmaceuticals in the last few years. This has been especially true for specific drugs whose classification was moved from Schedule III to Schedule II—such as amphetamines, barbiturates, and methaqualone.

CHAPTER 2

Drugs and Drug Use

Drugs are both chemical substances and social, cultural, and symbolic phenomena that are perceived, dealt with, and used in certain ways by the general society and by groups within it. We must therefore examine the social climate surrounding drug use in order to understand its causes, extent, and consequences. Sociological factors always affect a drug's pharmacology. It is a bit misleading to discuss the effects of drugs without emphasizing that drug effects are dependent or *contingent* on a number of key factors. What a drug does to the mind and body of a user depends on how it is taken. Drugs never do anything in the abstract. While different drugs do have a certain *potential* for specific effects on humans, whether this potential is actually realized is not a simple matter of biochemistry. All drug use takes place within a certain social context or setting. Customs and personal factors determine key variables that may, in turn, have strictly physical effects. That a drug can have certain effects on humans in a hospital or a clinical setting, or on animals in a laboratory, is no assurance that it will do so in real life, in actual drug-taking situations, simply because people in the street may not take it the way experimenters administer it in a research context.

For instance, alcohol does have the effect of debilitating motor coordination. But it is people who decide whether or not to drive while intoxicated. These are social, cultural, and personal considerations; they are not dictated by the objective properties of the drug itself. As we'll see in the chapter on alcohol, this drug's effects are highly variable from one culture to another. It is the custom to chew coca leaves in the South American Andes. In the United States, this is a highly unusual method for ingesting cocaine; recreational users here generally sniff or snort doses containing 10 to 50 percent cocaine. Again, the sociological factors surrounding the use of cocaine determine how it is used—and, as a consequence, what effects it has. The cocaine Americans take to get high is diluted as a result of the drug's criminal status: Here, too, sociological factors enter the picture. Pure cocaine may have specific effects on the human mind and body, but what users actually take is itself dependent on the type of society we live in.

FACTORS THAT INFLUENCE DRUG EFFECTS

At the same time, it would be a mistake to ignore how and why a drug works in a strict laboratory setting. That is, we must explore both *pharmacological* and *extra-pharmacological* factors influencing drug effects (remembering, of course, that extra-pharmacological factors, like the legal climate, always affect the pharmacological). Pharmacology, a scientific field of study that examines changes in organisms produced by chemical substances, especially drugs, would look at the impact that the following factors have on drug effects: (1) identity, (2) dose, (3) potency and purity, (4) drug mixing, (5) route of administration, and (6) habitation. It is relatively unlikely to study (7) set, and (8) setting, factors more within the scope of the social scientist.

The notion of a drug effect is extremely broad and all-encompassing. At the very least, effects should be divided into those that can be called "objective" and those that are "subjective." Some effects can be seen and measured by an outside observer (someone like a physician or a scientist) fairly precisely; other effects are experienced by the user and can be known only in a secondhand fashion, by means of verbal reports from users, to those who do not take the drug themselves. In short, some effects happen mainly in the body, while others happen mainly in the mind. Both are equally "real," although subjective effects tend to be more difficult to study; they are also a great deal more interesting to the sociologist. Some drugs have a relatively superficial impact on the workings of the mind, but powerfully influence certain functions or organs of the body; other drugs work in the opposite fashion. Still others work in both ways.

It should be strongly stressed that subjective effects are not those that the user mistakenly thinks happen, as contrasted with objective effects, which the scientist correctly sees are truly occurring. Subjective effects are no less real than objective ones; they simply exist in different dimensions. Some subjective experiences do have an "objective" referent—for instance, believing that one can drive better under the influence of alcohol than sober. In this case, we have an incorrect subjective belief and a correct objective fact: One's ability to drive actually does deteriorate under the influence. But most subjective effects have no objective referent at all; they are not about what is happening in the physical world. They are about what is happening in the user's mind under the influence. The experience is the ultimate truth here.

A second dimension distinguishing between different types of effects is the *acute-chronic* dimension. Some effects are short-term and take place *under the influence* of a drug, specifically during the minutes or hours subsequent to its ingestion; these are called its *acute* effects. Others take place over the long run, in the months or years of continued use, even when the user is not under the influence; these are called its *chronic* effects. It is improper to assume that acute effects automatically occur at the chronic level as well. This is a matter to be investigated scientifically. For instance, a given drug may induce acute memory loss under the influence, but may not do so over the long run, when users are not under the influence. Basically, then, there are three different types of effects: *acute subjective, acute objective,* and *chronic.* An example of an acute subjective effect would be the euphoria many users of cocaine feel when they take that drug. An example of an acute objective effect would be an increase in heartbeat rate that can be measured in users under the influence of marijuana, or the decline in motor skills that follows the ingestion of alcohol. And a chronic effect of the heavy, long-term use of barbiturates would be the development of a physical dependence, or the damage to the liver of the alcoholic. When we examine drugs and drug use, we must keep in mind the different levels or dimensions on which drug effects manifest themselves.

Identity

The identity of a drug is both simple and yet crucial: *Is the drug as advertised?* What is the substance being taken or administered? No matter how influential social factors are, it still makes a great deal of difference just what drug the user is ingesting. A great many of the substances that are illegally sold on the street are something other than they are said to be. Chemical analyses of street drugs have turned up a high proportion of bogus substances. Very little of what is sold today as mescaline is actually real mescaline. Street dealers have been known to sell canned mushrooms bought in supermarkets and dipped in LSD as psilocybin. Many pharmaceutical "lookalikes" contain nothing but caffeine, and are sold as stimulants or cocaine. (*The PharmChem Newsletter* publishes a monthly analysis of the chemical composition of street drugs.) So before we can talk about a drug's effects, we have to be certain just what drug we are really discussing. Many people who claim to have taken a certain drug have not actually had any experience at all with it.

Dose

The dose of the drug taken makes an absolutely crucial difference. Any discussion of drug effects is completely meaningless without a discussion of dose. A drug's chemical and pharmacological properties remain only a potentiality until the matter of dose is considered. There are dosage levels at which no drug would have any discernible effect on anyone, and there are other levels at which any drug would have extremely harmful effects on anyone. It is easier to die of an overdose of marijuana than of an overdose of heroin—if the dose of marijuana is several pounds, eaten, and that of heroin several micrograms. But the fact is, no one eats pounds of marijuana at a time, and consequently, no one dies of an overdose of the stuff. Likewise, heroin users and addicts do not take doses as small as several micrograms—doses are generally several hundred times this amount—and as a result, some heroin addicts do die after injecting the drug.

Thus the questions that have to be asked, even before the issue of drug effects is discussed, are "What is the customary dose of the drug that users take?" and "What are the drug's effects *at those dosage levels*?" Traditions have evolved for each drug in every society, and among groups within them, concerning what is an appropriate dose of one or another drug. Most drugs exhibit what pharmacologists call a *dose-response curve*—that is, specific effects occur at specific doses of the drug in question. As a general rule, the higher the dose that is taken of a given drug, the more extreme the effect, whatever the effect we select. After a given point, the effect usually reaches a kind of plateau, and greater doses do not have more extreme effects. In order to know a drug's effects, then, it is first necessary to know the dose of the drug that is taken.

Potency and Purity

Potency refers to the quantity of a drug that will produce a given effect. The lower the dose it takes to produce a given effect, the higher the potency of that drug. Marijuana is naturally variable in potency. Some batches will contain 1 percent THC (tetrahydrocannabinol, a group of chemicals scientists believe brings about the marijuana "high"); other batches will be as potent as 10 percent; still others are so weak that no one could possibly get high smoking them.

Purity is just what the word suggests: the percent of the batch or sample that is actually composed of the drug in question. Most of the drugs sold on the street vary enormously in purity. Consequently, it is misleading to discuss the ingestion of a given drug by itself. In fact, users take batches or samples that contain varying amounts and proportions of the drug in question. One bag sold on the street as heroin might be composed of 3 percent actual heroin, and will contain three milligrams of the drug itself. (The rest will be made up of relatively inert and nonpsychoactive substances that don't get the user high, such as quinine and lactose or milk sugar.) Another bag might be 10 percent pure, and contain ten milligrams of heroin. And a third sample could contain no heroin at all. Likewise, cocaine varies in purity, from about 5 percent to as much as 50 percent at the retail level. Both heroin and cocaine are "hit," "cut," or "stepped on" with cheap, nonactive fillers. From the laboratory to the street, a given batch may have been diluted a half-dozen times by sellers at each level of dealing.

Drug Mixing

Drug mixing is extremely common nowadays. Many people who take one drug also use another in combination with it. A popular street drug called a "speedball" contains a combination of heroin and cocaine, or heroin and amphetamine. (In 1982, the comic actor John Belushi died after injecting a mixture of cocaine and heroin. If he had taken either by itself, it is unlikely that he would have died.) Cocaine is commonly snorted while the user is also high on marijuana. Users frequently take methaqualone (Quaalude, Sopor) while they drink beer. In the pharmacological phenomenon known as *synergy,* certain drugs, taken simultaneously, have a stronger effect than if they are taken separately. Alcohol and barbiturates exhibit synergistic effects. For instance, the chance of dying of an overdose as a result of taking both together is greater than the chance taking twice as much of either separately. This multiplier effect is characteristic of many drug combinations.

Route of Administration

The way a drug is taken influences the effects it has on users. Some drugs are taken, almost always, in only one way in a given society. In large part, the culture determines a certain route of administration as proper and customary. Marijuana is nearly always smoked in the United States. In other cultures, it may be sprinkled or mixed in certain foods (as in India and the Middle East), or brewed in tea (as in Jamaica). Experimenters who study marijuana's effects are fond of administering marijuana to their subjects orally in the form of THC tablets; this produces effects that are quite different from those users experience if they smoke the stuff.

Intravenous injection (or "mainlining") is one of the most efficient means of delivering a drug to the bloodstream; it also produces one of the strongest effects. Intramuscular injection (also called "skin popping" or "joy popping"), injecting a drug right into the muscles of the leg or arm, is less efficient than mainlining, but it does the job for more experimental and less involved users. Snorting a drug into one's nostrils is even less efficient than skin popping. And taking a drug via oral doses, in the form of tablets or capsules, or in the form of a drink, or mixed with food, is the least efficient of the most widely used methods of administering drugs; it takes more to get you high, or have any given effect, and consequently, the dose must be larger than for other routes. Certain drugs cannot be taken by means of specific routes. For instance, marijuana is not injected, partly because it is not soluble in water. It is almost never sniffed or snorted, in part because the leaves will not dissolve in and be absorbed by the nasal membranes.

Habituation

Habituation refers to how accustomed one is to taking a certain drug. Since the continued use of most drugs leads to *tolerance,* or a build-up of the quantity necessary to produce a given effect, habituated users can and will take more of a given drug than the drug-naive individual. Junkies inject a quantity of heroin that produces euphoria in them, but would bring about a painful death by overdose in nonusers. In addition to the strictly pharmacological factor of tolerance, there is also *behavioral tolerance*: users become increasingly experienced with the drug and learn to handle its effects. An experienced drinker requires more alcohol to produce discoordination than an alcohol-naive nondrinker. There is, of course, a limit to behavioral tolerance; at a certain level, everyone who is administered alcohol will manifest significant discoordination.

Set and Setting

The term "set" refers to the psychic, mental, and emotional state of the individual taking the drug. It includes expectations, intelligence, personality, imagination, mood, and so on. "Setting" refers to the social and physical environment within which drug use takes place. It could refer to the user's immediate surroundings, such as a living room in one's own house, or it could refer to the broader social and cultural scene—for instance, the legal climate of a country with respect to drug use and possession, or the degree of condemnation of use and users. Setting involves such matters as whether one takes a drug with friends or with strangers, in surroundings that one is comfortable or uncomfortable with, while engaged in activities that are compatible with or clash with the drug state—such as driving or interacting with strangers. Clearly, setting in part determines set.

A CLASSIFICATION OF DRUGS AND THEIR EFFECTS.

All classifications of drugs and their effects are a least a bit misleading. Classifications put things into categories. But categories are significant and meaningful to the human mind, not to nature. We invent reasons why the world should be divided in a certain way. Drugs do not "belong" together in a certain category and apart from others in another category as a result of an edict from reality, science, or nature. The truth is, we latch on to certain traits as a relevant basis for a classification scheme. One of the basic principles in pharmacology is that *all drugs have multiple effects.* This means that one effect of a drug will lead a pharmacologist to place it in one category, while another effect will place it in an altogether different category. Which category does the drug "belong" in? The answer is, it depends on what is of interest to observers; it does not depend on the characteristics of the substance itself. For instance, cocaine has a stimulating effect on many organs and functions of the body, so that it can be classified as a stimulant. But it also has the property of being a local anesthetic: it numbs the sensation of pain upon contact with tissue. Its pain-killing property puts it in a category that shares a trait with many depressants that have, in nearly all other ways, effects opposite to those of stimulants.

But classify we must, for, as misleading as the process is, it is also necessary: the human mind cannot work in any other way. Since the actions of drugs are so complex, any classification scheme will omit most drugs, as well as most effects of the drugs it does classify. A very small proportion of the hundreds of thousands of psychoactive chemicals that are synthesized, isolated, or discovered actually end up being used on a widespread basis.

One way of classifying drugs is to look at their effect on the central nervous system (CNS)—the brain and the spinal cord. Drugs can directly *stimulate* or *depress* the CNS, or they can have no effect on it, or they can have a complicated or contradictory effect. The action of the central nervous system is of great interest to anyone concerned with human behavior, and therefore any drug that has a significant impact on it should concern us.

Central-nervous-system *stimulants* produce arousal, alertness, even excitation; they inhibit fatigue and lethargy. Such stimulants as amphetamines, cocaine, caffeine, nicotine, and ritalin speed up signals passing through the CNS.

Depressants have the opposite effect: They inhibit and slow down signals passing through the central nervous system. There are two basic types of depressants. The first is made up of the *analgesics,* which inhibit one main action of the CNS—the perception of pain. Narcotics are the most important type of analgesic for our purposes; this category includes opium and its various derivatives—morphine, heroin, and codeine—as well as synthetic and semisynthetic narcotics, like Percodan, methadone, and meperidine (or Demerol). All narcotics produce a physical dependency, often called an addiction. There are several drugs that also have the narcotics' pain-killing property, but do not produce an addiction or a "high" when ingested; they are simply referred to as *non-narcotic analgesics.* Aspirin is the best-known and most widely used representative of this drug type; Darvon and Talwin are two others.

Although narcotics have a very powerful and relatively specific impact on a single function of the body—the perception of pain—what are called *general depressants* are far more wide-ranging in their action. They induce an inhibition of many organs and functions of the body, and they produce relaxation and inhibit anxiety; at higher doses, they result in drowsiness and, eventually, sleep. Alcohol (or, technically, ethyl alcohol, or ethanol) is a general depressant, as are sedatives (like the barbiturates) and tranquilizers (such as Valium). Originally, pharmacologists thought that tranquilizers relieved anxiety without producing the mental cloudiness, drowsiness, and, for heavy, chronic, long-term use, physical dependence that is characteristic of the sedatives. However, today it is clear that tranquilizers are far more similar to sedatives than was previously believed; often, mental clouding and drowsiness result from their use and, if the drug is taken at a high enough dosage for long enough, an actual physical addiction results.

Tranquilizers are divided into "major" and "minor." "Major" tranquilizers are those taken for "major" mental illnesses; they are called *antipsychotics,* and are administered to mental patients. "Minor" tranquilizers are used for "minor" mental problems, such as anxiety and insomnia. In sufficiently high doses, they can induce an intoxication or high, and they are frequently sold and used illegally. Sedatives include two categories of barbiturates—long-acting and short-acting. Long-acting barbiturates (such as phenobarbital) take a long time to produce an effect, and are not used very much for recreational purposes. Short-acting barbiturates (Tuinal, Seconal, Amytal, and Nembutal) produce a high and are used with a fair amount of frequency on the street. Methaqualone (Quaalude, Parest, Sopor) produces effects

Table 2.1 A Classification of Psychoactive Drugs

NARCOTICS
  Opium and Derivatives ("Opiates"): Opium, Morphine, Heroin, Codeine,
    Dilaudid
SEDATIVES AND TRANQUILIZERS (GENERAL DEPRESSANTS)
  Short-Acting Barbiturates: Amytal, Nembutal, Seconal, Tuinal
  Long-Acting Barbiturates: Phenobarbital, Fiorinal
  Nonbarbiturate Sedatives (Methaqualone): Quaalude, Sopor, Parest, Alcohol
  Minor Tranquilizers: Valium, Librium, Equanil/Miltown
  Major Tranquilizers: Thorazine, Stelazine, Mellaril
STIMULANTS
  Amphetamines: Dexedrine, Benzedrine, Desoxyn, Biphetamine, Dexamyl,
    Methedrine
  Nonamphetamine Stimulants: Cocaine, Ritalin, Caffeine, Nicotine
HALLUCINOGENS
  LSD, Mescaline, Psilocybin, MDA
MARIJUANA
INHALANTS
  Amyl Nitrite, Butyl Nitrite, Nitrous Oxide, Aerosol, Toluene (glue, etc.)

very similar to those of the barbiturates, and is fairly popular as an illicit recreational drug.

Hallucinogens (once also called psychedelics) have effects on the central nervous system that are not fully understood and cannot be reduced to a simple stimulation-depression dimension. They occupy their own category and include LSD, mescaline, psilocybin, and MDMA. Marijuana has at different times and by different experts been classified as a stimulant, a depressant, and, most recently, a hallucinogen. Many observers now feel that it belongs in a category by itself. Recently, a drug that was once used as an animal tranquilizer, PCP ("angel dust"), or Serynil, has entered into some classifications as a hallucinogen because it is capable of producing hallucinations. Yet it shares none of the other major properties of hallucinogens; I prefer to classify PCP as a kind of sedative with paradoxical and unpredictable effects.

Pharmacologists pay very close attention to two phenomena they call *cross-tolerance* and *cross-dependence.* As a general rule, drugs that are put into a specific drug category can replace or substitute for one another. If one is addicted to heroin and the effects begin to wear off, one can avoid undergoing withdrawal symptoms by taking another narcotic, such as morphine or methadone. This is an example of cross-dependence. If one takes LSD every few hours for several days, tolerance will set in: it will take more and more of the drug to get high. Eventually, it will become almost impossible to get high unless one stops taking it for a while. (But if one takes a different category of drug, one can still get high on that drug.) If one takes another hallucinogen, like mescaline or psilocybin, one still won't be able to get high; it will have more or less the same noneffect as LSD. One has become tolerant to the effects of all the hallucinogens simply by taking one frequently. This is an example of cross-tolerance. Marijuana is not cross-tolerant with any of the hallucinogens. This is one reason why many observers feel that it does not belong in this category.

Lastly, there is a category of drugs whose members are classified by their route of administration, and not by their effects. These are the *inhalants*—drugs that are gaseous and are inhaled or sniffed, and not drunk, smoked, swallowed, or injected. Inhalants include nitrous oxide ("laughing gas"), amyl nitrite and butyl nitrite ("poppers," "snappers," "amys," or "rush"), and various substances that contain toluene, such as solvents and glue. In addition, aerosol cans are sometimes broken into and their contents sniffed for the effect.

There are a number of other drugs or drug categories that do not fit into this classification scheme—for instance, antidepressants, or "mood elevators." However, the drugs presented here make up the overwhelming majority of those that are used illegally for recreational purposes.

ADDICTION AND DEPENDENCE

Although it has been known for at least 2,000 years that certain drugs "have the power to enslave men's minds," it was not until the nineteenth century that the nature of physical addiction began to be clearly understood. At that time, a "classic" conception of addiction was formed, based on the opiates—at first, opium and morphine, then, after the turn of the century, heroin as well. Much later, it was recognized that alcohol, sedatives, such as barbiturates, and "minor" tranquilizers also produced most of the symptoms of "classic" addiction.

What is "classic" addiction? If a person takes certain drugs in sufficient quantity over a sufficiently long period of time, and stops taking it abruptly, the user will experience a set of physical symptoms known as *withdrawal.* These symptoms—depending on the dose and the duration—include chills, fever, diarrhea, muscular twitching, nausea, vomiting, cramps, and general bodily aches and pains, especially in the bones and the joints. It does not much matter what one thinks or how one feels about the drug, or even whether one knows one has been taking an addicting drug. (One may not attribute one's discomfort to the drug, but these physical symptoms will occur nonetheless.) These symptoms are not psychological—that is, "all in the mind." They are physiological, and most of them can be replicated in laboratory animals. The withdrawal syndrome is the nervous system's way of "compensating" for the removal of the drug after the body has become acclimatized to its presence and effects.

Although the label "addicting" has been pinned at some time or another on practically every drug ever ingested, it began to be recognized that certain drugs simply do not have physically addicting properties. Regardless of the dose administered or the length of time the drug is ingested, the same sort of withdrawal symptoms exhibited with heroin, alcohol, or the barbiturates cannot be induced in humans or animals taking LSD, marijuana, or cocaine. Users will not become physically sick upon the discontinuation of the use or administration of these drugs. In a word, these substances are not addicting in the "classic" sense of the word. If we mean by "addicting" the appearance of "classic" withdrawal symptoms after prolonged use and abrupt discontinuation, then certain drugs are addicting and others are not.

This bothered a number of officials and experts a great deal. Saying that a drug is not addicting seemed to border perilously close on stating that it is not very dangerous. Something had to be done. Some new concept or terminology had to be devised to make nonaddicting drugs sound as if they were in fact addicting. In the early 1950s, the World Health Organization, in an effort to devise a new terminology that would apply to the "abuse" of all drugs, and not simply those that are physically addicting, adopted the term "drug dependence." As it appeared in its final form in a later statement, drug dependence was defined as:

> . . . a state of psychic dependence or physical dependence, or both, on a drug, arising in a person following administration of that drug on a periodic or continued basis. The characteristics of such a state will vary with the agent involved, and these characteristics must always be made clear by designating the particular type of drug dependence in each specific case. . . . All of these drugs have one effect in common: they are capable of creating, in certain individuals, a particular state of mind that is termed "psychic dependence." In this situation, there is a feeling of satisfaction and psychic drive that require periodic or continuous administration of the drug to produce pleasure or to avoid discomfort (Eddy et al., 1965, p. 723).

Under the new terminology, each drug has its own characteristic type of dependence: There is a "drug dependence of the morphine type," a "drug dependence of the cannabis [marijuana] type," a "drug dependence of the alcohol type," and so on. In other words, the new terminology is a definition, or a series of definitions, by enumeration, for it was felt that no single term could possibly cover the diverse actions of the many drugs in use (or "abuse").

The new terminology was extremely imprecise and clearly biased. The intent of the drug experts who devised this terminology was ideological: To make sure that a discrediting label was attached to as many widely used drugs as possible. Under the old terminology of "classic" addiction, it was not possible to label a wide range of drugs as "addicting." It thus became necessary to stigmatize substances such as marijuana and LSD with a new term that resembled "addicting." In other words, the scientists and physicians who devised the new terminology of "dependence" were in effect disseminating propaganda to convince the public that nonaddicting substances were just as "bad" for them, that they could be just as dependent on them as on the truly "addicting" drugs. Medical authorities labeled the continued (or even the sporadic) use of nonaddicting drugs as "dependence" in large part because they were unable to understand why anyone would want to take them in the first place.

Physical dependence is a powerful concept. With a great deal of accuracy, it predicts what will happen physiologically to an organism that takes enough of a certain drug for a long enough period of time. Can psychological dependence be an equally useful concept? Does the fact that it was devised for propagandistic purposes mean that it is automatically meaningless?

During the 1970s and 1980s, researchers began to see some strong parallels between physical and psychological dependence. To put it another way, the fact that one drug is physically addicting and another is not does not seem to predict the patterns of their use very well. Some crucial facts and findings have emerged in the past generation—since the World Health Organization's notion of psychological dependence was formulated—to suggest that perhaps the concept of psychological dependence may not be meaningless.

First, as we'll see in Chapter 10, *most* regular users of heroin are not physically addicted in the classic sense. They take wildly varying amounts of heroin on a day-by-day basis, often go a day or two without the drug and do not suffer powerful withdrawal symptoms, take several doses a day for the next several days, and so on (Johnson et al., 1984; Johnson, 1984; Zinberg, 1984). If physical addiction were so crucial in determining use, this pattern would be unlikely, perhaps even impossible.

Second, even the heroin users who are physically addicted and withdraw—whether because of imprisonment, the intervention of a treatment program, or self-imposed withdrawal—usually go back to using heroin; roughly nine addicts in ten who withdraw become readdicted within two years. If physical dependence were the major factor in continued use, we would predict a much lower relapse rate than this. If the physical compulsion or craving is absent, why return to a life of addiction?

Third, many of the drugs that are not physically addicting are often used in much the same way that the addicting drugs are—that is, frequently, compulsively, in large doses, at an enormous personal and physical toll on the user. How could an addicting drug like heroin and a nonaddicting drug like amphetamine or cocaine produce similar use patterns? If addiction—the product of a biochemically induced craving—is the principal explanation for compulsive use, then how is this possible?

Fourth, and perhaps most crucial, was the hold that cocaine, a supposedly nonaddicting drug, was found to have on laboratory animals. The researchers who conducted these experiments wanted to answer several basic questions: How reinforcing is cocaine? How dependent do animals become on the drug? How much will they go through or put up with to continue receiving it? They discovered that animals will go through practically anything to continue receiving their "coke."

Three key sets of experiments establishing cocaine's dependence potential were conducted. In all three, a catheter was inserted into the vein of a laboratory animal (rats, monkeys, and dogs were used). A mechanism, usually a lever, was rigged up so that animals could self-regulate intravenous (IV) administration of the drug. In one set of experiments, animals were given a choice between cocaine and food; they could have one or the other, but not both. Consistently, laboratory animals chose to continue receiving cocaine instead of food, to the point where they literally died of starvation.

In a second set of experiments, the cocaine was abruptly withdrawn; pressing a bar no longer produced any cocaine. The researchers reasoned that the longer that unreinforced bar-pressing behavior continued, the more dependency-producing a drug is: The more frequently that animals press the bar before they give up—before bar-pressing is "extinguished"—the greater the dependence potential of the drug. Not only did animals that had taken cocaine over a period of time continue to press the bar many times after the drug was withdrawn, but, even more remarkable, they did so far longer than did those animals that had taken heroin—a clearly addicting drug! (A summary of the experiments conducted on the dependence potential of cocaine in animals may be found in Johanson, 1984.)

In a third experiment, one set of laboratory rats was allowed to self-administer cocaine; and a second set, heroin. Both groups could do this continuously and ad libitum—that is, at will, as much or as little as they chose. Those rats that self-administered heroin developed a stable pattern of use, maintained their pretest weight, continued good grooming behavior, and tended to be in good health. Their mortality rate was 36 percent after thirty days. Those self-administering cocaine ad libitum exhibited an extremely erratic pattern of use, with "binges" of heavy use alternating with brief periods of abstinence. They lost 47 percent of their body weight, ceased grooming behavior, and maintained extremely poor physical health. After thirty days, 90 percent were dead (Bozarth and Wise, 1985).

It is absolutely crucial to emphasize that humans are not rats, and experimental conditions are not the same as everyday life. What animals do in the laboratory may not tell us even in a rough way what humans do in real life. At the same time, laboratory experiments give us the framework within which drug effects can be understood. They establish the inherent pharmacological properties of drugs. Just *how* people take them is another matter; for that we have to examine drug use in naturalistic settings. Laboratory experiments give us an important *clue* as to how drugs might be taken in real life; they do not provide the whole story.

The facts and findings that these experiments brought to light point to the inescapable conclusion that the concept of psychological, or psychic, dependence is a meaningful, powerful mechanism. In fact, the results of the many studies conducted on the subject "indicate that psychological dependence might be more important than physical dependence" in much drug use, including narcotic addiction. "Psychological dependence, based on reinforcement, is apparently the real driving force behind even narcotic addiction, and tolerance and physical dependence are less important contributors to the problem" (Ray and Ksir, 1987, p. 26). Taking a highly reinforcing or intensely pleasurable drug over a period of time does not necessarily lead to physical addiction, but it does lead to a powerful desire to repeat the experience, and to make enormous sacrifices in order to do so. The more intensely pleasurable or reinforcing the experience is, the more psychologically dependency-producing it is.

But aren't many activities or substances pleasurable? In a letter to the editor of *Trans-action* magazine, one observer (Freidson, 1968, p. 75) commented on the assertion that marijuana produces a "psychic dependence" by saying: "What does this phrase mean? It means that the drug is pleasurable, as is wine, smoked sturgeon, poetry, comfortable chairs, and *Trans-action.* Once people use it, and like it, they will tend to continue to do so *if they can.* But they can get along without it if they must, which is why it cannot be called physically addicting."

Clearly, we run into a conceptual dilemma here. On the one hand, many activities or substances are pleasurable; does it make any sense to dub all of them psychologically dependency-producing? To do so is to be guilty of using a concept that is so broad as to be all but meaningless. On the other hand, certain drugs do produce a syndrome that is clearly distinct from, but as powerful as—indeed, in some ways, even more powerful than—physical dependence. Unlike several of the activities or substances mentioned above, such as comfortable chairs, poetry, and smoked sturgeon, an alarmingly high proportion of users *cannot* get along without certain drugs—cocaine being the outstanding example. We are led to the following inescapable conclusions with respect to drugs and dependence.

First, psychic and physical dependence are two separate and to some degree independent phenomena. That is, someone, or an organism of any species, can be psychologically dependent on a given drug without being physically dependent. Likewise, the reverse is also true: it is possible to be physically dependent on a drug without being psychologically dependent— for instance, as a result of having been administered that drug without realizing it (in an experiment, for instance, or in the form of a medicine or painkiller in a hospital).

Second, substances vary in their potential for causing psychological dependence—with cocaine ranking highest, heroin next, possibly the amphetamines after that, and the other drugs trailing considerably behind these three. It is highly likely that this potential is closely related to how reinforcing each drug is—that is, the intensity of the pleasure that each delivers to the user. The more reinforcing the drug, the higher its potential for psychic dependency.

Third, psychological dependence is a continuum, with gradations between substances, whereas physical dependence is probably more of an all-or-nothing affair. The potential for psychological dependence is a matter of degree. Heroin, barbiturates, and alcohol are clearly dependency-producing drugs; this property can be demonstrated in laboratory animals. Drugs either *are* or *are not* physically addicting. In contrast, drugs can be arranged along a continuum of psychic dependency—with cocaine ranking high on this dimension, and marijuana ranking considerably lower on it.

Fourth, substances vary in their "immediate sensuous appeal" (Lasagna et al., 1955; Grinspoon and Bakalar, 1976, pp. 191–194). This is not quite the same thing as the capacity to generate pleasure. It is, more precisely, *the capacity to generate intense pleasure without the intervention of learning or other cognitive processes.* For the most part, one has to learn to enjoy marijuana (Becker, 1953; Goode, 1970, pp. 132ff.). The same is true of alcohol. It has been asserted for heroin, but it may be less true than has been previously assumed (McAuliffe and Gordon, 1974). Certainly it is true of many pleasurable activities and substances—including eating smoked sturgeon, reading certain books and magazines, and appreciating fine art. Here, the pleasure is great but cultivated. In any case, it is not true of cocaine and, to a lesser degree, amphetamines. Subjects who take these substances without knowing what they are taking tend to enjoy them the very first time and want to take them again. In short, they have an immediate sensuous appeal (Lasagna et al., 1955).

Fifth, different routes of administration are differentially capable of generating intense and immediate pleasure in individuals who take drugs by these means. As we've seen, intravenous injection is the fastest way to deliver a drug to the brain; smoking—especially of cocaine—is also an extremely rapid and efficient means of drug-taking and is therefore highly reinforcing and more likely to cause psychological dependence. Injecting and smoking cocaine have been described as being like "a jolt of electricity to the brain." On the other hand, chewing coca leaves, which contain less than 1 percent cocaine, is far less instantly reinforcing and is far less likely to lead to dependency (Weil and Rosen, 1983, p. 46).

And sixth, individuals vary with regard to their degree of susceptibility or vulnerability to becoming psychologically dependent on varying substances or activities. Clearly, the variation from one person to another in this respect is vastly greater than from one animal to another of the same species, or even from representatives of some animal species as compared with those of others.

The term "behavioral dependence" is sometimes used as a synonym for psychological dependence (Ray and Ksir, 1987, p. 25). This is not entirely accurate. Psychological dependence can refer to both a potentiality and an actuality: We can say that cocaine has a high potential for psychological dependence, and we can say that a specific individual, John Doe, is psychologically dependent on cocaine. On the other hand, the concept of behavioral dependence always refers to an actuality. It makes no sense to refer to a drug having a high potential for behavioral dependence; we can only say that John Doe is behaviorally dependent on a particular drug.

Behavioral dependence refers to actual, concrete behavior enacted by an actual, concrete person taking an actual, concrete drug. What has John Doe gone through or given up in order to take or continue taking a specific drug? What is John Doe now going through to do so? What will John Doe go through? To continue taking their drug of choice, some individuals have lost their jobs, destroyed their marriages, given up all their material possessions, gone into enormous debt, ruined their health, threatened their very lives. They exhibit behavioral dependence. While psychological dependence can be inferred from someone's behavior, behavioral dependence is what we see concretely—an actual person sabotaging or giving up concrete values and possessions previously held in esteem to take a specific drug. We recognize behavioral dependence by the sacrifices a particular user makes to get high. Behavioral dependence has been known for some time to be common among alcoholics and heroin addicts. It is now known that cocaine causes similar manifestations in users as well.

In short, although physical dependence (or "classic" addiction) is a very real and very concrete phenomenon, behavioral dependence does not depend on physical addiction alone. In many ways, the distinction between physical dependence and true psychological dependence—for the drugs that are powerfully reinforcing—is largely irrelevant. Chronic users of drugs that are produce "only" psychological dependence behave in much the same way (that is, are *behaviorally dependent*) that addicts of physically dependency-producing drugs do. On the other hand, to throw drugs that produce a weak psychological dependence (such as marijuana) into the same category as drugs that produce a powerful one (such as cocaine) is misleading. Many experts "now regret" the distinction they once drew between cocaine as a "psychologically addictive" drug and narcotics like heroin that are "physiologically addictive." Heroin is "addictive" in a different way—it is both physically and psychologically dependency-producing. But both drugs activate pleasure centers in the brain in such a way that users feel impelled to take them again and again. Some users can overcome this message, but it is a factor that all users have to contend with. "We should define addiction in terms of the compulsion to take the drug rather than whether it causes withdrawal," says Michael A. Bozarth, an addiction specialist (Eckholm, 1986a).

APPENDIX: DRUG NAMES

Some drugs are manufactured, sold, and used legally for medical and psychiatric therapy; they are prescribed by physicians and are called *prescription* drugs, or *pharmaceuticals*. Prescription drugs typically have at least four different kinds of names: (1) the name that identifies their general category or type, (2) a *generic* or chemical name, (3) a *brand* or specific name, and (4) a *street* name (or names), a slang term. For instance, methaqualone (generic name), a nonbarbiturate sedative (category name), is sold under various brand names (Quaalude, Sopor, Parest, Somnafax, Optimil); it is known among users as "ludes," "soaps," or, in England, "wallbangers." Generally, a brand or specific name is capitalized; all the others are spelled with lower-case letters.

Often, a general drug type will encompass a number of different drugs, each one with its own brand as well as generic name. For instance, "minor" tranquilizers include Valium (diazepam), Librium (chlordiazepoxide), and Miltown (meprobamate). Sometimes a drug will be referred to most often by its brand name, sometimes by its generic name. Although it might seem confusing, it should be kept in mind that different terms may actually refer to the same drug.

Illegal drugs taken for recreational purposes (that is, to get high) may also have several names. Marijuana is known to science as *cannabis,* because it is taken from a plant with the botanical name *Cannabis sativa.* Moreover, technically, marijuana is not even a drug; it is a vegetable substance that contains a drug, or a series of drugs, referred to as tetrahydrocannabinol, or THC. In addition, marijuana has acquired a number of nicknames, including "pot," "grass," "dope," "weed," and "smoke." Every drug will be referred to by different names in different contexts or situations.

CHAPTER 3

Theories of Drug Use

Dozens of explanations have been proposed for drug use and abuse. In the early 1980s, the National Institute of Mental Health (NIDA) published a volume that spelled out more than forty theories of drug abuse (Lettieri et al., 1980). The dictionary defines "theory" as an explanation for a general class of phenomena. To most people, a "theory" of drug use, therefore, would be an explanation as to *why people use and abuse drugs.* However, not all the theories that have been proposed address this issue. Most theories do not attempt to explain the entire spectrum of use; most concentrate either on illicit use (often referred to as "abuse") or on alcoholism. Some focus entirely on addiction, usually to narcotics. Some focus on the drug experience—the consequences of experiencing the drug high in a certain way—and do not deal at all with the question of why people use drugs. Some focus on the individual; others on society; still others on the individual's relationship to society. While a number of theories deal with initiation into drug use, several focus on continued or habitual use. And nearly all these theories are partial in scope: they select one or a limited number of factors that are believed to cause drug use or abuse. Most theorists admit that the factor they focus on, *in combination with others,* influences drug-taking. Hardly any researcher in the field believes that one factor, and one alone, explains the phenomenon under investigation. Moreover, a factor is not a theory; most theories put together several factors to make up a coherent explanation, an argument with several different pieces articulating with one another. All of this means that most theories of drug use are not contradictory or in competition; most, in fact, cover different aspects of the same phenomenon, and may be regarded as complementary rather than contradictory.

There are three broad *types* of explanations for drug use: (1) *biological* theories, (2) *psychological* theories, and (3) *sociological* theories. Each focuses on a different range of factors as crucial in determining why people use and abuse psychoactive substances. Of course, within each broad type, there is a range of specific theories.

Before inspecting the theories in different disciplines or fields, it might be useful to mention that the most widely accepted general approach to drug use and abuse—not exactly a theory but a way of looking at the phenomenon—cannot be located in any particular field. It is adhered to by much, probably most, of the public, and by most practitioners, such as physicians, psychiatrists, psychologists, social workers, and therapists, who work directly with drug abusers. It is called the *medical* or the *pathology* model, and its basic assumption is that nonmedical drug use is very much like a disease—a malfunction, an abnormality, a pathology (Young, 1971, pp. 49–79; Goode, 1973a, pp. 26–37). It is not "normal" to use drugs outside a medical context; only a drug-free existence is normal. No one uses psychoactive drugs to get high unless there's something identifiably wrong with him or her. When things are working right, there's no "need" to take drugs. There is nothing valuable about the illegal drug experience; it is inauthentic, illusory, seductive; nothing but harm can come of it. Drug use should be purged from the face of the earth; it does not deserve to exist.

Not only are drug use and abuse caused by a pathology of some kind, they also *cause* a wide range of serious pathologies—in other words, "evil causes evil." One cannot fool around with drugs and remain unscathed; there is no such thing as "harmless recreation" when it comes to drugs. Recreational drug use violates the proper rules of nature, science, and medicine. It is the job of the drug researcher to find a way to eliminate it. This basic assumption, or set of assumptions, underlies not only much popular thinking about drugs, but provides the underpinning for several of the theories to follow. In other words, several of the biological, psychological, and sociological theories discussed below adopt the medical or pathology perspective toward recreational drug use. However, several do not; pathology-normality is a major dimension distinguishing different theories of drug use.

BIOLOGICAL THEORIES

Biological theories are those that postulate innate, constitutional physical mechanisms in specific individuals that impel them either to experiment with drugs, or to abuse them once they are exposed to them.

Genetic Factors

One line of thinking argues that the genetic make-up of individuals influences their predisposition toward drug abuse and alcoholism. A combination of genes influences specific biological mechanisms relevant to substance abuse—such as being able to achieve a certain level of intoxication when using drugs, becoming ill at low doses as opposed to much higher doses, lowering or not lowering anxiety levels when under the influence, or the capacity to metabolize chemical substances in the body. Clearly, all of these could vary from one individual to another, or from one racial, national, or ethnic group to another, and could influence continued use. This "genetic loading," in combination with environmental and personality factors, could make for a significantly higher level of drug abuse or alcoholism in certain individuals or groups in the population (Schuckit, 1980). Indeed, the tendency to prefer alcohol to other beverages can be bred in animals (Davison and Neale, 1986, pp. 259–260; Health and Human Services,

1987a, p. 28), suggesting the relevance and strength of the genetic factor in drug use and abuse.

Most of the research attempting to demonstrate a genetic factor in drug abuse has focused on alcoholism. Studies have shown that adopted children have rates of alcoholism closer to those of their natural parents than to those of their adoptive parents (Schuckit, 1984, p. 62). One study found that 30 to 40 percent of the natural children of alcoholics become alcoholics themselves, as opposed to a rate of 10 percent for the general population (Kolata, 1987). Some experts conclude that the rate of heritability of alcoholism—the chance of inheriting the disorder—is "similar to that expected for diabetes or peptic ulcer disease" (Schuckit, 1984, p. 62).

No researcher exploring the inherited link with alcoholism asserts that genetic factors make up the only or even the principal factor in compulsive drinking. Rather, they posit a genetic *predisposition* toward alcoholism. Inheritance is one factor out of several. Alone, it does not "make" someone a destructive drinker. In combination with other factors, genetic factors may facilitate the process, however.

What are some precise mechanisms that may push someone in the direction of alcoholism? One study found that the sons and daughters of alcoholics tend to be less affected by alcohol than the sons and daughters of nonalcoholics; their coordination is less debilitated, their bodies produce a lower hormonal response, and they feel less drunk when they imbibe a given quantity of alcohol. According to researchers Marc Schuckit, Jack Mendelson, and Barbara Lex, 40 percent of the children of alcoholics exhibit a significantly lower sensitivity to alcohol in these three respects, while this was true of only 10 percent of members of control groups (Kolata, 1987). In addition, researcher Henry Begleiter found that boys who do not drink but whose fathers are alcoholics have brain waves significantly different from boys who are sons of nonalcoholics—brain waves that are similar to those of alcoholics (Kolata, 1987). While some researchers doubt that such differences produce real-life differences in drinking patterns, others point out that inherited mechanisms, in combination with other factors, could lead to an increased likelihood of compulsive, destructive, chronic drinking.

Metabolic Imbalance

A second theory postulates metabolic imbalance as a possible causal factor in at least one type of drug abuse—narcotic addiction. Developed by physicians Vincent Dole and Marie Nyswander (1965, 1980; Dole, 1980), this theory argues that heroin addicts suffer from a metabolic disease or disorder, much like diabetics. Once certain individuals begin taking narcotics, their physiology "craves" opiate drugs in much the same way that diabetics crave insulin. Repeated doses of a narcotic complete their metabolic cycle; narcotics act as a stabilizer, normalizing an existing deficiency. The narcotics abuser can never be withdrawn from drug use because his or her body will continue to crave opiates, just as diabetics cannot be withdrawn from insulin; in both cases, the substance provides what the body lacks and cannot provide.

No precise biological mechanism corresponding to metabolic imbalance has ever been located. The best that can be said about this theory is that the treatment program based on it, methadone maintenance, has helped a certain proportion of addicts—a far lower proportion than its proponents claim, and a higher proportion than its critics claim. We'll explore the various available drug-treatment modalities in more detail in the Epilogue. Here, it is enough to know that hormonal imbalance has been proposed as a factor influencing drug abuse in certain individuals, even though its existence has never been established empirically. The only evidence supporting it is that some addicts behave *as if* they suffer from a metabolic imbalance. Comparing their early with their later writings on the subject, it is clear that the proponents of the metabolic imbalance theory have retreated somewhat from their original insistence on the importance of this factor. It is possible that the theory is relevant only on the clinical and not the theoretical, etiological, or the causal level. Indeed, it may remain as a relevant theory only in order to justify the maintenance of addicts on methadone for life.

PSYCHOLOGICAL THEORIES

Theories relying on psychological factors fall into two basic varieties: those that emphasize the mechanism of reinforcement, and those that stress that the personalities of the drug user, abuser, and especially the addict, are different from those of the abstainer. The mechanism of reinforcement is fairly straightforward: people tend to maximize reward and minimize punishment; they continue to do certain things because they have a past history of being rewarded for doing them. Drug users are individuals who have been rewarded for use, and hence they continue to use. The precise personality configuration that is said to produce drug use varies with the theorist; there is a range of personality factors invoked here. The key factor that binds these *psychodynamic* theories together, however, is that certain individuals, it is argued, have a type of personality that impels them to use and abuse drugs.

Reinforcement

A major psychological theory underplays the idea of personality differences between users and nonusers and emphasizes the role of *reinforcement*. Even animals use certain drugs compulsively under the right experimental conditions, casting doubt on the need to invoke psychodynamic variables in the development of addiction (Wikler, 1980, p. 174; McAuliffe and Gordon, 1980, p. 139). In addition, experiments have shown that, independent of personality factors, human subjects who are administered opiate drugs without knowing what they have taken wish to repeat taking the drug; their desire grows with continued administration (McAuliffe, 1975). Thus, at least for some aspects of the drug-taking process, a consideration of personality variables is not necessary. (At the same time, there is individual variation in reactions to and experiences of drug effects.)

There are two distinctly different types of reinforcement—positive and negative—and, consequently, two different theories that cite reinforcement as a mechanism in continued drug use. (Actually, some approaches make use of both of these mechanisms—different types of reinforcement for different types of drug abusers.) *Positive reinforcement* occurs when the individual receives a pleasurable sensation and, because of this, is motivated to repeat what caused it. In brief, "The pleasure mechanism may . . . give rise to a strong fixation on repetitive behavior" (Bejerot, 1980, p. 253). With respect to drug use, this means that getting high is pleasurable, and what is pleasurable tends to be repeated.

According to this view, the continued use of all drugs that stimulate euphoria is caused by their "extremely potent reinforcing effects" (McAuliffe and Gordon, 1980, p. 137). In the way that users behave, it is difficult to draw a sharp distinction between a strong psychological and a physical dependency. Taking drugs for intense pleasure and being physically dependent form a "continuous variable rather than [representing] qualitatively different state[s]" (McAuliffe and Gordon, 1980, p. 138). Indeed, physical dependence is not even a necessary mechanism for the proponents of the theory of positive reinforcement. What is referred to as addiction is simply an end point along a continuum and indicates that "a sufficient history of reinforcement has probably been acquired to impel a high rate of use" in the user (McAuliffe and Gordon, 1980, p. 138). This also means that continued, even compulsive, use and abuse do not require the mechanism of a literal physical addiction to continue taking place. Many users are reinforced—that is, they experience euphoria—from their very first drug experience onward, and the more they use the more intense the sensation and the greater the motivation to continue use.

Negative reinforcement occurs when an individual does something to seek relief or to avoid pain, thereby being rewarded—and hence motivated—to do whatever it was that achieved relief or alleviated the pain. In the world of drug use and addiction, when someone who is physically dependent on a particular drug undergoes painful withdrawal symptoms upon discontinuing the use of that drug, and takes a dose to alleviate withdrawal distress, he or she will experience relief with the termination of the pain. Such an experience will motivate the addict to do what has to be done to avoid repeating the painful sensations associated with withdrawal.

While positive reinforcement can occur with any euphoric drug—indeed, with any pleasurable sensation (Bejerot, 1972, 1980)—the theory emphasizing the mechanism of negative reinforcement as a major factor in drug abuse is largely confined to drugs that produce physical dependence, especially the opiates. Relatively little attempt has been made to apply this theory to explain either the continued use of nonaddicting drugs or the use of opiates that does not involve literal physical dependence. (However, some nonaddicting drugs, such as cocaine and marijuana, may provide relief from depression; this factor has been mentioned as a reason for continued use.)

The argument invoking negative reinforcement goes as follows. Initially, the use of heroin may or may not be pleasurable; still, at this stage, pleasure dominates as a motivating force in use. The first few weeks of narcotic drug use can be called the "honeymoon" phase. However, the user gradually becomes physically dependent without realizing it. Because of the body's tolerance to narcotics, the user, in order to continue receiving pleasure, increases the doses of the drug—eventually to a point at which addiction takes place. If use is discontinued—whether because supply has been disrupted, because there is not enough money to purchase the drug, or for whatever reason—painful withdrawal symptoms wrack the addict's body. By recognizing that doses of a narcotic drug can alleviate these symptoms, an intense craving is generated for the drug over time.

According to Alfred Lindesmith (1947, 1968), the earliest proponent of this theory:

> The critical experience in the fixation process is not the positive euphoria produced by the drug but rather the relief of the pain that invariably appears when a physically dependent person stops using the drug. This experience becomes critical, however, only when an additional indispensable element in the situation is taken into account, namely a cognitive one. The individual not only must experience withdrawal distress but must understand or conceptualize this experience in a particular way. He must realize that his distress is produced by the interruption of prior regular use of the drug" (Lindesmith, 1968, p. 8).

In short, "The perception of withdrawal symptoms as being due to the absence of opiates will generate a *burning* desire for the drug" (Sutter, 1966, p. 195). According to this theory, addicts continue taking their drug of choice *just to feel normal.*

Recent evidence suggests that addicts and other compulsive drug abusers do, in fact, experience euphoria, and that this is a major factor in their continued drug use. In one study of addicts, all of whom used heroin at least once a day, 98 percent of the sample (sixty-three out of the sixty-four interviewed) said that they got high or experienced euphoria at least once a month, and 42 percent got high *every day* (McAuliffe and Gordon, 1974, p. 804). In this sample, euphoria was consciously desired and sought. In fact, 93 percent said that they wanted to be high at least once a day, and 60 percent wanted to be high *all the time* (McAuliffe and Gordon, 1974, p. 807). Clearly, heavy, compulsive heroin users continue to seek, and achieve, euphoria, and its attainment is a major motivating force behind their continued use.

A resolution to the apparent controversy between the positive and the negative reinforcement models of drug addiction has been offered. (While the negative reinforcement school argues that only the avoidance of pain feel normal motivate the addict, the positive reinforcement ... ...at both factors, as well as others, are operative.) It is likely ... actually two types of narcotic addicts—the *maintainers* and the ...seekers. The maintainer takes just enough narcotics to avert with-...wal distress. Some addicts lack the financial resources, and are unwilling enough to engage in a life of crime, to obtain enough heroin to attain euphoria. They are simply staving off the agony of withdrawal, "nursing" their habit along (McAuliffe and Gordon, 1974, p. 826). To achieve the high they really want would require taking such substantial quantities of the drug that their lives would be transformed utterly and completely. They would have to work very hard and run a substantial risk of danger and arrest. Not all users want to commit crimes to get high; not all think the chance of arrest is worth threatening such valued aspects of their lives as their job, family, and freedom to come and go where and when they want. They prefer to "maintain" a habit to risking what they have in order to achieve euphoria. They have retained most of their ties with conventional society, and "let loose only periodically" (McAuliffe and Gordon, 1974, p. 822).

In contrast, the pleasure-seeking addict takes narcotics in sufficient quantities and at sufficiently frequent intervals to achieve euphoria. This habit is extremely expensive, and hence typically requires illegal activity to support it. In addition, the lifestyle of the euphoria-seeking addict is sufficiently disruptive that a legal job is not usually feasible; he or she must resort to criminal activity instead. It is also difficult for the nonaddict to fit in with and be capable of tolerating the addict's lifestyle, so marriage and a family are typically not possible. Further, since heavy opiate use depresses the sexual urge, intimate relationships with the opposite sex are difficult.

In short, the euphoria-seeking addict has sacrificed conventional activities and commitments for the hedonistic pursuit of pleasure; and to engage in this pursuit, a commitment to a deviant and criminal lifestyle is also necessary. Such sacrifices make no sense "if they were directed solely toward reducing withdrawal symptoms, which could be accomplished with much less effort, as every addict knows" (McAuliffe and Gordon, 1974, p. 828). *"For it is the frequency of euphoria, more than anything else, that stratifies the addict social system."* Among the addict subculture, the greater the success in achieving euphoria, the greater the prestige someone holds. "In this sense, hard-core addicts are the true elite, and the addict stratification system itself points to the fundamental importance of euphoria" (McAuliffe and Gordon, 1974, p. 828).

Inadequate Personality

Several psychological theories of drug use rely on the notion of a psychological *pathology, defect,* or *inadequacy:* there is something wrong in the emotional or psychic life of certain individuals that makes drugs attractive to them. They use drugs as an "escape from reality," as a means of avoiding life's problems and retreating into euphoric bliss and drugged-out indifference.

Euphoria, says one inadequate-personality theorist, is adaptive for the immature individual who lacks responsibility, a sense of independence, and the ability to defer hedonistic gratification for the sake of achieving long-range goals (Ausubel, 1980, pp. 4–5). Although drug use is adaptive for the defective personality in that it masks some of life's problems, it is adaptive only in an exclusively negative way: the problems never get solved, only covered up, and, meanwhile, drug use itself generates a host of other, more serious problems. Normal people, who do not share this inadequacy, do not find drugs appealing, and are not led to use them. Of course, not all drug users share personality inadequacies and defects to the same degree; some will be impelled to experiment or use simply because of social pressure or availability. However, the more inadequate the personality, the greater the likelihood of becoming highly involved with drug use, and the more that use becomes abuse and eventually addiction. In short, for the weak, drug abuse is a kind of "crutch"; for the strong, experimentation leads to abstention, not abuse.

Thus, for the inadequate-personality theorist, drug abuse is an adaptation or a *defense mechanism*:

> Drug use is preeminently a pharmacologically reinforced denial—an attempt to get rid of the feeling import of more or less extensive portions of undesirable inner and outer reality. It is a defense making the emotional significance of a perception of the outer or inner reality unconscious, inoperative, irrelevant. . . . Anxiety of an overwhelming nature and the emotional feelings of pain, injury, woundedness, and vulnerability appear to be a feature common to all types of compulsive drug use (Wurmser, 1980, pp. 71–72).

This theory posits that, although all users, and certainly all compulsive users and abusers, share an inadequate personality, each drug type offers a somewhat different adaptive mechanism; each drug is used to deal with "unmanageable" emotions—"narcotics and hypnotics are deployed against rage, shame, jealousy, and particularly the anxiety related to these feelings; stimulants against depression and weakness; psychedelics against boredom and disillusionment; alcohol against guilt, loneliness, and anxiety" (Wurmser, 1980, p. 72).

One major variety of the inadequate-personality approach is the *self-esteem* or *self-derogation* perspective. This theory holds that drug use and abuse, like deviant and criminal behavior generally (Kaplan, 1975), are responses to low self-esteem and self-rejecting attitudes. (Clearly, it does not apply in societies in which drug use is practically universal and normatively accepted by the majority.) Low self-esteem could come about as a result of "peer rejection, parental neglect, high expectations for achievement, school failure, physical stigmata, social stigmata (e.g., disvalued group memberships), impaired sex-role identity, ego deficiencies, low coping abilities, and (generally) coping mechanisms that are socially disvalued and/or are otherwise self-defeating" (Kaplan, 1980, p. 129). For some, normatively approved activities and group memberships are sources of painful experiences; deviant or nonapproved activities and memberships, however, are effective sources of self-enhancement. Drug use provides exactly such a deviant activity and group membership, and one that permits a deadening of the painful feelings stirred up by self-rejection.

Problem-Behavior Proneness

A third type of psychological theory of drug use sees the phenomenon as a form of *deviant or "problem" behavior.* In sociology and in social psychology, the branch of psychology most influenced by sociology, the term "deviant" has no negative, pejorative, or pathological connotations. It refers to behavior that is not in accord with the norms of, and that tends to be condemned by, the majority. Likewise, "problem" behavior is not necessarily bad or pathological; the term simply denotes behavior that has a certain likelihood of getting the individual who enacts it in trouble. Social psychologists have found that drug users typically have attitudes, values, a personality, and norms that depart significantly from those of the nonuser majority. And these, in turn, make it likely that he or she will engage in behavior that, likewise, departs from the conventional path somewhat. Of course, these are statistical, not absolute, differences—many users and nonusers may be similar to one another in a number of ways, and many users, and nonusers, differ substantially from one another in important respects. Still, the statistical differences are there, and they are often quite striking. What are they?

With respect to users' personality and attitudes, a great deal of research (Smith and Fogg, 1977, 1978; Jessor, 1979; Jessor and Jessor, 1977, 1980; Robins, 1980) demonstrates that users, in comparison with nonusers, tend to be more rebellious, independent, open to new experience, willing to take a wide range of risks, tolerant, accepting of deviant behavior and transgressions of moral and cultural norms, receptive to uncertainty, pleasure-seeking and hedonistic, peer-oriented, nonconformist, and unconventional. Users tend to be more *transition-prone:* that is, they tend to be more accepting of engaging in behavior that marks the transition from one stage of life to the next—from child to teenager, from adolescent to adult. For instance, among teenagers, drinking alcohol and engaging in sex are defined as activities appropriate to older and more mature youngsters; hence, the transition to engaging in them will be made earlier by users than nonusers. Users' personalities also tend to be less religious, less attached to parents and family, less achievement-oriented, and less cautious. This personality manifests itself in a wide range of behavior, much of it not only unconventional, but problematic for the individual and for mainstream society: earlier sexual behavior, and with a wider range of partners; underachievement in school and on the job; and mildly delinquent behavior.

Researchers who emphasize the unconventional personality as a key factor in drug use argue that they can apply the conventional-unconventional personality dimension to predict in advance, with a high degree of accuracy, which youngsters will experiment with and use psychoactive substances and which ones will not. With respect to personality, the adolescent less likely to experiment with and use drugs "is one who values and expects to attain academic achievement, who is not much concerned with independence, who treats society as unproblematic rather than as an object for criticism, who maintains religious involvement and a more uncompromising attitude toward normative transgression, and who sees little attraction in problem behavior relative to its negative consequences." The adolescent more likely to experiment with and use drugs "shows an opposite pattern: a concern with personal autonomy, a lack of interest in the goals of conventional institutions like church and school, a jaundiced view of the larger society, and a more tolerant view of transgression" (Jessor and Jessor, 1980, p. 109). In other words, a "single summarizing dimension underlying the differences between users and nonusers might be termed conventionality-unconventionality" (Jessor and Jessor, 1980, p. 109).

The researchers who follow this line of reasoning have conducted *longitudinal* surveys of drug use—studies that follow the same individuals for a number of years. They study youngsters *before* they have used any drugs, determine their personalities at that time, and predict which ones will use drugs in the future and which ones won't. Then they study the youngsters again a year or two later. The predictive accuracy of the dimension of unconventionality is extremely high, and seems inarguable.

Like most theories, the view that drug users are more unconventional and risk-taking than nonusers sees the relationship as a matter of degree. That is, the more unconventional the youth, the greater the likelihood that he or she will use drugs. In addition, the more unconventional, the more serious the drug involvement. *Mildly* unconventional youngsters are likely to drink, experiment with marijuana, and little else. *Moderately* unconventional youngsters will drink alcohol more heavily, use marijuana regularly, and experiment with other drugs. *Very* unconventional youth have a much higher chance of becoming seriously involved not only with alcohol and marijuana, but also with more dangerous drugs as well.

SOCIOLOGICAL THEORIES

Biological and psychological theories tend to emphasize individualistic factors, although the researchers who propose them usually indicate that broader factors are at work. For instance, two psychologists associated with the "problem-behavior proneness" line of thinking (Jessor and Jessor, 1980, p. 105) incorporate the environment or, to be more specific, the "perceived environmental system"—especially parents and friends—into their model. However, their focus is on the characteristics of the individual.

In contrast, sociologists tend to make broader, structural factors the focus of their theories. For the sociologist, the most crucial factor to be examined is not the characteristics of the individual, but the situations, social relations, or social structures in which the individual is or has been located. More specifically, it is the individual *located within* specific structures.

Four partially overlapping sociological theories have been proposed to help explain drug use: (1) social learning; (2) social control; (3) subculture; (4) selective interaction/socialization.

In the 1930s, sociologist Robert K. Merton generated what came to be referred to as the *anomie* theory of deviant behavior (1938, 1968, pp. 185–248), that deviant behavior—drug use included—occurs when the avenues to material success are blocked off. The theory has been applied to drug use and abuse (Cloward and Ohlin, 1960, pp. 178–184; Palmer and Linsky, 1972, pp. 297–301), but never successfully. Devastating critiques have attacked anomie theory and its application to drug use and abuse (Lindesmith and Gagnon, 1964, is one of the most thorough), and nowadays, the theory is pretty much completely ignored (Kandel, 1980a, p. 250). In fact, to some researchers, it is so completely irrelevant to an understanding of the etiology, or causality, of drug use that it is something of an embarrassment. Thus I will not discuss it as a relevant contemporary theory of drug use. At the same time, however, it is regarded as something of a "classic" theory, and the original article that spelled it out (in which, drug addiction and alcoholism were only mentioned in passing) is probably the single most cited article in the entire sociological literature.

Anomie theory, as Merton developed it (1938, 1957, pp. 131–160; 1968, pp. 185–248), argued that in a competitive, materialistic, achievement-oriented society, in which success is extolled as attainable for all members *but* where success is, in fact, attainable to only a relative few, individuals who do not succeed must devise "deviant" or disapproved adaptations to deal with their failure. Those who have given up on achieving society's materialistic goals, whether by approved or disapproved means, become retreatists. "In this category fall some of the adaptive activities of psychoticsm, autists, pariahs, outcasts, vagrants, vagabonds, tramps, chronic drunkards, and drug addicts" (Merton, 1957, p. 153). An extension of this theory holds that the person who is most likely to become a drug addict is someone who has attempted to use both legal (or legitimate) and illegal (or illegitimate) means to achieve success, and has failed at both. The addict is a "double failure," and has "retreated" into the undemanding world of addiction (Cloward and Ohlin, 1960, pp. 179–184).

Anomie theory has long been regarded as fanciful, generated in the almost total absence of knowledge of the world of drug use and addiction (Lindesmith and Gagnon, 1964; Preble and Casey, 1969). The model addict that predominates in this theory is that of the Chinese opium addict, puffing on his pipe in a dreamy, somnolent slumber. In fact, the world of the addict is anything but undemanding. It is a brutal, abrasive world requiring extreme skill and maximum effort to survive. Moreover, it is not the poorest members of poor communities—the most clear-cut "failures"—who turn to heroin, but those who are a rung above them financially and occupationally. Anomie theory seems to explain no significant feature of drug use, abuse, or addiction.

Social Learning

The theory that criminal or deviant behavior is a product of learning was first elaborated by sociologist Edwin Sutherland in the third edition of his textbook *Principles of Criminology* (1939). He called this formulation the theory of *differential association* because the key mechanism in becoming criminal or deviant is the fact that one associates differentially with social circles whose members define crime and deviance in favorable terms. The central tenets of this theory are that crime and deviance are learned in intimate, face-to-face interaction with *significant others,* or people to whom one is close. A person engages in deviant and criminal behavior to the extent that the definitions to which one is exposed are favorable to violations of the law—that is, because of an excess of definitions favorable to legal and normative violations over definitions unfavorable to such violations. The key to this process, according to Sutherland, is the *ratio* between definitions favorable and those unfavorable to legal and normative violations. When favorable definitions exceed unfavorable ones, the individual will turn to deviance and crime.

The learning approach has been extended by several sociologists who have blended Sutherland's theory of differential association with the principles of behaviorism in psychology. *Social learning theory* holds that behavior is molded by rewards and punishment, or reinforcement. Past and present rewards and punishments for certain actions determine the actions that we continue to pursue. Reward and punishment structures are built into specific groups. By interacting with members of certain groups, people learn definitions of behavior as good or bad. It is in the group setting, differentially for different groups, where reward and punishment take place, and where individuals are exposed to behavioral models and normative definitions of certain behavior as good or bad.

Social learning theory has a clear-cut application in explaining drug use: It proposes that the use and abuse of psychoactive substances can be explained by differential exposure to groups in which use is rewarded. "These groups provide the social environments in which exposure to definitions, imitations of models, and social reinforcement for use of or abstinence from any particular substance take place. The definitions are learned through imitation, and social reinforcement of them by members of the group with whom one is associated" (Akers et al., 1979, p. 638). Thus drug use, including abuse, is determined "by the extent to which a given pattern [of behavior] is sustained by the combination of the reinforcing effects of the substance with social reinforcement, exposure to models, definitions through association with using peers, and by the degree to which it is not deterred through bad effects of the substance and/or the negative sanctions from peers, parents, and the law" (Akers et al., 1979, p. 638). Social learning theory, then, proposes that the "extent to which substances will be used or avoided depends on the extent to which the behavior has been differentially reinforced over alternative behavior and is defined as more desirable" (Radosevich et al., 1980, p. 160).

Control Theory

A major theory in the fields of criminology and deviant behavior is *control theory.* Used extensively in the study of delinquency (Hirschi, 1969; Krohn and Massey, 1980; Wiatrowski et al., 1981), control theory has been applied specifically to drug use and abuse only as part of a more general framework, and then usually only implicitly (Kandel et al., 1978; Bachman et al., 1984; Clayton and Voss, 1981). Still, it provides a penetrating and systematic way of looking at drug use, and it should be examined.

Social control theory has a number of similarities with subcultural theory, discussed below, but there are important differences as well. While subcultural theory approaches the issue of drug use from the point of view of "Why do they do it?"—that is, what group processes facilitate the use of drugs—the social control model holds that it is is more fruitful to ask, "Why *don't* they do it?" In other words, it does not see a departure from conventional norms as problematic, and it takes for granted the lure of such deviant behavior as recreational drug use. What has to be explained, control theorists argue, is why most people *don't* engage in deviance, why they *don't* use drugs to get high. What causes drug use, like most or all deviant behavior, is the absence of the social control that causes conformity. Most of us do not engage in deviant or criminal acts because of strong bonds with or ties to conventional, mainstream social institutions. If these bonds are weak or broken, we will be released from society's rules and we will be free to deviate—and this includes drug use. It is not so much the drug users' ties to an unconventional subculture that attracts them to drugs, but their lack of ties with the conforming, mainstream culture that frees them to use drugs.

Of course, delinquency, deviance, and criminal behavior—including recreational, nonmedical drug use—are matters of degree. Just as most of us engage in at least one technically illegal act in our lives, a very high proportion of the American population eventually uses at least one drug outside a medical context. Control theory does not assert that individuals with strong ties to conventional society will never engage in *any* deviant action, regardless of how mild, including using a drug recreationally. It would, however, assert that both deviance and control are matters of degree: The more attached we are to conventional society, the lower the likelihood of engaging in behavior that violates its values and norms. A strong attachment does not absolutely insulate us from mildly deviant behavior, but it does make it less likely.

The more *attached* we are to conventional others—parents, teachers, clergy, employers, and so on—the less likely we are to break society's rules and use drugs. The more *committed* we are to conventional institutions—family, school, religion, work—the less likely we are to break society's rules and use drugs. The more *involved* we are in conventional activities—familial, educational, religious, occupational—the less likely we are to break society's rules and use drugs. And the more deeply we *believe* in the norms of conventional institutions—again, family, school, religion, and occupation—the less likely we are to break society's rules and use drugs. Drug use is "contained" by bonds with or adherence to conventional people, institutions, activities, and beliefs. If they are strong, recreational drug use is unlikely.

Subculture

The central thesis of the subcultural theory is that involvement in a particular social group with attitudes favorable to drug use is the key factor in fostering one's own drug use, and that involvement in a group with negative attitudes toward drug use tends to discourage such use. Drug use is expected and encouraged in certain social circles and actively discouraged, even punished, in others.

It must be emphasized that there is not one drug subculture, but a number of them. There is some division by race and ethnicity—at the very least, there are white, Black, and Hispanic drug subcultures. Age also partially separates members of certain drug subcultures—somewhat distinct high school, college, and young adult drug subcultures exist side by side. In addition, and perhaps even more important, the drug or drugs of choice that are used distinguish subcultures from one another. There are, at a minimum, the alcohol-abuse subculture, the marijuana subculture, the cocaine subculture, the heroin-injecting subculture, and the multiple drug-use subculture (Johnson, 1980, p. 115). The crucial point here, however, is not that these subcultures are to some degree different, but that they *overlap*— there is some measure of similarity among them (Kandel, 1978; Johnson, 1973, 1980). Some individuals are members of two or more subcultures, and thus, what happens to him or her in one affects what happens in the others. The fact that the overlap is extremely imperfect is irrelevant; the fact that there is a significant overlap is a crucial dynamic element in subcultural influence.

The first systematic application of subcultural theory to drug use was made by Howard S. Becker (1953, 1955, 1963), who focused on the process of becoming a marijuana user. Becker, like the other interactionists, was not concerned with the question of etiology or cause-and-effect explanations; the traditional question of why someone uses marijuana did not not capture Becker's attention. His focus was not so much on the characteristics that distinguish the user from the nonuser—what it was about the user that impelled him or her to the drug—but rather, *how does someone come to use and experience marijuana in such a way that it will continue to be used to achieve pleasure?* For this to take place, three things must happen, according to Becker's model.

First, one must learn how to use marijuana so that the drug is capable of yielding pleasure—that is, one must learn the proper technique of smoking marijuana. Second, since the effects of the drug are subtle and ambiguous, one must learn to perceive them: One must learn that something is happening to one's body and mind, and that it is the marijuana that is causing this effect. And third, one must learn to enjoy the effects. By themselves, the sensations that the drug generates are not inherently pleasurable; without knowing what is happening to one's body, the feelings attendant upon ingesting marijuana may be experienced as unpleasant, unsettling, disorienting, uncomfortable, confusing, even frightening. The drug's effects must be conceptualized, defined, and interpreted as pleasurable. How do these three processes come about? They depend, Becker says, "on the individual's participation with other users. Where this participation is intensive, the individual is quickly talked out of his feeling against marijuana use" (1963, p. 56).

Learning to enjoy marijuana "is a necessary but not a sufficient condition for a person to develop a stable pattern of drug use" (Becker, 1963, p. 59). Marijuana use is, after all, a deviant and criminal activity (and it was even more so in the 1950s and early 1960s, when Becker wrote about the subject). The individual must also, therefore, learn how to deal with the social control that exists to punish users and eliminate use. Deviant behavior can flourish when "people are emancipated from the controls of society and become responsive to those of a smaller group" (p. 60)—that is, a subculture or, in Becker's words, a "subcultural group." To continue smoking marijuana, users must ensure a reliable supply of the drug, keep their use from relevant, disapproving others, and nullify the moral objections raised by mainstream society. These three processes, again, require normative and logistic support from the marijuana-using subculture.

To ensure an adequate supply of the drug, the user must "begin participation in some group through which these sources of supply become available" (p. 62). Where a prospective user is isolated from the subculture, and therefore from sources of supply, use is not possible. (Becker did not consider the possibility that users would grow their own supply, a less common activity in the 1950s than it is in the 1980s.)

Secrecy, too, develops as a result of contact with the marijuana-using subculture. Heavily involved users are often so immersed in the subculture that "they simply have a minimal amount of contact with nonusers" (p. 70), in which case the problem of secrecy is minimized.

And novice users learn from more involved users how to cope with the disapproval of conventional society. "In the course of further experience in drug-using groups, the novice acquires a series of rationalizations and justifications with which he [or she] may answer objections to occasional use if he [or she] decides to engage in it" (p. 74). For instance, users "learn" from the subculture that alcohol is more harmful than marijuana, that marijuana is not a particularly harmful drug in comparison with some, and that the drug's effects are mainly beneficial. "In short, a person will feel free to use marijuana to the degree that he [or she] comes to regard conventional conceptions of it as the uninformed views of outsiders and replaces those conceptions with the 'inside' view he [or she] has acquired through his [or her] experience with the drug in the company of other users" (p. 78).

An interesting feature of Becker's model is that it turns the traditional view of drug use on its head. Far from motives causing use, Becker proposed the opposite—that *use causes motives.* One does not learn that drug use is acceptable, and then use drugs as a result; rather, one first uses drugs, and, *during the course of use,* one learns the necessary justifications and explanations that provide the motivation for further use. In a group setting, one is furnished with "reasons that appear sound for continuing the line of activity" one has begun (1963, p. 39). As Becker summarized:

> To put a complex argument in a few words, instead of deviant motives leading to the deviant behavior, it is the other way around; the deviant behavior in time produces the deviant motivation. Vague impulses and desires . . . are transformed into definite patterns of actions through the social interpretation of a physical experience which is in itself ambiguous. Marihuana use is a function of the individual's conception of marihuana and of the uses to which it can be put, and this conception develops as the individual's experience with the drug increases (1963, p. 42).

In short, the individual's involvement with the marijuana-using subculture is the key factor in use. People do not begin using the drug on their own; individualistic theories cannot account for use. The characteristics of individuals count for nothing in the absence of social circles whose members explain use to the novice, supply the drug, and provide role models. It is only through contact with other users, Becker reminded us, that use, especially regular use, can take place.

In fact, Becker's model does not include *any* discussion of specific individual *or* group characteristics that are compatible with use. It is, in fact, very close to a "pure" subcultural model, discussing the processes and mechanisms of the socialization of the novice without mentioning the fact that only certain types of individuals and only certain types of groups are likely to be attracted to marijuana use. Becker seems totally uninterested in the fact that people who have certain attitudes, beliefs, personality characteristics, or who engage in certain forms of behavior, are a great deal more likely to be attracted to subcultural groups who use drugs. Becker's model seems to presuppose an almost random recruitment into drug subcultures (although, once an individual is recruited, selective interaction and socialization are the major mechanisms at work).

Other schools—most notably the selective interaction/socialization perspective—share the central concepts of the subculture school, but have taken them in a direction in which Becker would not have gone. It should be noted that, for Becker, the content of the user subculture—apart from its use of the drug and its definition of the drug and its use—is secondary. Becker did not touch on any potentiating factors in use at all; he does not explain which individuals are more likely to be attracted to the use of the drug, or which individuals are likely to be attracted to other individuals or groups who are users. He does not deal with the issue of the compatibility between a given individual and the content of a specific subculture—what it is that draws a novice to a circle of individuals who specifically use marijuana. Following the interactionist approach, Becker underplayed the question of cause or etiology. Why someone finds himself or herself in the company of others who smoke marijuana, and actually ends up using the drug—rather than turning down the chance—is something of an unexplained factor in Becker's analysis. He assumed that the user's subculture is favorable toward use and defines it as such. But he made no assumptions about any other values or behavior that might or might not be consistent or compatible with use itself.

A few years later, Goode (1969) applied the subcultural perspective to multiple drug use among marijuana users. He was not so much interested in why people used marijuana as he was in the processes that influenced marijuana users to go on to use other, more dangerous drugs. There is something of a "decompression chamber" phenomenon operating here— using a drug that is widely used and regarded as less dangerous prepares one to use a less widely used, more dangerous drug. Every study that has ever been conducted on the subject has found that the use of any drug is strongly correlated with the use of any other drug; this holds for both legal and illegal drugs. Clearly, this is not an accidental pattern; it prevails for a reason. And that reason is subcultural involvement. The more involved one is in the values and behavior of the subculture of a less serious drug, and the more involved one is with its adherents, the greater the likelihood that one will progress to the use of a more serious drug. The central or "core" members of the marijuana subculture, who use frequently and have many marijuana-using friends, are highly likely to progress to the use of more dangerous drugs; marginal or "peripheral" members of the marijuana subculture, who use infrequently and have few marijuana-using friends, are unlikely to progress to the use of more dangerous drugs.

Goode found a strong correlation between one's friends' use of marijuana and the frequency with which one used the drug. More than six daily users in ten said that more than 60 percent of their closest friends were regular (weekly or more) marijuana users; for the less-than-monthly users, this figure was only about one in ten (9 percent). As a general rule, heavy users were more involved with friends who used marijuana, and other drugs as well, and were more involved in the drug-using subculture—that is, a community of users who defined use in favorable terms. Heavy users were more likely than light users to think it important whether or not a new acquaintance used marijuana; to prefer that their friends smoke marijuana; to "turn on" a younger sibling to marijuana use; and to buy and sell marijuana. Buying and (especially) selling marijuana were excellent indicators of one's involvement in the drug subculture: buyers and sellers were far more likely to "progress" to the use of other, more dangerous drugs, especially the hallucinogens, such as LSD (Goode, 1969).

Light users are only marginally and superficially connected with the drug subculture; their interactions are more frequent and intimate with nonusers than with users. The definitions that predominate in their social world are unfavorable to regular marijuana use and to experimentation with drugs more dangerous than marijuana. They rarely become involved in activities that bind them to or indicate strong drug-subcultural involvement. Consequently, their use of drugs other than marijuana is infrequent—for most, nonexistent. Heavy users, on the other hand, have many marijuana-using friends and friends who use other drugs as well. The definitions favorable to drug use to which they are exposed in their social world vastly outweigh the unfavorable definitions. In addition, heavy users are involved in drug-related activities other than use, such as selling, that both indicate and reaffirm their connection with the drug subculture. As a consequence, their use of drugs in addition to marijuana (multiple drug use) is extremely common.

Selective Interaction/Socialization

The term "selective interaction" refers to the fact that potential drug users do not randomly "fall into" social circles of users; they are *attracted to* certain individuals and circles—subcultural groups—because their own values and activities are compatible with those of current users. There is a dynamic element in use: *even before* someone uses a drug for the first time, he or she is "prepared for" or "initiated into" its use—or, in a sense, *socialized in advance*—because his or her values are already somewhat consistent with those of the drug subculture. As a result, one chooses friends who share these values, and who are also likely to be attracted to use and to current users. I call this process "selective recruitment" (Goode, 1972a, p. 247). In addition, once someone makes friends who use drugs, one *becomes* socialized by a using subcultural group, both into those values compatible with use as well as by values consistent with use. This is why I have called this the *selective interaction/socialization* model (1972, p. 248). Johnson (1980) calls it the subcultural model, and Kandel (1980a, pp. 256–257) calls it the socialization model. It is, in fact, both a "subcultural" and a "socialization" perspective, but it does not follow the lines of Becker's classic argument, and it is a somewhat different process of socialization from the traditional model.

In his examination of multiple drug use among marijuana users, discussed above, Goode (1969) adhered more or less closely to Becker's "pure" subcultural model; selective interaction was only an implicit feature of his approach. However, in a fuller report on marijuana use (1970), of which the article on multiple drug use was a part, it is clear that he was interested in the content of the marijuana-using subculture, aside from its use and definition of the drug itself. Users, he found, are more likely than nonusers to have certain characteristics—to be alienated from religion, sexually permissive, less authoritarian, politically left-wing, and so on (Goode, 1970, pp. 27–49). Even before they use marijuana for the first time, young people who share these values are more likely to be attracted to social circles of users. Marijuana use is attractive to novices because they enjoy the company of those who use, and they enjoy the company of those who use in part because they share subcultural values with them. There is a subcultural *compatibility* between potential and current users.

Studying drug use in a college setting, Johnson (1973) made use of both the subcultural and the socialization models. He demonstrated that drug use occurs because *adolescents are socialized into progressively more unconventional groups* (p. 5). Briefly stated, Johnson's argument holds that the more that adolescents are isolated and alienated from the parental subculture, and the more involved they are with the teenage peer subculture, the greater the likelihood that they will experiment with and use a variety of different drugs. The peer subculture provides a transition between the parental and the drug subcultures. For the most part, the parental generation is conventional and antidrug, and also opposes a number of other unconventional and "deviant" activities. Adolescents who are strongly attached to, influenced by, and committed to the parental subculture tend to adhere more closely to its values and follow its norms of conduct; as a consequence, they are more likely to abstain from drugs than the teenager who is isolated from his or her parents and involved with peers, who favors more unconventional norms, and therefore is more likely to accept certain forms of recreational drug use, especially marijuana smoking.

Not only does the peer subculture exist somewhat independently of the conventional parental generation; it also emphasizes activities in contexts where parental control is relatively absent. There is something of a competition for prestige and status ranking within peer groups. Higher status is granted in part as a consequence of engaging in activities and holding values that depart significantly from parental demands and expectations. These include alcohol consumption, marijuana use, the use of certain hard drugs, some delinquent activity, including what Johnson calls automobile deviance (speeding, driving without a license, and so on), shoplifting, "hanging out," "cruising," and so on.

Johnson's study found that if one has marijuana-using friends, one tends to use marijuana; if one does not have marijuana-using friends, one tends not to use marijuana. The more marijuana-using friends one has, the greater the likelihood of using marijuana regularly, buying and selling marijuana, and using hard drugs. In addition, having marijuana-using friends and using the drug regularly tend to be strongly related to sexual permissiveness (having sex early and with a number of partners, and approving of sex in a wide range of circumstances), political leftism, planning to drop out of college, and engaging in delinquent acts (Johnson, 1973, p. 195). Note that marijuana use is instrumentally involved in this process: using marijuana vastly increases the chance of engaging in numerous other drug-related activities. But Johnson's study suggests that it is not the physiological action of the drug itself that does this, but *the subcultural involvement that marijuana use entails.* [1] Marijuana use is an index or measure of subcultural involvement,

---

[1]Clayton and Voss (1981) make exactly this confusion between marijuana use per se—that is, the physiological action of the drug itself—and the impact of *use as a subculture activity.* This

and the more involved one is with the drug subculture, the more socialized by it, influenced by its values, and engaged in its activities one is.

The selective interaction/socialization model of drug use has been explored most systematically and in the greatest empirical detail by sociologist Denise Kandel. In fact, Kandel can be said to be the principal proponent of the perspective. Kandel's approach is eclectic and makes use of concepts taken from learning theory, the social control model, and the subcultural approach. She places less of an emphasis on "selective recruitment"—the fact that young people who eventually use drugs are different from those who never use, even before use takes place—and relatively more on the processes of selective interaction and socialization.

Adolescents vary with respect to a range of individual and social background characteristics. Likewise, adolescent social gatherings or groups have different and varying characteristics. Some are more compatible with a given adolescent's own traits; some are less so. As a general rule, people of all ages, adolescents included, tend to gravitate to groups whose characteristics are compatible with or similar to their own, and to avoid those that are incompatible or dissimilar. However, in early adolescence, young people tend to be "drifters"—that is, their early drug use, mainly of beer and wine, or nonuse is dependent mainly on accidental, situational factors. If they are in a circle of adolescents who drink, their chances of drinking are greater than if they are in a circle of nondrinkers. Early on, general peer climate powerfully influences patterns of substance use, and young adolescents are not strongly motivated to select a peer group that reflects their own interests and inclinations.

Adolescents are socialized by a number of different "agents." Socialization theorists locate four main agents of socialization: parents, peers, school, and media. Two are tightly related to drug use—parents and peers. Adolescents tend to internalize definitions and values and engage in behavior enacted and approved by significant others. The impact of the various agents of socialization depends on the values and behavior in question. For broader, long-term values and behavior, like religion, politics, and long-term goals, parents tend to be most influential; for more immediate lifestyle behavior and values, peers are most influential (Kandel, 1980a, p. 257).

The parental influence on the drug use of teenagers is small but significant: parents who use legal drugs (alcohol, tobacco, and prescription drugs) are more likely to raise children who both drink hard liquor and use illegal

---

sloppy conceptualization leads them to state that I said "the relationship between use of marijuana and use of heroin is spurious" (p. 160). If use is taken to mean an activity engaged in with intimates within a specific subculture, then I believe the opposite is true—the relationship between marijuana use and heroin use, as well as the use of all other drugs, is a strong causal one (Goode, 1969). If use is taken to mean a physiological effect that the drug touches off in the human organism, then I do believe that the causal explanation for the relationship between the use of marijuana and the use of heroin is a spurious one, as Johnson's study suggests. Clayton and Voss seem totally uninterested in making this crucial distinction, and, as a result, attribute a position to Johnson and to me that we do not hold.

drugs than are parents who abstain from drugs completely. In the earliest stages, parental example will influence substance use in the form of beer and wine and, a bit later on, hard liquor. However, peer influence on drug use is even more formidable. Teenagers, especially older ones, tend to associate with one another partly on the basis of similarities in lifestyle, values, and behavior—and drug use or nonuse is one of those similarities. Friends typically share drug using patterns: users tend to be friends with users; nonusers tend to be friends with nonusers. In fact, of all characteristics that friends have in common—aside from obvious social and demographic ones, like age, gender, race, and social class—their drug use or nonuse is the one they are most likely to share (Kandel, 1973, 1974).

Thus selective peer-group interaction and socialization comprise probably the most single powerful factor related to drug use among adolescents. Imitation and social influence play a significant role in initiating and maintaining drug use among teenagers. Over time, participation in specific groups or social circles reinforces certain values and patterns of activity. Association with friends whose company one enjoys reinforces the values shared and behavior engaged in with those friends. And the closer one's bond, the greater the likelihood of maintaining the values and behaviors that are shared. Note, however, that adolescents do not choose friends at random: they are, in a sense, socialized "in advance" for participation in certain groups, they choose and are chosen by certain groups because of that socialization process, and, likewise, participation in those groups socializes them toward or away from the use of illicit drugs. We have something of a reciprocal or dialectical relationship here.

Kandel's model of adolescent drug use is dynamic in that she does not stop her analysis with substance use per se—that is, at the point when someone has experimented with a psychoactive substance, or with continued use over time. Like Goode (1969) and Johnson (1973), Kandel is interested in the question of drug use *sequences*. Her analysis, however, is substantially more sophisticated, detailed, systematic, precise, and empirically documented. For her, to focus on a single drug is fallacious; adolescents use several drugs, and they use them in specific patterns and in specific "culturally determined" and "well-defined" developmental stages. The "use of a drug lower in a sequence is a necessary but not a sufficient condition for progression to a higher stage indicating involvement with more serious drugs" (Kandel, 1980b, pp. 120, 121). These stages can be reduced to four: (1) beer or wine, (2) cigarettes or hard liquor, (3) marijuana, and (4) other illegal drugs (1980b, p. 121). Adolescents rarely skip stages; thus drinking alcohol is *necessary* to smoking marijuana, just as marijuana use is necessary to moving on to more dangerous drugs such as cocaine and heroin.

Kandel supports the idea that unconventionality is related to drug use generally. However, she argues that the relevance and importance of specific variables are dependent on the young person's stage in life and the drug in question, in other words, there is a *time-ordering* of specific factors. In the early stages of substance use, early in adolescence, as I said above, the most important drugs used are beer and wine, and the most crucial causal factor is general peer climate. The less serious the drug use (beer and wine versus heroin and cocaine), and the more widespread it is, the more important the role played by accidental, situational features and by broad peer-subcultural attitudes and drug-related behavior. Here, most adolescents are "drifters" with regard to drug use; users' attitudes and beliefs about drugs are not significantly different from nonusers. At this point, most adolescents are "seduceable" with respect to psychoactive substances, particularly beer and wine.

At later stages, different factors come into play. For marijuana, in middle adolescence, attitudes toward the drug are very important, peer influence remains strong, and parental influence is fairly weak. In later adolescence, three factors loom especially large that were less crucial earlier. First, psychological pressures: more troubled adolescents will tend to progress from marijuana to "harder" drugs, less troubled ones will be less likely to do so. Second, relationship with parents: the more alienated an adolescent is from his or her parents, the greater the likelihood that he or she will progress from marijuana to more dangerous drugs. Intimate relations with parents tends to "shield" the adolescent from the more serious forms of drug use. And third, while peer climate in general declines in importance over time, having at least one specific friend who uses one or another dangerous drug assumes central importance. Here, the adolescent breaks away from peer circles who do not favor the use of more dangerous drugs toward specific individuals who use them. "The individual who progresses to the use of other illicit drugs may, as a result of his drug-related behavior, factors of availability, or family difficulties, move away from long-term friendships and seek less intimate relationships with those who share his attitudes, behaviors, and problems" (Kandel, Kessler, and Margulies, 1978, p. 36). This adolescent is no longer a "drifter" but a "seeker."

CONCLUSIONS

Clearly, a number of factors are at work in encouraging drug use; no single factor or variable can possibly answer the question of why some people use drugs and others do not. However, not all of these theories are equally useful to us. Negative reinforcement is clearly a factor in continued use by a certain segment of narcotic addicts, but it does not describe the use of all addicts, as McAuliffe and Gordon (1974) make clear. Positive reinforcement applies to all drug use, insofar as administration generates euphoria; on the other hand, can it explain why some individuals who experience euphoria continue taking a given drug, while others, who also experience euphoria, discontinue its use?

Do drug users and abusers have "inadequate personalities"? Users' personalities are no doubt different from nonusers'. However, this would have to be established *before* use takes place, since socialization by user groups is likely to transform one's personality, or at least one's values. Likewise, what some psychiatrists and psychologists call "inadequate" may simply be subcultural variation. For instance, one value common in deviant or unconventional groups is self-deprecation—self-criticism, along with criticism of society and life in general. Does this indicate "inadequacy"? Some personality theorists think so; their critics are skeptical.

To me, the "problem-behavior proneness" perspective is a different kettle of fish altogether. Clearly, individuals with certain kinds of personalities and values are more likely to get into trouble than are those with other personalities and values. This can be predicted in advance by the degree of the individual's unconventionality: someone who strays from society's mainstream values and behavior in one dimension, as well as in general, is likely to stray in other dimensions as well (Robins and Wish, 1977). Users are more rebellious, critical of and alienated from conventionality, independent, open to new experience, pleasure-seeking, peer-oriented, risk-taking, and less mindful of real-life consequences than are nonusers. The evidence linking "traits, values, and behaviors indicative of unconventionality and rejection of social institutions" and the use of psychoactive drugs "is overwhelming" (Kandel, 1980a, p. 266). One problem that arises, however, is: Are these personality characteristics, or are they subcultural in nature? Sociologists would tend to see them as originating in the subcultural group, as values that characterize certain social circles. On the other hand, psychologists would emphasize their individualistic, psychodynamic origin. This dispute is unlikely to be resolved overnight. Still, the differences between users and nonusers are statistically significant, powerful, and causally connected to use, and they increase in relevance with higher levels of involvement. Clearly, they cannot be ignored.

All of the sociological perspectives shed light on the phenomenon of substance use and abuse (with the exception of anomie theory, something of a relic of a bygone age). Drug use is learned and reinforced within a group setting. Future drug users interact with current users and learn appropriate definitions of the drug experience, which has a strong impact on their future experiences and behavior. Users learn how to use, how to recognize and enjoy drug effects, how to ensure a drug supply, and how to keep their use secret from conventional society. All of this is part of the "lore" of the user subculture.

However, the interaction and the subcultural perspectives do not address themselves to the question of why some people use and others don't. Here, the selective interaction/socialization approach must be mobilized. Personality factors, especially "problem-behavior proneness," must be combined with group and subcultural factors. Background, parental, personality, behavioral, and value characteristics predict which young people will gravitate toward one another—toward peer circles whose values and behavior are compatible with use. Once someone is selectively "recruited" into such a circle or group, his or her liklelihood of use increases rapidly.

Young people are socialized into values favorable to drug use by the social circles they interact in and are involved with. The more consistent these values, and the more concentrated and intense the interaction, the greater the likelihood of use. In addition, involvement in a using circle also provides role models for use, so imitation comes into play here. Youngsters do not magically and independently devise a solution to a psychological problem they may have, and rush out, looking for a chemical substance to alleviate that problem, as the inadequate-personality theory would predict. Future users turn to drugs because they have friends who use and endorse use, and because they are relatively isolated from circles that don't use and discourage use.

However, as Kandel emphasizes, the relative importance of certain dimensions, factors, and variables shifts with the time period in a youngster's life, with his or her drug history, and with the drug in question (1980b; Kandel, Kessler, and Margulies, 1978). The dynamics or causal sequence of using (or not using) different drugs is somewhat different for each stage. In early adolescence, beer and wine are the drugs of choice, and here, peer factors—simply falling into or drifting toward a certain circle of users—play the most prominent role. Moreover, parents set a pattern for alcohol use: Parents who drink are more likely to raise children who also drink. Warnings not to drink have little impact in the face of parental examples. Once in a specific social group, the process of socialization takes over, and such socialization prepares the youngster for more serious drug use—initially, the use of cigarettes and hard liquor and, a bit later on, marijuana. In middle adolescence, general beliefs and values, especially about drugs, play a more prominent role, and as does peer influence, now more strongly selected by the individual. Now strong differences in values and lifestyles predict marijuana use, and these differences increase with greater levels of use and involvement (Kandel, 1984, p. 208). Marijuana users generally display a far lesser involvement in conventional roles, values, and activities than nonusers. In later adolescence, a progression from marijuana to more dangerous drugs may occur. In this process, parental influences—especially in the form of degree of intimacy of the adolescent with his or her parents—loom especially large, as does the example of one friend, not necessarily an intimate, who provides a role model for illicit drug use while generalized peer influence begins to retreat into the background somewhat. Psychological problems assume prominence at this time, and predict the use of drugs more serious and dangerous than marijuana. Kandel's model shows that explaining drug use is not a simple matter. A number of factors play a key role, they fit into a coherent system or pattern of causality, and each plays a somewhat different role according to the time in someone's life and the drug in question. Anyone peddling a simplistic theory of drug use cannot be taken seriously.

CHAPTER 4

The Extent of Drug Use in America

At least two dimensions distinguish the many varieties of drug use: *legal status* and the *goal* or *purpose* of use. With respect to legal status, the use, possession, and sale of some drugs are criminal acts; they are against the law, they are crimes. Someone may be arrested if caught in the act of using, possessing, or selling certain drugs; if convicted, he or she may be sent to jail or prison. Heroin and LSD may not be possessed, purchased, or used by anyone for any purpose (with a tiny number of exceptions for approved medical experimentation). On the other hand, the same drugs are legal. Any nonincarcerated person above a certain age may legally buy alcoholic beverages. A number of drugs may be found in a wide range of legally purchasable substances, including nicotine (in cigarettes and other tobacco products), caffeine (in coffee, tea, cola, and chocolate), psychoactive chemicals in such over-the-counter remedies as aspirin, Tylenol, No Doz, Sominex, Allerest, Dexatrim, and so on. In addition, many drugs are legal with a physician's prescription, if taken within a medical context, but are illegal without a prescription.

Of course, the legal picture is not identical the world over, as I pointed out in the Prologue. In Iran, Saudi Arabia, and parts of India, the purchase of alcohol is illegal. In Nepal and parts of India, marijuana is legal. Even in the United States, there is some variation as to the legal status of certain drugs. For instance, in eleven states, the possession of small quantities of marijuana is an offense, not a crime, punishable by a small fine, much like a traffic ticket. An individual caught with small quantities of marijuana may not be arrested, cannot be convicted of a crime, and will never serve a jail or prison sentence. In addition, in more than half the states, marijuana may be used legally for certain medical purposes, such as treatment of glaucoma and nausea following chemotherapy for cancer. The legal picture in a given jurisdiction depends in part on history, accident, pressure groups, custom, religion, and public opinion; it does not solely reflect the objective effects of the drugs themselves.

With respect to the second dimension of drug use, goal or purpose, it would be a mistake to assume that all drugs are used for the same purpose by everyone. Even the same drug will be used for a variety of reasons by different users, even by the same user, in different situations. As we saw earlier, all drugs have multiple effects; some users will seek one effect from a given drug, while others will take it for another of its several effects. Amphetamine produces euphoria and mental alertness in low to moderate doses. Thus millions of individuals who need to stay awake for many hours at a stretch will use amphetamine for its ability to offset drowsiness and fatigue, such as long-haul truck drivers, students cramming for an exam, interns and other medical professionals on continuous twenty-four- or thirty-six-hour rounds. Here, we have instances of *illegal instrumental use*: users are taking the drug not because they enjoy the effects they experience when they take it, but in order to achieve more effectively a goal that most members of this society approve—working at a job, pursuing an education, or advancing a career. In this case, although the goal is approved, the means by which it is attained are considered unacceptable and illegitimate to most Americans.

On the other hand, if one were to take that same drug, amphetamine, for the purpose of euphoria or getting high, one would be engaged in *illegal recreational use*. Calling an activity "recreational" does not imply that it is harmless. Many recreational activities are extremely dangerous, as I said earlier—racing motorcycles, hang-gliding, flying ultralights, mountain climbing, cave exploring, skydiving, scuba diving. However, it does mean that the activity is considered enjoyable by some. Recreational drug use is taking a chemical substance to receive the pleasurable effects the drug causes in the user—to get high. Here, the effects are pursued not as a means to an end, but as an end in themselves.

Clearly, there are vast and important differences among the effects of different drugs, as we have seen, both in quality or kind, and degree or intensity. Some drugs take you up, some down, and some take you in a different direction altogether. The effects of some drugs are mild in the doses typically taken, and, for most activities, the user can cope with the everyday world, although usually less effectively than normally. The effects of other drugs are far more intense, even in fairly low doses, and the user must withdraw from the demands of the everyday world while under the influence, or else suffer the consequences. Thus we cannot equate drinking two glasses of wine during dinner with an intense eight-hour LSD "trip." But the two activities do share at least one characteristic: Both represent taking a chemical substance for the effects themselves, for the pleasure or euphoria the user experiences when taking the drug.

Combining these two dimensions—legal status and goal—yields four quite different types of drug use: (1) legal instrumental use; (2) illegal instrumental use; (3) legal recreational use; and (4) illegal recreational use. The combination of these two dimensions can be schematically represented below:

Types of Drug Use

		Status	
		Legal	*Illegal*
GOAL	INSTRUMENTAL	Taking Valium with a prescription	Using amphetamine to study all night
	RECREATIONAL	Drinking alcohol	Taking LSD to get high

Each of these types of drug use will attract different users whose patterns and frequencies of use contrast significantly.

LEGAL INSTRUMENTAL USE

There are two principal forms of *legal instrumental* drug use—over-the-counter and pharmaceutical. (Drinking coffee to stay alert might constitute a third variety—with a somewhat milder effect than the first two.)

Over-the-counter (OTC) drugs are also called *proprietary drugs.* They may be purchased directly by the public, off the shelf, without a physician's prescription. Examples of OTC drugs include aspirin, No Doz, Sominex, Allerest, and Dexatrim. The retail sales of OTC drugs totaled about $10 billion per year in the late 1980s. OTC drugs are not strongly psychoactive and are rarely used for the purpose of getting high. (At least, not intentionally. Some OTC drugs contain caffeine and are manufactured to look like prescription drugs, mainly amphetamines. They are sold on the street as "lookalikes," and naive customers will purchase and take them as if they were the stronger psychoactive pharmaceutical.)

OTC drugs are fairly safe if used instrumentally, and they do not normally represent a threat to human life. But no chemically active substance can be completely safe, and deaths have been known to occur with these proprietary products. As we'll see shortly, through a program called DAWN (the Drug Awareness Warning Network) the federal government collects information on hospital emergencies and deaths by drug overdose in areas with roughly one-third of the population of the United States. Two OTC drugs, Tylenol and aspirin, caused more than 11,000 nonlethal hospital emergencies and 370 deaths by overdose in these areas, indicating that these drugs are far from entirely harmless. However, in relation to their total use, the toxicity of OTC drugs is extremely low, and they need not be considered in detail in this book.

Prescription drugs are also called *ethical drugs* because they are advertised only to professionals—pharmacists and physicians—and not to the general public. They are also called *legend drugs* (from the ancient meaning of the word "legend," denoting an inscription). Prescription drugs are manufactured, bought, sold, and used legally, for legitimate medical purposes. They are prescribed by physicians to patients for the alleviation or cure of physical or psychiatric ailments, and the prescriptions are filled and sold at licensed pharmacies. In the United States, there are 315,000 physicians legally permitted to write prescriptions, and 150,000 pharmacists working at 60,000 locations legally permitted to fill these prescriptions and sell the prescribed drug.

We'll describe the prescription drug situation in the United States a bit later in this chapter. Here, it is enough to know that prescription drugs— those taken legally, via prescription, for medical and psychiatric problems— are a major source of psychoactive drug use. The pharmaceutical drug industry sells about $30 billion worth of drugs each year at the retail level. Some 1.5 billion prescriptions are written in the United States each year; about one in seven of these drugs is psychoactive. (The others work almost exclusively on the body, such as penicillin and antibiotics.)

One reason why presciption drug use is so interesting to us is that, if a drug is psychoactive, it rarely remains exclusively within the confines of approved medical usage. Heroin, cocaine, morphine, barbiturates, sedatives, tranquilizers, amphetamines—these widely used street drugs were all originally extracted or synthesized, then marketed, for medical purposes, and they then eventually escaped into recreational street usage. In fact, many of the psychoactive plants of the world—marijuana, the coca plant, and psychedelic mushrooms and cacti—have been used for both healing and euphoria, often within a religious context. Thus it is misleading to think that medical and recreational use occupy totally distinct worlds. In fact, many of the drugs used in both worlds are identical, and the major motives for use in each of these two worlds—taking a drug to feel better—are not radically different from one another. In fact, the licit medical and the illicit recreational worlds of drug use overlap.

LEGAL RECREATIONAL USE

Legal recreational use refers mainly to the use of alcohol, tobacco, and caffeine products. In each case, a psychoactive substance is consumed in part to achieve a specific mental or psychic state. Of course, not every instance of the use of these three legal substances is purely for pleasure or euphoria. Still, these drugs are consumed for a desired psychic state. Coffee drinkers do not achieve a high with their morning cup, but they do use the caffeine as a "pick-me-up" to achieve a mentally alert state, a slight "buzz" to begin the day. Many cigarette smokers are driven by a compulsive craving rather than the psychic pleasure achieved by smoking; still, they do achieve, if not a true high, then at least a psychic state that is more pleasurable to them than abstinence. Most individuals who engage in a form of behavior have mixed motives for doing so, and subeuphoric pleasure cannot be discounted as a major reason why most people use alcohol, tobacco, and, to a lesser degree, caffeine products. What is important about legal recreational drug use is not that it is identical to illegal recreational drug use (clearly, there are interesting differences between these two types of drug use) but that there are some interesting similarities and continuities that must be explored. Moreover, pleasure must be viewed not as an either-or proposition, but as a continuum.

The National Institute on Drug Abuse (NIDA) sponsored a survey based on a nationally representative sample of the American population age 12 or older (to be described below). According to this survey, roughly 85 percent of all Americans have at least tried alcohol, and about six out of ten (59 percent), or 113 million individuals, have used it in the past month and can be defined as "current" users. A third (32 percent) of American youth age

12 to 17 have consumed an alcoholic beverage within the past thirty days; this is true of seven in ten (72 percent) young adults age 18 to 25; and six out of ten (61 percent) adults age 26 or older. About a third (32 percent) of all Americans, or 60 million individuals, can be considered current users of cigarettes (NIDA, 1986).

Clearly, then, the extent of legal recreational drug use is immense. The most popular legal recreational drug, alcohol, is used by a majority of the American population. Even the second most commonly consumed legal recreational drug, tobacco, is used by more individuals *than are all illegal recreational drugs combined.* In fact, of all drugs, tobacco, in the form of cigarettes *is used most frequently*: Smokers use their drug of choice ten to twenty times a day, whereas drinkers do not use alcohol that much, on average, during an entire week. Indeed, alcohol and tobacco are so important as drugs of use that a separate chapter (Chapter 5) will be devoted to the first, and a major section of Chapter 8 to the second.

ILLEGAL INSTRUMENTAL USE

Illegal instrumental use, as I explained above, includes taking drugs without a prescription for some instrumental purpose of which society approves, such as driving a truck, studying for an exam, working at an all-night job, falling asleep, achieving athletic excellence, or calming feelings of anxiety. Individuals who purchase drugs illegally, without a physician's prescription, typically do not think of themselves as "real" drug users. They do not (primarily, at least) seek the intoxication or high associated with ingesting the drug, but rather they aim to achieve a goal of which conventional members of society approve. These users regard their behavior as merely technically illegal, therefore not criminal in nature, and completely normal and nondeviant. They do not make a sharp distinction between the use of legal, over-the-counter drugs and the use of pharmaceuticals without a prescription. Both types of drug use have the same goal: to achieve a psychic or physical state to facilitate the accomplishment of a socially approved goal. These drug users are only half right: most Americans would approve of their goal but disapprove of the means they have chosen to attain it. And because they approve of the goal, most Americans would not condemn illegal instrumental use as strongly as they would drug use for the primary or exclusive purpose of achieving euphoria or intoxication. Again, illegal instrumental use highlights the continuities among different kinds of drug use.

As we'll see when we explore the use of some of these prescription drugs, taking chemicals illegally but instrumentally can occur through criminal diversion of legally manufactured pharmaceuticals; the mercenary, unethical, unprofessional, and thoroughly illegal writing—for a fee, of course—of prescriptions by "script mill" doctors for anyone who asks for them; the illicit, clandestine production, either in the United States or abroad, of chemicals that are otherwise used in the manufacture of legal prescription drugs; and the illicit importation into the United States—smuggling—of quantities of drugs that are manufactured elsewhere. Of course, the same drugs, derived from the same source, can be used for the purpose of instrumental use or intoxication.

ILLEGAL RECREATIONAL USE

The sums spent on illicit drugs are enormous, almost incomprehensible. Said one journalist, "There is more money in illegal drug traffic than in any other business on earth" (Gonzales, 1985, p. 104). It is almost certain that more money is spent on drugs in the United States than anywhere else on earth; one estimate holds that Americans consume 60 percent of the world's output of illegal drugs (Lang, 1986, p. 48). The overwhelming bulk of the illicit drugs we use originate, for the most part, in another country.

How much is spent on drugs worldwide? One author (Mills, 1987, p. 3) claims to have seen classified documents containing statistics prepared by the Central Intelligence Agency (CIA) and the National Security Agency that provide an estimate of the volume of the worldwide drug trade. While we need not take this estimate as gospel, it might be worthwhile to take note of it:

> The inhabitants of the earth spend more money on illegal drugs than they spend on food. More than they spend on housing, clothes, education, medical care, or any other product or service. The international narcotics industry is the largest growth industry in the world. Its annual revenues exceed half a trillion dollars— three times the value of all United States currency in circulation, more than the gross national products of all but a half-dozen of the major industrialized nations. To imagine the immensity of such wealth consider this: a million dollars in gold would weigh as much as a large man. A half-trillion dollars would weigh more than the entire population of Washington, D.C. (Mills, 1987, p. 3).

In the early 1980s, William French Smith (1982), an official of the Justice Department, which encompasses the Drug Enforcement Administration (DEA), estimated that the total retail sales of illicit drugs in the United States for 1980 were close to $80 billion. Heroin, he said, was an $8 billion industry; $29 billion was spent on cocaine; $24 billion on marijuana; and $17 billion on "dangerous drugs"—that is, hallucinogens and illegal stimulants and sedatives. Criticism of this estimate was intense and harsh; it was branded as wild speculation with only the flimsiest relation to hard fact.

Since that time, DEA officials have been unwilling to speculate on the value of street drug transactions; one official said to me, "It's anybody's guess." The estimated figure, he said, ranges between $30 and $130 billion, clearly a huge and imprecise territory. *U.S. News and World Report* estimated that sales of illicit drugs total $100 billion, "more than the total net sales of General Motors, more than American farmers take in from all crops"

(Lang, 1986, p. 48). The National Organization for the Reform of Marijuana Laws (NORML) estimated the worth of the 1986 cash crop of home-grown marijuana at $26.3 billion (NORML, 1987). Since the value of marijuana imports from other countries certainly equals or surpasses this figure, NORML believes that Americans spend well over $50 billion on marijuana alone. Two pharmacologists (Ray and Ksir, 1987, p. 72) estimate the cocaine industry to be worth $50 billion a year. If these figures are even remotely accurate, then the lower end of the spectrum of estimates for money spent on all illicit drugs in the United States, $30 billion, must be far too low. It should be sufficient, therefore, to say simply that a great deal of money is spent on illegal drugs in the United States—certainly tens of billions of dollars. And clearly these huge sums, even if they are nearer the low end of the spectrum than the high end, reflect a huge demand for drugs.[1]

Tens of millions of Americans use illicit psychoactive substances on a regular basis. How many Americans use illegal drugs, and which ones do they use? The amount of research conducted on drug use in the United States, legal and illegal, is enormous. However, very little of that research deals specifically with the *extent* of use of illegal drugs. For legal drugs, information on per capita consumption is fairly easy to locate because total sales of legal products are a matter of public record. Thus we know how many drug prescriptions are written and how many packs of cigarettes and gallons of alcohol are purchased each year. Sales figures for most legal products are fairly "hard" data; they have a great deal of validity, and we can be sure that they are quite accurate.

However, no such information is available on the use of illegal drugs such as heroin, LSD, and marijuana. How do we know what quantities of these drugs are sold and consumed? What proportion of the population— how many people in the country—has used each of these drugs at least once, in the past year, the past month? In order to get a sense of the extent of the use of illegal drugs, we must rely on sources of information that are "softer" and less valid than sales figures for legal products.

A second reason why, of all the studies conducted on drug use, only a minuscule handful tells us anything about extent is that such studies must be large-scale and therefore extremely costly. To determine the effects of a given drug, a researcher need only administer it to a few dozen subjects under controlled experimental conditions. Such a study may make a major contribution to the scientific literature, but it is almost always small in scale and rarely very expensive.

[1]Clearly, reconciling the many different estimates from these different sources is an impossibility. For instance, if more than half the illegal drugs, in terms of value, are sold in the United States, and the value of the drug sales here totals $100 billion per year, then the worldwide yearly monetary gross cannot be half a trillion dollars. Clearly, these estimates are rough, most are wide of the mark, and it is likely that the total value of illicit drug sales is unknowable. Still, all observers agree that the total profit is immense and, at the very least, considerably greater than that of all but the biggest legal industries.

Even a sociological study designed to determine causes, patterns, and sequences of drug use, or to identify who is likely to use, does not have to sample respondents from the entire country, nor even to be a representative sample of a given area. Generally, such studies are based on samples from a few schools or neighborhoods, rarely from an entire state—but almost never from the entire country. Many of these studies are excellent, and tell us a great deal about certain aspects of drug use; in fact, we'll be looking at dozens of them in this book. However, a survey that can tell us about the extent of use of a variety of illegal drugs in the society as a whole must have a huge representative sample of respondents. Such a survey is extremely expensive to administer and analyze. Consequently, very few such such studies are conducted. Fortunately, two nationally representative surveys are conducted, and they will provide much of the information that follows on the extent of drug use in the United States in the 1980s.

Each year since the late 1970s, the Institute for Survey Research (ISR) at the University of Michigan has surveyed a nationally representative sample of roughly 16,000 high-school seniors concerning their use of and attitudes toward both legal and illegal drugs. In addition, beginning in 1986, young adults who completed high school one to ten years earlier and who were included in previous surveys, were also questioned. The ISR high-school survey considers four different measures of drug use—*lifetime prevalence* (use of a drug at least once in the respondent's lifetime); *annual prevalence* (use of a drug at least once during the previous year); *thirty-day prevalence* (use at least once during the past month); and *thirty-day prevalence of daily use* (use twenty times or more during the past month). This huge, well-conducted survey provides us with an excellent overview of year-by-year illicit drug use among high-school students (and now young adults as well) in the United States. (Alcohol and cigarettes are also asked about, but they are also illegal for most high-school seniors.) And since this survey has been repeated yearly for more than a decade, it provides a look at recent national *trends* in drug use—that is, changes over time—for high-school seniors, as well as young adults who were studied when they were high-school seniors. How extensive is the use of marijuana and cocaine in high school? Is the use of these drugs among adolescents increasing or decreasing over time? The ISR survey provides an almost definitive answer to questions such as these.

A second large-scale study on drug use has been conducted every two or three years since the early 1970s—in 1972, 1974, 1976, 1977, 1979, 1982, and 1985. Sponsored by the National Institute on Drug Abuse (NIDA), this survey is based on a nationally representative sample of Americans age 12 and older. NIDA divides its sample into three segments—youth, age 12 to 17; young adults, age 18 to 25; and older adults, age 26 and over. It uses more or less the same measures of drug use as the ISR high-school survey—lifetime prevalence, annual use, and use during the past month, or "current" use—but it does not have a measure of daily use.

Table 4.1   Number and Percentage of Americans Using Various Drugs, 1985 (Nonmedical Use Only)

	TOTAL POPULATION, AGE 12 AND OLDER: 190,790,000			
	Percent Who Ever Used	Number Who Ever Used	Percent Who Used in the Past Month	Number Who Used in the Past Month
Alcohol	86	164,360,000	59	113,070,000
Cigarettes	76	144,510,000	32	60,280,000
Marijuana	33	61,940,000	10	18,190,000
Cocaine	12	22,240,000	3	5,750,000
Stimulants	9	17,610,000	1	2,690,000
Tranquilizers	8	14,750,000	1	2,180,000
Inhalants	7	12,940,000	1	1,940,000
Hallucinogens	7	12,880,000	1	960,000
Analgesics	7	12,620,000	1	2,450,000
Sedatives	6	11,540,000	1	1,710,000
Heroin	1	1,930,000	*	—

*Less than 0.5 percent.
—Figure too small to estimate precisely.
Total numbers may not correspond precisely to percentages due to rounding.
SOURCE: NIDA, 1986.

Table 4.2   Percent Using Various Drugs, 1985 (Nonmedical Use Only)

	Youth Age 12–17		Young Adults Age 18–25		Older Adults Age 26+	
	Ever Used	Use in Past Month	Ever Used	Use in Past Month	Ever Used	Use in Past Month
Alcohol	56	31.5	93	71.5	89	60.7
Cigarettes	45	15.8	76	37.2	81	32.8
Marijuana	24	12.3	61	21.9	27	6.2
Cocaine	5	1.8	25	7.7	10	2.1
Stimulants	6	1.8	17	4.0	8	0.7
Tranquilizers	5	0.6	12	1.7	7	1.2
Hallucinogens	3	1.1	12	1.6	6	*
Analgesics	6	1.9	11	2.1	6	0.9
Sedatives	4	1.1	11	1.7	5	0.7
Heroin	*	*	1	*	1	*

*Less than 0.5 percent.
"Ever used" figures rounded off; "use in past month" figures not rounded off.
SOURCE: NIDA, 1986.

It is clear from these studies that illegal drug use is vast, extensive, and deeply ingrained in American society. Tables 4.1 and 4.2 tell the story of drug use, legal and illegal, in the United States. While it is true that no illegal drug is used by as many people in the United States as is alcohol, and no illegal drug is used, on a dose-for-dose basis, as much as tobacco, we should expect this to be true because alcohol and tobacco are legal and freely available, and have a long history of widespread use in this country. While illegal drugs are not nearly as popular as our two favorite legal drugs, the extent of illicit drug use in the United States is substantial. As of 1985, some 70 million Americans age 12 or older—37 percent of the U.S. population— had at least tried one or more illegal drugs once or more during their lifetime. Just under one American in five, 37 million Americans, had used an illicit substance in the past year. And roughly one American in eight, or 23 million individuals, had used one or more illegal drug within the past month (NIDA, 1986). As a source of criminal behavior, drug use is formidable and impressive.

It should come as no surprise that the country's most popular illicit or illegal drug is marijuana. In fact, it is possible that roughly half of all episodes of illicit drug use involve marijuana alone. As of 1985, fully a third of all Americans age 12 or older—some 62 million individuals—had at least tried marijuana. One in ten, 18 million people, had used it within the past month. Cocaine is the country's number-two illegal drug; 12 percent of all Americans age 12 and older (22 million people) had used cocaine at least once in their life, and 3 percent, 5.7 million individuals, had used it in the past month. Of the six major drug types asked about—hallucinogens, stimulants (other than cocaine), sedatives, tranquilizers, analgesics, and inhalants—between one American in eleven and one in seventeen had used each at least once, and about one in 100 had used one in the past month. Of all drugs asked about, by far the *fewest* Americans used heroin (NIDA, 1986).

Table 4.3 tells the story of nonmedical, mostly recreational, drug use among America's high-school seniors for 1986. The picture drawn from this ISR survey of high-school seniors is similar to NIDA's nationally representative household survey, but there are interesting differences as well.

As every other survey of the question has revealed, marijuana is the illicit drug of choice among the nation's high-school seniors. Just over half of the study's respondents (51 percent) had tried marijuana; just under four in ten (39 percent) had used it during the previous year; and a bit fewer than a quarter (23 percent) had used it within the past month. No other drug was used by even remotely the same proportion of the sample. Stimulants and cocaine, the next most popular drug types, were used by considerably less than half as many high-school seniors as was marijuana for all three indicators: 23 and 17 percent respectively for lifetime prevalence; 13 and 13 percent for annual prevalence; and 6 and 6 percent for thirty-day prevalence. For the thirty-day figure, the proportion of users was roughly one-quarter that of marijuana's. As an illegal recreational drug, marijuana is clearly in a class by itself.

Both the NIDA and the ISR surveys examine the question of *continued* use. Which drugs are users most likely to "stick with"? Which ones are they more likely to use infrequently, or to abandon? Some drugs are tried a few

Table 4.3   Use of Various Drugs, High-School Seniors, 1986

	Lifetime Prevalence	Annual Prevalence	30-Day Prevalence
Alcohol	91	85	65
Cigarettes	68	*	30
Marijuana	51	39	23
Cocaine	17	13	6
Stimulants	23	13	6
Sedatives	10	5	2
Barbiturates	8	4	2
Methaqualone	5	2	1
Tranquilizers	11	6	2
Hallucinogens	10	6	3
LSD	7	5	2
Inhalants	20	9	3
PCP	5	2	1
Heroin	1	0.5	0.2
Other Opiates	9	5	2

*Not tabulated.
SOURCE: Johnston et al., 1987, pp. 47, 48, 49.

Table 4.4   Nonmedical Drug Use, High-School Seniors and Young Adults, 1986

	High-School Seniors		Young Adults	
	Annual Prevalence	30-Day Prevalence	Annual Prevalence	30-Day Prevalence
Alcohol	85	65	89	75
Cigarettes	*	30	*	31
Marijuana	39	23	37	22
Cocaine	13	6	20	8
LSD	5	2	3	0.9
Stimulants	13	6	11	4
Sedatives	5	2	3	1
Barbiturates	4	2	2	0.7
Methaqualone	2	1	1	0.2
Tranquilizers	6	2	5	2
Heroin	0.5	0.2	0.2	0.1
Other Opiates	5	2	3	1

*Not tabulated.
Note: Not all drugs that are included in high school senior tables are also included in young adult tables. Young adults are follow-up respondents 1 to 10 years beyond high school.
SOURCE: Johnston et al., 1987, pp. 48, 49, 162.

Table 4.5   Ratio of Recency of Use (Past 30 Days) to Lifetime Use (Ever Used)

	Youth Age 12–17	Young Adults Age 18–25	Older Adults Age 26+	Total
Alcohol	.56	.77	.68	.69
Cigarettes	.34	.49	.41	.42
Marijuana	.52	.36	.23	.29
Cocaine	.35	.31	.22	.26
Analgesics	.33	.19	.18	.19
Stimulants	.32	.23	.09	.15
Sedatives	.26	.15	.13	.15
Tranquilizers	.14	.14	.15	.15
Inhalants	.39	.08	.12	.15
Hallucinogens	.36	.14	*	.07
Heroin	*	*	*	*

*Not tabulated due to small numbers.
SOURCE: NIDA, 1986.

times, or are used heavily for a time, and then given up or are used extremely infrequently. Others attract a more loyal following: they are less likely to be given up, and are more likely to be used regularly.

There are various ways of measuring the notion of continued use. One way is to calculate the ratio of recency of use (use in the past thirty days) to lifetime use. Imagine a large circle—all the people who have ever used a given drug. Then imagine a smaller circle inside the larger one—all the people who have used the drug recently, say, in the past month. If people use a drug, then give it up or use it extremely infrequently, the inner circle will be much larger than the outer one. On the other hand, if a lot of people who try a drug go on to use it regularly, and continue doing so, the inner circle will be almost as large as the outer one. A lot of people who *ever* used the drug are *still* using it—and and have done so recently.

Which drugs rank high on this "recency" index? Which ones rank low? NIDA's study shows that our two legal drugs, alcohol and cigarettes, rank highest in user loyalty, with alcohol considerably ahead of cigarettes. Nearly 70 percent of all Americans who have used alcohol at least once in their lives can be considered "current" users—that is, used it within the past month. The loyalty of cigarette smokers is a lot lower than this, but is still higher than for any illegal drug: 42 percent of all those who ever used cigarettes smoked within the past month. Marijuana and cocaine attract the greatest loyalty among the illicit drugs: 29 percent of all at-least-one-time marijuana users, and 26 percent of all at-least-one-time cocaine users, took their drug of choice in the past month. For all other drugs or drug types, recency of use was considerably lower; for the hallucinogens, for example, it was a paltry 7 percent. Not enough heroin users fell into in the sample to make the calculation for this drug meaningful (NIDA, 1986). There seems to be something of a relationship between the extent of use of a drug and the recency, or "loyalty," of its use among users.

TRENDS IN DRUG USE SINCE 1960

It is a cliché that use of drugs, especially of marijuana and the hallucinogens, was commonplace in the 1960s, far more so than in the conservative 1980s. Unfortunately, in the 1960s, no surveys were conducted even remotely like the high-school (Johnston et al., 1987) and the general population (NIDA, 1986) surveys we have looked at. Fortunately, the nationally-representative survey conducted in 1979 (Fishburne, Abelson and Cisin, 1980) "reconstructed" trends backward, relying on "retrospective estimates"—that is, based on the respondent's age and the age at which he or she began using the drugs asked about (Miller and Cisin, 1980, pp. 13, 32–33). This survey clearly shows that the use of marijuana, cocaine, and the hallucinogens—the three most widely used illicit drugs—was extremely low in 1960. Only 6 percent of young adults age 18 to 25 had used marijuana even once. This figure rose gradually between 1960 and 1967, when it stood at roughly 15 percent. Between the late 1960s and the early 1970s, it rose much more sharply, and stood at 48 percent in 1972, the first year of the national survey (Miller and Cisin, 1980, pp. 15–18). The same pattern holds for the other age groups, although at a significantly lower level, and for the other drugs, also at a significantly lower level. Thus, for the 1960s, the trend line for most illicit drugs rose throughout the decade—at first gradually, then more dramatically.

For the 1970s, the two surveys do not agree on every detail; for one thing, NIDA's surveys began in 1972, and the Institute for Social Research's high-school survey did not begin until 1975. For each drug, the story is a bit different. And for each indicator of use—lifetime, annual, and thirty-day prevalence—the trend lines are a bit different as well. Still, the overall pattern is roughly this: Illicit drug use rose throughout the 1970s and peaked late in the decade—for many drugs, in 1979. In fact, according to the high-school survey, annual prevalence increased after 1975 and reached its highest level for a majority of the illicit drugs asked about—marijuana, inhalants (amyl and butyl nitrites), hallucinogens (including LSD), PCP, barbiturates, and tranquilizers—in 1979. For the nationally representative survey, the pattern is not quite so clear-cut, but it does hold for marijuana; for many of the other drugs, the peak year was 1977, 1979, or 1982. And for most illegal recreational drugs, there was a decline in use throughout the 1980s.

This, then, is the trend line for the prevalence and incidence of most illegal drug use: a gradual rise between 1960 and 1967, a fairly sharp rise between 1967 and 1972, a moderate rise between 1972 and 1979, and a moderate-to-substantial decline after 1979. There are exceptions to this pattern, but it covers many of the illegal drugs most of us are interested in—especially marijuana. The one major exception to the overall pattern, as we'll see, is cocaine.

Tables 4.6 and 4.7 tell us the story of changes or trends in drug use in recent years. Did drug use, licit and illicit, rise, decline, or remain stable between 1979 and the mid-1980s? The answer is, although it depends on the drug, for *most* drugs, the trend is clearly downward.

For marijuana use, the three measures of use for high-school seniors (Table 4.7) between 1979 and 1986 are all strikingly lower in the latter year than in the former—for lifetime prevalence, a decline from 60 to 51 percent; for annual prevalence, from 51 to 39 percent; and for thirty-day prevalence, from 37 to 23 percent (Johnston, O'Malley, and Bachman, 1987, pp. 47, 48, 49). The NIDA household survey shows a decline in annual prevalence between 1979 and 1985 in all age groups except for older adults—among youth, a drop from 24 to 20 percent; among young adults, from 47 to 37 percent; and among older adults, an almost imperceptible rise from from 9.0 to 9.5 percent.

The use of hallucinogens, likewise, unquestionably fell during this period—for all three indicators for the ISR high-school survey, and in two out of three age groups for the NIDA household survey. (Unfortunately, the ISR survey categorizes PCP as a hallucinogen, which it most decidedly is not; I have used this study's "unadjusted" figures, which do not include the use of PCP.) In the high-school study, the use of LSD is also down.

Sedative use, including the use of barbiturates and methaqualone, declined by nearly half between 1979 and 1986 in the national survey. (However, it was slightly higher in two out of three age groups.)

The indicators for stimulants were down for the ISR study, but up for the NIDA survey. However, the high-school study was sensitive to the fact that many respondents who claimed to have taken a stimulant actually took a fraudulent nonstimulant "lookalike." This study, therefore, corrected for this tendency for respondents to overreport stimulants. Unfortunately, all of the ISR's stimulant figures are unadjusted between 1975 and 1983, and all of them are adjusted for 1984, 1985, and 1986. Thus comparability during our time period is questionable.

The use of PCP, not asked about in NIDA's study, declined sharply during 1979–1985 in the ISR survey.

The number of respondents taking heroin was too small in either survey to draw any firm conclusions that we can place much faith in. Still, among the high-school students, heroin use did seem to decline a bit during the period in question.

For cocaine, the trend for the high-school survey was very slightly up; for the national survey, it was also up in two out of three age groups. This was especially true of the older adults, age 26 and over. The changes in the number and proportion of Americans using cocaine from the late 1970s to the mid-1980s were modest but significant, according to these surveys. What was striking was not so much that new individuals used cocaine but that, among cocaine users, *frequency of use* increased. This is reflected less in the lifetime and the yearly figures than in the monthly figure. NIDA estimated that "current" use of cocaine—use within the past month—among the 26-and-over age group more than doubled between 1979 and 1985;

Table 4.6 Annual Nonmedical Drug Use, National Household Survey, 1979–1985 (By Percent)

	Youth Age 12–17		Young Adults Age 18–25		Older Adults Age 26+	
	1979	*1985*	*1979*	*1985*	*1979*	*1985*
Alcohol	53.6	52.0	86.6	87.4	72.4	73.6
Marijuana	24.1	20.0	46.9	37.0	9.0	9.5
Hallucinogens	4.7	2.6	9.9	3.7	0.5	1.0
Cocaine	4.2	4.4	19.6	16.4	2.0	4.2
Heroin	*	*	0.8	0.6	*	*
Stimulants	2.9	4.4	10.1	10.4	1.3	2.7
Sedatives	2.2	3.1	7.3	5.4	0.8	2.0
Tranquilizers	2.7	3.7	7.1	6.7	0.9	2.9
Analgesics	2.2	4.4	5.2	6.7	0.5	3.1

*Less than 0.5 percent.
Note: Questions about cigarette use for 1979 not comparable with those asked in 1985.
SOURCE: NIDA, 1986.

Table 4.7 Trends in High-School-Senior Nonmedical Drug Use, 1979–1986 (By Percent)

	Lifetime Prevalence		Annual Prevalence		30-Day Prevalence	
	1979	*1986*	*1979*	*1986*	*1979*	*1986*
Alcohol	93	91	88	85	72	65
Cigarettes	74	68	*	*	34	30
Marijuana	60	51	51	39	37	23
Inhalants	18	20	9	9	3	3
Hallucinogens	14	10	10	6	4	3
LSD	10	7	7	5	2	2
PCP	13	5	7	2	2	1
Cocaine	15	17	12	13	6	6
Heroin	1	1	0.5	0.5	0.2	0.2
Other Opiates	10	9	6	5	2	2
Stimulants	24	23	18	13	10	6
Sedatives	15	10	10	5	4	2
Barbiturates	12	8	8	5	3	2
Methaqualone	8	5	6	2	2	1
Tranquilizers	16	11	10	6	4	2

*Not included in survey.
Note: Inhalants figures are adjusted for underreporting. Hallucinogens figures are not adjusted. (PCP is mistakenly classified as a hallucinogen in adjusted figures.) Stimulants figures for 1979 are not adjusted; for 1986, they are adjusted for overreporting. (A consistent classification is not available.)
SOURCE: Johnston et al., 1987, pp. 47–49.

between 1982 and 1985, the number of Americans in all age categories who had used cocaine in the previous month increased from 4.2 to 5.8 million. Since the lifetime prevalence figures increased only modestly during these periods, nearly the entire increase in cocaine use represented an increase in frequency of use among those who were already using.

In a follow-up study of high-school seniors one to ten years after graduation, use of nearly all drugs showed a slight post-high-school increase. The one exception was cocaine, for which the increase was *massive.* Lifetime prevalence for the 28-year-old cohort (those who had graduated in 1976) had *quadrupled* since their senior year—from 10 to 40 percent. (Lifetime prevalence for the senior class of 1986 was 17 percent.) Annual prevalence increased from 6 to 20 percent, and thirty-day prevalence from 2 to 8 percent (Johnston et al., 1987, pp. 47–49, 160). Clearly, cocaine is a drug that is used considerably more by individuals in their twenties than in their teens. And just as clearly, when today's high-school students are in their mid- to late twenties, their use of cocaine will probably be significantly higher than it is now.

Alcohol consumption for the high-school population was down slightly; for the national population, it was remarkably stable.

Only two comparisons can be made for cigarette use for the time period, and both reveal a drop in use.

To summarize, the drugs whose use *declined* between 1979 and 1985 were marijuana; the hallucinogens, including LSD; sedatives, including barbiturates and methaqualone; inhalants; cigarettes; and PCP.

The drugs whose use remained more or less *stable* during this period were opiates other than heroin.

The drugs whose use clearly *increased* during this period were cocaine and analgesics.

And the drugs for which the data appear somewhat mixed are stimulants, tranquilizers, heroin, and alcohol.

SHORT-TERM TRENDS: 1986–1987

In 1988, the Institute for Social Research released a news bulletin summarizing its findings on the drug use of high school seniors and young adults beyond high school for 1987. The 1986–1987 drug use trends continue those that have taken place throughout the 1980s—but with one major surprise. Between 1986 and 1987, for all three categories studied (high school seniors, young adults one to ten years beyond high school, and college students one to four years beyond high school), for all illicit drug categories, and for all indicators of use, drug use declined or remained at the same level. (The only exception, college heroin use, involved so few cases that it is questionable that the figures reflect a real trend.) The researchers sum up the findings by saying that "the unhealthy romance between many of America's young people and illicit drugs continued to cool in 1987" (news release, University of Michigan, News and Information Services, January 12, 1988).

For the most part, this overall decline in drug use has been taking place throughout the 1980s, and so this is not major news. However, the major surprise in this survey is that cocaine use declined along with the use of the other drugs. In fact, for all three categories of respondents—high school seniors, young adults one to ten years beyond high school, and college students—and for all indicators of cocaine use, there was a decline. For annual prevalence, for high school seniors, cocaine use dropped from 13 to 10 percent; for young adults beyond high school, from 20 to 16 percent; and for college students, from 17 to 14 percent. This was the first time that any indicators of cocaine use declined in this survey since the late 1970s. This may very well represent a turning point; it is entirely possible that a long-term trend is in the making.

Before we become too optimistic, however, it is necessary to register three important reservations. First, the level of illicit drug use for American youth is higher than it is in any other industrialized nation on earth. Second, the percent of high school students who have ever used crack stood at 5.6 percent for the 1987 survey, with an annual prevalence of 4.0; as we'll see, crack can be an extremely dangerous drug. And third, while licit drug use has been declining in concert with illicit drug use for American youth, during the 1986–1987 period that parallel decline was reversed. For high school seniors and for post-high school youth, annual prevalence of alcohol consumption increased slightly, reversing a previous trend. Table 4.8 details these recent changes in drug use.

ATTITUDES TOWARD DRUG USE

Recent changes in drug use are interesting, and for some drugs, striking—cocaine's upward direction and marijuana's downward trend, for example. However, *attitudes* toward drugs and drug use have changed even more radically during the 1980s. This is especially true of attitudes toward the legality or illegality of drugs and drug use. (Technically, in most jurisdictions for most drugs, it is not use itself that is illegal, but possession and sale, but it is use that tends to be asked about in surveys.)

This shift is documented by the high-school-senior study. The proportion of high-school seniors who believe that marijuana should be entirely legal dropped *by half* between 1977 and 1986, from 34 to 15 percent. At the other extreme, the proportion favoring criminalization of marijuana use *doubled,* from 22 percent in 1977 and 1978 to 43 percent in 1986. The proportion favoring decriminalization, however, remained more or less stable, at slightly more than a quarter. For marijuana, as for no other drug, a fairly sharp distinction was made between using the drug in private versus using it in public: 79 percent favored criminalizing the public use of marijuana, but only 44 percent felt this way about the private use of the drug.

Table 4.8   Trends in Annual Prevalence for Eleven Types of Drugs, 1986–1987:

HIGH SCHOOL SENIORS, RESPONDENTS 1–10 YEARS BEYOND HIGH SCHOOL, AND COLLEGE STUDENTS 1–4 YEARS BEYOND HIGH SCHOOL

	High School		Respondents 1–10 Years Beyond High School		College Students 1–4 Years Beyond High School	
	1986	*1987*	*1986*	*1987*	*1986*	*1987*
Marijuana	39	36	37	35	41	37
LSD	5	5	3	3	4	4
Cocaine	13	10	20	16	17	14
Heroin	0.5	0.5	0.2	0.2	0.1	0.2
Other Opiates	5	5	3	3	4	4
Stimulants	13	12	11	9	10	7
Sedatives	5	4	3	3	3	2
Barbiturates	4	4	2	2	2	1
Methaqualone	2	2	1	1	1	1
Tranquilizers	6	6	5	5	4	4
Alcohol	85	86	87	89	92	91

SOURCE: News release, January 13, 1988, University of Michigan, News and Information Services, Tables 8, 24, and 28.

Interestingly, a substantial proportion felt that public cigarette smoking (45 percent) and public drunkenness (52 percent) should also be outlawed.

Thus what has happened in roughly a decade is a fairly sharp upswing in a conservative mood—a significant increase in the proportion favoring legal penalties against marijuana. The same conservative mood extends to other drugs as well; for the other illicit drugs, this feeling has become substantially stronger, and for the two now legally available drugs, alcohol and tobacco, it has become substantially weaker. In sum, then, "In recent years American young people have become more supportive of legal prohibitions on the use of illegal drugs, whether used in private or in public. The fairly tolerant attitudes of students in the late '70s toward marijuana use have eroded considerably as substantially more think it should be treated as a criminal offense and correspondingly fewer think it should be entirely legal to use" (Johnston, O'Malley, and Bachman, 1987, p. 132).

There has been a corresponding increase in the proportion of high-school seniors who think that people who use marijuana run a risk of harming themselves. In 1978, only 35 percent felt that there was a risk of harm in regular use; by 1986, this had doubled, to 71 percent. However, surprisingly, for no other drug type and for almost no other level of use did a rise occur, and for none did a comparable attitude change take place. In fact, for some drugs and some levels of use, there was a small drop in the perception that use is harmful. Table 4.9 presents the figures

Table 4.9   Trends in Perceived Harmfulness of Drugs, 1978–1986

QUESTION: "HOW MUCH DO YOU THINK PEOPLE RISK HARMING
THEMSELVES (PHYSICALLY OR IN OTHER WAYS), IF THEY . . .

	Percent Saying "Great Risk"	
	1978	*1986*
Try marijuana once or twice	8	15
Smoke marijuana regularly	35	71
Try LSD once or twice	43	42
Take LSD regularly	81	83
Take cocaine once or twice	33	34
Take cocaine regularly	68	82
Try heroin once or twice	53	46
Take heroin regularly	87	87
Try amphetamines once or twice	30	25
Take amphetamines regularly	67	67
Try alcoholic drinks once or twice	3	5
Take 1 or 2 drinks nearly every day	20	25
Take 4 or 5 drinks nearly every day	63	67
Smoke 1 or more packs of cigarettes a day	59	66

SOURCE: Johnston, O'Malley, and Bachman, 1987, p. 120.

on changes in perceived harmfulness of the use of various drugs between
1978 and 1986.

In sum, then, a moderate proportion of high-school seniors in 1978
believed that experimenting with most illicit drugs entailed "great risk"; in
1986, about the same proportion felt that way. The overwhelming proportion believed that regular use of these drugs involved "great risk" in 1978;
in 1986, the same picture prevailed. Alcohol, at commonly consumed levels,
was not perceived to be much of a threat to health at all. In fact, even
consuming one or two alcoholic drinks per day was not widely perceived to
be a risk. However, at the level of four or five drinks per day, a majority—
seven respondents out of ten—believed alcohol consumption to be risky.
Regular cigarette smoking was perceived as risky, and this attitude became
more widespread between 1978 and 1986. The one truly striking change in
beliefs about the possible medical consequences of drug use was the increased feeling that marijuana poses a substantial risk to physical and mental
well-being: twice the proportion felt this way in 1986 as in 1978. This
represents a truly substantial change in attitudes toward the use of this drug.

DRUG USE AND SOCIOECONOMIC STATUS

Sociologists measure social class or socioeconomic status (SES) by three
dimensions—level of education, the prestige of one's occupation, and income. Socioeconomic status exerts a decided influence on drug use, but its

effect is far from simple or unidimensional. Until very recently, the relationship between education, occupational status, and income on the one hand, and drug use on the other, varied to some degree independently for each drug or drug type. Some drugs were used more heavily at the top of the SES hierarchy, while others were more heavily used toward the bottom.

As we'll see in Chapter 5, the higher the socioeconomic status, the *greater* the likelihood that someone will drink alcohol; the lower the SES, the greater the likelihood that someone is a total abstainer. On the other hand, among those who drink, the higher the SES, the lower the chance of drinking heavily or being an alcoholic; the lower the SES, the higher is that chance (Armor et al., 1976).

Heroin's relationship to socioeconomic status has been unambiguously negative for a number of generations. In spite of the inroads the drug made into affluent communities in the 1960s and 1970s, it remains overwhelmingly a drug of poor, inner-city residents. Most slum areas in large cities have a serious heroin problem; very, very few middle-class suburban communities have even remotely as serious a heroin problem.

For generations, cocaine's relationship to social class was strongly positive. Because of its extremely high cost, cocaine tended to be used significantly more among the affluent segments of society than among those with more modest incomes.

In the 1960s and 1970s, the sons and daughters of higher-SES parents were more likely to use marijuana. While marijuana use was far from uncommon in poorer areas, statistical correlations in numerous surveys conducted in the 1970s showed a positive relationship: the higher the SES, the greater the likelihood of marijuana use.

Psychedelics or hallucinogens were largely the province of young people with more affluent, better-educated parents who worked at higher-prestige occupations. Youngsters with poorer, less well-educated parents who worked at lower-prestige jobs were significantly less likely to use these substances.

There are strong indications that, with illegal drugs at least, these patterns changed drastically in the 1980s. What seems to be evolving is something of a two-tier drug-using population, with the affluent and the poor diverging more in their use of drugs than ever before. At the higher end of the SES hierarchy, drug use is dropping significantly over time; on the other hand, at the lower end, use of several drugs may actually be increasing. "We are dealing with two different worlds here," says David Musto, a drug historian (Kerr, 1987d).

For the most part, the people who are turning away from drug use belong to the better-educated and more affluent segments of society. Among the poorest and least well-educated socioeconomic levels, drug use has increased or remained constant. Drug use has peaked or is declining in the nation generally; in the poorer areas, for several drugs—crack especially—there is actually an increase.

In the 1982 national survey of drug use (Miller et al., 1983), among young adults age 18 to 25, cocaine use correlated positively, and strongly, with education: the respondents most likely to use the drug were college graduates (11 percent used cocaine in the past month), while those who had never finished high school were significantly less likely to have done so (4 percent). But by 1985, the picture had reversed itself precisely; only 3 percent of college graduates said that they had used cocaine in the past month, while more than three times as many among those who had never graduated from high school (10 percent) had done so (Kerr, 1987d).

This situation has been compounded by the recent upsurge in the use of crack, a crystalline form of cocaine that is smoked rather than snorted. While it had been used by a small number of individuals in a few neighborhoods since the 1980s, it was not until late 1985 or early 1986 that its use exploded onto the national scene. In part because of its low cost, it has made deep inroads into poorer neighborhoods. While there have been exceptions, middle-class areas have not taken it up to the same extent. In one study—using education and educational plans as one measure of social class—college students were only one-third as likely to have used crack in the last year as were their non-college-age peers. In addition, high-school seniors who planned to go to college were less than half as likely to have used crack as were seniors who did not. For the most part, crack remains a "poor person's drug." And it is far likelier to be used in large cities than in nonurban communities (Johnston et al., 1987, pp. 16–17, 38). Its impact in certain inner-city neighborhoods has been described as devastating.

PRESCRIPTION DRUGS: AN OVERVIEW

Each year, as I said above, about 1.5 billion prescriptions are written in the United States; half of these are new prescriptions, and the other half are refills. Each prescription cost an average of $14.00 to fill in 1986. The pharmaceutical industry is a $30-billion-a-year industry, big business by anyone's standard. In order to introduce a drug onto the market, a pharmaceutical company must demonstrate that the product is both safe and effective. To do this, the firm must conduct extensive laboratory tests on animals and clinical tests on humans. Such research is extremely time-consuming and very, very costly. Developing, testing, and marketing a new drug cost a pharmaceutical company an average of $10 million (Julien, 1985, p. 33), and as much as $70 million (Ray and Ksir, 1987, p. 69), and there is no guarantee that the drug will be therapeutically effective at the end of the tests, or profitable even if it is. A pharmaceutical firm's patent on a drug is permitted to last only seventeen years; after that, any drug company may manufacture and market the generic version of the substance. A *generic* is the same chemical as the brand, except that it is packaged differently—the tablet or capsule will be a different color, size, or shape—and it will be sold under the generic name of the drug instead of the patented brand name.

For instance, Hoffmann-LaRoche introduced the drug diazepam, a tranquilizer, in the mid-1960s under the trade name Valium; it quickly became the best-selling prescription drug in America, and has been enormously profitable for the company, with sales of a quarter-billion dollars per year (and with total sales—for the company, the suppliers, and the pharmacies combined—of roughly $500 million). In 1975, a peak of 61.3 million prescriptions for Valium were written; after that, sales dropped sharply, and, by 1980, only 33.6 million prescriptions for Valium were sold—although it was still the number-one prescription drug in the country.

In 1980, Hoffman-LaRoche's patent expired, a development the company fought in the courts, claiming that generics do not deliver the drug to the body as efficiently or as effectively as trade versions do. In 1982, Valium fell to third place in prescription sales, and to fourth in 1983. In 1984, the Food and Drug Administration ruled that three drug companies could market the generic diazepam (Ray and Ksir, 1987, p. 76). In that year, Valium remained at number four, but by 1986, it had fallen to eleventh place; its ranking will likely continue to decline, as generics compete for its share of the market. In 1986, for the first time, the generic diazepam, manufactured by Parke-Davis, made an appearance on the list of the top 200 drugs, at the 199 position. Clearly, sales of generics, like sales of prescription drugs generally, is big business. In 1986, generics accounted for a total of about 14 percent of all new prescriptions written, a figure that has been rising yearly, and will probably continue to increase.

The pharmaceutical industry has been criticized for its aggressive marketing procedures. Profits have higher priority than the alleviation of suffering. Drugs are advertised and sold for every ill that befalls humankind. The industry spends roughly $2,500 per physician on advertising every year, and most of what many physicians know about prescription drugs they've learned from the clearly biased representatives of a drug company, whose primary interest is to sell as many prescriptions as they can. Some companies have resorted to deception and even outright fraud in compiling information about their products, underplaying their dangers and exaggerating their therapeutic effectiveness. The legal drug industry is said to be "very large, growing, and profitable." Authors write of "the legal drug epidemic." Valium, it is said, "would become the opiate of the people." Drugs, it is said, "are the almost perfect alternative to the police state dominated by troops, secret police, and prison camps." Troublesome people are supposedly "drugged into pacification" (Little, 1983, pp. 193, 195). In the United States, "central-nervous-system agents are the fastest-growing sector of the pharmaceutical market" (Illich, 1976, p. 64). Drug abuse is said to be "just what the doctor ordered"; prescription drugs are described as "political control in the name of health and illness" (Hills, 1980, pp. 117–138). Prescribing psychoactive drugs has been termed "mind control," with "a nationwide drug-dealing mental-health cabal" engaged in "sizing you up for a chemical straitjacket" (Schrag, 1978). The drug industry has been called "the pusher in the gray flannel suit"; the responsibility of the doctor, "to push more pills" (McKinley, 1978).

Many of these charges are valid; in fact, I made some of them myself in the first edition of this book (Goode, 1972a, pp. 123ff.). However, one feature of this line of criticism is not true: the allegation that prescribing psychoactive drugs is on the rise. In fact, the frequency of prescribing psychoactive drugs for medical purposes has declined sharply in the past generation. (As I said above, the number of prescriptions written in general—for both psychoactive and nonpsychoactive drugs—has remained fairly stable throughout the 1980s at 1.5 billion a year, and psychoactive pharmaceuticals make up 14 percent of all prescription drugs.) For a number of drugs—the amphetamines and the barbiturates are good examples—this decline began in the late 1960s. But by the early 1970s, the number of prescriptions written for the overwhelming majority of all psychoactive pharmaceuticals was clearly on a downward trajectory. Thus this trend should have become evident to all observers by the mid-1970s. Unfortunately, though, some observers are more interested in getting their own message across or proving their own theories than determining the facts.

Criticism of the overprescribing of psychoactive pharmaceuticals was extremely common in the late 1960s and early 1970s; many observers felt that certain drugs were being overused, and that they were neither safe nor effective. In part, as a result of these criticisms—some of which appeared in medical and pharmaceutical journals—physicians became decreasingly likely to prescribe psychoactive drugs for medical or psychiatric purposes, and their use dropped sharply during the 1970s and into the 1980s. In some cases, this decline was extremely sharp. As I noted above, Valium reached a peak of 61.3 million prescriptions written in 1975; in 1980, this figure had fallen to 33.6 million (Boffey, 1981; Rosenblatt, 1982); by 1986, Valium was only the eleventh most popular prescription drug. In 1975, 22.8 million prescriptions were written for barbiturates in the United States; by 1979, this figure had declined to 12.8 (Reinhold, 1980). The total number of prescriptions for painkillers (such as Darvon) dropped from 120 to 104 million between 1975 and 1979. One-sixth as many prescriptions were written for Benzedrine, an amphetamine, in 1981 as in 1976, and one-fourth as many for Biphetamine.

Can we use the number of prescriptions written per year as a rough index of the amount of use of each drug? One observer (McKinley, 1978, p. 230), noting the drop in the number of prescriptions written in the years before 1978, claimed that "doctors are prescribing more pills per prescription." Is the size or the number of the doses increasing as number of prescriptions drops? No. What we actually see is a decline on all fronts. In 1975, the prescribed daily dose for new prescriptions for Valium averaged 14.9 milligrams per patient; in 1985, it was 14.2. For Librium, the prescribed daily dose in 1975 was 53.3 milligrams per patient for new prescriptions; in 1985, it was 40.7 (Baum et al., 1986, p. 28). In 1980, 7.7 doses were prescribed for Valium per 1,000 Americans per day; in 1985, this figure had dropped to 5.1. For Librium, the comparable figures were 2.0 and 1.7 respectively (Baum et al., 1986, p. 33). Clearly, neither the size nor the number of doses has been increasing as the number of prescriptions has been dropping; if anything, there has been a significant decline. In short, we can use the number of prescriptions written as a rough measure or index of the volume of use of pharmaceutical drugs.

Table 4.10 tells the story. The National Prescription Audit (IMS America) tabulated the number of prescriptions written on a year-by-year basis; 1961 represents the base year, and so all the prescriptions written in that year are assigned the value of 100. (If the drug was not available in 1961, the earliest year it became available is taken as the base year.) If, for a later year, the number of prescriptions rose, the figure in the table will be higher than 100; if it dropped, the figure will be lower. Moreover, each specific time period can be examined to determine whether the number of prescriptions written rose or declined in that period. For instance, if the figures for 1986 are lower than those for 1981, it is clear that psychoactive prescription drug use declined; if higher, they rose.

For the 1981–1986 period, for twenty-two out of twenty-five drugs, fewer prescriptions were written at the end of the period than at the beginning for the 1971–1986 period, this was true of twenty-three out of twenty-five drugs. Indeed, for the fifteen-year stretch between the early 1970s and the mid-1980s, the decline of some prescription drugs was spectacular. For the barbiturates, fewer than one-tenth as many prescriptions were written in 1986 as in 1971. For the amphetamines, the drop was only slightly less dramatic. Between 1966 and 1971, the number of prescriptions for the methaqualones (such as Quaalude) rose ten times; between 1976 and 1986, it plummeted to nothing—the drug is simply not being prescribed any longer. Only Dilaudid, a potent painkiller and a semisynthetic derivative of morphine, seems to be holding its own. All indications point clearly to the fact that far fewer prescriptions are being written today for psychoactive pharmaceutical drugs than was the case in the past. This decline is one of the more significant changes in drug use in the past two decades.

THE DRUG ABUSE WARNING NETWORK (DAWN)

The federal government, through a program called the Drug Abuse Warning Network (DAWN) collects information on the incidence of crucial drug-abuse indicators in certain cities—specifically, (1) emergency room (ER) episodes, and (2) fatal drug overdoses, also called medical examiner's (ME) reports. Whenever someone in one of these cities comes or is brought to a hospital emergency room experiencing a drug-related reaction, it is counted as an "emergency room episode." These episodes include panic reactions, hallucinations, or other undesirable psychic effects, and overdose reactions requiring medical care, such as suicide attempts. Fatal overdoses are reported by the area's medical examiner, who conducts autopsies on nonroutine deaths; if drugs are thought to have been a contributing factor in the death, the death is counted as a fatal overdose. Up to four drugs can

Table 4.10   New Prescriptions Written For Psychoactive Drugs, 1961–1986 (all figures for base year 1961=100)

		1966	1971	1976	1981	1986
	Codeine	69	81	63	33	11
	Demerol	84	92	75	56	56
NARCOTICS	Dilaudid	147	149	200	206	277
	Morphine	74	52	43	22	60
	Percodan	106	215	315	215	138
NON-NARCOTIC ANALGESICS	Darvon	170	233	105	63	33
	Talwin	*	100	86	72	43
BARBITURATES	Amytal	148	101	66	22	5
	Nembutal	140	114	70	25	10
	Seconal	125	117	57	21	9
	Tuinal	146	138	96	35	12
SEDATIVES	Methaqualone	100	1,176	1,086	392	0
	Dalmane	*	100	465	513	236
MINOR TRANQUILIZERS	Valium	100	377	660	385	252
	Librium	160	160	131	64	37
	Equanil	84	75	35	15	7
	Miltown	76	68	31	13	6
MAJOR TRANQUILIZERS	Mellaril	289	683	842	720	506
	Thorazine	136	172	127	74	35
	Stelazine	136	116	104	60	·38
AMPHETAMINES	Dexedrine	117	83	67	48	32
	Benzedrine	65	97	89	14	0
	Desoxyn	169	96	119	67	16
	Biphetamine	157	213	249	58	12

*The drug was not available during this year.
Note: The year 1961 is used as the base year in this table (or, if drug was not available until a later year, that year is taken as the base year). If the number in later years is higher than 100, this indicates that more new prescriptions were written during that year than during the base year; if the number is less than 100, then fewer were written.

SOURCE: National Prescription Audit, IMS America, Ltd., 1986. Reprinted by permission.

be counted for a nonlethal emergency-room episode; 41 percent of DAWN's ER episodes entail the use of more than one drug. Up to six drugs can be counted in a fatal overdose; 72 percent of the ME reports mention two or more drugs. DAWN's data base covers 744 hospitals, two-thirds of the total of all hospitals in twenty-seven cities, which comprise one-third of the U.S. population. In addition, seventy-five medical examiner's offices report all the drug-related deaths they investigate. The total number of ER episodes and drug deaths reported by DAWN does not represent even remotely close to the total for the entire United States. Even some of the information from areas included in DAWN (for instance, ME reports from New York City) is incomplete.

Several factors can influence the number of emergency room mentions of nonlethal drug overdoses and medical examiner's reports of fatal overdoses from year to year, from city to city, and from drug to drug. Clearly, one of these factors is *purity*: A street drug that is, on average, 5 percent pure is considerably less likely to lead to both fatal and nonfatal overdoses than a drug that is 50 percent pure—even if the number of users remains constant. Second, there is *dosage*: The quantity of a given drug users take during a typical episode varies somewhat. If the dose is high, an overdose is more likely; if it is low, overdosing is less probable. If, during one year, the average purity of street heroin is 3 percent, and several years later, it is 30 percent, more users will drop dead in the latter year than in the former—even though the total number of users during both years may be the same. Third, there is *frequency of use*: If the average frequency of use is twice a day, users are more likely to overdose than if it is twice a week. A fourth factor is *drug mixing*: Typically taking a drug by itself is less likely to produce harmful effects than typically taking it in combination with other drugs. Also, the adulterants in batches of drugs sold on the street will influence negative reactions. Batches that contain adulterants that are relatively inert and do not interact with the main drug are less likely to result in medical complications; batches with adulterants that do interact with the main drug are more likely to do so. A fifth variable is the *route of administration*: When a drug is taken by certain routes of administration (for instance, injection), it is more dangerous than when it is taken by means such as snorting or oral ingestion. Thus, when DAWN figures change over time for a given drug, we cannot be sure whether the number of users attracted to that drug that is changing or whether one of these five other factors is responsible. At the same time, huge differences over time usually do indicate changes in the number of users.

In 1986, there was a total of 119,263 nonlethal ER episodes in DAWN areas; 188,199 drug mentions were involved with these incidents. Clearly, for some episodes, several drugs were cited. In addition, in the area covered, 4,138 individuals were determined by a medical examiner to have died of a drug overdose; some 9,528 drug mentions were associated with these deaths (DAWN, 1987, pp. iii–iv). If more than one drug is ingested in a given episode, we cannot ascertain which one is involved in the overdose. If an individual drinks alcohol, snorts cocaine, and injects heroin within a short period of time, and then dies shortly thereafter, how can we be sure which of the three drugs is responsible for the death? In truth, if we were to rely solely on DAWN's data, we could not be sure at all. All we know is that when a drug shows up many times in DAWN's figures—especially if it is the only drug taken—it is likely to be dangerous, at least given the manner in which it is currently used.

DAWN's data are severely flawed as an overall index of drug abuse in the United States, and as a basis of making comparisons among different cities, time periods, or drugs. A major problem is that emergency-room data are based on drugs *mentioned by the patient,* and clearly, the patient, especially in the throes of a medical crisis, is not the most reliable source of information on the drug he or she ingested. Possible sources of bias are rampant—conscious deception on the user's part, forgetfulness, confusion, disorientation, and so on. A second problem is that alcohol appears on DAWN's list *only if it is used in combination with another drug,* yet most acute alcohol-related medical complications, both fatal and nonfatal, occur with alcohol alone. Thus we cannot even remotely estimate alcohol's potential for abuse from DAWN's data.

Laboratory analyses of drugs actually found in patients in DAWN's studies have been conducted. In one study of 643 emergency-room patients and 1,008 drug mentions, great deal of error was found in DAWN's tabulations. In only 20 percent of the cases, the drugs reported to DAWN and those that turned up in the laboratory report were identical; in 10 percent of the cases, the drug reported differed from the drug(s) actually found; and in fully 70 percent[2] of the cases, DAWN's reports were incomplete—drugs were found in the patient's body that he or she had not reported to DAWN's physicians (Ungerleider et al., 1980). Laboratory tests revealed significantly more multiple drug use than DAWN's figures indicated. Thus, in most cases, if a patient reports to an emergency room physician that he or she has taken a given drug, the chances are moderately high that the drug was actually taken; on the other hand, the chances are also high that he or she failed to report one or more drugs that were actually taken. Thus, it can be said that DAWN's data are more likely to be incomplete than totally erroneous. They must be interpreted with great caution.

However flawed DAWN's data may be, they do provide a rough picture of the consequences of drug use and abuse in the United States. Most important, DAWN's tabulations can give us a very approximate idea of the relative contribution that each drug makes to nonfatal ER episodes and to fatal overdoses. By any reasonable reckoning, a drug that appears very frequently on these two lists can be said to be commonly abused.

Let's keep in mind an absolutely crucial qualification, however: We must always calculate the abuse potential of a given drug in terms of how widely used it is. For instance, DAWN reported that, together, Tylenol and aspirin caused, contributed to, or were implicated in 370 deaths in its jurisdiction in 1986; methadone was responsible for only 133 (DAWN, 1987, p. 54). Does this mean that Tylenol and aspirin are nearly three times as dangerous as methadone? Clearly not, because roughly a hundred times as many people use Tylenol and aspirin as use methadone. The contribution of each drug to fatal and nonfatal overdoses must always be assessed in light of the number of people who use it and its frequency of use.

Remember that DAWN's data refer only to *acute* complications; incidences of *chronic* medical ills do not appear in these figures at all. If an alcoholic dies of cirrhosis of the liver, or if a three-pack-a-day cigarette

---

[2]In the text of the article, the figure 60 percent is cited. However, in the abstract, 69 percent appears. A calculation shows 369 patients with "some correct information" to be 69.9 percent of the 528 total patients tested. Clearly, a typographical error was involved here.

smoker dies of lung cancer, it will not be tabulated by DAWN. Certain drugs (such as tobacco) manifest their harmful effects almost entirely in the form of chronic ailments. Thus DAWN's data do not deal with all of the ravages of drug abuse, only with the acute ones that come to the attention of emergency rooms and medical examiners.

Two sorts of conclusions about DAWN's data might be drawn: The comparative contribution that each drug makes to lethal and nonlethal drug overdoses, relative to the frequency of its use; and the changes that have taken place for each drug, both relatively and absolutely, in the recent past. The first conclusion that might be made—and this should come as no surprise to anyone—is that narcotics, specifically heroin, are extremely dangerous in terms of their ability to cause acute medical complications. More than a sixth (17.6 percent) of all ER drug mentions involved a narcotic drug, as did a nearly a third (30.4 percent) of all fatal overdoses; heroin and morphine specifically made up 60 percent of all narcotic mentions. When we keep in mind the fact that heroin—and narcotics as a category—is among the least commonly used drugs in America, we realize that it has an immensely high potential for abuse. Narcotics, specifically heroin, make a contribution to fatal and nonfatal acute complications far out of proportion to their use in the population. In the household survey of drug use in the general population discussed earlier (NIDA, 1986), only 1 percent of Americans age 12 and older had even tried heroin; the same proportion was found in a survey of high-school seniors (Johnston et al., 1987, pp. 47–49). We therefore must conclude that heroin is a very dangerous drug indeed.

Even though alcohol's role has been downplayed by DAWN's conventions—it is counted *only* if used "in combination" with another drug—it nevertheless shows up as the number-two drug in contributing to emergency-room episodes and fatal overdoses. Alcohol accounted for 15 percent of all drug mentions in nonlethal ER episodes, and for more than a sixth (17.8 percent) of all drug mentions in medical examiner's reports on lethal overdoses. Keeping in mind the fact that alcohol is used more or less regularly by six Americans in ten—113 million individuals age 12 and older it is a commonly abused drug by anyone's lights.

Another pattern that DAWN's data reveal involves suicide attempts. If there is a supply of a given drug in the medicine cabinet—barbiturates, tranquilizers, aspirin, Tylenol, and sedatives such as Dalmane and Quaalude, come to mind as candidates—there is a greater chance that it will be used in a suicide attempt. In fact, more than a third (36 percent) of all ER episodes entailed a suicide attempt, and more than a quarter (29 percent) of medical examiner's reports dealt with a successful suicide (DAWN, 1987, pp. iii–iv). Thus the drugs used for this purpose will show up in overdose statistics not because they are inherently unsafe *as they are typically used,* but because a supply is available and can be taken with deliberate self-destructiveness.

The relative role of two drugs—marijuana and LSD—in these figures deserves mention. Marijuana is by far the most widely used illicit drug in

America, possibly outstripping all other drugs combined; it is entirely possible that close to half of all instances of illegal drug use entail the use of marijuana. Some 62 million Americans have used this drug, and more than 18 million do so more or less regularly. And yet only some 6,000 emergency-room incidents reported by DAWN (mostly panic reactions) involved marijuana; these episodes also included use of another drug. In addition, twelve people were found dead—nearly all with another drug in their bloodstream—and marijuana was judged to be a causative factor. Taking extent of use into account, it must be said that the acute safety of marijuana is quite remarkable.

The use of hallucinogens (excluding PCP, which I have tallied separately because it is not a true hallucinogen)—primarily LSD—likewise generated very few lethal or nonlethal overdoses. Only about 1,000 ER episodes involved one of the hallucinogens, and in only one case was LSD deemed to be a contributing factor in a user's death by overdose (DAWN, 1987, pp. 26–30, 53–54). Again, given their fairly widespread use, the hallucinogens do not play a major role in ER episodes or, especially, medical examiner's reports.

Perhaps more interesting than the relative contribution that each drug makes to fatal and nonfatal overdoses at a given point in time are the *changes* that have taken place in the use of these drugs in the recent past. Here, we note some dramatic developments. Certain drugs are much less frequently associated with acute medical complications today than was once true. (Since the population of the areas studied by DAWN did not change significantly during this time period, we can simply look at the absolute number of lethal and nonlethal mentions as indicators of abuse.)

Between October 1981 and September 1982 (DAWN, 1983, p. 11; Goode, 1984, p. 44), 3,921 emergency-room episodes and 121 fatal overdoses involved the use of methaqualone, or Quaalude. In 1986, only 306 ER episodes and 4 fatal overdoses involved methaqualone. Clearly, the abuse of methaqualone has plummeted in the past few years. In 1981–1982, barbiturates contributed to more than 7,000 ER episodes and some 650 deaths; in 1986, these figures were less than 3,000 and 459 respectively—again, representing a significant drop in abuse.

With some drugs, the comparison yields a mixed message; "minor" tranquilizers, amphetamines, alcohol, PCP, and antidepressants showed a rise in one abuse indicator and a decline in the other—interestingly, and inexplicably, in all cases, a decline in ER episodes and a rise in fatal overdoses. With marijuana, the number of ER incidents remained stable, but its mention in ME reports increased. (As I said above, the vast majority of all marijuana complications entail the use of the drug in combination with another drug.)

With a few drugs, there was a significant and unambiguous rise in incidence of abuse indicators: among the narcotics, for example, there was a substantial increase—from 19,000 ER mentions to 25,279, and from 1,539 ME reports to 2,502. The most striking change, however, involved cocaine.

Table 4.11 Drugs Mentioned in Nonlethal Emergency-Room (ER) Episodes and Lethal Medical Examiner's (ME) Reports in 1986

Drug/Drug Type	Drugs Mentioned in ER Episodes Nonlethal *Number*	Drugs Mentioned in ER Episodes *Percentage*	Drugs Mentioned in ME Reports (Lethal) *Number*	Drugs Mentioned in ME Reports *Percentage*
Narcotics	25,279	17.6	2,502	30.4
Alcohol-in-combination	21,801	15.2	1,463	17.8
Cocaine	24,847	17.3	1,092	13.3
Antidepressants	7,204	5.0	808	9.8
"Minor" tranquilizers	18,453	12.9	750	9.1
Barbiturates	2,944	2.1	459	5.6
Non-narcotic analgesics	13,933	9.7	400	4.9
PCP	6,421	4.5	245	3.0
Nonbarbiturate sedatives	6,725	4.7	187	2.3
Amphetamines	3,475	2.4	176	2.1
Antipsychotics	5,134	3.6	123	1.5
Marijuana	6,046	4.2	12	0.1
LSD	1,002	0.7	1	*

*Less than 0.5 percent.
Note: "Percentage" reflects drug mentions, not drug episodes or overdoses, thereby taking multiple drug abuse into account. There was a total of 188,199 drug mentions for emergency room data (143,246 for the drugs listed above), and 119,263 total drug-abuse episodes. For ME data, there was a total of 9,528 drug mentions (8,220 for the drugs listed above), and 4,138 drug-abuse deaths. Clearly, several drugs were mentioned in a given episode or death, "All other drugs" equal 23,783 for ER reports, 994 for ME reports. "Drugs unknown" equal 12,930 for ER reports, 25 for ME reports.
SOURCE: DAWN, 1987, pp. 26–30, 53–54.

In 1981–1982, there were 5,800 emergency-room episodes and 198 fatal overdoses associated with cocaine; in 1986, these figures were respectively 24,847, a more-than-fourfold increase, and 1,092, a more-than-fivefold increase (DAWN, 1987, pp. 26–30, 53–54). There doesn't seem to be any doubt that cocaine is used much more today than in the past, is administered via more potentially lethal routes (smoking and injecting versus snorting), and is used more frequently and in larger quantities by those who use. As a result, its use is now far, far more likely to result in fatal and nonfatal overdoses. The use and abuse of cocaine have been rising faster than the use and abuse of any other drug, and the indicators of complications associated with it have been rising fastest as well. Clearly, in terms of these signals, cocaine is the drug to watch in the late 1980s and 1990s.

CHAPTER 5

Alcohol

In terms of its impact on the workings of the human mind, alcohol is a drug in precisely the same sense that LSD, heroin, and cocaine are: They are all *psychoactive*. Likewise, in the sense that alcohol is used in large part, although not entirely, for its effects on the drinker (the user takes it to get high)—alcohol is a drug not essentially different from marijuana and cocaine: It is a *recreational* drug. With respect to its capacity to induce a *physical dependence* in the drinker, alcohol is a drug in the same way that heroin and the barbiturates are: Alcohol is "addicting," that is, it generates severe withdrawal symptoms when the heavy, long-term drinker discontinues its use. In fact, alcoholism is by far our most common form of drug addiction. Estimates hold that there are roughly 10 million alcoholics and only half a million heroin addicts in the United States. The typical drug addict, then, is an alcoholic, not a street junkie. In that a sizable minority of drinkers displays a pattern of *behavioral dependence*—they continue to drink heavily in spite of the social cost to themselves and to others that they care for—alcohol is a drug no different from cocaine, amphetamines, and heroin.

In the bodily sense, then, *all drinkers are drug users*. There is no internal, chemical feature of alcohol that sets it off from the substances people think of as drugs. There is no biochemical aspect of drinking that is qualitatively different from what most of us regard as "drug use."

There are two ways in which alcohol cannot be regarded as a drug, however: first, most of the public does not consider alcohol a drug (Abelson et al., 1973, p. 512; Abelson and Atkinson, 1975, p. 97), and second, legal controls on the purchase of alcohol are minimal, which is not true for most drugs. Almost any adult may buy it almost anywhere in the country. This chapter will consider some of the similarities and differences between alcohol and the substances that are universally regarded as drugs and what relevance these similarities and differences have to human behavior. To us, how a drug is regarded and what it does to us physically are equally important; moreover, the two mutually influence one another. Still, in many respects, there is a yawning chasm between the "objective" properties of some drugs and their image in the public mind. Alcohol is one of these drugs.

Alcohol has an ancient and checkered history. Fermentation was one of the earliest of human discoveries, dating back to the Stone Age. Alcohol emerges spontaneously from fermented sugar in overripe fruit; the starch in grains and other food substances also readily converts to sugar and then to alcohol. Because this process is simple and basic, the discovery of alcohol by humans was bound to be early and widespread. It is also no accident that alcohol's "remarkable and seemingly magical properties as the ability to induce euphoria, sedation, intoxication and narcosis" (Health, Education, and Welfare, 1971, p. 5) and its "great capacity for alleviating pain, relieving tension and worry, and producing a pleasurable sense of well-being, relaxation, conviviality, and good will toward others" (Straus, 1976, p. 184) have made it an almost universally acceptable and agreeable beverage. Consequently, we have been ingesting beverages containing alcohol for something like 10,000 years. It is also the most widely used drug in existence; alcohol is ubiquitous, almost omnipresent the world over.

Actually, what is generally referred to as "alcohol" is one of a whole family of alcohols. Pharmacologists call it *ethyl alcohol,* or *ethanol.* Other representatives of this family include wood alcohol (methyl alcohol) and rubbing alcohol (isopropyl alcohol), which are outright poisons, even in small quantities. It is therefore no accident that ethyl alcohol, the most pleasant and one of the least toxic of all the alcohols, has come to be identified with the general term. I will refer to ethyl alcohol simply as "alcohol."

Societies differ vastly in their average level of alcohol consumption. What proportion of their members drink at all, and how much, each drinker consumes on the average varies enormously from one nation to another, and even from one group to another within a country. In addition, every society that has some acquaintance with alcohol has devised and institutionalized rules for the proper and improper consumption of alcohol. There is, then, intersocietal variation on the behavioral and the normative levels. Although there are indeed biochemical "effects" of alcohol, both short-term and over the long run, most of them can be mitigated or drastically altered by the belief in and the observance of these cultural rules. Heavy, long-term alcohol use is associated with certain medical maladies, but the extent to which intoxication leads to troublesome, harmful, or deviant behavior varies considerably from society to society. In many places, alcohol use poses no social problem according to almost anyone's definition. The drug is consumed in moderation and is associated with no untoward behavior. In other places, alcohol use has been catastrophic by any conceivable standard. The overall impact of alcohol, then, is not determined by the biochemical features of the drug itself, but by their *relationship* to the characteristics of the people drinking it. This is not to say that alcohol can have any effect that the members of a society expect it to have. There is a great deal of latitude in alcohol's effects, but it is a latitude within certain boundaries.

As with illegal drugs, the effects of alcohol can be divided into short-term or *acute* effects while under the influence, and long-range, or *chronic* effects. Even this breakdown is crude. The acute effects can be further subdivided into those that rest within the "objective" or strictly physiological and sensorimotor realms; the realm of behavior under the influence, called *drunken comportment*; and the "subjective" realm, or what it feels like to be drunk, how the intoxication is experienced. The sensorimotor effects are fairly specific and easily measured in mechanical and mental performance, such as motor coordination, memory, and the ability to achieve a given score on certain psychological tests. Drunken comportment, in contrast, refers to the vast spectrum of free-ranging, real-life behavior: what people do with and to one another while under the influence. A sensorimotor effect would be driving more poorly under the influence; drunken comportment might refer to whether or not one even gets into a car while drunk in the first place. The long-range effects can be divided, at the very least, into *medical* effects and *behavioral* effects—what happens to one's daily life after ingesting certain quantities of alcohol over a lengthy period.

ACUTE EFFECTS OF ALCOHOL

The potency of alcoholic beverages is measured by the percent of *absolute alcohol* they contain. Pure ethyl alcohol is 100 percent absolute alcohol. Beer contains about 4 or 5 percent. Wine is about 12 percent; it is the most potent drink we can concoct through the natural fermentation process. ("Fortified" wine, in which alcohol is added to the natural substance, may be no higher than 20 percent alcohol. The wines skid-row alcoholics drink are usually "fortified." Sherry is a wine fortified with brandy.) However, the process of distillation (boiling, condensing, and recovering the more volatile, alcohol-potent vapor from the original fluid, and adding an appropriate proportion of water) produces drinks, like Scotch, vodka, gin, rum, and tequila, that are about 40 to 50 percent alcohol, or 80 to 100 "proof." Consequently, in order to consume roughly an ounce of absolute alcohol, someone would have to drink two 12-ounce cans of beer, or one 8-ounce glass of wine, or a mixed drink containing about 2½ ounces of Scotch or gin. According to *the rule of equivalency*—which states that the effects of alcohol are determined mainly by the volume of absolute alcohol that is drunk, rather than the type of drink itself—these drinks would be roughly equal in strength, and would have approximately the same effects on one's body.

Alcohol, when it enters the body, is translated into what pharmacologists call *blood-alcohol concentration* (BAC), or *blood-alcohol level* (BAL). This corresponds fairly closely to the percent of one's blood that is made up of alcohol after it is ingested. There is a relationship between blood-alcohol concentration and what we do under the influence. The effects of alcohol are, to a large degree, dose-related: the more that is drunk, the greater the effect it has. There are, of course, person-to-person variations in this respect. And there are many qualifications that must be noted.

The effects of alcohol are influenced by many factors. Some of them are directly physiological. Since alcohol registers its impact via the bloodstream, the *size* of the drinker influences blood-alcohol concentration; the larger the drinker, the more alcohol it takes to make him or her drunk. The presence of food and water in the stomach will retard and space out over time—by as much as two times—the rate of absorption of alcohol into the bloodstream. Consequently, the less one has in one's stomach, the less it takes to get one drunk. The *faster* one drinks, the less able the body is to metabolize the alcohol within a standard period of time, and the drunker one will become. One can drink small quantities of alcohol continually without demonstrating any effects at all, if the drinks are taken slowly enough. The presence of carbonation in an alcoholic beverage—as, for example, in champagne or sparkling Burgundy—will speed up the metabolism process and can make one drunker more quickly.

As with practically all drugs, alcohol builds pharmacological tolerance: It takes more to have an effect on a regular drinker than on an abstainer, more on a heavy drinker than an infrequent drinker. Much of this is behavioral tolerance: simply learning to get used to alcohol's effects. But biochemical tolerance does develop as well. There is a kind of "plateau," however: It requires something like twice as much alcohol to have an effect in the sensorimotor realm in the heavy, long-term drinker as in the moderate drinker.

Alcohol's strictly physiological effects include cellular dehydration (a major reason for a hangover the day after), gastric irritation (which may lead to an upset stomach after drinking too much), vasodilation (an increase of blood flow through the capillaries), a lowering of body temperature (though the surface of the skin does become flushed, creating an illusion of greater body warmth), some anesthesia, and a depression of many functions and activities of the organs of the body, especially the central nervous system. Alcohol also disorganizes and impairs the ability of the brain to process and use information.

One ounce of alcohol consumed in less than an hour will result in a blood-alcohol concentration of roughly .05 percent in a person of average size (see Table 5.1). This produces in most people a mild euphoria, a diminution of anxiety, fear, and tension, a corresponding increase in self-confidence and, usually, what is called a "release" of inhibitions (an effect I'll have to qualify shortly). Decreased fear also typically results in a greater willingness to take risks; this effect has been demonstrated in laboratory animals (Health, Education, and Welfare, 1971, p. 39). Alcohol is, for most people, at low doses, a mild sedative and a tranquilizer. This is by no means universally the case, however. There are many people for whom alcohol ingestion results in paranoia, distrust, heightened anxiety, and even hostility. These "effects," however, typically occur, when they do, at high doses. And at low doses, alcohol will result in little or no diminution of motor and intellectual performance.

Alcohol's effects on motor performance are familiar to us all: clumsiness; an unsteady gait; an inability to stand or walk straight; slurred speech. One's accuracy and consistency in performing mechanical activities decline dramatically as blood-alcohol concentration increases. And the more complex, the more abstract, and the more unfamiliar the task, the sharper the decline. The most noteworthy example is the ability to drive an automobile. It is crystal clear that drinking, even moderately, deteriorates the ability to drive, and contributes to highway fatalities.

**Table 5.1   Alcohol Intake and Blood-Alcohol Level (BAL)
(for a 150-pound individual, in one hour of drinking)**

Absolute Alcohol (Ounces)	Beverage Intake	Blood-Alcohol Level (BAL) (grams/100 milliliters)
½	1 can beer 1 glass wine 1 oz. distilled spirits	.025
1	2 cans beer 2 glasses wine 2 oz. distilled spirits	.05
2	4 cans beer 4 glasses wine 4 oz. distilled spirits	.10
3	6 cans beer 6 glasses wine 6 oz. distilled spirits	.15
4	8 cans beer 8 glasses wine 8 oz. distilled spirits	.20
5	10 cans beer 10 glasses wine 10 oz. distilled spirits	.25

Note: The less someone weighs, the higher the BAL, other things
being equal; the more someone weighs, the lower the BAL. The BAL
of males tends to be slightly lower than that of females.

SOURCE: Adapted and simplified from Ray and Ksir, 1987, p. 155.

How intoxicated does one have to be to lose the ability to perform
mechanical tasks? What does one's blood-alcohol level have to be to display
a significant decline in motor coordination? And how many drinks does this
represent? The answers depend on a number of factors, as I just said,
experience with alcohol being crucial. It is true that seasoned drinkers can
handle themselves better at the same blood-alcohol level than novices can,
but experienced drinkers are typically far too overconfident about their
ability to function while under the influence. In fact, since alcohol tends to
dull anxiety and tension, drunk drivers typically think that they perform
better than they actually do—and are surprised, even incredulous, when
their ineptitude is demonstrated to them—so that the problem becomes
more than a simple deterioration in mechanical ability. All drinkers experience a loss of motor skills at a certain point, and it occurs at a fairly low BAC.
However, many drivers are quite willing to get behind the wheel while
intoxicated: In 1986 in the United States, there were 1.8 million arrests for
drunk driving.

There is a kind of "zone" within which alcohol impairment occurs. At
about the .03 percent blood-alcohol level, some very inexperienced and

particularly susceptible individuals will display significant negative changes in the ability to perform a wide range of tasks. (See Table 5.1 for an indication of how much alcohol this entails for a 150-pound person.) The Federal Aviation Administration (FAA) sets a .04 percent BAC as representing an alcohol-influenced condition, and prohibits pilots from flying at this level of intoxication. As we can see from Table 5.1, this is less than two typical drinks. At the .10 level, even the most hardened, experienced, and resistant drinker will exhibit some impairment in coordination. Most states set a BAL of .10 as constituting legal intoxication—a far too conservative a level, in the view of most experts. At the .04 percent level, for most people, there is no measurable increase in the likelihood of having a highway accident. But at the .06 percent level, the risk doubles. As we can see, this is only slightly more than two typical mixed drinks, or two beers, or two glasses of wine. At the .10 level, one's driving ability deteriorates by 15 percent, and one's likelihood of having an accident shoots up six or seven times, according to one estimate (Brodie, 1973, p. 32). According to another estimate, at a .08 BAL, one's risk of being involved in a fatal car crash triples, and at .12, it increases fifteenfold (Ray and Ksir, 1987, p. 157). At the .15 level of blood-alcohol concentration, which constitutes "driving while intoxicated" (DWI) everywhere in the United States, one's skill at handling an automobile drops by one-third and one's chances of smashing up increase by between 10 to 50 times (Brodie, 1973, p. 32).

Motor-vehicle crashes are the most common cause of "non-natural" death in the United States; they account for more fatal injuries than any other type of accident. The proportion of drivers involved in fatal crashes whose BAL tested at .10 or higher was 50 percent in 1980. This figure declined through the 1980s to 38 percent in 1985 (Brooke, 1986), but in 1986, the number of deaths from drunk driving increased a bit (Stevens, 1987). Taking all traffic fatalities together—drivers, passengers, pedestrians, and cyclists—42 percent were alcohol-related in 1983. The National Highway Traffic Safety Administration reported that 60 percent of fatally injured drivers of motorcycles had a BAC of .10 or higher; for fatally injured drivers of heavy trucks, this was only 20 percent. Even pedestrians vastly increase their chances of being killed by an automobile—more than five-fold!—if they are intoxicated. A third of pedestrian fatalities in one study had a BAC of .15 or higher, whereas only 6 percent of the control group randomly selected at the same time and place were this intoxicated (Brodie, 1973, p. 32).

Automobiles are not the only source of fatal alcohol-related accidents. The National Transportation and Safety Board estimates that nearly 70 percent of drownings are alcohol-related. The U.S. Coast Guard estimates that of all boating accidents that result in a drowning, 88 percent are alcohol-related. Nearly half (46 percent) of all burn victims had been using alcohol at the time of their injury. In roughly a quarter of all suicides (23 percent), a measurable level of intoxication was found in the victim's body (Health and Human Services, 1987a, pp. 8–11). In an unpublished study supplied by the chief medical examiner of North Carolina, the following figures represent the percent of people who died of each cause who registered a BAC of .10 or higher: drowning, 41 percent; fire, 58 percent; stabbing, 68 percent; firearms, 40 percent. Another study examined a thousand consecutive violent or accidental deaths in New York City in 1972. A BAC of .10 or higher was found in a third of all victims—33 percent for victims of falls, 44 percent for vehicular drivers or passengers, and 32 percent for pedestrians (Haberman and Baden, 1974). Numerous studies (Combes-Orme et al., 1983; Abel and Zeidenberg, 1985; Goodman et al., 1986) show that close to half of all homicide *victims* were drinking at the time they were killed, and one-third had a BAC of .10 or higher. Adding it all up, one estimate holds that in 1980 alone, alcohol was responsible for nearly 60,000 premature deaths from accident (38,000), suicide (8,000), homicide (12,000), and other non-disease-related sources (Ravenholt, 1984; Health and Human Services, 1987a, p. 6). Thus, in one year, alcohol was responsible for the loss of more American lives—not even counting the illnesses it caused—than was the Vietnam War.

Beyond the .15 blood-alcohol level, one's ability to function plummets. At the .20 level, the drinker is somewhat dazed, confused, and distinctly uncoordinated; any movement at all becomes risky and problematic. Driving is extremely hazardous. At the .30 level, any response to the stimuli of the outside world becomes an insurmountable chore. One's ability to perceive and comprehend what is happening is reduced to a bare minimum. At the .40 level, most people pass out and lose consciousness; this is regarded as the LD-50—the point at which half of all drinkers die from an overdose. At .50 percent, if the drinker is still alive, he or she has entered a coma, from which he or she can be aroused only with the greatest difficulty. At .60 percent, overdoses are increasingly common; death occurs as a result of the inhibition and paralysis of the respiratory centers. Almost anyone whose blood is .80 percent alcohol will die.

DRUNKEN COMPORTMENT

When we look at alcohol's effects, we must be careful to distinguish clearly those that are more or less standard from those that manifest themselves in almost endless variation. There is no doubt at all that alcohol, if drunk in sufficient quantity, results in a significant and measurable impairment in the drinker's ability to perform sensorimotor activities. In this sense, alcohol's effects are to a large degree specific. But in another realm, they are more or less completely dependent on the individual who is drinking and the culture in which drinking takes place. Does alcohol make the drinker depressed or euphoric? Gregarious or withdrawn? Vicious or pleasant? Energetic or passive? Most of us feel that alcohol universally "releases inhibitions," allowing us to show our uglier, more animalistic side, ordinarily kept in check by the restraints of our civilization. Alcohol, this homespun view theorizes, acts in a fairly standard fashion on the human animal.

An extensive survey of the impact on human behavior that alcohol has in many of the societies of the world was undertaken by two anthropologists, Craig MacAndrew and Robert B. Edgerton, and reported in a book entitled *Drunken Comportment* (1969). MacAndrew and Edgerton demonstrate that this folk view of alcohol universally acting as a "releaser of inhibitions" is false. Human emotions and behavior are far more subtle and labile than that. People are not simply under the control of alcohol; the precise effects of alcohol are under the control of the society in which drinkers grow up and live. Behavior under the influence, or drunken comportment, is sensationally and dramatically different from one society to another. MacAndrew and Edgerton report, for example, that when drunk, the Yuruna, an Indian tribe living in South America's tropical rain forest, become withdrawn, acting "much as though no one else existed" (1969, p. 17). In Takashima, a tiny rural fishing village in Japan, drunkenness results in "camaraderie, laughter, jokes, songs and dances" (MacAndrew and Edgerton, 1969, p. 33). The residents of Aritama, a village made up of mestizo, or part-Indian, part-Spanish people, in northern Colombia, are a somber, controlled, almost morose people. And, "regardless of the degree of intoxication that is achieved" by Aritama drinkers, their "rigid mask of seriousness stays in place"; they remain "unobtrusive and silent," seemingly incapable of enjoying themselves (MacAndrew and Edgerton, 1969, pp. 25–27). The Camba of Bolivia, another mestizo people, drink a concoction they call, appropriately enough, "alcohol"; it is a sugar cane distillate that is 89 percent alcohol—almost 180 proof! In the early stages of their intoxication they are convivial, high-spirited, gregarious, voluble. The more they drink, the more stupefied and thick-lipped they grow, staring silently at the ground. Many simply pass out and fall asleep. Throughout their drinking bouts, there is a complete absence of verbal or physical aggression.

The Mixtecs of Mexico drink, we are told, truly prodigious quantities of alcohol, frequently to the point of passing out, stupefied. Along the way to becoming drunk, do they become violent? Angry? Hostile? Dangerous? These Indians specifically deny that alcohol is capable of producing violent behavior in them. And that is, indeed, exactly what happens: They are never observed to become loud, aggressive, or violent. Drinking coconut toddy among the Ifaluk, residents of a tiny island in the Pacific, results in no anger or violence either. Instead, a "warm feeling of good fellowship" spreads through everyone, "and every man becomes a brother and the world is a paradise" (MacAndrew and Edgerton, 1969, p. 29).

Not only is drunken behavior markedly different from culture to culture, but it also varies strikingly in the same culture *from one social setting to another.* Among traditional Papago, an American Indian desert-dwelling people, a cactus wine was drunk ceremonially to await the coming of a brief, sparse rainy season. The people became drunk, often hopelessly so, and vomited copiously. Drunkenness was approved during this period and no one acted unruly; fighting was entirely absent. The most violent activity observed was singing. With the intrusion of whites into Papago territory, initiating the ready availability of liquor and its use during times other than the rainmaking ceremony, the Papago became violent during drunkenness. Getting drunk took on a nontraditional, nonceremonial, and even deviant character. Here we have two kinds of drinking, leading to precisely opposite behaviors under the influence. Clearly this difference cannot be explained simply by the nature of alcohol itself (MacAndrew and Edgerton, 1969, pp. 37–42).

Beer drunk in tribal villages by South Africans results in behavior that is "free of rancor" and lacking in physical aggression. But the very same beer drunk by the very same tribespeople when they migrate to the urban South African slums frequently results in arguments, fights, brawls, and stabbings. "While the beverage of the South African Bantu has not changed, the circumstances surrounding its consumption most certainly have. And as these circumstances have changed, so, too, has their drunken comportment" (MacAndrew and Edgerton, 1969, p. 53). In rural Okinawa, the Japanese residents drink sake. There are, however, two distinctly different types of drinking occasions. When men and women drink together, behavior is "completely free of drunken aggression." When men drink by themselves, they become quarrelsom, noisy, and often physically violent. When the Indians of Tescopa drink pulque among themselves, the result is harmony and contentment, a feeling of fellowship; violence is unheard of. When Tescopans drink with outsiders, violent, bloody fights frequently erupt (MacAndrew and Edgerton, 1969, pp. 55–57).

Exactly the same pattern that we observe with violence prevails with regard to the connection between drinking alcohol and sexual licentiousness. In some societies, drunkenness produces no departure at all from the usual puritanical sex code. This is true, for example, of the Abipone of Paraguay and the Pondo of South Africa. The Camba of Bolivia, when sober, stress "interpersonal harmony" and a "rigorously enforced puritanical approach to all things sexual." Does intoxication produce a dissolution of these inhibitions? Not only does alcohol "fail to produce tidal waves of aggression and sexuality, it does not even produce ripples" (MacAndrew and Edgerton, 1969, p. 33).

In other societies, when alcohol is drunk, a normally reserved people may become amorous—but always within certain specific limits. The Tarahumara of Mexico, normally an extremely chaste, puritanical, and timid people, when drunk engage in mate swapping, a practice that is absolutely unheard of and never engaged in when they are sober. Or alcohol may make some amorous peoples even more so. The Lepcha of Sikkim are one of the most sexually active and permissive people on the face of the earth. They have intercourse extremely early in life, at age 10 or 12 and continue to do so vigorously into old age. Adultery is common, even expected, and no cause for anger on the part of the spouse. Sex, it has been said, constitutes the principal recreation among the Lepcha. It is their main topic of conversation as well as an inexhaustible wellspring of humor. During the annual harvest festival, large quantities of home-brewed liquor are drunk. The normally relaxed sexual customs blossom into almost unbridled promiscuity. Lepcha theory is that the more couples that copulate, and the more often they do so, the richer the harvest. If someone sees his or her spouse having sex with someone else, it is bad form to interrupt or even to mention it to anyone later. Four- or 5-year-old children imitating copulation with one another are encouraged by adult onlookers. Yet, throughout this festival of carnality, the incest taboos are never broken. The Lepcha feel a sense of horror about incest; it is believed that if enacted by even one couple, it will bring disaster to the whole community. What is interesting is that the Lepcha have an extremely broad interpretation of incest, one that encompasses a very high proportion of the population, including second, third, and fourth cousins (what we would call "kissing cousins"), any in-laws no matter how remote, blood relatives on the father's side for nine generations, and so on. Every child of 10 has learned and knows which members of the community are legitimate sex partners and which ones are to be shunned sexually. Even when the Lepcha are drunk, these rules are never broken, in spite of the huge number of relatives with whom one may not have sex, and in spite of the very powerful norms propelling almost every Lepcha into the arms of many partners of the opposite sex. Alcohol may relax sexual custom, but when it does, it does so only in a pattern that is socially and culturally approved.

There is, then, a time, a place, and an object selectivity, both for violence and for sex under the influence: disinhibition takes place within limits set by the community. In other words, "however great the difference may be between persons' sober and drunken comportment . . . it is evident that both states are characterized by a healthy respect for certain socially sanctioned limits" (MacAndrew and Edgerton, 1969, p. 85). By itself and in and of itself, "the presence of alcohol in the body does not necessarily conduce to disinhibition, much less inevitably produce such an effect" (pp. 87–88). It is possible, then, to speak of *the socially organized character of drunken comportment.* How does socially approved drunken behavior arise? "Over the course of socialization, people learn about drunkenness what their society 'knows' about drunkenness; and, accepting and acting upon the understandings thus imparted to them, they become the living confirmation of their society's teachings" (p. 88). There is in nearly every society a zone of behavior that is permissible *only under the influence.* Being drunk is considered a kind of time out. The norms of what is acceptable behavior while intoxicated—and what is not—are already spelled out well before one gets drunk. The behavior may be thoroughly reprehensible if one is sober, but if committed while drunk, one may *invoke* the disinhibiting effect of the alcohol one has drunk. The otherwise deviant act becomes an excused transgression. This doesn't work for all behavior. Societies allow the excuse of drunkenness for some forms of behavior but not others. It matters not to the law of the United States that one is drunk when murdering one's spouse, though it may count in one's own mind. In some other societies, drunkenness may be a mitigating circumstance in homicide, considerably reducing the penalty one will receive.

Behavior under the influence, then, does not follow a predetermined, biochemically fixed pattern. It, too, has its norms, although they may be a bit different from those that influence behavior when one is sober. It is not the drug, alcohol, that truly *makes* anyone do anything. Alcohol is merely one component in a vastly intricate scheme.

With regard to alcohol use and violent behavior in the United States, two facts are clear: The first is the enormous range in the drug's impact on Americans, and the second is that alcohol is associated with a great deal of violence here. Clearly, many Americans view being drunk as a legitimate occasion for engaging in brawling and sexually aggressive behavior. It is far too simple to say that alcohol consumption is *the* or even *a* cause of violent behavior. But in our society, alcohol consumption and violence often appear together. The more violent the crime, the greater the likelihood that the offender was drunk while committing it. One classic study reported that in 60 percent of all murders the killer had been drinking prior to his attack on the victim (Wolfgang, 1958). A later study, conducted in Chicago, found this figure to be 53 percent (Voss and Hepburn, 1968). Thus, although alcohol cannot be said to *cause* people to kill one another, it is certainly involved in an extremely high proportion of all homicides in the United States.

The same holds true of sexual aggression. The massive study conducted by the Institute of Sex Research (the "Kinsey Institute") on convicted, incarcerated sex offenders indicated that alcohol plays a significant role in sex crimes—especially those involving force, as well as those against young children. In about 40 percent of all acts of male sexual aggression against adult women (mostly rape and attempted rape), the offender was classified as drunk. Exactly two-thirds of all aggressive sexual offenses against young girls, or child molestation, involved drunkenness (Gebhard et al., 1967, pp. 761–763, 813). Another study found that 45 percent of the men arrested in the city of Cincinnati on the charge of rape had a blood-alcohol concentration of .10 percent or higher (Shupe, 1954).

ALCOHOL CONSUMPTION AND CONTROL IN THE UNITED STATES

Alcohol consumption should be interesting and instructive to any student of human behavior for a variety of reasons. For one thing, legal controls have been applied to the manufacture and sale of alcoholic substances, with mixed results. Moreover, the use of alcohol has been regarded as respectable during most of the nation's history—indeed, to refuse to drink has been seen as unacceptable, unfashionable, even slightly deviant. Yet during the period between roughly 1850 and the 1920s, drinking became an atypical, minority activity. The typical American disapproved of it on principle. Perhaps equally important, "respectable" Americans were *most* likely to oppose alcohol consumption; the less prestigious, less affluent, and less powerful social and ethnic groups tended to be more favorably inclined toward drinking. The dominant attitude of conventional Americans was that moderate drinking was not possible: one either abstained altogether or become an incurable alcoholic—there was no in-between territory.

During this period, there was an attempt, as there invariably is today in other areas of life, to demonstrate a *moral* point by mobilizing credibility and a rational-sounding argument. The fact is, Prohibitionist elements in America opposed the use of alcohol on moral grounds: They considered the practice evil, an abomination. In their denunciations of drinking, the line between what the drug does to the user and the inherent degeneracy of the practice itself was extremely fuzzy. In order to see drinking as a morally tainted activity, Prohibitionists wished to convince others that it was an irrational, illogical, damaging activity as well, that it had consequences in the real world that any reasonable person would disapprove of. All that was necessary was the dissemination of the "correct" point of view.

Thus alcohol has had a fascinating cyclical history in America. The Indians who greeted Columbus brewed and drank beer. (They were not, however, acquainted with distilled spirits.) The Puritans, although remembered for their abhorrence of sensual and physical pleasures, arrived on the shores of New England with ample supplies of beer, wine, and hard liquor. The *Arbella,* which arrived in the Boston area only a few years after the *Mayflower,* "set sail with three times as much beer as water, along with 10,000 gallons of wine." In addition, most settlers brought along a supply of distilled spirits as well. "So liquor was more than a luxury in the colonial mind; it was a necessity to be kept close at hand" (Lender and Martin, 1987, p. 2). Increase Mather, a Puritan minister of some distinction and the author of *Woe to Drunkards* (1673), while warning against overindulgence, said, "Drink is in itself a good creature of God, and to be received with thankfulness." Drinking "constituted a central facet of colonial life. Indeed, two of the key characteristics of early drinking patterns were frequency and quantity. Simply stated, most settlers drank often and abundantly" (Lender and Martin, 1987, p. 9).

Drinking in colonial America was "utilitarian, with high alcohol consumption a normal part of personal and community habits." Beer and cider were common at mealtime, with children often partaking; collective tasks, like clearing a field, were typically accompanied by a public cask. Farmers usually took a jug into the fields with them each morning. Employers often gave their employees liquor on the job. Political candidates usually "treated" the electorate to alcoholic beverages, including at polling places on election days. The Continental Army supplied its troops with a daily ration of 4 ounces of rum, when it was available, or whiskey. Drinking was extremely common in seventeenth- and eighteenth-century America, considerably higher than it is today. One estimate holds that in 1790, when the first national census was taken, the per capita alcohol consumption for the American population age 15 and older was 5.8 gallons of absolute alcohol per year, more than twice its present level (Lender and Martin, 1987, pp. 9–10, 205).

Drinking in seventeenth- and eighteenth-century America was rarely considered a serious social problem; in fact, there was a remarkable lack of anxiety about it. While heavy drinking and even alcoholism certainly existed, most drinkers consumed alcohol in a family or a community setting, and strong social norms kept excessive drinking within acceptable bounds, and prevented unacceptable and potentially dangerous behavior under the influence from getting out of hand. Drinking, though heavy by today's standards, was fairly well socially controlled. "As the colonial period drew to a close, most Americans still held to the traditional view of drinking as a positive social and personal good" (Lender and Martin, 1987, p. 34).

High as alcohol consumption was at the turn of the eighteenth century, it actually rose significantly into the nineteenth—from 5.8 gallons of absolute alcohol per person age 15 and older per year in 1790 to 7.1 in 1830. Moreover, the proportion of the alcohol consumed in the form of distilled spirits, in contrast to beer and wine, was 40 percent in 1790; in 1830, it was 60 percent. Said one observer in 1814, "the quantity of ardent spirits" consumed in the United States at that time "surpasses belief." Drinking "had reached unparalleled levels." The notion "that alcohol was necessary for health remained firmly fixed. It was common to down a glass of whiskey or other spirits before breakfast. . . . Instead of taking coffee or tea breaks," Americans customarily took breaks at eleven and four for a few pulls on the jug. "Even school children took their sip of whiskey, the morning and afternoon glasses being considered 'absolutely indispensable to man and boy.' " Distilled spirits "were a basic part of the diet—most people thought that whiskey was as essential as bread." In the early nineteenth century, "the idea that the problem drinker could cause serious social disruption had occurred to relatively few people; drinking behavior, even when disruptive, remained largely a matter of individual choice" (Lender and Martin, 1987, pp. 205, 46, 47, 53).

Reacting to these apparent excesses, the temperance movement began to take shape. Perhaps the most influential of the early advocates of prohibition, who wrote when he was but a voice in the wilderness, was Benjamin Rush, Philadelphia physician, signer of the Declaration of Independence, surgeon general of the Continental Army, and author of *An Inquiry into the Effects of Ardent Spirits on the Human Mind and Body* (1784). Rush challenged the conventional view that drinking was an unmixed good. Rush did not condemn drinking per se, only heavy, uncontrolled drinking, nor did he condemn alcoholic beverages per se—his primary target was hard liquor. "Consumed in quantity over the years," he wrote, distilled spirits "could destroy a person's health and even cause death." Rush was the first scientist or physician to label alcoholism a disease characterized by progressively more serious stages; it was accompanied, he said, by addiction. Rush felt that community constraints on drinking in late eighteenth- and early nineteenth-century America had broken down, destroying drinkers' lives, families, and ability to function as breadwinners and citizens.

Although he conveyed a powerful sense of urgency, Rush was not optimistic about reform. However, he had friends who were influential in religious affairs, and "he had sown the seeds of reform movements to come." The first temperance society was founded in 1808, and by 1811, the temperance movement, uniting a number of scattered and independent organizations, was formed. In 1826, the American Society for the Promotion of Temperance (later the American Temperance Society) was founded. Initially, the society, like Dr. Rush, preached the gospel of moderation. It "helped organize local units, sent lecturers into the field, distributed literature (including Rush's *Inquiry*), and served as a clearinghouse for movement information." Within three years, more than 200 state and local antiliquor organizations were active. By 1830, temperance reform "constituted a burgeoning national movement" (Lender and Martin, 1987, p. 68).

By the 1830s, the adherents of total abstinence carried the day in the movement. The Temperance Society boasted 1.5 million members who proselytized righteously for their cause. Employers stopped supplying liquor on the job. Politicians ceased being so free and easy about "treating" their constituency and supporters with alcohol. An extremely effective tactic of the temperance movement was to influence local and county politicians to refuse granting licenses to taverns, undercutting major centers of heavy drinking. Although the movement lost some steam before and during the Civil War, while more pressing matters were settled, the 1870s and 1880s witnessed a rebirth of even stronger prohibitionist activity.

Alcohol consumption plummeted between 1830 (7.1 gallons of absolute alcohol per person age 15 and older per year) and 1840 (3.1 gallons). Between 1850 and 1920, when national alcohol prohibition took effect, alcohol consumption remained, with relatively small decade-to-decade fluctuations, at about 2 gallons per year for every adult age 15 and older in the population.

The Volstead Act, bringing about a complete national prohibition on the sale of alcohol, took effect in 1920. After its passage, the author of the Volstead Act, Senator Morris Sheppard, representing the state of Texas, uttered the classic statement: "There is as much chance of repealing the Eighteenth Amendment as there is for a hummingbird to fly to the planet Mars with the Washington Monument tied to its tail." But by 1933, Prohibition had been declared a failure and was abandoned as a social experiment. (The Eighteenth Amendment is the only one ever to be repealed in American constitutional history.) What happened in the historically brief intervening fifteen years?

During Prohibition, at a time when people were actually drinking less than they did before, *drinking alcohol was becoming considered more and more respectable*. Attitudes and behavior are not always perfectly correlated. So the question becomes: What happened socially, economically, and politically during the course of Prohibition? I contend that people's attitudes toward the use of alcohol per se were tangentially related to whether Prohibition worked or not. And they were not based on the medical effects of this drug. Something else changed the people's minds. What was it?

Many forms of behavior that become criminalized pose no direct threat in any way to their practitioners, nor to the other members of a society. But they may be considered deviant by self-righteous, morally indignant conventionals. The struggle between alcohol drinkers and Prohibitionists in the years before the passage of the Volstead Act can be looked at primarily as a struggle between status groups and lifestyles. Supporters of Prohibition were primarily rural dwellers, native-born members of the native-born parentage, either white-collar or middle class or owners of farms, and overwhelmingly Protestant. Opponents of Prohibition were far more likely to be urban dwellers, immigrants or the sons and daughters of immigrants, manual laborers, and Catholic. "Prohibition stood as a symbol of the general system of ascetic behavior with which the Protestant middle classes had been identified" (Gusfield, 1963, p. 124). A number of historical changes took place during the twentieth century that directly impinged upon the issue of alcohol and Prohibition. First, the old Protestant middle class suffered a serious decline in prestige as a social group. Second, urban dwellers, Catholics, the non-Anglo-Saxon ethnics, all secured far more political power than they had held previously. Third, the "new" middle class rose in numbers, in power, and in status. The urban, cosmopolitan, college-educated, technically trained executive working for a nationally based corporation became the symbol of the middle class. The old-time locally based entrepreneur lost hold on the American consciousness as the model representative of the middle class. *And it was specifically this "new" middle class that abandoned abstinence and took to recreational drinking.* The Volstead Act was passed because abstinence was identified with a prestigious and powerful group in American society. Prohibition failed because it was the powerful, prestigious middle class that abandoned abstinence as a legitimate and respectable way of life. Temperance ceased to be necessary to a respectable life; its symbolic connection with respectability was severed. And lastly, the Depression loomed before the American public and the government, and relegalizing alcohol manufacture and sale brought with it the prospect of jobs and tax revenue (Gusfield, 1963, pp. 111–138).

By the time that repeal actually did take place, the idea of Prohibition had become so unpopular that the population of no area of the country wanted to retain the Volstead Act. A study conducted in 1932 by a magazine of the time, the *Literary Digest,* found that adults favoring the retention of Prohibition ranged from a scant 19 percent in the populous, urban northern states of New York, New Jersey, and Pennsylvania to 41 percent in the rural Bible-belt southern states of Mississippi, Alabama, Tennessee, and Kentucky. Thirty-nine states actually voted on the repeal of Prohibition in 1933. Repeal carried by three to one (15 million for, 5 million against). Again, as with the *Literary Digest* poll, in northern, urban, and heavily Catholic states like New York, New Jersey, and Rhode Island, repeal was chosen by more than 80 percent of the voters. But in rural, Protestant southern states like Alabama, Arkansas, and Tennessee, the vote was between 50 and 60 percent for repeal. Only in North and South Carolina did a majority vote to retain Prohibition.

We've all learned that Prohibition was a catastrophic failure, perhaps the least successful effort to control behavior in the nation's history. Many of us even believe that alcohol consumption rose during this period—after all, we say, outlawing an activity will only encourage people to engage in it. In fact, the truth is exactly the opposite from this gem of conventional wisdom: All indications point to the fact that alcohol consumption declined sharply during Prohibition, and rose once legal restrictions were lifted.

Of course, we do not have hard data on alcohol consumption between 1920 and 1933; since sales were illegal, no record of them was kept. We must, therefore, make inferences about use by relying on more indirect indicators of alcohol consumption. One such indicator is the incidence of cirrhosis of the liver, which is very closely correlated with alcohol consumption in the population. The rate of death from cirrhosis of the liver remained between 12 and 17 per 100,000 in the population each year between 1900 and 1919. But it dropped to between 7 and 9 per 100,000 in the 1920s and early 1930s, a reduction of almost half. In the mid-1930s, it began to rise again (Grant et al., 1986).

In addition, the number of people arrested and jailed in the state of Connecticut on the charge of public drunkenness fell from more than 7,000 in 1917 to fewer than 1,000 in 1920. And the number of automobile fatalities—also strongly correlated with alcohol consumption—declined 40 percent between the years immediately preceding Prohibition and the 1920–1933 period (Burgess, 1973, p. 152). Putting together a number of indicators, two authors (Lender and Martin, 1987) estimate the yearly adult per capita alcohol consumption in the United States for the 1920–1930 period at 0.9 gallons of absolute alcohol, less than half of what it had been in 1916–1919. Use did not skyrocket immediately after Prohibition; most people simply got out of the habit of drinking and it took several years for them to resume the habit. In 1934, consumption rose to 0.97 gallons; by 1935, to 1.20, and the prewar 1936–1941, to 1.54. In fact, alcohol consumption rose steadily between the end of Prohibition and the late 1970s, as we'll see shortly.

Why do many people believe that drinking increased rather than decreased during Prohibition? That's not hard to answer: It's a much more entertaining and interesting story. We tend to focus on "speakeasies" and honky-tonks, jazz clubs, secret passwords, bathtub gin, silver hip flasks, Al Capone, gang warfare, corruption, payoffs, a few honest, crusading crime-fighters—all of this is exciting stuff. It sticks in our minds. We tend to exaggerate the frequency of the unusual and underplay that of the routine, the everyday. We assume that most people were engaged in these exciting alcohol-related activities that we've heard so much about. People living in a given age often think that everyone who lived at a different time was engaged in that period's most memorable and noteworthy activities. In fact, people who actually lived through another time will tend, upon recollection of it, to exaggerate their participation in these unusual activities. The truth about Prohibition is, therefore, relatively unexciting. In general, most

Americans did not drink during Prohibition, and those who did drank significantly less, and less often, than they did before or after.

Today, Americans age 15 or older consume about 2.58 gallons of absolute alcohol per person per year (Lender and Martin, 1987, p. 206). This is a fairly "hard" or reliable statistic because it is based on sales and not simply what people say they drink. This works out to just under 1 ounce of absolute alcohol per person age 15 or older per day. Of course, some people drink a lot more than this, some less, and some not at all. Roughly one-third of all Americans are more or less total abstainers. Thus it makes sense to tabulate the quantity of alcohol consumed specifically for drinkers, and leave abstainers out of the picture entirely. Adult drinkers consume a bit more than 1½ ounces of absolute alcohol per day. This represents two and a half 12-ounce bottles or cans of beer *or* one and a half 8-ounce glasses of wine *or* one 3- or 4-ounce drink of hard liquor per day for every drinking adolescent and adult in the country.

During the 1980s, the American population became more moderate in its use of psychoactive substances. We saw earlier that the use of illegal drugs (except cocaine) declined between 1979 and the mid-1980s. More or less the same has been true of alcohol consumption. The use of alcohol rose more or less steadily from the end of Prohibition (an average of 1.20 gallons of absolute alcohol in 1935) to 1978 (2.82 gallons), and declined after that. In 1980, the per capita yearly alcohol consumption for Americans 15 and older was 2.76 gallons of absolute alcohol per year; in 1985, as I just said, it was 2.58 (Lender and Martin, 1987, p. 206). It is likely that this downward trend will continue for the foreseeable future.

Recorded yearly alcohol sales can be backed up with information on the proportion of the American population who says that it drinks. Every year or so, the Gallup Poll asks a sample of Americans the following question: "Do you have occasion to use alcoholic beverages such as liquor, wine, or beer, or are you a total abstainer?" This question was first asked in 1939, when 58 percent defined themselves as drinkers, 42 percent as abstainers. In 1945, 67 percent said that they drank; the percentage declined between 1945 and 1949, then rose steadily throughout the 1950s and 1960s, and reached a peak of 71 percent in 1976 and 1978. It declined thereafter, and stood at 64 percent in 1984, but rose slightly to 67 percent in 1985 and 1986 (Gallup, 1980, p. 236; 1986, pp. 80–81; 1987, pp. 18–19).

The National Institute on Drug Abuse survey I cited so often in earlier chapters (NIDA, 1986) also contains information on alcohol consumption. The questions NIDA asks are a bit different from Gallup's; NIDA is more specific about the time periods in which the alcohol consumption took place—that is, has the respondent ever drunk alcohol, and has he or she drunk alcohol within the past month. As can be seen in Table 5.2, there has been a noticeable decline in self-reported alcohol consumption between 1979 and 1985 for all ages.

For youth age 12 to 17, the proportion who ever drank dropped from 70 to 57 between 1979 and 1985, and from 37 to 32 percent for those who

Table 5.2   Alcohol Consumption, 1979–1985

	1979		1985	
	Ever	*Last Month*	*Ever*	*Last Month*
Youth (12–17)	70	37	57	32
Young Adults (18–25)	95	76	93	72
Older Adults (26+)	92	61	89	61

SOURCE: Fishburne, Abelson, and Cisin, 1980, p. 89; NIDA, 1986.

drank within the past month. For young adults age 18 to 25, the decline was less substantial, from 95 to 93 percent and from 76 to 72 percent respectively. For older adults, there was a decline in the "ever" statistic, from 92 to 89 percent, but the proportion drinking within the past month remained stable at 61 percent (Fishburne, Abelson, and Cisin, 1980, p. 89; NIDA, 1986). Clearly, then, the NIDA survey, like the sales figures and the Gallup Poll, shows a significant decline in alcohol consumption during the 1980s. The trend, then, must be regarded as real and not the artifact of one particular measuring device. Moreover, it must be taken as part of a more general trend in the decline of the use of all psychoactive drugs (except cocaine) in the 1980s.

What accounts for this recent decline in alcohol consumption? Partly a shift to lighter, lower-alcohol-content drinks. In 1977, distilled spirits accounted for 40 percent of the alcohol consumed in America; in 1985, this figure had decreased to 35 percent. Correspondingly, wine increased from 48 to 52 percent. While in principle this would not necessarily decrease the nation's overall alcohol consumption—drinkers might conceivably consume more wine to get the same amount of alcohol—in practice, the switch has resulted in decreased use. In addition, many young drinkers are turning to wine "coolers," with an alcohol content of 5 to 6 percent. To the extent that wine coolers are being substituted for regular wine, this represents a decline in the total quantity of alcohol consumed by the drinker; on the other hand, if wine coolers are substituting for beer, there is a very slight increase.

Another significant development in the 1980s is the fact that all states in the United States except Wyoming have instituted a 21-year-old drinking age, while in 1979, only fourteen had such a law. Although conventional wisdom says that young people will find a way to drink in spite of legal restrictions (for an article making this claim, at least for college students, see Ravo, 1987), the same fallacy applies here as to Prohibition: When legal controls exist and are enforced, drinking will decline significantly for the relevant age group; although many will break the law, enough will comply to bring down the average level of alcohol consumption significantly. According to one study, a year after New York state raised its drinking age to 21, alcohol purchases among 16- to 20-year-olds declined by 50 percent, and use itself declined by 21 percent. When the legal age was 18, 25 percent of 17-year-olds and 20 percent of 16-year-olds said that they had purchased alcohol during the previous month. When the drinking age was raised to 21, more than a quarter of the 19- and 20-year-olds surveyed said that they had purchased alcohol within the last month; but only 9 percent of the 18-year-olds, 14 percent of the 17-year-olds, and 6 percent of the 16-year-olds said that they had done so. The same systematic tendency toward a decline prevailed for use, and, other studies indicate, the same pattern holds for the country generally (Kolbert, 1987).

The most important reason for the decline in the consumption of absolute alcohol, however, has been a consistent decline in drinking overall. As we saw, it is not simply a reduction in the use of lower-alcohol-content beverages that has brought these consumption figures down; that would reduce the sales and total consumption figures, but not the proportion of the population who have ever drunk or the proportion who drank within the past month. The simple fact is, fewer people are drinking, and, among those who drink, a higher proportion is drinking less when they drink, and less frequently as well. The same pattern prevails as with the illicit psychoactives: Americans are using fewer psychoactive drugs nowadays than they were a decade ago.

The decline in drinking in the population generally, and for teenagers specifically, along with stricter law enforcement with respect to drinking and driving, have translated into a significant decline in alcohol-related deaths in auto accidents. The National Highway Traffic Safety Administration estimated, as I said above, that 38 percent of all drivers in a fatal automobile accident in 1985 had a BAL of .10 or higher, a significant decline from nearly 50 percent in 1980 (Wald, 1986). In 1982, the administration estimated, 16,790 drunk drivers were involved in fatal crashes, whereas the figure for 1985, with more total cars on the road, was 14,650. A survey by Louis Harris in 1983 found that 32 percent of those questioned said that they had driven a car after drinking during the past year; by 1986, this figure had declined to 26 percent. In Minnesota, random roadside checks indicated that roughly 5 percent of all drivers on the road at night were legally drunk in 1976; in 1986, the figure was 2.5 percent. In that same state, in 1976, only 14,000 drivers lost their licenses in connection with alcohol-related offenses; in 1986, the figure was more than 45,000. Clearly, the result of increased police enforcement of the drunk-driving laws has been to reduce the number and proportion of drunks on the road and, consequently, alcohol-related deaths. However, such actions have mainly had an impact on the more moderate social drinkers. Heavy drinkers and alcoholics are undeterred by the crackdown; as a result, a higher proportion of alcoholics are now being arrested on the road than in the past. Said a Maine highway official, "We're getting into the hard-core alcoholics now. Before, they bagged social drinkers, and heavy drinkers got by. . . . Now that social drinkers aren't out there, the alcoholics are getting caught" (Malcolm, 1987).

WHO DRINKS? WHO DOESN'T?

Just as interesting as the overall figures on alcohol consumption and their changes over time is group-to-group variation in drinking. Who drinks and who doesn't? Are certain groups or categories significantly and consistently more likely to drink than others?

A study by public-opinion pollster Louis Harris and his associates (summarized in Armor et al., 1976, pp. 53–62), explored the social correlates of drinking.[1] Two basic measures of alcohol consumption were used: the percent of abstainers in each group, and the mean daily alcohol consumption among nonabstainers for each group. There was a relationship between what percent of each population drank at all (that is, the percent of nonabstainers in each group) and the average quantity consumed, but the correlation was far from perfect. In fact, a major finding of this study was that for many groups there was a high proportion of abstainers, but among those who did drink, their average level of consumption was surprisingly high; among other groups, it was exactly the reverse.

Social class, or socioeconomic status (SES)—a combined measure made up of income, occupation, and education—also showed a complicated relationship with drinking. The higher the social class, the greater the likelihood of drinking at all: 79 percent of upper-class respondents drank, as opposed to 66 percent of middle-class people and only 48 percent of the lower-class respondents. Yet, among those who did drink, the daily ethanol consumption did not vary much across class lines. Education alone correlates very strongly with drinking, too. The 1985 Gallup Poll found that only 49 percent of respondents who were not high-school graduates said that they drank; 69 percent of high-school graduates did so; 74 percent of respondents with some college did; and fully 80 percent of college graduates said that they were drinkers. Clearly, then, there is a strong and powerful correlation between drinking and education and SES in general. The higher the SES the greater the chances that someone will drink. However, this relationship makes an interesting flip-flop when it comes to drinking to excess or getting into trouble as a result of drinking. When these same respondents were asked, "Has drinking ever been a cause of trouble in your family?" 24 percent of those who had not graduated from high school said yes, but only 17 percent of college graduates did so, with the in-between categories also in between on their answers to this question. Clearly, while high-SES people

---

[1]The rather large discrepancy between these figures on the average daily alcohol consumption and those just cited for the national average is due to the fact that the national average figures are based on alcohol *sales*, a reliable set of statistics, while the figures cited here are *self-reports*, in which consumption tends to be underestimated by more than half. In a paper delivered at the San Diego Symposium on Alcohol and Cardiovascular Disease, Dr. Charles Kaelber reported that a comparison of self-reports of alcohol consumption from national household surveys with figures on alcohol sales revealed the former figure to be less than half (less than 0.40 ounce of alcohol per day) the latter (close to 1.0 ounce per day). This study was summarized in the October 3, 1980, issue of *ADAMHA News* (vol. VI, no. 20).

are more likely to drink, they are also less likely to get into trouble for drinking, while for lower-SES individuals, the reverse is true (Gallup, 1986, pp. 80, 81).

The Catholic-Protestant difference in drinking tends to be large nationally. In the Louis Harris poll (Armor et al., 1976, pp. 53–62), 42 percent of the Protestants were total abstainers, nearly twice as high a figure as for the Catholic respondents (22 percent). This statistic was also backed up by the Gallup Poll: 60 percent of Protestants said that they drank, and 78 percent of Catholics did so. The majority of Southern Baptists, a highly abstemious denomination, said that they were abstainers—only 45 percent drank at all. However, interestingly, Southern Baptists were also more likely to get into trouble for drinking, possibly indicating a lower degree of acceptance of any level of drinking whatsoever in the Southern Baptist milieu.

Both the Harris and the Gallup polls consistently find a strong correlation between geographical residence and drinking. In the Harris Poll, a majority (54 percent) of all southerners were abstainers, while this was true of only about half as many northerners (28 percent). In the Gallup Poll, the results were not quite so striking: 56 percent of all southerners said that they drank, but about seven respondents in ten from the other regions of the country drank—72 percent for easterners, 70 percent for midwesterners, and 73 percent for residents of the West (G. Gallup, 1986, p. 80). Although the exact magnitude of the figures differs, the same relationship can be observed: Southerners drink significantly less than northerners.

Gender or sex, too, correlates strongly with drinking. In fact, of all variables, perhaps gender correlates most strongly with alcohol consumption. Men are consistently more likely to drink than are women, and they drink more when they do drink. In the Harris Poll, three-quarters of the men (74 percent) were drinkers, while only a slight majority (56 percent) of women were. Likewise, men who drank consumed considerably more than—in fact, twice as much (.91 ounces of absolute alcohol per day) as—women (.44 ounces). In the Gallup Poll, again, the differences were not quite so striking: 72 percent of the men said that they drank, while 62 percent of the women did so.

Age, too, strongly predicts drinking. In the Harris Poll, the vast majority of under-30 respondents drank: Only 23 percent were abstainers. The older the respondent, the greater the likelihood of being an abstainer: Almost half (49 percent) of the over-50 respondents said that they had not consumed any alcohol in the previous year, twice as high a percentage as in the youngest category. More or less the same pattern prevailed in the Gallup Poll: 74 percent of the 18-to-29-year-olds, and 74 percent of the 30-to-49-year-olds drank, and 54 percent of the over-50-year-olds did so—again, twice the proportion of abstainers in the older category.

Drinking's correlation to race and ethnicity has been studied extensively and in detail, and clear-cut differences among groups remain in spite of generations of assimilation (Greeley, McCready, and Theisen, 1980; Cahalan and Room, 1974; Health and Human Services, 1987a, pp. 18–20;

Health, Education, and Welfare, 1971, pp. 23–25). Consistently, individuals of the following ethnic backgrounds are highly likely to drink: Irish, Italians, Jews, northern WASPs (white Anglo-Saxon Protestants), Slavs, Scandinavians, and Germans. Members of the following ethnic groups are more likely to be abstainers and not drink at all: Blacks, Latins, southern WASPs, and Asians.

Of all groups, the Irish are most likely to drink a great deal, and to get into trouble when they drink. In one study (Health, Education, and Welfare, 1971), fully a third of individuals with an Irish-born father were defined as heavy drinkers, far higher than the proportion for any other category. In another study (Greeley et al., 1980, pp. 9, 10), Irish-Americans were most likely to drink two or more times per week (42 percent versus 15 percent for Italians and Jews and 24 percent for WASPs), and most likely to drink three or more drinks at a sitting (33 percent versus 11 percent for Jews, 14 percent for Italians, and 24 percent for WASPs). Another study (Cahalan and Room, 1974) devised several measures of heavy drinking and getting into trouble as a result of drinking. Jews were extremely unlikely not to drink at all (only 8 percent were abstainers), but they were also extremely unlikely to drink heavily or to get into trouble as a result of drinking. Irish and Italian Catholics had almost exactly the same proportion of drinkers (only 4 and 5 percent abstainers respectively). But Irish-Americans were far more likely to drink heavily and to get into trouble when they drank (Cahalan and Room, 1974, p. 101). Clearly, some alcohol-related aspect of Irish culture seems to be preserved even after one or more generations of residence in the United States. In a survey of twenty-two countries by the Gallup organization, a majority of the Irish surveyed (51 percent) answered yes to the question "Do you sometimes drink more than you think you should?" The average for the respondents from all countries was 29 percent, and it was 32 percent for residents of the United States (G. Gallup, 1986, p. 186).

THE PROBLEM DRINKER

By defining the alcoholic simply as someone who drinks a given average quantity of ethanol per day over a certain period (with all due respect to the qualifications registered earlier), we avoid the trap of thinking that alcoholism necessarily means any more than that. What *else* it means is an empirical question, something we have to investigate, not something we can define in the first place. By defining alcoholism along a single line we can actually determine whether this behavior, heavy drinking, is related to other things in the drinker's life. What most people mean when they refer to the alcoholic is actually what might better be called the *problem drinker* (Cahalan, 1970).

Are alcoholics and problem drinkers the same population, different points along the same spectrum, or totally different groups? Heavy drinkers may (and often do) become problem drinkers; problem drinkers are usually (but not necessarily) heavy drinkers. Getting into various kinds of trouble is one possible outcome of drinking a lot, but not a necessary one. The notion of the problem drinker is sociologically useful because it is the opposite of the "objective" definition of alcoholism proposed below—the consumption of 15 centiliters of absolute alcohol per day. The notion of a problem drinker is based on *how people see what happens to the drinker's life*, supposedly as a result of unwise or excessive drinking. Being considered a problem drinker is a result of a combination of drinking and how this behavior is reacted to by others as well as by the drinker.

Heavy drinking is associated with a number of social and legal problems, but these problems will vary in kind and in intensity. And part of the reason for the variation can be traced to the social and cultural context in which heavy drinking takes place. Alcohol may or may not directly cause these problems. They are closely connected with alcohol's social image, with conventional drinking practices in a given culture, with what one generally does or is expected to do when drunk, with the demands placed on one's performance, and with how the drunk is dealt with by other members of a society, particularly his or her intimates. In other words, when we examine the problem drinker, we have to understand *the social organization of alcohol-related trouble.* It is absolutely crucial, however, to keep in mind that *what is considered a problem in the first place* and *what specific problems we are considering* will vary from place to place. A problem drinker, then, is quite simply someone who gets into trouble—directly or indirectly—because of consuming alcohol.

Problems come in many forms, and drinking, likewise, assumes a number of guises. When we discuss "problems," we are referring to anything that is connected to values and conditions that are threatened, damaged, or destroyed (or thought to be) as a result of drinking. One can be a problem drinker because one has a glass of wine at meals from time to time in a completely abstemious community: One can be labeled a deviant because of it, and be condemned or ostracized. "Problems" are socially defined and created; alcohol consumption can be measured independently of what anyone thinks. The two may or may not be related in a given case. That is for us to find out—in terms of where, when, and how.

The "consequences" of one's drinking depend in part on what one does when drunk and in part on community standards regarding drunkenness and intoxicated behavior. Breaking the drinking codes of one's group, or threatening strongly held values by being drunk, gets one assigned to the category of alcoholic more swiftly than the bare fact of drinking. In a study of the drinking practices of a nationally representative sample of men age 21 to 59, Don Cahalan and Robin Room (1974) found some impressive correlates of heavy drinking and problem drinking. They found, among other things, that getting into trouble as a result of drinking was not a simple function of the quantity of alcohol consumed; other factors played a role as well. They devised a scale of "problems" that drinkers sometimes become entangled in—problems on the job, problems with their wives, problems with friends and neighbors, financial problems, problems with the police, and so on. One of the factors related to problems among drinkers was local attitudes toward drinking and drinking customs. The "drier" the community—the less the per capita alcohol consumption, and the more opposed a certain proportion of the community was to drinking—*the less drinking it took to get a man in trouble.* The "wetter" the community was, and the greater the tolerance there was for heavy drinking, the greater the quantity of drinking it took to get a man in trouble (Cahalan and Room, 1974, p. 81). For instance, drunk-driving arrests were significantly *higher* in states where there was *less* drinking. This was because community standards were stricter with regard to drunken driving (Cahalan and Room, 1974, p. 82).

WHO IS THE ALCOHOLIC?

The writings and research on alcoholism are controversial, contradictory, and confusing. Most of the major and pressing questions as yet have no definitive answers. Is alcoholism a disease? Can recovered alcoholics drink in a moderate, controlled fashion? On what criteria should a definition of alcoholism be based? Can the cause of alcoholism be located primarily in the substance, alcohol, itself, or in the characteristics of the drinker? Is biological make-up a major component in the etiology of alcoholism? For any imaginable answer to these questions, there are fervent supporters and critics. Very little is conclusively agreed upon in this field.

There are four common definitions of or criteria for alcoholism (Schuckit, 1985, p. 5). First, the *quantity* and *frequency* of alcohol consumed (De-Lindt and Schmidt, 1971): alcoholics are individuals who drink a substantial quantity of alcohol over a period of time. Second, *psychological dependence* (see the essays in Blane and Leonard, 1987): Someone is an alcoholic if he or she "needs" alcohol psychologically, cannot function without it, suffers extreme discomfort and anxiety if deprived of it under specific circumstances. Third, *physical dependence*: Someone is an alcoholic to the extent that he or she would suffer *withdrawal symptoms* upon discontinuation of drinking (Mendelson and Mello, 1985, pp. 265–269). And fourth, the *life problems* definition (Schuckit, 1984): Whoever drinks and incurs "serious life difficulties" as a consequence—divorce, being fired from a job, being arrested, facing community censure, harming one's health, being accident-prone, and so on—and continues to drink in spite of it, is an alcoholic.

Each of these definitions poses serious problems, and has been criticized for its deficiencies.

Defining alcoholism by the quantity of alcohol consumed has the drawback that the same amount of alcohol may be relatively innocuous for one person (for instance, a healthy 28-year-old) but harmful to another (an ill 68-year-old). Further, someone may drink no alcohol at all, but have the potential for developing a pattern of heavy consumption subsequent to taking up drinking. Is this individual to be regarded as exactly the same animal with respect to alcohol as the abstainer whose potential alcohol experience is likely to be positive and moderate?

Psychological dependence has been criticized for being vague and difficult to test. Questions supposedly tapping the "signs" of alcoholism include: "Do your friends drink less alcohol than you do?" "Do you drink to lose shyness and build self-confidence?" "Do you occasionally drink heavily after a disappointment, a quarrel, or when the boss gives you a hard time?" "Are there certain occasions when you feel uncomfortable if alcohol is not available?" A yes answer to these and similar questions is supposedly a sign that one is dependent on alcohol—and therefore an alcoholic. The problem is that many moderate drinkers could also give a yes answer to such questions. Psychological dependence on alcohol is extremely difficult to pin down; in the words of one expert, "determination of this attribute is very subjective" (Schuckit, 1985, p. 5).

The physical dependence or withdrawal criterion of alcoholism is an absolutely certain sign of the condition—but it is far too restrictive. Indeed, anyone who is physically dependent on alcohol must be regarded as an alcoholic by any reasonable definition, but many other drinkers who would also be called alcoholics are not physically dependent on the drug.

The life-problems definition is dubious because it is contingent on the nature of one's social milieu, as we saw in the previous section. In some areas, one can get into a great deal of trouble with an extremely moderate amount of alcohol consumption—as, for example, in contemporary Iran or in a fundamentalist Christian community. On the other hand, many communities and cultures worldwide tolerate extremely high levels of alcohol consumption, and "cushion" the drinker from many serious problems and consequences that drinking may entail elsewhere. Moreover, medical complications consequent to high levels of drinking appear on a statistical, rather than an absolute, basis. Not all heavy drinkers develop cirrhosis of the liver; is one who does an alcoholic and one who drinks just as much, but doesn't contract the disease, not an alcoholic?

Alcoholism is one of those phenomena that is difficult to define, but most experts would say that they "know one when I see one." The four above criteria overlap in practice; most drinkers encompassed by one definition will also be encompassed by at least one of the others. A clear, reliable, and valid definition is far more important for theoretical purposes than for practical or clinical reasons.

Perhaps the bitterest controversy in the field of alcohol research in the last decade has been the question of whether or not recovered alcoholics can drink in moderation after treatment. The controversy has, in fact, spilled over into the courts and scientific review panels in both Canada and the United States, as one team of researchers accused other investigators of scientific fraud, and filed a $96 million lawsuit against them for their study and its results. While the charges of fraud were dismissed (Maltby, 1982; Boffey, 1982b, 1984), the debate rages on.

On one side of the controversy stand researchers who argue that formerly heavy and problem drinkers, and even a substantial proportion of victims of severe alcoholism, can learn to drink sensibly, in moderation, and in a controlled fashion. Uncontrolled, heavy, damaging drinking, they contend, is a *reversible behavioral disorder*; behavior that is learned can be unlearned, at least, in a substantial proportion of cases. These researchers do not claim that all alcoholics can drink moderately—some say one in ten, others say a majority—but that controlled drinking is not only possible, but a feasible long-term treatment goal for many alcoholics. This approach is especially likely to be endorsed in Europe (Boffey, 1983; Heather and Robertson, 1981) and in Canada (Sobell and Sobell, 1978, 1984), although some American researchers accept it as well (Armor, Polich, and Stampul, 1976; Polich, Armor, and Braiker, 1980).

On the other side, the more traditional and orthodox approach, and the one most likely to be adopted in the United States, is that alcoholics are incapable of drinking in a controlled, moderate fashion; the only possible alternative is total abstinence (Pendery, Maltzman, and West, 1982). Alcoholism, say the advocates of this position, is an *irreversible disease*; the alcoholic is sick, and *cannot* return to drinking. The National Institute on Alcohol Abuse and Alcoholism (NIAAA) has consistently adhered to the view that "abstinence is the appropriate goal of alcohol treatment." In a 1981 report to Congress, the NIAAA stated that, "while a substantial minority of alcoholics are capable of engaging in controlled drinking for a short period of time, it is difficult to predict in advance who they are and it is not likely that they can control their drinking over the long run" (Boffey, 1983, p. C7).

The abstinence-only school argues that studies showing the possibility of controlled drinking are flawed—that they rely on self-reports of drinking by alcoholics, who lie notoriously about their alcohol consumption; they select heavy drinkers and problem drinkers, but not true alcoholics as subjects (so-called gamma, or physically dependent, alcoholics); they do not use a long enough follow-up period to determine whether their subjects have relapsed into dangerous drinking behavior; they have been careless about following up their subjects and often fail to record the disastrous lives these individuals are leading, even the fact that some of their subjects have died of alcoholism. (Pendery et al., 1982, summarizes most of these points.) These objections, says the abstinence-only faction, render valueless and misleading the results of studies showing that controlled drinking is possible.

Some of these objections are valid for some of the controlled-drinking studies that have been conducted. However, enough such studies have been done without these flaws to make it clear that some alcoholics can drink in a moderate, controlled, nonproblem fashion. The only question is the size of this category. Is it one in ten, as a report by the National Academy of Sciences suggested in 1980? Or six out of ten, as others argue? (Boffey, 1983, summarizes several of these studies.) Perhaps future research will yield better data than we have today.

In one study, alcoholics were studied four years after their release from a variety of federal treatment programs. These programs were not geared specifically toward training recovered alcoholics to drink sensibly, so its results must be taken as a conservative estimate. More than half of the nearly 1,000 subjects in the study (54 percent) were still drinking heavily enough to be considered problem drinkers. More than a quarter (28 percent) had abstained completely from alcohol during the six months prior to the study, and thus fit the "abstention-only" model. The remainder, less than a fifth (18 percent), were drinking in a more or less moderate or "nonproblem" fashion, half drinking an average of 3 ounces of absolute alcohol per day; the other half, less than 2 ounces per day (Polich, Armor, and Braiker, 1980, p. 51).

Abandoning the "abstention-only" model for treated alcoholics—even if they constitute only a substantial minority—represents something of a revolution in thinking about the subject. If the notion of the alcoholic's inevitable "irreversible impairment" when drinking has to be abandoned, then the very idea of alcoholism as a disease must also be rejected, and the notion of alcoholism as a modifiable behavior has to be introduced (Heather and Robertson, 1981, pp. 247–248). Given the fundamental systems of thought on which these two assumptions are based—the medical model and the learning-theory model of alcoholism—it is likely that this controversy will be with us for some time to come.

ACCOUNT: ALCOHOLISM

The contributor of this account is an electrician in his forties.

> I started drinking when I was about 12. I used to go out with a bunch of other guys and we'd find some wino from the neighborhood and we'd give him a half a dollar and have him go into a store and get 4 or 5 quarts of beer. Then we'd go to the park and we'd drink there. Most of the guys, when they'd fill up, they'd leave and go home. But with me and maybe one or two other guys, if there was something left, we'd drink it up. Or if it was gone, I'd try to go out and get some more. Most of the time, I'd get drunk. I'd do this at least once-twice a week, usually more. My whole social life was drinking. I'd just hang around guys who drank. Or I'd be with girls who had babysitting jobs. I'd go with them and drink the booze that was around the house. During this time, I'd black out quite a bit. Later, the next day or something, I'd be told the funny and not-so-funny things I did when I was drunk—and I wouldn't even remember. I'd climb a pole or a tree, or I'd wind up getting in a fight, or getting nasty, and I wouldn't remember any of it. I didn't know it at the time, but I was having blackouts.
>
> When I was 16, I forged my birth certificate and I enlisted in the Army. They found out after four months and I got a minority discharge. Right after my discharge, I got drunk one night and I stole a car. I wasn't aware of stealing the car. In fact, I wasn't even aware I was in a *car*. I woke up when I smashed into the rear end of a police car waiting for a red light. The cops got out and asked me for my license and registration. I didn't have it. No license, no registration,

I was driving a stolen car, and I had smashed into a police car. They put me in a juvenile detention home for three or four weeks. When I turned 17, I enlisted in the Air Force for four years.

For most the time I was in the Air Force, I'd drink whenever I could. I drank a lot. The booze was plentiful. I'd drink maybe four-five times a week, probably. Like a fifth of Seagram's or if it was beer, maybe twenty-four bottles or cans. I'd drink from five in the afternoon to two or three in the morning. I used to get in a lot of fights. I got one court-martial. I drank like that until the age of 25. Basically, I was a periodic drinker for most of this time. I'd drink for four or five weeks, and then I'd quit for a week, and then I'd drink again. During this time, I got married. I'd stay out all night and I'd drink. I'd drink rather than pay my bills, just to feed my drinking habit. Relations with my wife were strained, to say the least. If she tried to admonish me, I'd say, "I drank before I knew you, and I'll probably die drinking." I never thought it was a problem, I thought the problem was with my wife, not me.

I was getting into a lot of car accidents. I'd wake up in a smashed-up car and not remember where I was. I had one really major car accident and that's when I swore off alcohol, for good, I thought. It was only for five-and-a-half years. And after all that time, when I picked up the first drink, it was just like it was before. I drank a beer at 10 A.M. and I kept drinking all day, till late into the evening, until I passed out on my brother's living room floor. I went right back into my periodic drinking pattern. I'd go for a few weeks and then give up for a week or two. And then I'd try to see if I could drink one or two drinks, and I could, that night, and then I'd go back the next night and drink till I had another blackout. This got worse and worse for the next eight and a half years. It came to the point where I no longer wanted to go out and have a drink. Then, I *needed* it, just to clear the cobwebs out. It got to be where it was a hopeless thing. When I picked up one drink, there was no telling what would happen—where I'd go, what I'd do, who I'd end up with.

The last three years of my drinking were almost daily—there were no off days. I did nothing but drink. I'd work only a couple days a week. My relationship with my wife was gone by then—she was just beaten down by it. The emotional turbulence in the lives of my six children was tremendous. A lot of pain was involved there. My teenage daughter would have to answer the phone, and it would be some woman I had wound up with—I would just go somewhere and the next day, I'd find myself with someone. My kids had to deal with that. I was never a father to my children. I just didn't bother coming home. And when I did, I'd get into an argument with my wife about the whole thing, and I'd want to go out and drink again. I'd wake up with guilt and remorse, and want to drink to drown it out.

One night, I sat down at my kitchen table and started going into a crying jag. I knew I was in trouble. The bottom had fallen out. My wife was in Al-Anon, which is an organization for the relatives of alcoholics. She suggested that I go to AA. She even dialed the phone for me. I went to a meeting that night. I listened to three speakers, and I thought they were nuts. I couldn't wait to get out of there and get a drink—which is what I did. I drank for three more months. That was the pits. I knew my life was really messed up. So I stayed off the booze for ten months. Still, my mind wasn't functioning properly, I couldn't concentrate, I couldn't work on the job. I'd work fifteen hours a day just to wear myself out. My marriage had fallen apart. I was still miserable. See, I was fighting it. I had quit drinking on my own, and I thought I was a self-sufficient person. I now realize I wasn't. So once again my wife suggested that I go to another AA meeting, and I went. I sat down and talked to some people I could talk to. This fellow shared his life with me. I realized that I wasn't unique, that I wasn't a freak. I came to see that I could have a decent life without booze, and that it was alcohol that was causing my problems. I saw that I had the choice of destroying the rest of my life or staying sober. I could have ended up on the Bowery or killing someone. That day was my last drink—August 13, nine years ago.

I lost my wife and kids. I lost a house. My business was down the drain. I was $40,000 in debt in back taxes and bills. I owed everybody. I even owed the garbage man—he wouldn't come and pick up my garbage. If I heard the phone ring, I wouldn't want to pick it up, I was afraid it was another bill collector. At the age of 38, I woke up and found out what life was all about.

In the beginning, I went to a lot of AA meetings. For three and a half years, I went to an AA meeting almost every day. I had a lot to work on. I had to learn to live with some kind of humility and self-acceptance. My life took a complete turnaround. Everything is right in my life now. I'm out of debt. I can put in a full day's work. I'm a responsible person. I've gotten remarried. Today, I feel good about my life.

If I were to give someone advice, I'd say, if you see the roadsigns coming down the pike, use them. When you pick up a few drinks and you can't tell what's going to happen—don't drink. Drinking robbed me of any kind of a relationship with anybody. I didn't know what it was like to be with somebody because I didn't know who I was. The only social occasions I wanted to go to was where booze was going to be served. If there was no booze, I didn't go. So if booze is pulling you away from what's out there, don't drink. I didn't care about the consequences of my drinking—sickness, the accidents, the fights, the destruction of my marriage, causing my kids nothing but misery. That's another sign: If you drink and don't care what happens, you're in trouble. And another thing. When I drank, I thought I was the person I wanted to be. It increased my self-confidence. I could always blame somebody else for what went wrong, put everything off on the external world. It wasn't me, it was everybody else. If I'd get something bad off somebody, I'd just go away from the people who were bothering me about my drinking, and I'd go to another bar and drink there. If you can't be who you are without drinking, don't drink. If you need booze to cover up your problems, don't drink. If you have to change your circle of friends because of your drinking, you need help.

In my heart I knew I didn't want to drink. But I suppressed it, I pushed it down. And what made it possible for me to do that—was drinking. I say these things not just to talk about my life. I would like to share my life with other people to help someone. I'd like someone to learn from my life. If they can't handle it, stay away from it. That's what I would tell them—don't drink.

The last thing I want to say is the most important—in fact, it's the point of the whole thing: I couldn't have stopped drinking without God's help. I could never stop drinking before. Only when I asked God for sobriety, to be relieved of the obsession to drink, was I able to quit. It was God who gave me the strength to stay sober. [From the author's files.]

CHAPTER 6

Marijuana

Technically, marijuana is not a drug, but a vegetable substance that contains a whole series of chemicals. What is sold on the street as marijuana in the United States are the dried leaves and flowering tops of the plant *Cannabis sativa* or, less commonly, *Cannabis indica.* The cannabis plant contains hundreds of chemicals; sixty-one of them, called cannabinoids, are found nowhere else. The primary psychoactive agent in marijuana is trans-delta-tetrahydrocannabinol, or THC. It is generally agreed that it is the THC that gets the user high. Different batches of marijuana contain varying proportions of THC. Analyses of street samples of marijuana indicate that the THC content of marijuana has been rising; during the 1960s and early 1970s, between 1 and 2 percent THC for a batch of commercial-grade Mexican marijuana was typical. Today, marijuana, imported mainly from Colombia, contains about 4 percent THC. Varieties specially grown without seeds, from California and Hawaii, called *sinsemilla* (meaning "without seeds" in Spanish), contain more than 6 percent THC. *Hashish* contains the resin of the marijuana flower with no leaves, and usually has a higher THC content than marijuana. Hashish usually comes from Asia and the Middle East; it is rarely available in the United States nowadays, although it is common in Europe.

One feature of marijuana that makes it different from alcohol as a recreational drug is that, while alcohol passes through the body fairly quickly, THC is stored in the body, specifically in the fatty tissue, for long periods of time. The half-life (the period of time after use when half the chemical is still in the body) of THC in the blood is nineteen hours, but its metabolites have a half-life of fifty hours. After one week, 25 percent of THC's metabolites remain in the body (Ray and Ksir, 1987, p. 308). The slow rate of the elimination of THC and its products suggests that if it is used regularly, some storage and accumulation take place, which may be medically harmful to the user. In addition, marijuana is usually smoked, perhaps in 95 percent of all episodes of its use in the United States. Taking the fumes of any combusted substance into the lungs is likely to have a number of medical consequences not characteristic of a drug taken orally, as any student of cigarette smoking will tell you.

[The first and most fundamental fact about marijuana use in the United States that needs to be emphasized is that it is pervasive, very nearly universal, among young Americans. This does not mean that every adolescent and young adult uses it, only that it can be found practically everywhere.]Nor does it mean that all who use it do so equally often; clearly, frequency of use is a variable, not a constant. Still, nearly all adolescents have to come to terms with the drug. This makes it necessary for teenagers "to confront choices and decisions about whether, when, and how to use." So much is this the case that at least one observer (Jessor, 1983, p. 22) argues that it is futile for parents, educators, and authorities to expect to eliminate the use of the drug among youth completely. It makes more sense, he argues, to attempt to reduce or delay its use, and to encourage young people to use it, if they insist on doing so, responsibly, moderately, and in relatively safe contexts. (Naturally, this approach has its critics; see Mann, 1987.)

It is true that marijuana use has declined during the 1980s—which is also true, as we have seen, of all other illicit drugs (except cocaine), and cigarettes and alcohol as well. Some observers have contended that marijuana use is passé, that the use of other drugs is more common, that cocaine has become more popular than marijuana. These claims are simply journalistic exaggeration and sensationalism. In fact, according to every reliable, systematic survey that has ever been conducted on the subject, marijuana has been, and is now, the most commonly tried or used illegal drug in the country, and it is likely to remain so. Even when other drugs are taken, marijuana is very often used in conjunction with them. In the 1982 national survey sponsored by the National Institute on Drug Abuse (Miller et al., 1983, p. 43), it was found that: "In every age group, the majority of those who have ever used cocaine say that they have used marijuana on the same occasion that they took cocaine." Thus the use of other illegal drugs usually also implies marijuana use, although the reverse is not necessarily true.

As we saw in the 1985 nationwide survey sponsored by NIDA, a third of the American population age 12 and older has tried marijuana—some 62 million individuals. And one in ten, a total of some 18 million Americans, are "current" users—that is, have used the drug within the past month (NIDA, 1986). Among high-school students, much the same picture prevails: marijuana is common—in fact, the most frequently used illegal drug. Just over half (51 percent) of the country's high-school seniors have used marijuana at least once, and nearly a quarter (23 percent) used it within the past month (Johnston et al., 1987, pp. 47, 49). There are three times as many individuals who have used marijuana as have used cocaine, and almost four times as many current users of marijuana as of cocaine. While the size of the cocaine-using population has grown substantially in the past half-dozen years compared with that of the marijuana-using population, the two are still not in the same league. Moreover, since marijuana tends to be used more frequently by the typical regular user than is true of cocaine, the total number of episodes of marijuana use is many times, perhaps ten times, the total number of episodes of cocaine use. It is possible that the total number of times that marijuana is used approaches, and may even exceed, the total for all other illicit drugs combined. Any discussion of the use of illegal drugs in America must begin with marijuana.

WHO USES MARIJUANA?

What factors and forces lead someone to "turn on" to marijuana? More important, what causes someone who tried the drug to become a regular user? It would be fallacious to assume that any behavior as complex as the use of drugs, or any one drug, can be completely explained by a one factor or variable, or even a single integrated theory. Many factors, forces, and mechanisms contribute to the use of drugs in general, and even to use by a specific individual. We have a number of empirical regularities describing illegal psychoactive drug use generally, and marijuana specifically. These correlations are not in doubt; they are, as statisticians are fond of saying, "robust" relationships, solidly documented, independently confirmed by different researchers in a variety of locales (within the United States and Canada, at any rate), and constant over time. The validity of the various explanations to account for these regularities, however, is still being debated, as we saw in Chapter 3.

A team of researchers (Radosevich et al., 1980) distinguished three interrelated sets of variables that are causally related to marijuana use: (1) *structural variables,* which include sociodemographic factors such as age, sex, social class, race, and community or region of residence; (2) *social-interactional variables,* which pertain to interpersonal relationships, or the likelihood of associating with and relating to individuals with varying degrees of involvement with marijuana or its correlates and accompaniments (an example would be one's friends' use of marijuana, or use patterns in one's peer group); (3) *attitudinal variables,* or attitudinal (and, ultimately, behavioral) factors pointing to one's views both of the drug itself and behavior associated with its use—beliefs about whether the drug is harmful and willingness to break the law are two examples of this dimension. Of course, these sets of variables overlap a great deal; they cannot be sharply or cleanly separated.

Age

The structural variable most strongly correlated with the use of marijuana is age. If we had to select one major characteristic to help in predicting whether a given individual uses or has used marijuana, we could not make a better selection than age. Children under the age of 12 are extremely unlikely to smoke marijuana, in spite of the fears of alarmists and propagandists. Only one young adolescent in twelve (age 12 to 13), or 8 percent, has even tried marijuana, and one-quarter of that (2 percent) have used it within the past thirty days. This percentage rises steadily throughout the teen years and peaks in the 18 to 25-year-old bracket (64 percent). There is a significant drop-off in the 35 to 49-year-old age range (24 percent have tried marijuana; 8 percent used it in the past month), and a very sharp drop in the over-50-year-old category (Miller et al., 1983, pp. 34, 38).

Two life circumstances that are connected with the adolescent to young adult age range (the mid-teens to early twenties) are (a) a growing independence from adult supervision, and (b) relative freedom from adult responsibilities. Older teenagers are in the process of discovering what it means not to be supervised by their parents as closely as a few years previously, and at the same time they have not yet assumed the responsibility of supporting a household or raising children. A team of researchers summarized a number of variables that are related to the use of drugs of all kinds, including and especially marijuana, and concluded that these variables have one thing in common: they all "have to do with the degree to which a young person is under the direct influence and/or supervision of adult-run institutions. . . . Those who most avoid such influence are also the most likely to be involved in all forms of substance use," marijuana included (Bachman et al., 1981, p. 67). High-school students who hold part-time jobs are also more likely to smoke marijuana than those who do not; far from being under adult supervision on the job, young workers tend to find themselves "surrounded by other young workers, including some slightly older and thus more experienced in the use of drugs" (Bachman et al., 1981, p. 67).

An indication that freedom from adult responsibilities is one reason why adolescents and young adults are more likely to smoke marijuana than individuals who are significantly older is that, even at the same age, married persons show the lowest rates of use, while the divorced and those living independently show much higher rates (Kandel, 1980a, p. 249). In fact, "being married is one of the most important correlates of abstention from the use of illicit drugs among adults 18 years and older" (Kandel, 1980a, p. 249; see also Cisin et al., 1976). In one nationally representative survey of young men age 20 to 30, 46 percent of the married respondents, 51 percent of those living in their parents' homes, 68 percent of those living by themselves, and 82 percent of those who lived with a woman to whom they were not married, had used marijuana once or more (O'Donnell et al., 1976, p. 21). Likewise, among all the employment categories, the lowest rate of marijuana use was registered by individuals who worked full-time or nearly full-time (52 percent), while much higher rates were displayed by those working fewer than thirty hours per week (74 percent). In short, there seems to be something of an inverse relationship between involvement in various forms of illegal drug use, including marijuana, and participation in the roles of adulthood, especially marriage and employment (Kandel, 1980a, p 249). Child-rearing would, of course, magnify this tendency.

Sex

At one time, the male edge in marijuana use was considerable. In the 1960s, approximately twice as many men as women used the drug. This was especially true among the heavier and more frequent marijuana users (Goode, 1970, pp. 32–34). Over the years, the male edge has become less pronounced. It has not, however, disappeared. Among high-school seniors, males are slightly more likely to have smoked marijuana (53 percent) than females (48 percent). However, males are more than twice as likely to be daily or almost daily smokers—6 percent versus 2 percent (Johnston et al., 1987, pp. 36, 41). In a nationally representative survey of the entire population, the male edge in lifetime prevalence is fairly small for adolescents (28 versus 25 percent); it is a bit larger for young adults (68 versus 60 percent), and it is fairly substantial for older adults (30 versus 17 percent). For each group, the gap increases at higher levels of use (NIDA, 1986). In sum, then, men are *slightly* more likely than women to use marijuana at all, *considerably* more likely to use it regularly, and *extremely* more likely to use it heavily. As a general rule, the greater the level or frequency of use, the more sizable the male edge.

This pattern holds for most, although not all, drugs (Clayton et al., 1986). The sex difference among adolescents in cigarette smoking has been erased and, in fact, recent studies indicate that it has actually reversed itself recently: Teenage girls are smoking more than boys (Johnston et al., 1987, p. 40). Women use psychoactive drugs under medical supervision much more than men do. There is some speculation that women are more likely to handle stress and crises with pharmaceuticals, while men turn more often to the heavy use of alcohol. A fairly valid generalization would be that, other things being equal, the more deviant an activity is, the greater the male edge in participation.

Peer Influences

While some studies have shown that parental example has some influence on adolescent drug use generally, and the use of marijuana specifically (Kandel, 1973), peer influence is a far more powerful factor in drug use. The use of marijuana by one's own friends is massively and overwhelmingly correlated with one's own use of the drug. Adolescents report more similarity with their friends in marijuana use than in any other activity. In fact, of all things that friends have in common—except for obvious demographic characteristics like age, sex, and race—they are more likely to have the use of marijuana in common than anything else (Kandel, 1973, 1974). Youngsters whose best friends have never tried marijuana are extremely unlikely to have tried the drug themselves. On the other hand, young people whose best friends smoke regularly are extremely likely to use marijuana themselves. Almost no one becomes involved in marijuana use who does not have marijuana-using friends. This influence is sometimes called *peer pressure,* but it also operates with all other aspects of one's life, both favorable and unfavorable; it is not unique to drug use.

The fact that marijuana use flows from friend to friend, within and among social intimates, demonstrates the fallaciousness of two classic beliefs concerning the drug—the "peddler" myth, that young people use drugs mainly because they are induced to do so by drug sellers, and the myth that someone tries and uses marijuana because he or she is frightened, lonely, isolated, or forlorn. Neither assumption is borne out by the facts: Young people are turned on by their friends, specifically because they value the opinions and activities of their friends. In countless studies on the subject, the principal motivating force underlying turning on is that one's friends use marijuana.

There are three ways that a friend influences a potential marijuana convert. (1) The friend provides an example, a kind of legitimation. If young people associated marijuana use only with "creeps," "lames," and "losers," they would want no part of it. But if they discover that contemporaries whom they respect and admire use marijuana, they will be eager to try it, to be part of the drug scene. (2) The friend defines the nature of the marijuana experience. He or she endorses its use and provides a rationale. He or she launches a miniature and semi-intentional advertising campaign. (3) The friend provides the drug itself. Contrary to popular belief, marijuana is not as easy to buy as bubble gum, but it is easily obtained if one is part of a network of other young people who use and sell it. More important, if a youngster is highly motivated to "score" marijuana, he or she will seek out those who are known to sell. Most neophytes, however, are somewhat dubious about marijuana to begin with, and they need a friend to coax them along. The factor of drug-related friendships is thus absolutely crucial in the earliest stages of marijuana use. The subtle process of acquiring attitudes favorable to marijuana use consists of having friends and acquaintances who define the experience of use in favorable terms, of having a general ideology that prepares one for initially accepting marijuana, and of being intimate with others who use it. All these factors then powerfully conspire to impel the young person in the direction of using marijuana.

In short, marijuana users tend to be "heavily involved in social networks in which marijuana use" is "prevalent and tolerated." The marijuana use of one's friends (and spouse or partner) increases "dramatically" with one's own use. In one study, 85 percent of young men age 24 to 25 who used marijuana four or more times a week said that most or all of their friends were also users, as opposed to 60 percent of those who used the drug between two or three times a month and two or three times a week; 23 percent of those who used less than once a month; 16 percent of those who used, but not in the past year; and only 7 percent of those who had never used marijuana. For women the same age, the comparable figures were 96, 68, 36, 14, and 6 percent (Kandel, 1984, pp. 205, 206). The association between friends' use of marijuana and one's own is truly remarkable.

Use of Other Drugs

As we saw in Chapter 3, a strong and significant relationship exists between the use of marijuana and the use of all other drugs (Goode, 1969; Johnson, 1973; Kandel, 1980b, 1984). This is true whether the other drugs are legal or illegal. The statistical chance that someone will use a given drug is increased if he or she uses any other drug, and decreased if no other drug is used. This means that if a teenager smokes tobacco cigarettes and/or drinks alcoholic beverages, he or she has a higher likelihood of eventually using marijuana than the teenager who does not smoke or drink. It also means that, subsequent to smoking marijuana, he or she stands a higher chance of using other drugs than the individual who has never used marijuana. That is, the people who use illegal drugs, marijuana especially, are fundamentally the same people who use alcohol and cigarettes—they just stand a bit farther along the same continuum.

As we saw in Chapter 3, there are four distinct developmental stages in adolescent drug use: (1) the use of beer or wine; (2) the use of cigarettes or hard liquor; (3) the use of marijuana; and (4) the use of other illicit drugs, such as cocaine or hallucinogens (Kandel, 1980b, p. 121). Using a drug or set of drugs in the sequence makes a progression to the next stage more likely; not initiating a given stage makes using the drugs later in the sequence less likely. The more involved one is with the drug or drugs at a given stage, the greater the likelihood that this progression will occur; the less frequently one uses the drug or set of drugs in a given stage, the less likely it is that one will proceed to the next. Other factors also facilitate or retard this progression, such as relations with one's parents, psychological problems, and, of course, peer relations. Moreover, experience with a given drug or set of drugs is something of a *necessary*, but by no means a *sufficient*, condition for the progression. Still, acquaintance with drugs early in the sequence does seem to ease the process along, at least in a statistical sense.

Clearly, then, marijuana users are more likely to be drawn from the ranks of users of legal drugs—alcohol and cigarettes—than from the ranks of abstainers. In fact, an adolescent who has never smoked a tobacco cigarette or drunk beer, wine, or hard liquor is unlikely to use marijuana. What happens after the young person has smoked marijuana for a period of time? What are the odds of a marijuana user trying and using other, more dangerous drugs, such as cocaine, the hallucinogens, or heroin? And what role does marijuana play in this progression? These are questions we'll examine when we look at some of the consequences of marijuana use.

Unconventionality

A large number of *attitudinal* and *behavioral* correlates and antecedents of marijuana use have been located by researchers. One such commonsensical variable is the perception and belief that the drug is relatively harmless. Individuals who believe that the effects of marijuana are benign, that the drug is not likely to harm them, are significantly more likely to try and use it than those who believe that it is harmful (Kandel et al., 1978, pp. 13, 28). Marijuana users have also been found to be more politically *liberal* than nonusers. The more politically conservative the individual, the lower the likelihood of his or her smoking marijuana; the more politically liberal or left-leaning his or her ideological views are, the higher is this likelihood (Johnson, 1973, pp. 54, 60; Kandel et al., 1978). The same holds for *aliena-*

tion from traditional religious expression. The stronger the religious belief and the more frequent the religious observance, the lower the chances of smoking marijuana; the less traditionally religious and the less religiously observant, the greater the likelihood of marijuana use (Johnson, 1973, pp. 54, 56–57; Jessor and Jessor, 1977; Smith and Fogg, 1978; Kandel et al., 1978). Lastly, marijuana users tend to be *less traditional* in the realm of *sexual belief and practice.* They are more likely to engage in sexual intercourse earlier in their lives, to have had intercourse with a greater number of partners, and to approve of more unconventional, unorthodox sexual practices. Nonusers tend to be more traditional in the sexual arena and have sex later in their lives and with fewer partners (Goode, 1972a; Johnson, 1973, p. 153f.; Hochman and Brill, 1973; Hochman, 1972, p. 104). Marijuana use does not "cause" this greater sexual activity, since it may exist even before the individual uses the drug for the first time.

What seems to be common to all of these attitudinal and behavioral correlates of marijuana use is a broader "lifestyle" dimension made up of several components: (1) a greater *tolerance for deviance,* (2) a greater willingness to engage in *risk-taking* behavior, and (3) a *less authoritarian* and a *more permissive* attitude generally. Marijuana users differ from nonusers "on a cluster of attributes reflecting unconventionality, nontraditionality, or nonconformity." They display "a more tolerant attitude toward deviance, morality, and transgression," greater rebelliousness from rules and regulations, especially those issuing from the parental generation, and a higher "expectation for independence or autonomy" (Jessor, 1979, pp. 343–344). Marijuana users, in short, tend to be more willing to break the norms of the society in which they live, to deviate from cultural prescriptions more frequently in a wide range of ways. They also tend to be *risk-takers,* in comparison with nonusers. They have a greater receptivity to new experience, "to uncertainty and change as against an emphasis on familiarity and inflexibility"; they are somewhat less likely to say "I shouldn't do that" when faced with an alternative that appears tempting but a bit risky or laden with danger (Jessor, 1979, p. 344).

In short, the use of recreational drugs generally, and of marijuana specifically, is strongly related to psychosocial unconventionality. Not only do all of these generalizations hold when comparing users with nonusers, but they also hold when comparing heavy and light users; unconventionality is a continuum, not an either-or proposition. This dimension covers many different areas of life; "the use of marijuana is not an isolated behavior but is part of a larger constellation of behaviors" (Jessor, Donovan, and Costa, 1986, p. 35). This includes, as we saw, precocious and unconventional sexual behavior, heavier involvement with other drugs, aggression and delinquency, and greater tolerance for unconventional and "deviant" behaviors. It also includes a lesser degree of involvement with traditional institutions. This manifests itself in a more critical attitude toward and greater alienation from conventional society, uncertainty about conventional social norms, a lower level of academic achievement, and a weaker

link with—indeed, indifference to—conventional religious beliefs and practices (Jessor, 1983, pp. 24–25).

In short, marijuana use correlates negatively with conformity (Kandel,
1984, pp. 204, 206). So strong is this relationship that, given several facts
about a young person's position on the conventionality-unconventionality
dimension, one could predict, with a high degree of accuracy, whether or
not he or she uses marijuana—and, if a user, what his or her level of use is.
Moreover, this greater unconventionality in a wide range of areas of life has
proved to be an extremely sturdy relationship: It was true in the past, and
it continues to be true now. In short, this pattern "has been shown to be
relatively invariant over time" (Jessor, Donovan, and Costa, 1986, p. 37).
In all likelihood, the connection between marijuana use and unconventionality will remain through the forseeable future.

ACUTE EFFECTS OF MARIJUANA

Arguments about drugs change over time. At one point, a given effect may
be attributed to a drug and considered important, while another will be
ignored. Later, the first effect will simply disappear from public discussion—
indeed, will widely be agreed to be mythical—and the second will assume
center-stage importance. Precisely this process has taken place with the
debate on marijuana. In the 1930s, the *acute* effects of the drug commanded
the most attention—specifically, that marijuana would cause users to go
crazy and become violent; men would rape and kill under the influence, and
women would become promiscuous. Publications from the period had titles
such as "Marijuana—Sex-Crazing Drug Menace" (Moise, 1937), "Marijuana—The Weed of Madness" (Rowell and Rowell, 1939), and "Marihuana: Assassin of Youth" (Anslinger and Cooper, 1937). Today, these
supposed effects receive no attention even in the most vigorous antimarijuana polemics (Nahas, 1975; Mann, 1985). Almost no observer
argues that, in a single episode of use, marijuana generates psychosis, violence, or sexual "excess" in the typical user. These issues are simply no
longer the focus of controversy.

While the acute effects were emphasized in the 1930s, it is the *chronic*
effects that have become the center of attention today. (See "Chronic Effects" below.) And it is, of course, the acute effects that the user seeks. (See
"Subjective Effects" below.) Interestingly enough, the purely physical short-
term effects of marijuana are extremely superficial and few in number. The
only ones that have been established beyond a doubt are (1) a reddening
of the eyes, (2) a slight increase in the rate of heartbeat, and (3) a dryness of the mouth. One effect long believed to be caused by cannabis is
dilation of the pupils. One "health" textbook informs the reader that the
effects of marijuana include "muscular twitching" and "dilation of the
pupils of the eyes," and directs him or her to a photograph of a wide-eyed
youth with pupils properly dilated (Jones et al., 1969, pp. 54, 28). In fact,

reliable laboratory studies have shown that marijuana does not dilate the pupils at all (Weil et al., 1968). Blood-sugar level, which regulates hunger, is also curiously unchanged under the influence of marijuana, despite the drug's spectacular impact on hunger.

Pharmacologists term the quantity of a given drug that will achieve a given effect in a subject as the *effective dose,* or simply ED. In laboratory research ED is generally treated in terms of the quantity that will have a given effect on half the experimental subjects, and it is called ED^{50}. Thus, if in an experiment one cigarette of a gram of marijuana containing 1 percent THC were administered to ten human subjects, five of whom demonstrated the three effects mentioned above, a gram of 1 percent THC marijuana would be the ED^{50} in humans. Another designation of importance is the *lethal dose,* or LD^{50}, the amount that will kill animals (or humans); others are lethal in very small doses. Another important measure is *the ratio between effective dose and lethal dose.* In some drugs the quantity that can get a subject high and the quantity that can kill him or her are very far apart; in other drugs they are fairly close together. Alcohol was once used for analgesic purposes during operations, but because its ED was so close to its LD, more effective drugs with fewer and less lethal side effects were adopted. With heroin, the margin of safety is razor-thin—the lethal dose is dangerously close to the effective dose. With marijuana, one of the important facts is the the ED and the LD are extremely far apart. A physician, Tod Mikuriya, calculated that roughly 40,000 times the effective dose can be lethal for mice—in other words, there is a "safety factor" on the order of 40,000 for marijuana or THC (Mikuriya, 1969). The safety factor for alcohol is about 10—thus alcohol can be considered 500 to 1,000 times more lethal than marijuana.

Although experimental animals have been killed with enormous doses of THC—much more than humans ever use—there have been no reliably reported human deaths from an overdose of THC, marijuana, hashish, or any cannabis preparation. Cannabis, or THC, is one of the least toxic drugs known to man. Considering the immense number of marijuana users, as well as the great variability in potency of the drug, that no one has ever died of an "overdose" of cannabis alone can be attributed only to the drug's relative lack of lethality.

Contemporary research suggests that marijuana's effects tend to be detrimental to motor coordination. The earliest systematic scientific report on this question, interestingly, indicated that marijuana does not deteriorate simulated driving skills (Crancer et al., 1969). Later research demonstrated beyond any doubt that the drug does deteriorate motor coordination, and impairs performance on driving tests. The more complex and unfamiliar the task, the more inexperienced the subject is with marijuana, and the more intoxicated the subject is on the drug, the greater the degree of discoordination (Canadian Commission into the Non-Medical Use of Drugs, 1972, pp. 62–63, 131–144).

One recent study (Barnett et al., 1985) found that levels of THC in the blood correlate significantly with lower performances on the motor tasks that are necessary for driving. Another study (Yesavage et al., 1985) tested experienced pilots one, four, ten, and twenty-four hours after smoking one marijuana cigarette. All four tests showed deterioration in the ability to perform a landing maneuver. During the test taken twenty-four hours after smoking, the subjects said that they did not feel high, which indicates that there is likely to be a lingering effect of residual THC in the bloodstream. In a posthumous sample of more than 400 male drivers in California age 15 to 34 who had been killed in an auto accident, 81 percent were found to have one or more drugs in their blood samples (Williams et al., 1985); alcohol was present in 70 percent of the cases, THC in 37 percent, and cocaine in 11 percent. THC alone was found in one of eight of these drivers. Data show that marijuana users are significantly overrepresented in fatal automobile accidents in terms of their numbers in the population (Petersen, 1980, p. 16). Clearly, marijuana use seems to contribute to a greater number of deaths and accidents on the highway. Of course, alcohol is still by far the number-one drug in this regard, although the additive effects of alcohol and marijuana should give anyone cause for concern.

SUBJECTIVE EFFECTS OF MARIJUANA

Long lists of supposed marijuana effects that were circulated in the late 1960s and early 1970s (Munch, 1966; Hill, 1971) were completely fraudulent and based on no knowledge of what the user actually felt under the influence of the drug. Nausea, vomiting, diarrhea, and psychotic episodes appeared frequently on these lists, and yet, when a cross-section of users is interviewed as to what they have felt and experienced under the influence of the drug, these effects appear so rarely as to be virtually nonexistent. With a growing sophistication on the part of the American public, these hysterical and inaccurate rosters of supposed acute marijuana effects went out of style. Today's descriptions of the marijuana experience tend to be more accurate. In fact, the marijuana controversy focuses much less on the drug's *acute,* and even less on its *subjective* effects, than on its *chronic* effects. Nonetheless, it is still crucial to know what someone *feels* under the influence of marijuana.

What do users describe as the subjective effects of marijuana? Before summarizing the surveys, it is essential to keep in mind the problems involved with such an endeavor. Laboratory studies, which put users in a hospital or clinical setting and administer a standard quantity of the drug to them, commonly by a route of administration that is unfamiliar to them, and record their responses to standardized tests are flawed because they do not examine real-life situations. Interview and questionnaire studies of users are flawed because they cannot control for the variability of the marijuana users' past experiences (variability in quantity and quality of the marijuana used, situational variability, and so on). This dilemma is insurmountable;

the only solution is to examine in detail both techniques of studying the phenomenon.

During interviews with about 200 marijuana smokers in New York, I asked each user to describe the effects experienced under marijuana (Goode, 1970). The most common response was that the user felt more peaceful, more relaxed, under the influence of marijuana; 46 percent mentioned this effect spontaneously—that is, without direct prompting or formal questioning on my part. Thirty-six percent said that they felt their senses were more "turned on," that they were more sensitive in almost every way than was true normally. Thirty-one percent said that they felt their thoughts were more profound, deeper—that their thoughts ran in a more philosophical and cosmic vein. Twenty-nine percent said that everything seemed much funnier than usual—that they laughed much more than they did when they were straight.

In another study conducted at roughly the same time, a California psychologist, Charles Tart, distributed checklist questionnaires to his students (after several years of informal interviews with users to find out what some common responses were) asking them to indicate what effects they experienced when stoned (Tart, 1971). Of the 750 questionnaires distributed, 150 were returned and analyzed. Since Tart's questionnaire was a forced-answer checklist, it should not be surprising that there are a higher percentage of respondents reporting a specific effect than in my study, where respondents had to think up the individual effects themselves without any presentation of choices. In my study, there is the possibility that they may have forgotten to mention effects that they actually experienced; in Tart's, there is the possibility that they checked a response merely because it was in front of them. In any case, although the exact percentages vary, the rankings of the various effects do not differ appreciably.

A third survey, conducted by three physicians, generally corroborated these findings (Halikas et al., 1971). One hundred regular marijuana smokers—that is, users who had smoked the drug at least fifty times in the six months prior to the study—were interviewed and given a checklist questionnaire on which they were asked to indicate whether each effect tended to occur "usually," "occasionally," or "once or never." The results revealed that some of the "effects" commonly enumerated in antimarijuana tracts were *never* experienced as "usual" effects, and most respondents experienced them infrequently: nausea (91 percent once or never), vomiting (98 percent once or never), diarrhea (95 percent once or never). On the other hand, euphoria turned up frequently, as did relaxation, a keener sound sense, a "peaceful" feeling, increased sensitivity, and increased hunger.

Even though the overwhelming bulk of the effects described were pleasurable, a significant minority of the respondents—16 percent—said that they usually experienced at least one unpleasant effect, and a majority of the sample said that they occasionally experienced one or more such negative effects. Of course, whether these negative effects are regarded as serious by users may be another matter; some effects may be felt as slight inconveniences, or even as neutral, whereas others may be seen as serious and distressing. Thus two points are noteworthy: (1) regular marijuana users experience mostly pleasant and positive effects from taking cannabis; and (2) some effects regarded as negative are occasionally experienced by some users.

A fourth study was conducted by two physicians at the student health center at the University of California at Los Angeles (Hochman and Brill, 1972). This random sample of UCLA's student body also used a forced-alternative checklist of effects with three categories of use frequency— "often or always," "occasionally," and "never." The study took the further step of dividing the sample into three levels of use—the heavy or "chronic" user, the "occasional" user, and the nonuser (the last having used marijuana less than ten times in the past year).

What is the general impression conveyed by these four studies of marijuana intoxication? What effects stand out as most common? Probably the most obvious and dominant impression is that *users overwhelmingly describe their marijuana experience in favorable and pleasurable terms*; in short, they like what they feel. This is not to say that they never experience unpleasant effects. Both my study and Hochman and Brill's survey bring out some indication of feelings of paranoia under the influence. (It must be kept in mind that, given the prevailing legal climate, the meaning of the term "paranoia" has changed from an unrealistic fear of persecution to any—and often a very realistic—fear of arrest.) But the pleasant effects are by far the most common. *Most users, most of the time, enjoy their marijuana experiences.*

A second impression conveyed by these descriptions is that *marijuana use is largely a recreational activity.* The vast majority of effects reported by users are whimsical in nature—happy, silly, euphoric, relaxed, hedonistic, sensual, foolish, and decidedly unserious. Moreover, marijuana use is commonly associated with highly pleasurable activities—eating, sexual intercourse, listening to music, watching a film, attending a party, socializing, and so on. The most common periods of use for most marijuana smokers are specifically during these recreational moments. The high is deliberately sought as a means of intensifying enjoyable experiences. The drug tends not to be used—or is used far less—during more serious periods, such as studying or reading. Moreover, these serious activities are felt to be *impaired* while under the drug, in contrast to the recreational activities, which are felt to be improved by the drug's effects. For instance, in my sample only a third had ever read anything while high, and of this group two-thirds said that the experience was worsened by the drug. But 85 percent had listened to music while high, 75 percent had had sexual relations, and 75 percent had eaten food; about 90 percent of those who reported these experiences said that they were more enjoyable while high.

One subjective effect that received a certain amount of attention in the late 1960s and early 1970s was psychotic episodes under the influence (Talbott and Teague, 1969; Schwartz, 1969). The issue does not receive much attention nowadays. This is not to say that some users do not experience panic reactions under the influence. However, these acute toxic reactions tend to be atypical, to take place among inexperienced, neophyte beginners, and to take place in settings in which the user is uncomfortable (Smith and Seymour, 1982). As a general rule, if someone experiences severe psychological distress under the influence of marijuana, he or she tends to discontinue the use of the drug. It is an effect that is rare enough not to be considered typical, but common enough to warrant caution.

CHRONIC EFFECTS OF MARIJUANA

In the 1970s, it looked like the antimarijuana forces were on the defensive. The drug had become decriminalized in eleven states making up a third of the nation's population, it looked as if a growing proportion of the public accepted the idea of decriminalization, and a declining proportion believed the drug to be harmful. Moreover, the number of new users grew with each survey conducted. But these developments seem to have spawned an antimarijuana "backlash," which resulted in increased federal funding for research on marijuana's medical effects, a growing volume of antimarijuana articles in mass-circulation magazines and newspapers, and a termination of the earlier trend toward decriminalization.

In 1974, fearing that a growing "epidemic" of marijuana use was taking place in the nation, Senator James Eastland conducted a series of Senate subcommittee hearings on the *Marihuana-Hashish Epidemic and Its Impact on United States Security* (Eastland, 1974). These hearings called two dozen witnesses and experts who presented data showing that marijuana is a dangerous, damaging drug. Eastland assembled witnesses and experts specifically known for their antimarijuana stance; any researcher who had conducted a study showing that marijuana was not harmful was not invited to deliver testimony. "We make no apology," Eastland stated, "for the one-sided nature of our hearings—they were deliberately planned that way" (Eastland, 1974, p. xv). Some of marijuana's ravages, these witnesses claimed, were brain damage and "massive damage to the entire cellular process," including chromosomal abnormalities. The drug "adversely affects the reproductive process," causing sterility and impotence. In addition, it causes cancer and, the only nonorganic entry in this list, a life of lethargy and sloth, called the "amotivational syndrome." Eastland concluded from this testimony that if the "cannabis epidemic continues to spread . . . we may find ourselves saddled with a large population of semi-zombies." Are Eastland's expert witnesses correct in viewing marijuana as medically dangerous? What is the consensus in the scientific and medical community on marijuana's long-term effects?

Such studies are fraught with complications. It may be that there is an empirical relationship between the use of marijuana and a certain medical pathology, but a cause-and-effect relationship may not exist at all; marijuana use may be related to a third factor that, in turn, actually causes the medical pathology. Some studies tracing the medical impact of marijuana have been shown to be faulty specifically because of this complication; the results obtained were based on experimental or measurement error. For instance, one study suggested that marijuana use may damage the liver (Kew et al., 1969). But a later study attempted to replicate this finding and failed to do so (Hochman and Brill, 1971); in fact, its findings refuted those of the original liver-damage study. It turns out that the original study had not controlled for the marijuana users' alcohol consumption. When the subjects were asked to refrain from drinking alcohol, their liver functioning reverted to normal. So the abnormal livers the researchers saw in their subjects were related not to the subjects' marijuana use, but to the fact that many of them also drank. In fact, one major difficulty in tracing marijuana's medical effects is that there are very few marijuana-only drug users. Many smoke cigarettes, most drink, and most have had experience with other illicit drugs as well.

One study purported to find that chronic marijuana users manifested a significantly lower testosterone level—testosterone is the major male sex hormone that, if insufficient, can lead to impotence and sterility (Kolodny et al., 1974). However, soon after this study was published, another one appeared that concluded that marijuana use had no connection at all to testosterone levels in the male (Mendelson et al., 1974).

One study revealed extensive chromosomal damage as a consequence of marijuana use (Stenchever et al., 1974). This study, one propagandist claimed, demonstrated that marijuana users exhibited "roughly the same type of degree of damage as in persons surviving atom bombing with a heavy level of radiation" (Jones, 1974, p. 210). However, another study did not bear out the original result; the chromosomes of users and nonusers turned out to be almost identical (Nichols et al., 1974).

One study purported to show that marijuana caused "cerebral atrophy"—a shriveling of the brain (Campbell et al., 1971). However, its research methodology turned out to be faulty. Its sample consisted of mental patients all of whom were also users of more dangerous drugs as well. Two more carefully conducted studies found no indication of cerebral atrophy in marijuana users (Kuehnle, 1977; Co et al., 1977).

One research team produced laboratory results that indicated that marijuana users' white blood cells demonstrated a lowered capacity to fight disease; their "cellular immunity" was distinctly diminished (Nahas et al., 1974). However, this finding is challenged by later research that shows no differences between users and nonusers in the resistance of their blood cells to disease (White et al., 1975; Lau et al., 1976).

The only finding that seems not to have been refuted or seriously qualified elsewhere is the one indicating that heavy, chronic cannabis use is related to an impairment in the functioning of the lungs (Tashkin et al., 1976; Morris, 1985). This makes a certain amount of sense. After all, marijuana is smoked just as cigarettes are smoked, and it is inhaled more deeply and held in the lungs for a longer period of time. When cannabis and tobacco cigarettes are smoked in the same way, marijuana produces more than twice as much tar as tobacco does (Rickert et al., 1982). Impaired pulmonary functioning is one finding that remains fairly "robust" when studied by different researchers.

The reason for the contradictory findings that have turned up is fairly clear. Except for brain studies, in which the drug seems to have no effect at all, and the studies on pulmonary functioning, where marijuana's effect is fairly clear-cut, for all other organs and functions of the body that have been studied, marijuana's effect seems fairly weak. With a weak effect, some studies will produce positive results and some will turn up negative ones—especially if different measures or instruments are used. For instance, cannabis produces some chromosome breakage, but very little, and it is likely to be detected only in extremely sensitive tests (Morishima, 1984). Marijuana may lower testosterone functioning in males, but even the lowered rate is typically within normal limits (Harclerode, 1984). Marijuana administered to pregnant animals decreases the birth weight some in offspring, but in humans, the amount of fetal birth weight loss is barely significant (Abel, 1985), if not nonexistent (Tennes et al., 1985). Moreover, 1½- to 2-year-old children born to marijuana-smoking mothers do not display poorer functioning on various intellectual and motor tests (Fried, 1985). The evidence that marijuana smoking lowers the body's resistance to disease and infection "remains inconclusive" (Cohen, 1987, p. 82).

THE AMOTIVATIONAL SYNDROME

One of the effects some observers have speculated is caused by the use of marijuana is what has come to be called the "amotivational syndrome." Users become apathetic, become ineffective in achieving conventional goals—even goals that they themselves valued prior to use—find themselves unable to carry out long-range plans, have difficulty in concentrating, and begin doing poorly in school. There is a dropping away of the will to succeed, a lack of interest in achievement, a life characterized by lethargy, sloth, and languor. In an early statement on this syndrome, psychologists William McGlothlin and Louis West spell out what happens to the regular marijuana user:

> . . . clinical observations indicate that regular marihuana use may contribute to the development of more passive, inward-turning personality characteristics. For numerous middle-class students, the subtly progressive change from conforming, achievement-oriented behavior to a state of relaxed and careless drifting has followed their use of significant amounts of marihuana. . . . It appears that regular use of marihuana may very well contribute to some characteristic personality changes, especially among highly impressionistic young persons. Such changes include apathy, loss of effectiveness, and diminished capacity or willingness to carry out complex long-term plans, endure frustration, concentrate for long periods, follow routines, or successfully master new material. Verbal facility is often impaired, both in speaking and writing. Such individuals exhibit greater

introversion, become totally involved with the present at the expense of future goals, and demonstrate a strong tendency toward regressive, childlike magical thinking (McGlothlin and West, 1968, p. 372).

If an observer were to watch a typical gathering at which marijuana is used, McGlothlin and West's contention that getting high and using marijuana regularly creates apathy might make a certain degree of sense. Compared with most of their waking hours, when users are not under the influence of the drug, there is certainly a significantly diminished quantity of activity taking place. Stoned, few people want to do anything very vigorous. Most lie about and listen to music, watch television, dream, gorge themselves on food, or perhaps engage in what seems like fanciful, disorganized, and nonsensical conversation. The most energetic behavior typically taking place is making love or going out to watch a film. Most heavy intellectual efforts are ignored, although some creative efforts, such as painting or writing poetry, may be undertaken. But considering that these activities form the bulk of nearly all recreational activities, whether or not the individual is stoned, we may wonder whether users are in any way unique in their participation in them. There is a necessary assumption built into the amotivational-syndrome position that marijuana users are high a considerable proportion of the time—or that marijuana has effects on the user long after he or she has stopped smoking. The typical user is under the influence of marijuana about 4 percent of his or her waking hours. Thus, on the surface, it is difficult to imagine how cannabis could continue to generate apathy in the user during hours of nonuse. However, some research has shown that traces of THC metabolites remain in the body for several days (Lemberger et al., 1970), although they disappear from the heavy user's body roughly twice as fast as from the novice's body (Lemberger et al., 1971). Could it be that some lethargy-inducing effects remain in these traces? What, then, is the empirical relationship between marijuana use and achievement?

Although several early studies seemed to point to similar academic achievement by marijuana users and nonusers alike, more recent surveys indicate that marijuana users have lower grades in school, miss more classes, are more likely to drop out of school before completing a given grade, are less likely to go on to college and to graduate, and manifest a greater gap between their ability and their academic achievement. Moreover, *the more the individual uses,* the more strongly these tendencies hold. And the *earlier* that use is initiated, the more that they prevail as well. Johnston (1973, pp. 142–144) found a negative relationship between use of marijuana (and other drugs as well) and grades in high-school seniors. However, he discounted the direct action of marijuana itself because, typically, a lower level of academic achievement began to appear *even before* the student began using marijuana (pp. 145, 147). He suggested that "membership in a deviant subculture" remains a possible explanation for the finding.

Interesting results were turned up on the issue in one study of high-school students in several affluent suburbs of New York City (Kleinman et al., 1987a). The students studied were asked what their overall grade average was at the end of the year prior to the survey. For *daily* marijuana users, 81 percent received grades of C or lower, as opposed to 62 percent for less-than-daily users, 54 percent for individuals who had used but were not current users, and 40 percent for students who had never used marijuana. Daily users were also more often truant from school, and spent significantly less time doing homework. Although objections have been raised to self-report surveys involving drug users (Voth, 1982, p. 23), in fact, independent checks of information provided by drug users always strongly corroborate the answers given in self-report surveys (Robins and Murphy, 1967).

Does marijuana directly cause lowered achievement in school? Is it the effects of the drug that leads to lower grades, skipped school, less motivation to work? In this study, daily marijuana users were quite unlike other individuals in a wide range of ways. Compared with nonusers, marijuana users were more likely to be male; less likely to be living with both biological parents; more likely to have parents who "get drunk on occasion"; more likely to drink three or more times a week, get drunk themselves, and to have been drunk at an early age; more likely to have used marijuana at an early age; more likely to have active and frequent relations with the opposite sex; more likely to smoke a pack or more of cigarettes a day; more likely to engage in delinquent activities; and more likely to rank high on a "rebelliousness" scale.

In short, marijuana use "is just one behavior in a constellation of related problem behaviors and personality and familial factors. School problems can thus be understood to result from many of the same forces that lead to substance abuse, rather than the specific effects of marijuana use." The very factors that lead a youngster to smoke marijuana are those that also lead him or her to have problems in school. Does this mean that marijuana is unrelated to school problems? "The answer is a qualified no. Marijuana is indeed related to school problems. However, the association appears to be related to the qualities or attributes that are intrinsic to marijuana, the substance, in only a secondary manner. The primary association appears to be produced by virtue of the fact that marijuana use is one element in a large and complex picture of interrelated problems and behaviors." When these other factors are held constant, "level of marijuana use is not significantly associated with school problems." In sum, then, "by the time a student enters high school, he or she has already developed the attitudes that will cause problems there" (Kleinman et al., 1987a, p. 7).

In addition to the personal and individual factors, the subcultural factor must be considered as a source of lowered academic achievement among marijuana users. Becoming involved with a nonachieving subculture has a powerful impact on a youngster's motivation to succeed. Involvement with illegal drugs, including marijuana, and especially at the higher levels of use, may be taken as a rough indicator of the individual's participation in a drug subculture. The more that one uses, the earlier in life that one has used, the more that one buys and especially sells illicit drugs, the greater are the proportion of one's friends who also use and the likelihood that one is involved in a drug-using subculture (Goode, 1969; Johnson, 1973), and the greater the likelihood that this subculture will be alienated from traditional values, including desire for achievement and conventional success. These correlations alone, even ignoring the pharmacological impact of the drugs one uses, would lead us to expect differences in academic achievement based on degree of drug use. The subculture impact appears to me to be much more the issue than any amotivational-syndrome potential inherent in a given chemical substance, marijuana included. As the Institute of Medicine noted:

> Interpretation of the evidence linking marijuana to "amotivational syndrome" is difficult. Such symptoms have been known to occur in the absence of marijuana. Even if there is an association between this syndrome and use of marijuana, that does not prove that marijuana causes the syndrome. Many troubled individuals seek an "escape" into use of drugs; thus, frequent use of marijuana may become one more in a series of counterproductive behaviors for these unhappy people. The available evidence does not allow a sorting of the various possibilities in the relationship between use of marijuana and the complex of symptoms in the "amotivational syndrome." It appears likely that both self-selection and authentic drug effects contribute to the "motivational" problems seen in some chronic users. . . . Persons who are experiencing loss of motivation, apathy, and the other aforementioned symptoms probably will worsen the situation by taking any sedating drug. They should be warned to avoid frequent use of marijuana, alcohol, and other nonprescribed drugs (Institute of Medicine, 1982, p. 125).

MARIJUANA USE AND THE PROGRESSION TO DANGEROUS DRUGS

As we saw earlier, the use of every psychoactive drug is correlated with the use of every other psychoactive drug. Individuals who take or use any given drug are statistically more likely to take or use any other drug than is true of someone who does not take or use that given drug. Adolescents who smoke cigarettes and drink alcoholic beverages are more likely to "go on" to use marijuana in the future than are those who have not and never will use tobacco or alcohol. Marijuana users, in short, are disproportionately drawn from the ranks of individuals who use legal drugs. When we ask who uses marijuana, our answer must include drinkers and cigarette smokers (Kandel, 1980b).

But, we are also interested in whether or not marijuana users are more likely to try and use other illegal drugs than is true of individuals who do not and will not use marijuana. And does level or quantity of marijuana use play a role in this relationship? Are heavy users more likely to progress to the use of more dangerous drugs, such as cocaine, heroin, and the hallucinogens, than is true of the light, infrequent, or episodic user? And is marijuana use a causal agent in the correlation? Does the use of marijuana per se activate this relationship, if it prevails, or is some other factor at work here?

The correlation between the use of marijuana and the use of all other drugs is an extremely robust one. Every researcher who has investigated the issue systematically and empirically, myself included, has found a strong positive relationship. There is no question about its existence: Marijuana users are more likely to use any and all illegal dangerous drugs than are nonusers; and the more that one uses, the greater is this likelihood. Moreover, the earlier in life that one uses, the greater the probability that one will try and use a wide range of illegal drugs, including cocaine, heroin, and the hallucinogens. In addition, the more that one uses marijuana, and the earlier in life one first does so, the greater the likelihood of becoming *seriously* involved with other illegal dangerous drugs. The evidence supporting these relationships is overwhelming, persuasive, and incontrovertible. No one in the field questions the validity of the strong, positive, and significant correlation between the use of marijuana and the use of other illegal dangerous drugs.

The only question that exists is the causal mechanism underlying the relationship. *Why* does it prevail? Why are marijuana users significantly more likely to use other drugs than nonusers, heavy users more than light users, and early users than later ones? What impels more of them to progress to other illegal psychoactive substances? There are two schools of thought on the question. The first could be called the *intrinsic* school; the second is the *sociocultural* school.

The proponents of the "intrinsic" school (Jones, 1974, pp. 236–237, 249; Jones and Jones, 1977; Nahas, 1973, p. 276) argue that there is something inherent in marijuana use itself—from the experience of getting high on the drug, to the pharmacology and physiology of use—that leads to the use of and dependence on more dangerous drugs. The causal mechanism here lies within the drug itself—or, more properly, within the interaction between marijuana and the human body. This mechanism does not rely on the intervention of any outside factors or variables. It would take place in the absence of social and psychological factors—indeed, in a cave or on the moon, if marijuana and other drugs were available there. It argues that the relationship between marijuana and the use of more dangerous drugs is a constant, and occurs in all social categories at a more or less uniform rate. A given number of marijuana smokers translates into another specific number of heroin or cocaine addicts after a given period of time—a smaller number, naturally, to take account of exceptions, dropouts, the use of substances which might be substituted for either—alcohol, for instance—and so on. The correlation between marijuana use and the use of other, more potent psychoactive substances is, in effect, caused by a biochemical reaction.

Artificial, drug-induced pleasure, the argument goes, is temporary. When drugs are taken for pleasure over a period of time, the user becomes tolerant and therefore desensitized to the pleasurable sensations the drug originally delivered. Thus the drug must be taken more often. The experimental, episodic user must increase his or her frequency of drug use until he or she takes the drug daily and becomes physically and psychically dependent. Still, desensitization continues, and the pleasure continues to diminish. Consequently, a drug with a more potent effect must be taken. "The demand for pleasurable sensations caused by *Cannabis* will require in time larger and larger amounts of the drug. A biological urge will develop to substitute more potent drugs for *Cannabis,* in order to reach a similar feeling of detachment from the world" (Nahas, 1973, p. 276).

One antimarijuana propagandist, Hardin Jones, claims that his "statistical computation" demonstrates that 10 percent of all daily marijuana users become heroin addicts within three years (Jones, 1974, p. 236). The mechanism? He claims that "cross-tolerance" is to blame, pointing to "some degree of chemical action," which is to be expected "because of the marked similarity in chemical structure between opiates and cannabinols." "In my studies," Dr. Jones states, "daily users who have transferred to heroin use do not show withdrawal symptoms," which is, he claims, "an indication of crosstolerance. Crosstolerance enables cannabis users to have increased sensual effects from heroin without the unpleasant withdrawal symptoms of cannabis" (p. 237).

The metaphor used by the "intrinsic" school is that of a *conveyor belt.* Heroin addiction, and the heavy, dependent of use of all dangerous drugs, is seen as a later stage of a process that begins with experimental marijuana use. If marijuana use is halted, slowed down, or diminished, fewer users of hard drugs will be produced at the other end (Goode, 1972a, p. 239).

The "sociocultural" argument holds that the progression from marijuana to other drugs takes place, when it does, not because of the physiological action of the drug itself, but because of the activities, friends, and acquaintances the user is involved with during the course of use (Goode, 1969, 1970, 1974; Johnson, 1973). Users tend to make friends who have attitudes toward drug use that are more favorable than those of nonusers; the more one uses marijuana, the higher the proportion of one's friends who use not only marijuana but other drugs as well, the more positive their attitudes toward use are likely to be, and the more opportunities they will offer the user to try other drugs as well. It is not the *physical experience* of marijuana use itself—that is, getting high on the drug—but the *activity* of use and all of its surrounding social features, that is the major factor influencing this drug progression.

The "intrinsic" argument was widely ballyhooed in the 1960s and 1970s. (Interestingly enough, prior to 1950, antimarijuana propagandists *denied* that progression from marijuana to other drugs took place because they wanted to focus on the dangers of marijuana itself; see Grinspoon, 1971, pp. 235–240, 1977.) Much as the proponents of this school claimed that evidence backed up their argument, in fact, their claims were never really tested; Jones's "statistical computations," when examined closely, turn out to be bogus; he presents no systematic studies or evidence to back up his statement. However, two sociologists (O'Donnell and Clayton, 1982) decided to test the validity of the "intrinsic" school; they claim that their evidence shows that "marijuana is a cause of heroin use in the United States." They make this claim on the basis of a rule that dictates that if (1) two variables are statistically associated, (2) one variable is prior to the other at the relevant time, and (3) the association does not disappear when the effect of a third variable is removed, then the relationship between the two variables is causal in nature.[1] They hold that this is in fact the case with marijuana use and heroin addiction, that the association between these two variables meets these three criteria.

Setting aside the question of whether or not such a simple formula or rigid set of criteria can determine causality between two variables, does O'Donnell and Clayton's evidence support their claim? Everyone agrees that criterias (1) and (2) obtain; there is no argument here. What about their claim that they have removed the effect of key third variables and still find a strong correlation between marijuana and heroin use? The sociocultural school argues that the drug use by friends influences the progression from marijuana to more dangerous drugs. O'Donnell and Clayton control for thirty-two different variables, only three of which—friends' use of alcohol, friends' use of marijuana, and friends' use of other drugs—are relevant here. But their controls are for friends' use of alcohol, marijuana, and other drugs *when the individual was a teenager,* and not when he (the researchers studied only men) was interviewed nor when he tried or used heroin. (The age range of their sample was 20 to 30.)

More crucial than this, however, is that O'Donnell and Clayton refuse to distinguish between marijuana use *as an activity* and *as an experience.* The authors seem to be saying there must be something direct and intrinsic about the impact of marijuana use; we don't know exactly what it is, but we're going to pretend that it's there. They never address the question of *what it is about marijuana use* that affects the causal sequence in question. They say that if using marijuana leads to selling marijuana, which leads to selling hard drugs, which leads to having heroin-using friends, which leads to using heroin, then this actually *strengthens* their argument, because the causal chain begins with marijuana use (O'Donnell and Clayton, 1982, p. 237). But they never address the issue of exactly what the causal mechanism in this process is. Is it the biochemical action of the drug itself? Is it the association with a drug-using subculture? They never say. What's more, they don't seem to care; all they know is that something they call "use" is the first step in this process. Thus their argument can best be described as a "crypto-intrinsic" one: They assert that the relationship between marijuana and more danger-

[1] I would argue for a somewhat different set of criteria. In fact, I believe that, if the introduction of a third variable significantly and drastically reduces the strength of a given empirical relationship, *even if that relationship remains statistically significant,* then causality may be called into question, because this reduction suggests the possibility that other variables will further diminish the strength of the original relationship.

ous drug use is intrinsic, but in fact, the intrinsic mechanism is a hidden variable.

A major problem surrounding this issue is the misuse of the term "spurious" both by O'Donnel and Clayton and by myself. As my graduate-school teacher Paul F. Lazarsfeld would have said, a *relationship* cannot be spurious—it is *the explanation accounting for that relationship that should be called spurious.* When I stated that the relationship between marijuana use and the use of other drugs is spurious (Goode, 1973b), I was using shorthand for saying that it is the "intrinsic" *explanation* for the relationship that is spurious. The relationship exists; it is real, and it cannot be said to be spurious. Clearly, *some aspect of marijuana use* is causally related to the use of more dangerous drugs. But what exactly is that aspect? As I clearly spelled out elsewhere (Goode, 1972a, pp. 237–250), it is the biochemical argument that I consider a spurious explanation for the drug progression. Nowhere do O'Donnell and Clayton address that issue. In short, the "intrinsic" argument cannot be said to have been demonstrated.

ACCOUNT: GETTING HIGH ON MARIJUANA

Below, two users describe what they feel like under the influence of marijuana.[2] At the time of the interview, the first respondent was a 22-year-old college senior who played in a rock band on weekends. When the interview was published, he was a student in a graduate business school, when he smoked marijuana twice a month during the school year and every day during the summer.

> Things started striking me funny—I mean, somebody would say something and I'd keep hearing it. Or I'd look at something, and I'd find myself looking at it for an overly long period of time, and all of a sudden I'd wake up and say, what the hell am I doing, looking at this for so long? When I'm high, I always listen to music. Music would begin to sound extraordinarily good. And then, after four or five minutes more, I would realize that I was high, and I'd get very happy. I spend most of my time high listening to music. I'd listen to the music, and I'd always concentrate on one instrument, it didn't matter which one. I could never listen to all at the same time, which is the only drawback I see to being high and listening to music, as opposed to being straight. But I could listen to what I consider good rock and roll, and just love it. It would be just about the most pleasing thing I've ever done in my life.
>
> I play the guitar. I prefer to play casually, informally, high. I will not play before an audience high, because it's too uncomfortable. I know that I have to perform, and I get scared. I start to think, what if I pass out, what if I don't have enough wind for the next song, 'cause I do get short-winded. I almost blew the whole thing in a night club last summer. But rehearsing, or getting together with

[2]These interviews originally appeared in: Erich Goode, *Marijuana,* New York: Lieber-Atherton, 1969, pp. 52–57. Reprinted by permission of the publishers, Lieber-Atherton, Inc. Copyright © 1969. All rights reserved.

the rest of the group when you're high, it's a great experience. I sit there and play and play and play. I play much better. I'm quite convinced that this is not a high fantasy. I *know* I'm playing better. 'Cause I don't make any mistakes, like I usually do. And I can anticipate what's coming. And throw phrases back and forth between guys, if somebody else is high. We had a job once at Bryn Mawr, where I played. We all smoked in the afternoon and came back to this room where we were going to play, and we sat down and played one song, one instrumental song, for forty-five minutes without stopping, and it was the best thing I've ever done.

I used to play games, I used to do things with my eyes, great things. Nothing that really ever scared me, because I could always be cautious not to go too high, so that I wouldn't have, you know, a bad time. I could always know where I was, what I was doing, unless I made myself forget. Sometimes I'd listen to the Byrds. I could lie down on the bed, and pick myself up, and throw myself down, sort of float down one of those concentric-ring, man-hole type things. Or there was one experience I had recently, where I was listening to them. And the notes were coming out, it's a very strident, shrill, crisp twelve-string electric guitar, and it's beautiful. He does Indian-type stuff on it. And the notes sounded to me as they came into my ears, it sounded as if I were a million miles away. I had a picture in my mind of sitting out in space and watching the notes come flying by. They were very sharp, coming by. I said to myself, the machine is making these notes, and these notes will be free from now on, they're coming out in a certain order to make a tune, and I saw them continuing out from the earth into space, and they could always be heard if you had sensitive enough ears. It was great when I was out there, for about ten seconds I was sitting out there, in space, looking at the earth, watching the notes come by. And it was all black around me. And then all of a sudden, I realized that everything, my whole world, was back there, several million miles away. And I got clutched for a minute. So I opened my eyes and I came back. I like to do stuff like that.

I have changed colors on some of those psychedelic posters. I've made them flash from red and white to black, and then changed it to blue. Very often I can place myself inside a concert hall when I'm listening to records. I can see the performance taking place in front of me. This happened the first time I got high. I saw the band, and they were dancing, and the drummer's feet, and all the performers' heads, came to a sharp point, because the music was very shrill, and the notes were sharp and pointed. And then during the solo, I remember the drummer got up and danced around his drums while he was playing them—on his points, the points of his toes.

Simultaneously, I thought of the guy I was with in the room. I realized that I was sitting on the floor with my ear next to the speaker, and I said, this must look very foolish. And then I said, well, it looks foolish, and if it looks foolish, I'll have to get up. But I don't want to get up. So I'll just pretend that it doesn't look foolish. You'll do almost anything to rationalize away something that gets in the way of your enjoyment.

There's always sex. If you don't want it, you get more turned off. If a girl repulses you, you definitely wouldn't think of going near her. But once you get the idea into your head that you want to get your hands on her, there's very little that can stop you. And you don't care. The easiest thing to do is to walk up to a girl, if you're at a party or something, and to let her know you're high, so she'll understand if you try to con her into bed in one minute. There's definitely a heightening of all the physical impulses high. They are much, much stronger, in every way. Pain, too. If you concentrate on pain, you'll really start to hurt. Sex is more purely physical high, that's the only problem. It's a lust orgy. When you are involved in it, you don't think about the girl at all, you just think about the physical pleasure. But the physical pleasure is just immense. However, it doesn't detract from my normal, straight sex life. I don't say, "Gee whiz, I wish I were high." But when you want it to, marijuana acts as a frighteningly powerful aphrodisiac. At least for me it does.

I get very, very, very thirsty when I'm high. My mouth dries out. In fact, the last time I smoked, my mouth dried out so much that I actually thought I was going to do some physical damage to it, because it got to the point where I couldn't speak, because my lips were sticking to the insides of my gums, and it was totally dry.

Just walking around feels good, nice, you know. You can groove on your own movements. In some cases I become pretty uncoordinated. I tried playing tennis once high, and it was a complete disaster. Whereas I can sit in my room with an imaginary set of drums and coordinate my two feet and two hands to different beats, which I could never do straight.

My eyes get very heavy. Hot.

At the time of the interview, the second respondent was an 18-year-old college student who smoked marijuana roughly once a week. She was smoking when the interview took place.

The sense of touch is—all the senses are heightened. Your senses are—your perceptions change. You look at something and you see, you perceive it, differently. It may be—you may see more. Maybe it's more defined to you, the outline may be more defined. Or you may see it in a different dimension. One dimension may stand out. Like looking at a painting. You look at it as if it is in another dimension, rather than just flat. And figures become more—their outlines become more defined. You can look at something and see the detail of it rather than look at a table and just see the many things on it. You actually see each individual thing in its own place.

A lot of times you can see yourself, you can look at yourself objectively, and almost feel as if you're talking, but it's somebody else talking, and you listen to yourself as if you're another person. So you can sort of get outside yourself. It feels that way most of the time I talk when I'm high. My voice doesn't sound like it's my own. I know it's mine, but I listen, I hear it as if it's another voice. Usually, straight, you can't hear your voice, you don't know what your voice sounds like. When you're high, it's like listening to a tape recording of your voice at the same time that you're speaking.

And your imagination—you let your imagination go more, so that you're more suggestive to different pictures of things, more relaxed. To a certain extent, I think either more creative thoughts, something that I've been thinking about, but I don't have time to think about when they come into my head, or some things that I'd hide when I was straight, that I may feel subconsciously. When I'm high, they come to me as actual thoughts. I'm more aware of them when they come. And the thoughts are much more clear. I remember them.

You're much more aware that you're saying one thing and possibly thinking another. And your thoughts go much faster than the time it takes to say them.

You can think two things at the same time, right next to each other, and see each one.

In the beginning, my throat gets dry, and it stings and burns.

And you may get tingly. I first get tingly in the sensuous spots. I don't know whether it's psychological, but that's where I feel it usually. It sort of slides down.

You feel very hungry. You can feel hungry after a while. When you do, it's a tremendous hunger. And you eat more than you probably usually would. And you *think* you're eating more, even when you don't actually.

And time is very . . . let's see, what does it do? Lengthened. Or shortened. It can be either way. You think you've been some place for a very long time and in fact, it's just been a few minutes, or vice versa.

My sense of hearing is heightened. I can hear the rain very distinctly right now. And the different noises that make up a sound separately. Music sounds much more vivid. You can break up the music into its different instruments, or you can hear it in different ways. You watch it and perceive it. You can watch it as you hear it, say, in your mind you want to hear the violins, you hear them more distinctly. Many times, I could never understand the words of Dylan straight, but high I have no problem at all. I didn't even make a conscious effort. All of a sudden, I understood the words, and I never understood them before.

Pot makes you a sex fiend. You don't necessarily want sex more, but you enjoy it more. You always want it the same. Since it allows your subconscious to express itself, subconsciously, you may want sex more, so when you are high, you want more—no, not more. You're just more aware of it.

And you feel your heart beat. You don't know whether it's getting faster, but you feel the presence of it beating.

CHAPTER 7

Hallucinogens

During the 1960s, hallucinogenic drugs were called psychedelics. This category includes LSD, peyote, mescaline, the psilocybin mushroom, DMT, DET, and MDA. Many other chemicals and botanicals are hallucinogenic in effect, but they are relatively infrequently used. The terms "psychedelic" and "hallucinogen" convey almost opposite points of view on the drug experience, and each is likely to be used by ideologues of directly contrary opinions. "Psychedelic" contains a not-so-hidden prodrug bias: it means that the mind is "made manifest" when it is under the influence of a psychedelic drug—that we can think and see more clearly, more acutely, more deeply. The ideology underlying the "psychedelic" philosophy is (or was when the term was in vogue in the mid-1960s) that we are creatures who have been lied to and blinded by the propaganda socialized into us from infancy. No one is able to see reality "as it really is," except a tiny number of genius visionaries. The vision and thoughts of nearly everyone are warped by the "games" imposed by a fearful and restrictive social order. The essential function that psychedelics serve, according to this view, is to strip away the impediments to a direct confrontation with reality; they allow the drug user to see things clearly, without society's lies. As Aldous Huxley exclaimed under the influence of mescaline upon witnessing the awesome "isness" of his trousers, his bookshelf, the legs of a chair: "This is how one ought to see, how things really are" (Huxley, 1963, p. 34). The psychedelicists claimed that far from providing an *escape* from reality, drugs such as mescaline and LSD offer a direct confrontation *with* reality, a plunge into a uniquely unadulterated world. And the term "psychedelic" captures this perspective. The ideology has to a great degree diminished in importance, but the word remains. In any case, I do not intend any prodrug bias when I use the term "psychedelic."

Almost the opposite point of view is summed up in the word "hallucinogen." Since we live in an age that thinks of itself as scientific, anything called a "hallucinogen" is something illusory—a deception, a fallacy, perhaps even the ravings of a madman, and hence something undesirable, the manifestations of a sickness calling for firm treatment. Another related term is "psychotomimetic"—having the quality of producing a state that "mimics" madness, very much like insanity in important respects. Both of these terms are obviously negatively charged and ideological in import. Actually, a true hallucination is relatively rare during the "hallucinogenic" drug experience. (Just as the mind being "made manifest," or operating most clearly, under a "psychedelic" drug is rare.) Again, when I use the term "hallucinogen"

I intend no ideologically overtoned meaning. I will use the terms as if they were neutral and simply descriptive, because no completely unbiased term exists.

What are the psychedelics, or hallucinogens? Lysergic acid diethylamide, or LSD-25, or simply LSD (or "acid"—almost the only slang street term that is used routinely), is by far the best known of all psychedelics. LSD is a semisynthetic drug derived from the principal active agent in the ergot fungus, a contaminator of rye; the fungus is itself psychotoxic—in fact, an epidemic that killed thousands of people in the Middle Ages was caused by the eating of rye bread contaminated by ergot. LSD was synthesized and named by the Swiss chemist Albert Hofmann in 1938 (LSD is an abbreviation of the German term *lyserg saure diethylamid*—if it had been discovered by an English-speaking chemist, it would have been abbreviated LAD), but its potent psychoactive properties were not discovered until 1943, when Hofmann accidentally inhaled a minute quantity of the drug. Describing his experiences (the first LSD "trip" in history), Hofmann wrote:

> I had to leave my work in the laboratory and go home because I felt strangely restless and dizzy. Once there, I lay down and sank into a not unpleasant delirium which was marked by an extreme degree of fantasy. In a sort of trance with closed eyes . . . fantastic visions of extraordinary vividness accompanied by a kaleidoscopic play of intense coloration continuously swirled around me. After two hours this condition subsided.

Later, after discovering that it was the LSD that caused these reactions, and after some additional self-experimentation, Hofmann wrote: "This drug makes normal people psychotic."

LSD is taken via a swallowed capsule or tablet; at one time it was taken in the form of sugar cubes impregnated with a drop of the chemical, but this method is totally unknown today. Even as minute a quantity as 25 micrograms of LSD is psychoactive for most people. (An ordinary headache tablet contains more than 300,000 micrograms of aspirin.) The usual dose of LSD is purported to be between 200 and 500 micrograms; however, since black-market LSD is both contaminated (often with amphetamine) and unstandardized as to potency, very few users of street LSD can be even remotely sure of the dosages they take, in spite of their claims. An LSD "trip" customarily lasts between five and twelve hours, although reactions, sometimes of an undesired, uncomfortable, and even frightening nature, can last for days. "Flashbacks," or recurrences of the LSD experience without taking the drug, also sometimes occur.

Mescaline ("mesc") is a naturally occurring psychedelic drug named after the Mescalero, an Apache tribe. It is in extremely infrequent use, though many naive users buy and take a chemical their dealers tell them is mescaline. (It is usually LSD, often cut with an amphetamine.) Mescaline is one of the eight or so psychoactive chemicals in the peyote cactus. Another naturally occurring psychedelic drug, psilocybin, is derived from *Psilocybe mexicana,* the so-called sacred or magic mushroom. Both peyote and the sacred mushroom are used in religious ceremonies by Native Americans, peyote mostly in the United States, and the sacred mushroom in Mexico. The peyote cult existed before the invasion of America by the Europeans, but it became widespread only with the destruction of much of Indian civilization. Members of the Native American Church take peyote as a sacrament—the drug represents the body of Christ—and this practice is legal in the United States.

Dimethyltriptamine, or DMT for short, and diethyltriptamine, or DET, are synthetic hallucinogens, and they deliver a powerful but extremely brief trip, sometimes lasting only fifteen minutes. For this reason they have been called the "businessman's" or "lunchtime" psychedelics. At one time, it was common to chew morning-glory seeds to bring on a hallucinogenic experience. Some genuses of morning-glory seeds contain a substance whose chemical structure is closely related to LSD's. Its psychoactive properties were known to the Aztecs, who referred to the plant as "ololiuqui." Today few young people eat morning-glory seeds, partly because the commercially sold variety began to be sprayed with a substance that induces vomiting.

There are also a number of more exotic and less frequently used hallucinogenic substances, both synthetic and naturally occurring. The mushroom *Amanita muscaria*, or fly agaric, has been used for centuries for its psychoactive properties by various Siberian tribes, such as the Chuckchee. It is almost unknown in America. The South American vine *Banisteriopsis caapi* produces a drug, usually called "yage" (pronounced "ya-hay"), that is used by some Amazonian tribes. Ingesting it produces a psychic state that could be called psychedelic or hallucinogenic. Some avant-garde literary figures, such as William Burroughs, journeyed to South America to experience the drug's effects and to write about it. In spite of its underground notoriety, I have never encountered anyone who claims to have taken yage. Another drug, bufotenine, is derived from the skin of one species of toad and seems to have some mind-altering qualities. It is almost never used in the United States. Common household nutmeg, if taken in sufficient quantities, produces an intoxication that might be called hallucinogenic. In spite of its use in prisons (described by Malcolm X in his autobiography), and in spite of its ready availability in the United States—which imports more than 5 million pounds yearly, mostly from Indonesia—it is not a frequently used drug. Relatively few young people are even aware of its consciousness-altering properties.

A tranquilizer that had been available on American streets since the 1960s made a resurgence in the late 1970s. It was originally called THC by drug dealers, but it was not the active ingredient in marijuana and hashish of the same name. Instead, it was a commercially manufactured animal tranquilizer known as PCP, with the chemical name of phencyclidine and the trade name of Serinyl. The Food and Drug Administration regards the drug as unsafe for human use, and it is used only to sedate and anesthetize large animals. It is now manufactured illegally and is sold as angel dust; it is often sprinkled in marijuana joints. Many observers classify this drug as a hallucinogen (Ray and Ksir, 1987, pp. 290–292; Johnston et al., 1987, pp. 28ff.). This is, I believe, a mistake, as a comparison between its effects and those of LSD will quickly verify. Except for hallucinations (often horrifying with angel dust, occasionally so with LSD) and psychotic episodes (more common with angel dust than with LSD) the two drugs have nothing in common. Angel dust has none of the major effects of hallucinogens. Objectively, these drugs are simply not in the same category, although most observers do classify them together.

SOME SUBJECTIVE EFFECTS OF HALLUCINOGENIC DRUGS

In one study I conducted (Goode, 1970), about half of the respondents had used at least one hallucinogen drug. I elicited from them descriptions of their experiences with this drug type. One commonly reported effect was what is called *eidetic imagery,* or "eyeball movies." Under the influence of LSD and other psychedelic drugs (and also on occasion with marijuana), the subject, with his or her eyes closed, "sees" physical objects, usually in motion, as sharply as if he or she were watching a film. Often these eidetic images are abstract and lacking in dramatic content; they frequently represent almost interminable repetitions of a pattern or design, much like moving wallpaper—but with the pattern constantly changing. This is by no means always the case; many respondents also reported striking imagery. One interviewee described his vision of eidetic imagery as follows: "Closing my eyes, I saw millions of color droplets, like rain, like a shower of stars, all different colors." Another young man put one of his experiences in these terms:

> I can't begin to describe them, even to myself, they happened so fast. I can only recall the vaguest hint of what they were like. One was hundreds of fleurs-de-lis, repeating themselves, moving in several lines. Very graceful and beautiful. Another, not so nice, was hundreds of iron crosses, repeating themselves in four lines at right angles to one another, receding into some point on the horizon. These two were by far the most banal of any I saw. Most of the others were literally indescribable. Red and green played a large part in the color parade. A lot of it was images thrown on a solid surface, like a woman's body.

Another psychedelic experience commonly reported was *synesthesia*—the simultaneous perception of the stimulation of several senses. Users reported "hearing" color, or "seeing" sounds. The subjective meaning attached to a stimulus perceived by one sense is felt to mean something in other senses as well—is felt to be translatable from one sense to another. One researcher described the experience as follows:

> The phenomenon of synesthesia occurs almost uniformly with a sufficient dose. Its most frequent and obvious form is exhibited when auditory stimuli produce changes in visual hallucinations. For example, the experimenter claps

his hands and the subject sees flashes of color in time to the clapping (Klee, 1963, p. 463).

An early researcher who took mescaline himself wrote: "I felt, saw, tasted, smelled the tone. I was the tone myself. . . . I thought, saw, felt, tasted my hands" (Guttman, 1936, pp. 209, 210). A woman I interviewed put it this way: "I really got into music on my trip. I was traveling on the notes. I felt as if I was on an arc of fireworks—a quiet explosion. I felt as if the music was inside me, I felt as if it was making love to me. It was beautiful."

A third effect of the psychedelics reported by my respondents was what might be called *perception of a multilevel reality.* Sometimes these levels relate to perspective perceptions. One subject told me: "You see things from seven different ways at once." Another young woman said: "I looked at any object, and it would breathe and move and also appear from all angles in one instant." Occasionally, this multilevel perspective invades scientific realms; the diverse levels are those that a scientist might explore one at a time. A young artist put it this way: "I was sitting on a chair, and I could see the molecules. I could see right through things to the molecules." A young woman had this experience: "I stared at my dog—his face kept changing. I could see the veins in his face, under his skin." Often these levels do not relate specifically to definite senses; their referential location is vague. A college student said:

It was a total explosion of customary thought pattern frameworks. I became totally open—all channels were open. I didn't view the world in my usual way. I had a specific train of thought with the acid that isn't the only pattern of thought—others were working simultaneously. My channels of thinking were widened. Different channels were working simultaneously—the poetic, the allegorical, the cosmic, the tragic levels. And I became aware of the interaction of all levels simultaneously—you break down the weave and are aware of the parts, while you are aware of the whole.

Another perception beyond the range of "normal" reality was that the world was continually *fluid.* This perceived dynamic quality of the universe was perhaps the most commonly mentioned of any of the varied aspects of the psychedelic trip. The static universe seems to explode into a shimmering, pulsating cosmos, a world in continual flux. "Things were oozing as if they were made of jelly," one interviewee said. Others reported: "A brick wall wobbled and moved." "Paint ran off the walls." "Every physical thing seemed to be swimming in a fluid as if a whole wall had been set in liquid and was standing there before me, shimmering slightly." "I saw wriggling, writhing images." "I saw flowers on the window sill, blowing in the breeze. I went to touch them, but there was no breeze, and the flowers were dead."

A fifth commonly reported psychedelic experience was *subjective exaggeration,* of anything—an object, an event, a mood, a person, a situation—a kind of baroque rendering of the world outside. The exaggeration may be in sheer number—perceiving more things than are there; or it may be the dramatization of a single characteristic of the stimulus, or an allegory on the nature of its essence. This type of experience ranges from modest exaggerations, some within the range of normal imaginative minds, to extravagant and detailed visions. A coed told me: "One pillow turned into 50 million pillows—all the pillows in the world." Another said: "The mind is very suggestible. Sudden appearances of things take on strange forms. A towel falling off the edge of my tub looked like a giant lizard crawling down. The mind works faster, and is more suggestible." A young man had this experience:

> When my girlfriend was peeling an orange for me, it sounded like she was ripping a small animal apart. I examined it carefully. It seemed to be made up of tiny golden droplets stuck together. I'd never seen an orange before. My girlfriend was eating scrambled eggs, and it was as if I was watching a pig with its face in a trough of garbage. A few bits of egg clung to her teeth, and it seemed as if gobs of garbage were oozing down her face and out of her mouth. But I knew I was imagining it.

This experience of subjective exaggeration of the things around one shades over into what some clinicians call the "eureka experience"—the feeling that what is usually seen and thought to be quite ordinary takes on extraordinary and even epic proportions.

Another common feature of the LSD experience was *emotional lability*—extremes in mood, great swings in temperament. Under the influence of the drug, a person can within seconds go from ecstasy to the depths of despair; sobbing and laughing may follow in swift succession. A divorcee described to me one such swing in mood:

> It started off beautifully. I looked into a garden and I saw full-blown jewels, you know, of different colors, and the smell was something that made me realize how I never really sniffed a scent before. And suddenly, it got terrible, because I saw a couple holding hands on a couch, and they reminded me of my husband and myself, what we didn't have, because they were in love. And I started to cry, you see. So all of a sudden, the whole beauty of the garden faded, and I started to cry. And then all of a sudden, the thought changed to my mother, when I was a little girl. And I got sad over that. And then, my attention wandered, and something else was happening, beautiful music was turned on, and I heard such exquisite things. Then suddenly I felt happy. And then I thought, My God! One moment after the next cancels out the preceding moment. And that time is a funny thing. That none of those incidents means more than the other one, because they're wiped out right after they've happened by the next thing that happens. There I saw that every incident just happening in a flash, and that a new stimulus could take away the old. And have equal importance.

Another description that emerged during my interviews with LSD users was a *feeling of timelessness*. Some users contrasted their LSD experiences strongly with those on marijuana. Marijuana slows things down—it seems as though more time has passed than actually has—but the difference is quantitative not qualitative. With marijuana, one might overestimate the duration of time by two or three times. With LSD, the change is much more radical. Time, in a sense, ceases to exist; it seems suddenly irrelevant. One young man described it this way:

> Has an hour gone by since I last looked at the clock? Maybe it was a lifetime. Maybe it was no time at all. I don't know what an hour means, anyway. What is a clock? Mechanical gears and springs. My body's pulse can tell me much more than a clock can about how much time has passed by. One burst, one gush, one throb, went by—that's how much.

Another young man exclaimed: "Music takes *endless* lengths of time on acid."

Another commonly mentioned subjective "effect" of LSD-type drugs was a sensation of what might be called *irrationalism.* The virtues of clarity, logic, cause-and-effect relationships, regimentation, objectivity, universalism, and so on seem somehow to lose force. The contrary values of intuition, tactility, emotive communication, and organicism seem to take on a cosmic significance. A rejection of western rationality seems to be associated with the ingestion of LSD. Users reported that under the influence of the drug they felt that an ineffable, nonlogical mentality was taking over, and they welcomed it with open arms. Suddenly what seemed important was the unique rather than the general, the implicit rather than the explicit, the preverbal rather than the verbal, participation and involvement rather than detachment and objectivity, the unpredictable rather than the predictable, the dynamic rather than the static. They preferred what Marshall McLuhan calls the "implosive"—the privatistic inward search—to the "explosive"— the aggressive, outward drive to understand and dominate. One casualty of this change was *words.* A young woman put it this way: "I felt that words were futile. We, my boyfriend and I, could think about the same thing, and *know* it, without words. Later, my thoughts were *images,* not in the form of words." Her sentiment was echoed by a young lawyer:

> One thing my trip taught me, was able to make me see, was the essential falseness of words. They are used for masking feeling, evading, dodging the issue. It isn't just that they are *inadequate* to explain, to convey, much of experience. It is that they actually convey a basically *distorted* impression of it. Much of human experience is completely untranslatable into words, into logical thought. Those cold, sterile little gnomes, words, cannot possibly get across something that is basically emotional, physical, perceptual, spiritual—illogical, in a sense. They aren't comparable systems of thought. It's almost like trying to eat money instead of an orange; the two just don't mean the same thing.

No doubt many of my respondents already had some sympathy with these "irrationalist" tendencies before taking any drugs. No doubt there is a considerable overlap between many of their perceptions and many antirationalist values within some dissident groups and subcultures in America, a large proportion of which also use psychedelic drugs. Many groups shared these values before drugs began to be taken on a mass basis—the bohemians of the 1920s and 1930s, the "beatniks" of the 1950s and early 1960s, the hippies of the later 1960s. Thus the people who experiment with hallucinogenic drugs and the people who move in the direction of rejecting western-style rationalism are in large part the same. It is difficult to sort out which factor is primary.

As noted earlier, the full-blown authentic hallucination, the perception of a materially nonexistent physical object created out of whole cloth and felt by the subject to be actually there, is a rarity under the influence of LSD. Usually, trippers know that the things they are seeing do not "really" exist. And often some sort of "actual" stimulus touches off the sensation. Perhaps "pseudohallucination" or "virtual hallucination" would be a more appropriate term for these sensations. One very common variety is the perception of one's own body in various unusual and never-before-seen states. Sometimes this occurs before a mirror; often a dynamic element is introduced into the perception—one sees oneself over time or repeated in space. A college student said: "I saw myself, my face in the mirror, developing from 5 years old to 40 years old." Another said: "In the mirror, I saw my clothes change into costumes from different periods of history." A young man had a similar sensation: "I could see ten images of myself on each side of me, like a tuning fork." Sometimes the body appears transmuted into a state that is both horrible and fascinating at the same time. A bizarre beauty clung to many of my respondents' descriptions of the self-metamorphosis. An artist reported: "The first thing that I noticed was that my arm was made of gold. This held my attention for a long time. It was beautiful." A young woman said: "I saw myself in the mirror with one eye. It was disturbing, but not horrible." Another subject exclaimed: "My eyelashes grew and became like snakes."

Another variety of "pseudohallucination" revolves around changed perceptions of other people. Users reported few differences in content between the transformations perceived in themselves and those seen in others. In both, malformations seemed to dominate. A schoolteacher said:

> The people outside, on the street, were horrible freaks. I never saw such twisted, distorted monsters in my life. Everyone was old, fat, or pathologically skinny, with twisted arms, hunchbacks, bloated bellies, turniplike tubers of flesh, flesh run rampant, a grotesque travesty of human flesh, the Gothic artist's ideal.

Inexplicably, animals figured more than occasionally in the content of these sensations, whether in transformation of actual humans or in completely original creations. A young woman said that she saw "a man with a frog's head walking down the street." Under the influence of DET, another subject described seeing "a painting of a landscape. Then I saw a little boy in the painting. A tree tried to capture the boy, and then the boy changed into a werewolf. Then I saw a rhinoceros making love to a woman. The rhino was leering at me." A schoolteacher I interviewed described the following experience under LSD:

> Several friends came by and tried to coax me to go the Bronx Zoo. When they asked me, it sounded as if I was in a jungle with a vegetable canopy above me,

and their pleas were like little gremlins squeaking. One of my friends said we can see the reptiles, and man, I really *saw* a reptile, right there in my living room, a silver, green, and black snake, slithering along my floor.

Unlike marijuana, which most users describe as being pleasurable most of the time, LSD seems to elicit a formidable sense of *ambivalence*. It does not necessarily sharpen the senses, but it does open up the psyche to *receive* sensations. Our normal psychological inhibitions enable us to limit what we see around us, to "attend" to a very narrow range of sensations. Otherwise, our day-to-day and even minute-to-minute existence would be fraught with overwhelming complications. Under LSD the mind is overloaded with sensory input, with impressions and sensations that we normally filter out. Emotional inhibitions are also lowered under LSD. Everything seems to be sensed as much more extreme and intense than normal. This means that what is pleasant will suddenly seem to be ecstasy, a magic voyage of the gods. And what is normally experienced as simply unpleasant will become dreadful—the absolute bottom circle of hell. Both may occur during a trip, often simultaneously. One of Aldous Huxley's books describing his mescaline experiences was entitled *Heaven and Hell*—testimony to the very powerful ambivalence most users experience during a trip on a hallucinogenic drug. Most of us do not find such extremes to our liking. Extreme swings of mood can be unsettling. Nearly everyone who emerges from a psychedelic experience, whether he likes it or not, is struck by this basic characteristic (Katz, 1970).

PSYCHOTIC EPISODES

The issue of the generation of temporary psychoses, psychotic episodes, or extreme emotional disturbances by hallucinogenic drugs is a crucial, though overplayed, aspect of the drug experience. There are several different schools of thought on this matter. One view, which may be called the traditionalist or positivist approach, is that any deviation from the "normal" everyday functioning of the mind is *by definition* abnormal and hence a psychosislike state. In its pure form this is certainly a dying view; however, somewhat weaker versions of it are still the norm in some commentaries on the subject. One observer, a physician, writes that LSD

> . . . impairs perception and cognition. The user does not perceive accurately the world around him. His capacity to think and reason is also adversely affected and there is a danger of becoming mentally ill after the use of the drug. . . . The "bad trip" can happen to any user of LSD and a recurrent psychotic reaction can occur in anyone who takes the drug. Hallucinations, anxiety, panic, confusion, depression, and other serious mental and emotional disorders may occur. The chronic users of LSD . . . are alienated, psychotic, schizophrenic, and totally unresponsive to education about the hazards of drugs. LSD does not improve creative talents, but on the contrary impairs the expression of abilities. The drug has been found to lower intelligence, to leave disturbed personalities unimproved or more

psychotic. . . . Those misguided persons who have preached to young people that they must go out of their minds in order to understand the true meaning of life have apparently failed to recognize that without a normally functioning brain man cannot understand the true meaning of anything (Byrd, 1970, p. 154).

Thus the traditionalist's view ranged from seeing all LSD reactions as psychotomimetic to seeing psychotic episodes as an extremely common feature of the LSD trip.

A second view is that the effects of the so-called mind drugs, of which LSD is the best-known representative, are almost completely unpredictable. According to this view, the nature of the experience cannot be forecast from any currently known variables, since the same individual in the same or similar settings will have radically, even violently, different experiences— one perhaps peaceful and rewarding, and another turbulent, frightening, and even psychotomimetic. Supporters of this position point out that even veterans of hundreds of psychedelic trips report psychotic episodes, or "bummers." Several experienced clinicians write of this phenomenon:

> . . . there is no single factor that guarantees immunity from an adverse LSD reaction . . . cases in which subjects used LSD 100 times or more with no adverse reactions and then subsequently developed psychiatric symptomology [were observed]. . . . Set and setting appear to help but not to guarantee against adverse complications (Ungerleider et al., 1968, p. 1490).

A third view, closer to my own, emphasizes the overwhelming importance of extrapharmacological variables in determining rates of psychotomimetic experiences under the influence of LSD and at the same time stresses the relative rarity of such episodes in comparison with the total number of nonpsychotic and nonpanic experiences. The classic and clearly erroneous view of a psychotic episode under the influence of a drug is that it is a function of a neurochemical reaction, and little else. Howard S. Becker, a sociologist, has developed an alternate hypothesis, emphasizing the social bases of the drug-induced psychotic reaction (Becker, 1967). His thesis is that the existence of socially created and maintained interpretations of what the drug experience means have a great deal to do with whether those taking the drug "freak out" or not. When a given drug is first introduced into a culture—say, in America, marijuana in the late 1920s and 1930s, and LSD in the early 1960s—few interpretations of the drug experience exist within the drug subculture. When reactions, or "effects," occur under the drug for which there is no handy explanation or interpretation, no cultural niche so to speak, these novel reactions are labeled—even by users—with the only available definition meaningful at the time: *insanity*. Thus, if people living and interacting within a "drug-subculture-poor" social environment—a society or group with only a rudimentarily developed drug-taking community and few interpretations and explanations of the drug experience—experience unusual reactions under the influence of a drug, such as seeing God, or believing that they have two heads, or observing buildings wobble, they begin to doubt their sanity, because this is the only way to interpret these reactions. Anyone in that society or subculture who believes or perceives those things *is* called crazy. Individuals under the influence of a strange drug—loosened from their traditional moorings, heavily sensitive to and influenced by the interpretations of their behavior by their equally naive companions—come to look upon their own behavior and experiences not merely as eccentric but as an unquestionable sign of actual insanity. The message of their companions flashes back to them: *I'm crazy!*, and their conviction of their own insanity, the novelty of the sensations they are experiencing, the interpretations of their friends, their negative feelings about letting go or losing control, all conspire to push them in the direction of an actual psychotic outbreak.

Becker's thesis is that over time, drug subcultures develop interpretations of the drug experience that take it out of the realm of insanity and place it within "normal" contexts; more and more users experience having two heads, seeing God, and so on, and such sensations lose their bizarre aspect. They are recognized as simply the kinds of things that one experiences under the influence of a drug—in this case, LSD. Such reactions are given an approved and fully rationalized status. By developing an ideology that views such feelings as acceptable and even positive, by setting them within the realm of expectation, by viewing them as more or less commonplace, the subculture channels these reactions into the "normal" experience of taking LSD. Consequently, according to Becker's hypothesis, fewer people come to view themselves as going insane, and fewer actually undergo psychotic reactions. The fact that LSD is even more commonly used today than in the mid-1960s (something I shall explore shortly) and that hospitals nonetheless see and report markedly *fewer* psychotic reactions than previously lends credence to the theory. (In addition, the drug is being taken in smaller doses today than it once was.)

Nearly all users report uncomfortable and unpleasant moments during their experiences with hallucinogenic drugs; at the same time, most report being able to handle the discomfort, and some claim that even the "bad trip" can be rewarding. This is not the place to debate the virtues or pathologies of the LSD experience, and certainly no one would find a true psychotic episode valuable or fulfilling. But it is crucial to emphasize the role of society and personality in shaping the nature of the drug reality. Any experience that influences perceptions in a direction radically different from that which is considered "normal" is unsettling. Some users are able to handle the ambiguity inherent in altered perceptions; others are not. People in civilizations with a tight rein on emotions and a narrow conception of what is "real" are more likely to experience panic when traditional moorings are loosened than those in civilizations with a more flexible affect and epistemology. A large number of anthropological studies indicate that the psychedelic effects of certain drugs, particularly peyote, are fruitfully woven into the religious and tribal life of many peoples without any ensuing medical or psychiatric complications (LaBarre, 1964; Slotkin, 1956; Efron, 1967; Bergman, 1971; Schultes and Hofmann, 1979). In a preface to one of these works, an anthropologist emphasizes the juncture between psychedelic drugs and epistemology:

> Anthropology has taught us that . . . the worlds of different peoples have different shapes. The very metaphysical presuppositions differ: space does not conform to Euclidean geometry, time does not form a continuous unidirectional flow, causation does not conform to Aristotelian logic, man is not differentiated from non-man or life from death, as in our world (Goldschmidt, 1968, p. vii).

The psychedelic drug experience is more compatible with some cultural world outlooks than others. And this difference in perspective inevitably shapes and acts back upon the experience. This view suggests that panic reactions under the influence of hallucinogenic drugs could be considerably diminished with an inculcation in users of an outlook that is capable of tolerating ambiguity, paradox, ambivalence, hyperemotionalism, and mystical insight.

How frequently does the LSD psychotic episode actually take place? Ever since such episodes began to be reported in large numbers in the medical literature and the media during the early 1960s, the temporary psychosis has been viewed as almost part and parcel of taking LSD-type drugs. But the total number of bad trips requiring psychiatric or medical attention, computed as a proportion of the total number of trips taken, is actually fairly small. Joel Fort estimates that the incidence of the less serious, "short-lived complications" is about one in 1,000 trips, and that the "most serious or longer-lasting ones" constitute roughly one in 10,000 (Fort, 1969, p. 184). Other investigators maintain that the incidence of bad trips on street LSD is significantly higher than this, partly because of inadequate preparation for and supervision of the experience, and partly because of the impurities contained in black-market substances (Snyder, 1970, p. xv; Irwin, 1970, p. 31).

Now, the *seriousness* of a psychotic outbreak would appear to be sufficiently great that even a small statistical chance would not seem to be "worth it" to the prudent individual. After all, the odds of shooting oneself in Russian roulette are much less than the odds of emerging alive—but what is the point? In any case, on a sheerly statistical basis the chances that the LSD user will experience a psychotic episode requiring psychiatric or medical treatment are relatively slim. However, the consequences of a single LSD trip can last, conceivably, for good or for ill, an entire lifetime, and the affect surrounding each trip is enormous and overwhelming. At one time it was believed that studying individuals under the influence of LSD would yield insight into schizophrenia, since the two mental states were considered very similar—this is the so-called model-psychosis hypothesis. But on the whole these efforts have been abandoned as fruitless, largely because of the basically dissimilar natures of these two mental states.

An incredible amount of nonsense has been written on the effects of LSD and the LSD-type drugs by commentators on both sides of the controversy. The *significance* of psychotic episodes has been confused with their *typicality,* or frequency. For most people the importance of the former outweighs the importance of the latter—the fact that *any* number of individuals experience a psychotic episode under the influence of LSD is so significant that the drug is thereafter regarded as one that produces psychotic episodes. Such a confusion leads to hysterical statements purporting to describe what *usually* happens under the influence of LSD. One researcher comments:

> Even with a positive set to begin with, most "triers" and users go through intensely frightening and terrifying experiences under the drug. . . . The "experimentation" carried on by groups of young people who obtain their LSD supplies through illegal channels and take the drug under highly unsupervised conditions *can only lead to tragic results* [my emphasis] (Smith, 1967).

Three other observers opine that "it is almost impossible to produce anything but an extreme reaction when taking illegally prepared doses" (Jones et al., 1969, p. 57). Both of these statements are, of course, complete nonsense. The many LSD experiences described to me, and to all other investigators of the psychedelic drug scene, vary enormously—some intense (or "extreme"), some mild and pleasant, some ecstatic, and some depressing or terrifying. Most trips are all of these, at different moments. But almost no user describes his experiences in the one-sided light that these observers would have us believe. On the other hand, the psychedelicist camp resorted to similarly absurd allegations. The proclamations of Timothy Leary, which asserted that LSD was a panacea for a wide range of ills, including frigidity, homosexuality, war and violence, crime, alcoholism, and mental illness, were the mirror image of unambiguously pathological assertions and were equally fallacious.

GENETIC DAMAGE

In March 1967, the prestigious scientific journal *Science* published an article by Maimon Cohen, a physician and geneticist, and two associates, reporting that when human blood cells were placed in a culture containing LSD the cells underwent some chromosome breakage. In addition, one schizophrenic mental patient who was treated with LSD fifteen times in a therapeutic setting was found to have a higher degree of chromosome damage than was typical or normal (Cohen et al., 1967). Within twenty-four hours, the news swept the country. These "findings" from an inadequately controlled study immediately became translated into the inescapable "fact" that LSD would damage one's offspring—that uncountable generations of infants would be born deformed if one took LSD. The thalidomide disaster of the early 1960s was invoked as a parallel. Popular magazines published articles on LSD, showing photographs of distorted babies and explaining that "If you take LSD, even once, your children may be born malformed or retarded." Just below the title of one such article was this statement: "New research finds it's causing genetic damage that poses a threat of havoc now and appalling abnormalities for generations yet unborn" (Davison, 1967, pp. 19–22).

An indication of how seriously these findings were regarded is the fact that even in the decidedly prodrug and pro–"legalization of marijuana" underground newspapers, such as *The East Village Other (EVO)*, many articles appeared during the summer of 1967 affirming that genetic damage would take place in anyone who ingested LSD. One such article published in *EVO* was entitled "Acid Burned a Hole in My Genes." Drug propaganda campaigns rarely fail to mention LSD's supposed "monster-producing" properties. The National Foundation–March of Dimes distributed a leaflet containing photographs of deformed, legless, or armless children pitifully attempting to perform simple tasks such as writing or picking up toys with their "flippers," artificial arms, or toes. The text contains the warning that "there is evidence that LSD and other similar drugs may cause chromosome breakage." Although the leaflet adds the qualification that "there is no proof yet that chromosome breaks cause birth defects in humans," the impact of the photographs is so devastating that the caveat is lost completely. The leaflet ends with the injunctions "Learn the facts about birth defects" and "Speak up to help replace myths and superstition with the facts." What *are* the facts on LSD and chromosomes?

An enormous range of factors influence the outcome of chromosome and fetal studies; controls are extremely important because when one variable is changed, the results of an entire experiment may be altered completely. In any study on drug effects, it is absolutely crucial to be aware of the "identity" of the drugs involved. Much street LSD contains impurities; thus it is important to know (1) whether any given subject whose chromosomes are examined took pure (rare) or contaminated (common) LSD and (2) how many times, at what dosage levels, and how recently the subject did so. Low doses of a drug may produce no measurable effect on chromosomes, but high doses may generate a significant effect. In addition, many users of LSD ingest other drugs as well. It then becomes necessary to sort out which of the various drugs ingested has an effect, if any; in most cases, this is impossible to determine. Effects in animals do not demonstrate effects in humans, and effects in vitro (cells in a solution or culture) do not imply effects in vivo (cells taken from a living being). Furthermore, chromosome breakage does not necessarily mean fetal damage. Even the occurrence of birth defects by itself may not be significant. About 4 percent, or about 140,000, of the infants born in the United States each year have some significant defect, irrespective of the factor of LSD use (Lyons, 1983). Thus the fact that a mother who has taken LSD gives birth to a child with certain congenital aberrations is not automatic evidence of LSD's mutagenic effect; the significant question is whether the birth defect rate among all mothers who have taken LSD is any different from that among non-LSD-taking mothers—assuming that all factors are controlled, which they rarely are.

Another crucial consideration is *when* the mother took the drug. No mother should ingest any drug during the first trimester of her pregnancy—and this includes alcohol, cigarettes, and aspirin. There is a certain degree of risk in ingesting any nonfood substance while the fetus is in its most formative stages.

After making an exhaustive study of the available findings reported in nearly one hundred scientific papers, four researchers reported that subjects who ingested pure LSD showed no in vivo increases in chromosome breakage, but that subjects who had taken "illicit, alleged" LSD, purchased on the street, had about three times the proportion of breaks normally found in the absence of a drug (Dishotsky et al., 1971). This strongly suggests that the breakages reported in the Cohen study were caused not by LSD but by the impurities in street LSD, as well as the various other illicit substances that LSD users take. These researchers conclude: "We believe that pure LSD ingested in moderate dosages does not produce chromosome damage detectable by available methods." Turning to the question of mutagenesis, they summarize several studies that indicate that in moderate, or "trip," doses LSD does not appear to induce true genetic damage, and that only in massive dosages (never ingested by humans) do any mutational effects occur in animals and insects: "We believe that LSD is, in fact, a weak mutagen, effective only in extremely high doses; it is unlikely to be mutagenic in any concentration used by human subjects." With regard to LSD's possible teratogenic effects (that is, its ability to induce birth defects), the authors state: "There is no evidence of a malformed child born to a woman who ingested pure LSD; there are six cases of malformation associated with exposure to illicit LSD. . . . Given, however, the high frequency of . . . birth defects, the rare occurrence of malformed infants born to women who used illicit LSD may be coincidental." The researchers conclude that "there is no evidence that pure LSD is teratogenic in man" (Dishotsky et al., 1971, p. 439). In short, LSD does not appear to damage chromosomes. The erroneous view was disseminated and accepted because there was a strong tendency to believe that a drug with such evil effects must inevitably harm the body in a wide range of ways. If the same mistaken research findings had been published (if, indeed, they would ever have been published) concerning the effects of a relatively innocuous substance, it would not have been news, and it would not have been accepted as true by the public. Clearly, our prejudices and preconceptions shape our view of reality and truth.[1]

[1]I would like to thank Dr. Elof Axel Carlson of the Department of Biology at the State University at Stony Brook for extremely useful criticisms of an earlier draft of this section on genetic damage. Dr. Carlson warns that the shoddy research done in the original LSD-chromosome articles should not lead to mistaken conclusions:

> . . . while some science is bad science, the bad science is driven out by the good science. A false piece of work does not usually get retracted (none of the LSD "scare scientists" admitted in print that they were in error). Rather, it withers away by neglect; no one cites it any more. . . . Students reading your book should not get the impression that the scientist is an establishment type out to fool the public or that scientists contradict one another, so why listen to anything they say. It is better to point out that the LSD controversy is

PATTERNS OF USE: INCIDENCES AND FREQUENCIES

The general public typically has an imperfect notion of the extent of a phenomenon taking place in society (Davis, 1952). If you were to ask ten people on the street whether the use of LSD and the other hallucinogens has risen or declined since the late 1960s, it is likely that at least seven would answer "declined." Actually, what has declined is the media attention devoted to psychedelic drug use. Using the number of articles published in mass magazines about LSD as an index of media coverage on the topic, we can see that this is a phenomenon confined almost entirely to the 1960s. No article is listed in the *Reader's Guide to Periodical Literature,* an index of articles published in the United States in popular magazines, on LSD earlier than 1954, when a *Look* story appeared, entitled, ominously and prophetically, "Step into the World of the Insane." In August 1962 a magazine story reported that the drug had leaked from the confines of the laboratory into the streets: "Hallucinogenic Drug Now Sold on the Black Market." In the entire decade before February 1963, only eleven articles were published on LSD in all of the popular magazines in the country indexed by the *Reader's Guide*—only one per year (not counting those appearing in *Science,* which, although listed in the *Reader's Guide,* is not really a popular magazine).

However, starting with the dismissal of Timothy Leary from a faculty position at Harvard in the spring of 1963, the stories began to mount. Between March 1966 and February 1967, fifty popular articles were published on LSD. That proved to be the zenith of the subject. In March 1967, a research article appeared that purported to demonstrate that LSD damaged human chromosomes; that angle proved to be a major theme in the thirty-three popular articles published in the subsequent year (again, excluding those appearing in *Science*). But by early 1968, LSD was no longer newsworthy; only thirteen articles were published in popular magazines in 1968–1969, and fewer than half that in each succeeding year. Only one article on LSD was published in the popular literature between March 1974 and February 1975; four appeared in 1975–1976. After that, no more than a handful were listed in the *Reader's Guide* for any given year. Clearly, as news, acid had had it.

However, media coverage and actual use are not the same thing. After 1967, as the number of articles on LSD was plummeting, the use of the drug actually rose sharply. The earliest surveys on the use of LSD were conducted among college students. The Gallup Poll, in its *Gallup Opinion Index* for February 1972, reported in four different surveys on the use of "LSD or other hallucinogens" among samples of college students. In 1967, only 1 percent said that they had ever used a psychedelic, including LSD; in 1969,

---

illustrative of the way science really works at all levels—good work replacing inadequate or bad work, with *time* being the essential basis for judgment (Elof Carlson, June 28, 1971, personal communication).

4 percent; in 1970, 14 percent; and in 1971, 18 percent. It is clear, then, that, in colleges at least, the use of LSD rose dramatically from the late 1960s to the early 1970s—at precisely the same time that the number of articles devoted to this topic actually dropped sharply.

To follow the use of LSD specifically, and hallucinogens generally, over time, we rely on the same two nationally representative surveys we've been using all along (Johnston et al., 1987; NIDA, 1986). These two surveys tell more or less the same story: the use of LSD rose throughout the 1970s, peaked in about 1979, and declined during the 1980s. Tables 7.1 and 7.2 tell the story. For the 12-to-17-year-old age group, in 1979, 7 percent said that they had used at least one of the hallucinogens; in 1982, this was 5 percent; and in 1985, this had declined to 3 percent. For young adults age 18 to 25, the comparable figures were 25, 21, and 11.5 percent respectively. And for adults age 26 and older, these figures were 4.5, 6.4, and 6.2 percent (NIDA, 1986). In 1975, 11 percent of the high-school sample had used LSD at least once; by 1986, this had declined to 7 percent. In 1975, 7 percent said that they had used LSD once or more during the past year; by 1986, this had shrunk to 4.5 percent. And the proportion who had used during the previous month was 2.3 percent in 1975; in 1986, it was 1.7 percent (Johnston et al., 1987, pp. 47, 48, 49). Clearly, then, although more than 12 million Americans had tried one or more of the hallucinogens at least once, and roughly a million had taken it within the past month (and are therefore classified as "current" users), LSD and the other hallucinogens

Table 7.1   Use of Hallucinogens, 1974–1985

	1974	1979	1982	1985
Youth, Age 12–17				
Ever Used	6.0	7.1	5.2	3.2
Used in Past Month	1.3	2.2	2.2	1.1
Young Adults, Age 18–25				
Ever Used	16.6	25.1	21.1	11.5
Used in Past Month	2.5	4.4	1.7	1.6
Older Adults, Age 26+				
Ever Used	1.3	4.5	6.4	6.2
Used in Past Month	*	*	*	*

*Less than 0.5 percent.
SOURCE: Miller et al., 1983; NIDA, 1986.

Table 7.2   Use of LSD by U.S. High-School Seniors, 1975–1986

	1975	1979	1982	1986
Ever Used	11.3	9.5	9.6	7.2
Used in Past Year	7.2	6.6	6.1	4.5
Used in Past Month	2.3	2.4	2.4	1.7

SOURCE: Johnston, O'Malley, and Bachman, 1987, pp. 47, 48, 49.

are now very much on the decline. Some experts believe that this downward trend will continue; others disagree, and feel that the LSD-type drugs will make a comeback in the 1990s. Whichever occurs, it is certain that our experience with the drug in the 1960s and 1970s is not likely to be repeated.

Users of the hallucinogenic drugs hardly ever take them frequently, chronically, or compulsively. Psychedelics tend to be used episodically, on a once-in-a-while basis. "The most important fact about chronic or long-term psychedelic drug use is that there is very little of it" (Grinspoon and Bakalar, 1979, p. 176). In the NIDA study cited above (1986), "current" use (use in the past 30 days) was compared with "ever" use. Of all drugs, alcohol commanded the highest user loyalty: 70 percent of all individuals who had used alcohol at least once had also used it within the past month. Marijuana and cocaine were the two illicit drugs that tended to be "stuck with" the most: roughly a quarter of all at-least-one-time users were still using them. In contrast, just over 7 percent of all "ever" hallucinogen users had used in the past month, the lowest proportion for any drug or drug type tabulated. LSD and the other hallucinogens are not even remotely addicting in the physical sense, nor do they produce psychological dependence. Judging by their behavior, laboratory animals dislike being high on LSD; they avoid taking it if they can. The drug thus does not have the "immediate sensual appeal" of cocaine and the amphetamines. Among humans, LSD is simply not a drug of frequent use, no matter what sort of myth may be used to explain its use. In fact, the concept of psychological dependence has less relevance to a discussion of the hallucinogens than it does for that of any other drug or drug type. It is practically impossible to have a psychedelic drug "habit." And the users of LSD seem to have learned from the experiences of earlier users; today, LSD is taken in much smaller doses than was once true—80 micrograms versus 200, 250, or 300 microgram doses.

There are at least two reasons why the hallucinogens almost never produce a dependency in users. First, the body builds up a tolerance or resistance to hallucinogens extremely rapidly—faster than for any other drug or drug type. Unlike all of the other drugs under consideration, LSD does not allow one to be high during all of one's waking hours, day after day, for a long period of time. And cross-tolerance sets in for the various psychedelics, so getting high on one will diminish one's ability to get high on another.

Second, the LSD experience requires a monumental effort. To go through eight hours of an LSD high—sensory bombardment, psychic turmoil, emotional insecurity, alternations of despair and bliss, one exploding insight upon the heels of another, images hurtling through the mind as fast as the spinning fruit of a slot machine—is draining and exhausting in the extreme. Most experienced marijuana users claim to be able to "get straight" during the marijuana high in the event of an emergency. They say that they would be able to go to work or to classes stoned without being detected, and to function in a reasonable manner. Perhaps this is possible; it depends on the individual. But almost no one claims to be able to do this with LSD. Users report that it is impossible to function normally, to "come down" at will. "You really are in another world," explained one heavy marijuana smoker of the psychedelic experience. In addition, more than any other drug used on the street, LSD has extremely *inconstant* effects; the experience varies markedly from trip to trip. One trip might be ecstatic; another might be horrifying; a third might be relatively uneventful. Most drugs are taken for some aspect of the intoxication, to achieve a certain kind of high. A drug as unreliable as LSD would not be used on a day-to-day basis by someone seeking a specific drug experience.

EPILOGUE

Have we closed the book on the psychedelics?

Most of the hallucinogenic drugs that are used on the street—including LSD, mescaline, peyote, psilocybin (the chemical, not the mushroom), DMT, and DET—are classified under the federal statutes as Schedule I drugs—that is, substances with high abuse potential and no medical utility. (So are marijuana and heroin—but not alcohol, and not tobacco!) It is extremely difficult—practically impossible—to do medical or psychological research on Schedule I drugs because they are extremely difficult to obtain legally, and it is bureaucratically cumbersome to secure official permission to administer them. In effect, Schedule I is a death sentence for scientific research on a given drug.

A number of experts regard LSD's legal classification as a serious scientific mistake. They argue that we barely began to understand the action of hallucinogenic drugs when the scientific book was slammed shut on the subject. The research potential of the hallucinogens, they say, is great, and their therapeutic potential is untapped. Psychedelic drugs do not pose a major threat or drug problem to society. "No one wants to see a revival of LSD use on the scale and in the style of the 1960s [and 1970s], and nothing is less likely . . . because people have learned better how and when to use and avoid it, and because it does not have the kind of attraction that makes people continue to use a drug against their better judgment" (Grinspoon and Bakalar, 1979, p. 292). Hysteria and sensationalism, not a rational consideration of their hazards and benefits, led to their present legal classification. The problem now is "not how to get them off the streets, which is probably impossible anyway, but how to get them back into hospitals, laboratories, and other supervised settings" (Grinspoon and Bakalar, 1979, p. 292). Say two experts, finding a sane and sensible way to use the psychedelic drugs, as they are used in many tribal societies, "is a test for humanity. We are facing that test now. The genie is out of the bottle, and we neither need nor are able to force it back in, so we must use our resources of intelligence, imagination, and moral discernment to find ways of making it serve us" (Grinspoon and Bakalar, 1979, p. 308).

ECSTASY: THE PSYCHEDELIC DRUG OF THE 1990S?

"Better living through chemistry," was a slogan that flourished during the psychedelic 1960s; it implied that synthetic and semisynthetic drugs such as LSD should be developed and used for their effects, making the world a more pleasant place in which to live. This motto was meant to be amusing, but no one could have foreseen the special significance it took on in the 1970s and 1980s, when a number of drug derivatives or analogues were developed from a few basic chemical formulas. These substances are called *designer drugs.* A chemist "fiddles" with the structure of a given chemical, changing a molecule or two and thereby producing a totally new drug—one that is both legal and psychoactive. (A compound is legal until declared otherwise.) It may be years from the time a drug is synthesized or derived, is marketed and hits the streets, is widely used, attracts police notice, is confiscated, and is then analyzed and tested by police chemists, to the time it is proposed as a controlled substance. Meanwhile, the enterprising chemists who "designed" the drug may have earned a great deal of money on a minuscule investment. The Drug Enforcement Agency (DEA) claims that by the mid-1980s, the designer-drug business became a billion-dollar-a-year industry in the United States (Gallagher, 1986a).

One of the remarkable things about the process of developing analogues is that the new substances often have very different effects from their parent drug. Consider MDMA, called "ecstasy" on the street (and "Adam" by some), is a synthetic derivative of amphetamine. Theoretically, ecstasy should be a stimulant—and it does have some effects similar to those of amphetamines—but many of its effects resemble those of the psychedelics. Actually, it was derived early in this century and patented by Merck as a possible appetite suppressant. It lay on a shelf for decades. Then the army tested it in 1953; in large doses, it turns out, MDMA kills animals. Quietly, psychiatrists began using it on their patients in the 1970s as an aid to therapy; according to one estimate, some 10,000 doses were administered in 1976. (As a parallel, LSD also began to be used in a psychiatric setting.) In about 1979, it began to be used recreationally on the street. By the mid-1980s, according to one estimate, some 30,000 doses were being taken per month (Klein, 1985, p. 42). By then, it had attracted the attention of law-enforcement authorities. In 1985, the Drug Enforcement Administration classified it as a Schedule I drug—high abuse potential, no medical utility. Anyone selling the drug could face a fifteen-year prison sentence. Ecstasy's classification is currently under appeal.

"Bill" is 50, a respected medical administrator. He is intelligent, soft-spoken, and he dresses conservatively. He says he's never used cocaine or LSD, and has experimented with marijuana only "once or twice." A friend, a writer, a man whom Bill respects "enormously," said "he had something I might like to try, a new drug. . . . He said it was interesting and safe. . . . He said I wouldn't hallucinate or lose track of reality." The drug was ecstasy; Bill tried it. And? "Well, this is going to sound ridiculous. What happened is, the drug takes away all your neuroses. It takes away the fear response. There is an overwhelming feeling of peace. . . . You feel open, clear, loving. I can't imagine being angry under its influence, or feeling selfish or mean or even defensive." At the same time, Bill adds, "You don't lose touch with the world. You could call your mother, and she'd never know." It is, he says, "the opposite of paranoia" (Klein, 1985, p. 38).

Some therapists agree with Bill's assessment. They claim that their patients open up under the influence of the drug, become less fearful and less defensive. There is a "sensory and verbal disinhibition," a "state of mutual trust and confidence between the subject and the therapist." The drug, they claim, generates a feeling that says, "Anything harmful will pass right through me" (Klein, 1985, p. 41). It allows patients to dredge up material from their past that they have been repressing for years, even in psychiatric treatment. Says psychiatrist Lester Grinspoon, "It helps people get in touch with feelings that are ordinarily not available to them. . . . It appears to help people [recall] things from their past. . . . If this is an accurate picture, you might just be able to break up some logjams in therapy with it" (Adler et al., 1985). Says Dr. Rick Ingrasci, a therapist who has treated some 200 patients with the drug, ecstasy "is a powerful tool—not an answer but a *catalyst.* . . . It enables people to look at the past without fear. . . . It can speed up the therapeutic process enormously. It facilitates healing" (Klein, 1985, p. 39). At the same time, these doctors claim, the drug does not cause disorientation or hallucinations, and it is extremely safe. Norman Zinberg, a professor of psychiatry at the Harvard Medical School and colleague of Grinspoon's, says that he's never seen a bad reaction to MDMA; "it has quite a low potential for abuse," he adds (Adler et al., 1985).

Some other therapists are skeptical of these assertions. For example, Dr. Ronald Siegel, a well-known drug researcher at UCLA, says he was once "burned" by thinking that cocaine isn't as harmful as we now realize it is. In the 1970s, cocaine's effects were relatively mild, partly because it was snorted in small doses, in powdered form. Now that it is smoked and injected, we realize that it has a massive potential for abuse. "The point is, you can't be cavalier about these things. There are doctors who swear by ecstasy, but they are only offering anecdotal evidence. . . . I think it's downright irresponsible to go around touting this drug without adequate research." When the dose is low, in a therapeutic setting, its effects often are benign. On the street, it is often a completely different matter. Siegel says that researchers are now seeing "hallucinations, disorientation, psychotic episodes. . . . We've had people locked in fetal positions for as long as seventy-two hours. We had a psychotherapist who took it, disappeared, and turned up a week later directing traffic" (Klein, 1985, p. 42).

Dr. Jeffrey Rosecan, director of the Cocaine Abuse Treatment and Research Program at Columbia Presbyterian Medical Center, agrees. Speaking of ecstasy, Rosecan says, "This could be potentially as devastating as cocaine or worse—it's longer-lasting, it's cheaper, and it's being hyped in the media as *the* new drug." Rosecan has treated two college students who have had serious and prolonged psychotic reactions to MDMA. One, having become convinced that his friends were going to kill him, locked himself in his dorm room for two weeks. The other "was hallucinating and was convinced that people were trying to kill him. He spent four weeks in the hospital, and never really recovered. He's now in a group home in Pennsylvania." While there were "mitigating circumstances" in both cases—one student had a history of nervous breakdowns, and the other was experiencing an acute family crisis—nonetheless, they cause Rosecan to be cautious about the drug's effects (Klein, 1985, p. 42). Said Siegel, "When doses are pushed, we get madness, not ecstasy" (Roberts, 1986, p. 14).

In addition, in a series of experiments on rats and guinea pigs by psychopharmacologists Lewis Seiden and Charles Schuster, it was discovered that the drug may cause long-term, possibly irreversible, damage to the brain. A neurotransmitter, serotonin, which helps to send signals to various organs of the body and regulates sleep, sex, aggression, and mood, was found to be at "alarmingly low levels." The brain, in fact, had been depleted of its supply of serotonin, and, eight weeks after the conclusion of the experiment, the researchers saw no indication of its return. Based on their animal experiments, Seiden and Schuster conclude that doses harmful to the brain are only two to three times those taken on the street (Roberts, 1986, p. 14).

Psychiatrist Lester Grinspoon (private communication) downplays the "bad trips," "flashbacks", and other negative psychological effects supposedly caused by ecstasy. However, he does insist that there is one potentially dangerous physical effect of the drug: it can cause arrhythmia of the heart. In individuals with Wolf-Parkinson-White syndrome—a fairly rare disorder whose presence shows up only on an EKG—this effect could be lethal. All individuals should be screened for the syndrome, Grinspoon says, and at-risk individuals should not take ecstasy. For most people, he insists, the drug is quite safe if taken under proper supervision.

Still, the debate continues. The supporters of ecstasy argue that the drug is far safer than those which have been given a less restrictive federal schedule, and the potential benefits of MDMA are overwhelming. Says Dr. Rick Ingrasci, "The real question . . . is how we use drugs in this society. . . . A tacit decision has been made that it's okay to use drugs to ease pain. It's okay to take aspirin or Valium, both of which may well be more dangerous than MDMA. But it's not okay to use drugs to gain insight. My hope is that MDMA will force us to re-evaluate our attitude about that" (Klein, 1985, p. 43).

ACCOUNT: THE ACID TRIP

At the time of this interview, the respondent was a 20-year-old college student.

Q: You said you took a hit of acid that was much stronger than anything you've ever taken before. And you said you had some experiences which seemed quite different from the general-run-of-the-mill acid experiences that most people have. How did this time differ?

A: Let me tell you first about the acid itself. The acid we took was in the form of a four-sided pyramid, about the size of a postage stamp, and it's raised in the center. It's hard, like a plastic or glass-like substance. And it's clear, like a crystal. It's green. It's like a flat piece of paper, with this raised pyramid in the center. It's three-dimensional, but there's no *base* to it. It's hollow inside. You could turn it upside down and fill it with a drop of water. And the whole thing *was* the acid, the whole piece, the whole material was acid. It was almost like a piece of glass. And we tried to cut it—we wanted to split it—and it just *shattered* into little pieces. We had to collect the pieces and swallow them.

Q: Tell me about the experience.

A: I'm really serious about this. I'm amazed that it happened. I've taken acid eight times before. I figure it would be like what a typical acid trip was. In the past, my acid experience has been a feeling of disorientation, not caring about certain things, timelessness. This time, for the first two hours, it was pretty much the same. It was a lot of intense colors. A spun-glass effect. Just beautiful. Incredible. Up until this time, I knew it was the acid that was having this effect on me. After two hours, the trip went into a new phase. It was two hours of a normal acid trip, a good one. Then, all of a sudden, everything changed. I was with my friend Jason in my dorm room, just the two of us. We started experiencing something. And he said to me, "Rob, everything's changing—this is not acid any more. I feel different. I can't control what I'm saying, and the things I say are not me." And then he said, "They want me." He told me, "Look out the window."

Q: Who's "they"?

A: At first, I didn't know what he was talking about. But what it comes down to is "they" were space men, extraterrestrial life. I walked to the next room and I looked out of the window. It sounds bizarre—but I saw space ships out the window. I said, "Oh, God, I don't believe it."

Q: Did Jason mention anything about space ships?

A: No. He just said "they." And he said, "They' *want* me, they really want me." And so there they were, eight space ships, hovering. They were in formation. I was really freaked. I walked back into the next room and I said, "Jason, I can't believe what I saw," and he said, "They're there—I *told* you they're there." I said, *"What are they?"* And Jason said, "That's *them.* They want me to go with them." And I said, "Well, you can't go." I mean, I seriously *believed* it. "What do they want to *do* with us?" I asked him. And he said, "They just want me. I don't know what they want with me, but I know that they want me, and you're here, and so I guess they'll take you, too. But don't worry—they won't hurt us." And I was just flipping out.

Q: He saw the same thing as you did? Did he describe what he saw to you?

A: Yes. Exactly the same thing. Same number of ships. Everything. I sat in the room and I said, "Let's sit down and smoke a joint and get our wits together. It's not out there, there's nothing there." And then all of a sudden, Jason went into a kind of trance. And I looked outside, and the ships were coming closer. They were, like, really *right* outside the window. And I was *petrified* of this unknown thing, which I definitely believed was out there. I sat in the chair and I smoked joints and cigarettes, wondering what I was gonna do. And I was hoping that they'll just go away. But I knew that they weren't. And then, all of a sudden, there was this intensely loud *sound*. It was the wind *roaring* through. And finally, Jason snaps out of his trance and says, "We gotta go, we gotta go with them, because you can see that they *want* us." I walked into the next room, and there was this *light* on the ceiling. It was shaped like a crown. I turned out the light in the room, and it was still there. I walked back into the other room, and I said to Jason, "Go and look in the next room, I see something on the ceiling; don't tell me what you see, just go in there and look at it, and come back and write it down on a piece of paper, and tell me if you're seeing the same thing as I'm seeing." And he walked in there and he walked out and he writes down on a piece of paper exactly the same thing that I saw. That freaked me out. I was convinced that very strange things were happening. Oh, yeah, another thing: at one point, I picked up the phone and it was dead, the line was dead.

Q: Were the ships gone by now?

A: No, the space ships were still out there, they're hanging in there, and they were *coming in*—into the room. You could feel this energy, this *presence* coming into the room.

Q: Did you see the movie *Close Encounters of the Third Kind?* Because there's a lot of parallels between your experience and the movie.

A: No, I didn't see it. Somebody I told this experience to asked me the same thing. I'd feel pretty foolish if I had seen it and then I came in here and told you about this stuff. I'm dying to see it. Anyway, this presence is coming into the room, I mean, I could really feel it, it was so intense. And Jason said, "Look at the ceiling, Rob." I looked up and all of a sudden, on the ceiling, there's this *mosaic.* Tiles and lines going through them. Brownish and black colors. And Jason says, "It's *them*—it's a *face.*" And there was this intense energy in the room. And I'm getting scared. And he says, "Calm down, they're not going to hurt us." Finally, I got to the point where I *knew* we had to go, there's no choice, they really want us to go with them. And I told Jason, "I don't want to be left alone." I said, "I know we have to go out there." My dorm room is on the third floor; Jason was just gonna walk right out the window. I stopped him, and he says, "Don't worry, Rob, I'll be all right." I told him, "I'll go with you." I was petrified, but I went anyway. I left this note to my girlfriend. I put it on the desk. I grabbed some stuff—a sweater, a brush, some pot, my glasses, a few other things—and I threw it in a duffel bag, I threw on my coat and we walked outside. There was *nobody* else around. We felt *completely* alone, like the rest of the world didn't exist. No cars, nothing. And there, in the sky, there must have been *thirty* of the ships. No creatures, just ships, hovering. It seemed like they were really far away and they were coming closer and closer, and getting bigger and bigger. I looked at Jason, and I said, "This is incredible—I can't take it, I can't deal with it, I'm really getting scared." And he said, "OK, go inside; if they want us, they're going to come after us." He said that he was getting scared at this point, too. So we went back inside. We sat down. And they were still there. If they're gonna get us, they can get us. And then it started to fade. And the sun started to come up. And all this incredible energy just *left.* And then it was just gone. And Jason and I stared at one another for a half hour, just freaking out a little bit. Everything became very calm with the sun up. And it was over. We just looked at each other. Is anybody ever gonna believe this? Did it really happen? And we started questioning each other—did you see this, did you see that?—and it all corresponded. We just took the day off, we walked to the beach, constantly talking about this experience. It was just so incredibly real. And I believe it, there's no doubt in my mind that they were there.

Q: A lot of people I've talked to about taking acid describe little episodes. They say, this happened, that happened; their minds get very easily changed from one thing to another. They see something and then look away, and look back, and it's gone. It sounds like your images all maintained themselves. Your experience wasn't just a series of discrete episodes. It had a beginning, a middle, and an end. It sounds like you kept the same visions throughout, that you weren't distracted from them.

A: Exactly. That's why it was so weird. It wasn't like changing things. It was as if the acid trip disappeared and it was a different energy thing. We were just taken over by what was out there.

Q: Also, it's amazing that, as you've described it, there didn't seem to be a great deal of suggestion. Often, in what somebody sees, there'll be some kind of suggestion, some kind of hint from the other person, and that'll build on a person's imagination. Whereas it doesn't sound like you were really giving any suggestions to one another.

A: We both were trying so hard to be very rational. We tried to make sense or reason out of this. We were trying to figure out if we were creating something. We were analyzing it, what was going on, what we were doing. We were being skeptical about the experience. That's why it was so freaky—we couldn't rationalize it away. It still gives me a weird feeling, because I still can't make any sense out of it. I just couldn't believe what was out there—but I couldn't deny it, even though I was trying to.

Q: I've never heard anything quite like that.

A: We tried to get hold of that same acid again. But we couldn't get it. Jason's still looking for it. He's totally convinced that that's not acid. He's done a *lot* of acid, he's probably done, like 200 trips, easily.

Q: What does he think it was?

A: He thinks it was . . . *planted* there.

Q: By the creatures?

A: By the creatures. He's convinced that they want him. It sounds bizarre.

Q: It's too much. Too much. It's freaky. [From the author's files.]

CHAPTER 8

Stimulants

Stimulants speed up signals passing through the nervous system; they activate organs and functions of the body, heighten arousal, increase overall behavioral activity, and suppress fatigue. In low doses, stimulants can heighten the body's sensitivity and improve mental and physical performance. At high doses, however, many of these functions seem to go haywire. Behavior becomes unfocused, supersensitivity translates easily into paranoia, and mental and intellectual performance become uncontrollable, ineffective, often compulsively repetitive.

The immediate subjective effect of the stimulants is euphoria and a sense of confidence and well-being. As I pointed out in Chapter 2, of all drugs or drug types, cocaine and the amphetamines are the two with the greatest *immediate sensual appeal* (Lasagna et al., 1955; Grinspoon and Bakalar, 1976, pp. 191–194)—that is, experimental subjects, without knowing what drug they have taken, enjoy their effects most and would rather take them again than any other drug. In experiments, rats, mice, and monkeys will self-administer cocaine in preference to food, and will even starve to death self-administering cocaine. If experimental animals receive cocaine as a result of engaging in a certain activity, and the researchers then discontinue administering the drug, these animals will go on engaging in that activity—thousands of times in an hour—at a higher rate than for any other drug type (Grinspoon and Bakalar, 1976, p. 193). In psychological terms, then, cocaine and the amphetamines are powerfully *reinforcing.* People (and animals) enjoy their effects. It should come as no surprise that they are widely used for recreational purposes—to get high.

AMPHETAMINE

The amphetamine drugs include Benzedrine, Dexedrine, Methedrine, Desoxyn, Biphetamine, and Dexamyl. They go by the street names of "speed," "ups," "crank," "splash," "pep pills," "meth," and "A." The first of the amphetamines (Benzedrine) was discovered in 1887, but it was not marketed as a prescription drug until the 1930s. Initially, Benzedrine was used as an inhaler for nasal congestion. Later, the amphetamines were used to treat narcolepsy (compulsive and involuntary sleep), depression, alcoholism, schizophrenia, obesity, hyperkenesis (it seems to have the paradoxical effect of calming down hyperactive children), Parkinson's disease, and fatigue. It became known fairly quickly that amphetamine drugs have a number of side effects—including euphoria—that make them attractive for recreational use. Throughout the 1940s and 1950s, prescription amphetamines were increasingly diverted into illegal channels, and by the 1960s, amphetamine had become one of the half-dozen most popular street drugs. In addition, amphetamines were used for instrumental purposes—to combat fatigue and drowsiness.

Amphetamines are used instrumentally and quasitherapeutically in tablet or capsule form; between 2.5 and 10 milligrams would constitute a typical dose. In such low dosages the typical bodily and mental effects of the amphetamines are: (1) a heightened competence in motor skills and mental acuity (measured IQ increases on the average by eight points under the influence of amphetamine in small doses); (2) an increased alertness, a feeling of arousal or wakefulness, a diminution of fatigue and drowsiness; (3) a feeling of increased energy; (4) a stimulation of the need for motor activity, particularly walking about and talking; (5) a feeling of euphoria, an inhibition of depression; (6) increased heartbeat; (7) an inhibition of appetite; (8) constriction of the blood vessels; (9) dryness of the mouth; (10) a feeling of confidence and even grandeur (Weiner, 1985, pp. 166–169).

Among most groups in the population, between the 1960s and the early 1980s, amphetamines remained the second most popular illicit drug or drug type in the United States. (Marijuana was, of course, the first, and remains so to this day. Today, for most groups, cocaine occupies the number two position.) In the past, amphetamines were used illegally mainly in three modes, circles, or scenes of use. Of these, only two remain, and two have been significantly scaled back.

The first type of illegal amphetamine use is instrumental. Amphetamines were immensely popular in the 1960s and 1970s as prescription "diet pills" (Grinspoon and Hedblom, 1975, pp. 207–217). When physicians cut off a patient's supply as a result of overuse, he or she readily found another supply illegally, on the street. The drug does inhibit the appetite, but any weight loss is temporary; most doctors today agree that taking amphetamine is not only ineffective but dangerous as well. Nowadays, hardly any physicians prescribe amphetamine for weight loss, and illicit use for this purpose seems to be less frequent as well. In addition, in past decades, amphetamines were used without a prescription by a large number of individuals who wished to allay drowsiness—long-distance truck drivers who had no time to rest or sleep, students cramming for an exam, executives, housewives, athletes, and so on. The instrumental use of the amphetamines for this reason still takes place, but controls on these drugs have diminished its frequency and extent. A typical dosage for someone using amphetamine instrumentally would be 2.5 to 10 milligrams.

The second type of illicit amphetamine use, which has existed for decades, is practiced by *recreational multiple drug users,* who take speed in combination with other drugs, especially alcohol, marijuana, and barbiturates or Quaalude. A recreational user might take two to four 10-milligram tablets or capsules at a time. This type of amphetamine use, like instrumental use, still exists, but is less common than it used to be.

The third category of illegal amphetamine use is the high-dose intravenous use of Methedrine, a sister drug of the amphetamines. (Methedrine is no longer legally manufactured in the United States.) This pattern of use sprang up and died out in the late 1960s, and will be discussed shortly.

During the 1980s, the illicit use of the amphetamines has declined significantly. In 1982, 20 percent of high-school seniors had used amphetamine within the past year; by 1986, this figure had declined to 13 percent. Among college students, the proportion dropped from 21 to 10 percent (Johnston et al., 1987, p. 17). Table 8.1 shows the trend in stimulant (mainly amphetamine) use between 1975 and 1986 for high-school seniors for three categories of use.

In the 1985 national survey, just under one American age 12 and older in ten (9 percent) said that they had taken amphetamine outside of a medical context at least once in their life—a total of 17.6 million individuals; 1 percent, or 2.7 million people, had used it within the previous month (NIDA, 1986). The lifetime-prevalence figure represented a slight rise from 1982, when 8 percent, or 14.6 million individuals, had used amphetamine; the thirty-day-prevalence figure, however, represented a slight decline from 1982, when just under 2 percent, or 2.8 million people, had taken the drug in the past month (Miller et al., 1983, pp. 4, 16–24).

Even with the recent dip in amphetamine use, it remains a frequently used drug. Among high school seniors, it is still the number-two illicit drug (after marijuana) in lifetime prevalence and annual prevalence, and it ranks third (after marijuana and cocaine) in thirty-day prevalence. In the national survey, only marijuana (30 percent in lifetime prevalence, 10 percent in monthly prevalence) and cocaine (12 percent and 3 percent respectively) ranked higher in illicit use (NIDA, 1986). Even today, although it attracts practically no publicity at all, and although it is used somewhat less often than in the past, amphetamine remains an extremely popular street drug. Of course, a substantial proportion of this use is made up of illicit instrumental use—for staying up all night to study for exams, driving cross-country, keeping alert on the job, performing well on the athletic field, and so on—and not recreational use.

Table 8.1   Stimulant Use by High-School Seniors, 1975–1986

	1975	1979	1982	1986
LIFETIME PREVALENCE	22	24	36	23
ANNUAL PREVALENCE	16	18	20	13
30-DAY PREVALENCE	9	10	11	6

Note: Figures for 1975 and 1979 are unadjusted; for 1982 and 1986, they are adjusted.
SOURCE: Johnston et al., 1987, pp. 47, 48, 49.

It should be pointed out that much of what passes for illicit amphetamine use in the United States is bogus. That is, tablets and capsules containing mild stimulants, such as caffeine, are manufactured to look exactly like amphetamines and sold as "energy" tabs and caps. They are called "looka-like" pills, and many young and naive users will take them, thinking they will experience the amphetamine high. After 1982, the researchers who con-ducted the high-school survey (Johnston et al., 1986, 1987) "adjusted" their statistics on amphetamine use to take account of the "lookalike" phe-nomenon. It is possible that the figures on amphetamine use in the national drug survey (NIDA, 1986) should also be scaled down because of overstat-ing due to the use of bogus sustances.

As we saw in Chapter 4, the prescription use of the amphetamines has literally dropped off the charts. Between 1971 and 1986, the number of prescriptions written for the amphetamines *declined by 90 percent*: Only 10 percent of the number of prescriptions written fifteen years ago are being written nowadays. For some of the amphetamines (methamphetamine, or Methedrine, and Benzedrine), no prescriptions are being written today at all. Currently, the number of medical and psychiatric ailments for which the amphetamines are being used is extremely limited.

As I noted above, a sizable "speed scene" developed and flourished on the street in the late 1960s. It consisted of tens of thousands of young men and women who took amphetamines or Methedrine in huge doses day in and day out. Use peaked in about 1967, and declined sharply after that. Many "speed freaks" (as compulsive, high-dose users of amphetamine were called) at the time became heroin addicts because they alternated the use of amphetamine, a stimulant, with heroin, a depressant, so that they could "come down." They used more and more heroin and less and less ampheta-mine, and eventually heroin took over completely. Incredible as it may seem, considering the way that amphetamine was used by the speed freaks, heroin was a safer and easier drug to take, and it had less of an impact on their lives.

Although the street "speed scene" did not last a very long time, it had a tremendous impact on the participants' lives. What was it like? The "speed freak" of the late 1960s took amphetamine or Methedrine to get high. More specifically, amphetamine was injected intravenously (IV) to achieve a "flash" or "rush" whose sensation was likened to an orgasm—a "full-body orgasm." Extremely large quantities of the drug were taken in this manner. While 5 or 10 milligrams of Dexedrine, Desoxyn, or Dexamyl taken orally, via tablet or capsule, is a typical therapeutic or instrumental dose, the speed freak may inject half a gram or a full gram (500 or 1,000 milligrams!) in one IV dose. Such massive doses of speed would cause unconsciousness or even death in a nonhabituated individual, but a pleasurable rush in the ex-perienced user. Since amphetamine inhibits sleep, IV use will cause long periods of wakefulness, often two to five days at a stretch (called a "run"), when the drug is injected into the user's system every four to eight hours.

This would be followed by long periods of sleep ("crashing"), often lasting up to twenty-four hours.

Such a pattern of heavy, compulsive amphetamine abuse inevitably had a dramatic impact on the user's life and body. Taking huge quantities of a strong stimulant, combined with chronic sleeplessness, produced a state of hyperactivity and hyperexcitement. Researchers believe that the "amphetamine psychosis" is an *inevitable* accompaniment of high-dose IV amphetamine abuse; its features include paranoia, a tendency toward violence, a schizophrenialike psychosis, hallucinations, delusions, and wild mood swings. One medical observer has noted that "anyone given a large enough dose [of amphetamine] for a long enough period of time will become psychotic" (Kramer, 1969, p. 10).

Another feature of heavy amphetamine use was the development of certain behavioral fixations, which are repeated over and over again, such as picking at bits of dust in a rug or spending a whole night counting the cornflakes in a cereal box. (This repetitive activity is called "punding," and can be induced in laboratory animals.) One speed freak I interviewed told me of a fellow user who had spent two years engaged in covering an entire wall with heads of George Washington, carefully cut out from canceled postage stamps; supposedly, he had pasted 60,000 of these figures on the wall. In addition, some chronic, compulsive users feel the sensation of bugs crawling under the skin.

Is amphetamine addicting? Specifically, does taking amphetamine in high doses, intravenously, in the manner of the speed freak of the 1960s, build a physical dependence? Discontinuing the use of amphetamine after taking it in quantity over a period of time does produce withdrawal symptoms, but they do not closely resemble those associated with withdrawal from heroin or the barbiturates. The amphetamine withdrawal consists of severe depression—often to the point of being obsessed with suicide—as well as anxiety, fatigue, lethargy, lassitude, sleeplessness, nightmares, irritability, fear, terror, constipation, and muscular aches and pains (Grinspoon and Hedblom, 1975, pp. 153–160; Ray and Ksir, 1987, pp. 109–110). A 19-year-old speed freak I interviewed at the height of the street speed epidemic describes his experience with withdrawal as follows:

> Now for the comedown. The amphetamine starts to go away. Wears off. You're still awake. And you can't get to sleep. You start to come down. And it's the worst feeling in the world. It's not as physical as heroin withdrawal. . . . It's a mental withdrawal, when all these illusions you've been having high come crashing down. It's like a celebration of disillusionment. All of a sudden, nothing in the world is right, nothing—absolutely nothing. Usually you just sit there with all your nerves burnt out, with your stomach shrunk, with your lips and mouth too dry to be comfortable so that you're always chewing, your eyeballs twitch, you're pretty nervous, but at the same time, you're too depressed and too nervous to do *anything,* you just sit there feeling miserable. It's the kind of thing where you wanna cry, but you usually can't cry . . . and so you just have to sit around and be the dregs. From people who have seen others when they're coming down, the

normal reaction is that they look like they're dead, 'cause that's what you look like. Your extremities are deprived of blood. Your nose is freezing cold, your cock shrivels up. . . . You're constantly chewing, but you can't swallow very well. And because you haven't been eating or sleeping, everything is worse. Your skin is all spiny and prickly, nervous, hot and cold at the same time, cold sweating, things like that, but they're all from the nervous system, so they're, like, half mental and half physical. You feel as if Genghis Khan had you chained to a pole for twelve hours (Goode, 1984, p. 183).

If addiction is defined by the "classic" abstinence syndrome described in Chapter 3, then amphetamine is not addicting. On the other hand, the withdrawal symptoms that are produced by amphetamine are serious, and many of them occur reliably. It is possible that what we call addiction is characteristic only of the depressants, and that other drugs produce a somewhat different set of withdrawal symptoms (Grinspoon and Hedblom, 1975, p. 153). Thus the question of which drugs are addicting in the physical sense seems partly a semantic question. Moreover, amphetamine, especially if taken IV in large doses, is strongly reinforcing, and thus causes a psychic or psychological dependence that is, in fact, nearly as great as cocaine's in strength. Consequently, the question of whether or not amphetamine is literally physically addicting seems irrelevant, since heavy, chronic users of amphetamine display a pattern of behavioral dependence that seems to be identical to those displayed by individuals who are physically dependent on drugs such as heroin or barbiturates; clearly, it makes little difference as to whether users are technically physically addicted or not.

The street speed scene is interesting today mainly for historical reasons. After about 1967, physicians began curtailing their prescriptions for Methedrine; fewer than one-third as many prescriptions for this drug were written in 1971 as in 1966. In the 1970s, Methedrine was outlawed as a prescription drug altogether, and classified as a Schedule I substance. Of course, it is still manufactured in clandestine laboratories, both in the United States and abroad, but the total volume of its use is a fraction of what it was in the late 1960s. Today, drug users take amphetamines more sporadically, less compulsively, in smaller doses than the 1960s speed freak—and almost never intravenously. Contemporary drug users take the amphetamines simply as one item on a total menu of multiple drug use—as just another of many drugs to get high on. In many respects, and for most groups in the population, cocaine has supplanted amphetamine as the number-two illicit drug in the country.

COCAINE

Cocaine gives an icy-cold high that freezes your heart and makes you believe that you are all-powerful, invincible, and righteously correct in all of your appetites and impulses. It is the most self-deceiving of drugs, and the most insidious, quietly turning every user into a Mr. Hyde. If grass is the drug of peace, cocaine is the drug of war. [Bogdanovich, 1985, p. 143]

Of all drugs, the effects of cocaine are most similar to those of amphetamine. Users describe cocaine's effects as more transient; they typically last no more than a half-hour, while amphetamine's effects last for several hours. Cocaine is also said to be more of a "head" drug and less of a "body" drug than amphetamine; its effects are more subtle; one has to learn to recognize and enjoy its effects. And, as we'll see shortly, while the recreational use of amphetamine is fairly stable, the use of cocaine is growing explosively.

The use of cocaine dates back more than 2,000 years. The coca (*not* cocoa) plant grows in the Andes Mountains in South America, and its leaves contain roughly 1 percent cocaine. The Indians living in the region chew these leaves to offset fatigue and hunger, and can work for long hours without stopping as a result of the drug's effects. The ancient Incan civilization regarded the coca plant as divine; one of the gods they worshiped was "Mama Coca" (Antonil, 1978). The Spanish invaders regarded coca's worship and even its use as an abomination, and tried to stamp out both. Coca leaves made their way to Europe, and scientists and physicians studied their effects. Cocaine was isolated from coca leaves about 1860. (The exact date, and the scientist who first did it, are in dispute.) Cocaine was hailed as a wonder drug by much of the medical profession, including Sigmund Freud (Byck, 1974), until its darker side became known.

Cocaine, in the form of coca leaves, was a major ingredient in many popular beverages sold in the late nineteenth and early twentieth centuries. Mariani's Coca Wine was one of the most popular of these; thirteen volumes were published that consisted of testimonials by prominent users (including popes, kings, and presidents) singing the praises of the concoction (Andrews and Solomon, 1975, pp. 243–246). Coca-Cola, too, contained coca leaves until 1903, when they were deleted because of pressure applied "by Southerners who feared blacks' getting cocaine in any form" (Ashley, 1975, p. 46).[1]

A major reason for cocaine's legal downfall, according to some observers, was racism. Although there is no reliable information documenting the fact that Blacks were more likely to use cocaine than whites, it was feared by some whites that this was so—and that Blacks were especially dangerous and violent under the influence. That fact that this myth was believed by the dominant white majority brought the drug under state and federal control. Numerous articles were written just after the turn of the century arguing that cocaine stimulated violent behavior in Blacks. In 1903, *The New York Tribune* quoted one Colonel J. W. Watson of Georgia as saying that "many of the horrible crimes committed in the Southern States by the colored people can be traced directly to the cocaine habit." A Dr. Christopher Koch asserted, in an article published in the *Literary Digest* in 1914, that "most of

[1]Coca-Cola still purchases coca leaves, which make up part of its ingredients, but includes it in its beverage only after the cocaine has been extracted.

the attacks upon white women of the South are a direct result of a cocaine-crazed Negro brain." Even the staid *New York Times* published an article on February 8, 1914, entitled "Negro Cocaine Fiends Are a New Southern Menace," detailing the "race menace," "cocaine orgies," "wholesale murders," and "hitherto inoffensive" Blacks "running amuck in a cocaine frenzy." (These articles are summarized in Ashley, 1975; Musto, 1973; and Grinspoon and Bakalar, 1976.)

"All the elements needed to insure cocaine's outlaw status were present by the first years of the twentieth century: It had become widely used as a pleasure drug . . .; it had become identified with despised or poorly regarded groups—blacks, lower-class whites, and criminals; it had not been long enough established in the culture to insure its survival; and it had not . . . become identified with the elite, thus losing what little chance it had of weathering the storm" (Ashley, 1975, p. 74).

By the time of the passage of the Harrison Narcotics Act in 1914—which included cocaine as a narcotic, which, of course, it is not—forty-six states had already passed laws attempting to control cocaine (only twenty-nine had done so with the opiates). This indicates that cocaine was seen by many legislators as the major drug problem at the time. There can be no doubt that this was directly related to racial hostility toward Blacks on the part of the dominant white majority.

It is impossible to know with any degree of accuracy just how frequently cocaine was used in the years following its criminalization. We have anecdotes and often hysterical newspaper stories, not reliable information. It is frequently mentioned as the drug of choice among rarefied, elite social circles in the 1920s. But after that came "The Great Drought": "Virtually every source I have consulted," writes one cocaine expert, "agrees that cocaine use was insignificant during the 1930s" (Ashley, 1975, p. 105). Its use remained insignificant and confined to a very tiny number of Americans more or less into the 1960s. And then the explosion occurred—paralleling the marijuana explosion, though on a smaller scale.

Most users sniff or "snort" cocaine. The drug is chopped into fine lines with a razor blade on a smooth surface; users inhale each line, usually one to a nostril, through a straw or a rolled-up bill. (To do it with a $100 bill is supposed to demonstrate flair.) Recently, two methods have become more common—although they are still atypical when compared with the total universe of use—freebase smoking and injecting. Freebase is a substance that is the product of dissolving coke in an alkaline solution and boiling it; what remains is a more potent form of the drug. Injecting and freebasing are far more efficient means of delivering the drug to the bloodstream than snorting it. They produce a powerful "rush"—an intense flash of extreme orgasmlike pleasure that is even more powerfully reinforcing than taking it in the nose. Injecting and freebasing are not only dangerous in themselves, but also are both associated with and tend to generate frequent, heavy, chronic cocaine use. Two experts argue that snorting cocaine results in "a pattern of continued use while supplies are available and in simple abstention when supplies are lacking. . . . It may interfere with other activities of the individual, but it may be a source of enjoyment as well." On the other hand, injecting or smoking coke "can lead to almost continual consumption and drug-seeking behavior, destructive to personal competence and productivity" (Van Dyke and Byck, 1982, p. 140).

What is the appeal of cocaine? Four researchers (Erickson et al., 1987, p. 79) assert that cocaine's appeal is greater than that of any other illicit drug; most users would probably agree. There is a feeling among recreational drug users toward cocaine that borders on reverence and awe; cocaine is called "the champagne of drugs," "caviar among drugs." Poet Michael McClure has dubbed it "The Ace of Sunlight." There is no doubt that snob appeal has a great deal to do with the spread of this drug (Grinspoon and Bakalar, 1976, p. 61). It is, by far, the most expensive widely used drug in America; in terms of cost per hour that the user is high, it is four times as expensive as heroin. The price of a gram (one-twenty-eighth of an ounce) ranges between $60 and $150, depending on the drug's purity and where it is purchased. Today, cocaine is far more abundant and far purer than it was even four years ago. A given gram may be as much as 50 percent pure cocaine. Wealthier users will purchase an ounce instead of a gram; today, an ounce of cocaine costs between $1,800 and $2,500.

The cocaine intoxication is extremely pleasurable; behavioral psychologists would call it highly reinforcing—more so than is true for any other drug. As we saw in Chapter 2, laboratory animals will give up food, sex, and water for self-administered doses of cocaine, and will even starve to death to continue receiving cocaine instead of food. Of course, these are animals, not humans, and presumably we are governed by more of a conscious will than laboratory animals are. Moreover, humans do not necessarily take cocaine via the same route of administration that laboratory animals are forced to do—that is, intravenously, and, as we know, route of administration strongly influences a drug's effects. Still, when all is said and done, cocaine is extremely reinforcing for both animals and humans. Cocaine's principal effect is exhilaration, elation, euphoria, well-being, a voluptuous, joyous feeling accompanied by grandiosity. William Burroughs, a novelist who was once addicted to heroin, and who has tried just about every drug known to humankind, described taking cocaine as "electricity through the brain." A second common effect of the drug is confidence, a sensation of mastery of and competence in what one does and is. A third effect is increased energy and the suppression of fatigue, a stimulation of the ability to continue physical and mental activity more intensely and for a longer period of time. South American workers can endure ordinarily exhausting conditions without food or rest for days on end because of the effects of the coca leaves they chew. Robert Louis Stevenson, a sickly man, wrote *Dr. Jekyll and Mr. Hyde*, a 60,000-word novel, in three days under the influence of cocaine. (To be more exact, he wrote one version in three days, was dissatisfied with it, tore it up, and wrote another version in three days.) Users frequently assert that in small doses, cocaine is an aphrodisiac (Gay, 1981)—

although, if it is taken in large doses, or used frequently over long periods, one often loses interest in sex.

Cocaine does not produce tolerance: One does not have to increase the dose over time to achieve the same effect. It does not produce a physical addiction or dependency; there are no physical withdrawal symptoms upon a discontinuation of heavy, long-term use. However, psychological consequences often follow discontinuing the use of this drug, including depression, irritability, and fatigue; some observers suggest a biochemical basis for this (Wesson and Smith, 1977a, p. 145). Users claim that cocaine is a safe, extremely nontoxic drug. This is partly true and partly false. Cocaine, if taken occasionally—less than weekly—in moderate doses, causes little if any physical or mental damage at all (Petersen, 1979). However, this pattern of use, and its attendant safety, has mainly to do with its cost, according to contemporary experts. A $150 gram is sufficient for about six doses; each dose generates a high that lasts less than a half-hour. Simple arithmetic tells us that a high costs $25, or $50 an hour for one person. Many users find its effects so pleasurable that taking cocaine once in a while is not enough; they want to take it again and again. Using it often is prohibitively expensive for the average recreational drug user, and thus its cost keeps its heavy use down.

Today, cocaine is news. Media attention to the drug exploded in the 1980s. More specifically, it grew steadily through the early and mid-1980s, then skyrocketed in late 1985 and early 1986. *The Reader's Guide to Periodical Literature,* as I've noted earlier, indexes a number of magazines and lists the subjects of the articles published in them each year. Of course, for any given subject, many more articles are published in magazines not indexed by *The Reader's Guide,* and many more than that appear in newspapers. Still, the *Guide* is a fairly accurate measure of the total number of articles published on a given subject over time. For 1981–1982, the *Guide* listed only six articles devoted to cocaine in the American magazines it indexes. In 1982–1983, it listed fourteen; in 1983–1984, twenty; in 1984–1985, twenty-five; and in 1985, the first year *The Reader's Guide*'s tabulation coincided with the calendar year, it listed thirty-one. In 1986, there were fifty-seven articles nationally on cocaine and twenty-three on crack, for a grand total of eighty—a tripling in less than two years. Clearly, by the mid-1980s, cocaine entered the national consciousness perhaps as never before in the country's history.

As we saw in Chapter 4, cocaine is now the only drug we looked at whose indicators of use are mainly on the upswing. Interestingly, not all indicators point upward for cocaine use—although most do. However, more significant than the rise in indicators of use is *the rise in the frequency of cocaine use among those who use the drug.*

In the national survey cited earlier (NIDA, 1986), the annual use of cocaine remained more or less stable for 12-to-17-year-olds between 1979 (4.2 percent) and 1985 (4.4 percent); decreased slightly for 18-to-25-year-olds (19.6 percent versus 16.4 percent); and doubled for adults age 26 or older (2 to 4.2 percent); use within the past month also doubled for the over-26-year-old category. The number of Americans using cocaine during the previous month rose from 4.2 to 5.8 million between 1982 and 1985. In the high-school survey, cocaine use was remarkably stable between 1979 and 1986—15 to 17 percent for lifetime prevalence; 12 to 13 percent for annual prevalence; and 6 to 6 percent for thirty-day prevalence. However, the proportion of *daily* cocaine users jumped from 0.2 percent to 0.4 percent (Johnston et al., 1987, pp. 47, 48, 49, 50).

The fact that heavy cocaine use is increasing fairly sharply is indicated by the Drug Abuse Warning Network (DAWN) data. As we saw, there are problems with using this information (Ungerleider et al., 1980); still, if massive differences are observed in overdose figures over time, it probably tells us something important. In the year between October 1979 and September 1980, DAWN recorded 3,757 nonfatal emergency-room cocaine-associated episodes, and 127 cocaine-related deaths; in 1981–1982, there were 5,830 ER cocaine mentions, and 198 lethal cocaine-associated overdoses, a substantial increase. During 1985, there were 13,501 emergency-room episodes and 643 lethal overdoses attributed to cocaine. However, in the single year between 1985 and 1986, ER episodes increased by 84 percent, and medical examiner's lethal drug mentions increased by 70 percent! In 1986, cocaine ER mentions numbered 24,847—17 percent of all drug mentions. And medical examiners reported 1,092 lethal overdoses in which cocaine was present—13 percent of all mentions (DAWN, 1987, pp. 26, 53). Since cocaine overdoses, both lethal and nonlethal, occur mainly in the very heavy user, and specifically when the drug is smoked or injected, these figures, however flawed, point to a *massive* increase of heavy cocaine use by means other than snorting.

Cocaine has burst onto the street drug scene as never before in the nation's history. It is being used on a startlingly frequent basis by men and women who make their living committing predatory street crimes. One study showed that among men arrested for serious crimes in New York's borough of Manhattan, the proportion who tested positive for cocaine *nearly doubled* between 1984 and 1986. When they were guaranteed anonymity, 85 percent of the men arrested for felonies agreed to be tested for the presence of drugs. In 1984, 42 percent tested positive for cocaine use; in 1986, 78 percent did. Among all categories of arrestees, robbers were most likely to have cocaine in their body: 90 percent tested positive for the drug. The rise was especially sharp among the young. For 16- to 20-year-olds, in 1984, 28 percent tested positive, but by 1986, this had risen to 71 percent; for 21- to 25-year-olds, the respective figures were 43 and 91 percent (Bronstein, 1987).

Is cocaine addicting? Much of the controversy over drug addiction becomes tangled in semantics—what words mean rather than what's happening in the real world. If we mean, does cocaine produce a physical addiction in the classic sense of the word, complete with heroinlike withdrawal symptoms, then the answer is a qualified no. On the other hand, if we mean, is it possible for a sizable proportion of users to develop a craving so intense that they will give up many of the things they value—money, possessions, relationships, jobs and careers—in order to continue taking the drug, then the answer is an emphatic yes. Many cocaine users become behaviorally dependent on the drug. Admitting this, however, does not mean that it is cocaine and cocaine alone that determines the user's pattern of use. Recall the discussion in Chapter 1 on what I called the *chemicalistic fallacy.* Pharmacology alone does not determine how a drug is used. The social and personal characteristics of the individual, too, make a great deal of difference.

As David Smith, a physician and founder of the Haight-Ashbury Free Medical Clinic, says: "What you're taking does not matter as much as who you are. Some people will take the drug—any drug—and not get addicted. Others will take it once and be inexorably drawn to it. The drug is the same; the people are different. . . . Interestingly," Smith adds, "the person who is addicted to cocaine responds differently the very first time he uses it. Later, he'll use terms that are qualitatively different from those that others use to describe the experience of taking cocaine the first time: 'This is the greatest thing that's ever happened to me,' or words to that effect." Smith estimates the proportion of more or less regular users of powdered cocaine who become behaviorally dependent on the drug at roughly one in ten, the same as with alcohol. In addition, Smith estimates that 30 to 40 percent will experience at least one episode of dysfunction—a seizure, a coke binge that makes them sick, or some other effect that forces them to feel the ill effects of the drug. All of this means that some people "can experiment with the drug and not abuse it." He is quick to add, however, that this is an extremely dangerous experiment, certainly not worth the odds (Gonzales, 1984, p. 114).

Ronald Siegel, a psychologist who recently completed an eight-year study of cocaine users, agrees—but with one important qualification. He distinguishes between cocaine taken in powdered form intranasally, or snorted, and cocaine that is smoked. Today, most smoked cocaine is in the form of crack, but until 1985–1986, cocaine was smoked in the form of freebase. Freebase is cocaine that has been chemically purified by removing the adulterants, thereby producing a cocaine "base" that is smoked. Siegel began with ninety-nine "social-recreational" users of cocaine; all began as intranasal users, and all stayed that way for roughly three years. However, after three years, Siegel's sample evolved into two distinct populations: intranasal users (90 percent) and freebase smokers (10 percent). Half of the users remained social-recreational users, a third were "situational" users, who took cocaine occasionally when it was offered to them, 8 percent were heavy, "intensified" users, and 10 percent were chronic, compulsive users who could be considered behaviorally dependent on the drug. Of the 10 percent of Siegel's sample who became addicted to cocaine, all smoked it freebase (Siegel, 1984, p. 100). "Essentially," says Siegel, "there is no such thing as a social-recreational freebaser" (Gonzales, 1984, p. 199).

Intranasal users averaged 20 milligrams per administration if a coke spoon was used, and 50 milligrams if "lines" were used; they averaged between 1 and 3 grams per week when they used. In contrast, the smokers averaged 100 milligrams per administration (or "hit"), and 1.5 grams per day. The temporal spacing of hits, the total duration of a smoking episode, and, hence, the total quantity of use varied enormously for smokers. For some, hits were taken every five minutes for periods ranging from a half-hour to four days straight. Consumption ranged from a gram to 30 grams during a twenty-four-hour period; one subject consumed 150 grams in seventy-two hours was recorded in the study. For compulsive users, smoking continued until supplies of the drug were depleted or when the user fell asleep from exhaustion (Siegel, 1984, p. 100).

For social-recreational users, negative effects were reported in 40 percent of episodes, and included restlessness, irritability, perceptual disturbances, an inability to concentrate, fatigue, lassitude, and nasal problems. Smokers reported these reactions in 71 percent of their episodes of use. None of the social-recreational users reported the more serious physical or psychological reactions. On the other hand, in roughly 10 percent of the smokers' intoxications, severe toxic reactions were experienced, including chest pains, nausea or vomiting, difficulty in breathing, seizures, convulsions, a loss of consciousness, hallucinations with "violent loss of impulse control," and attempted suicide. In addition, psychomotor agitation, depression, and paranoia were extremely common (Siegel, 1984, p. 102).

In short, "many of the social-recreational cocaine users do not change their long-term pattern of use and do not appear to develop toxic crisis reactions." Social-recreational users "maintained relatively stable patterns of use [even] when supplies were available." The hypothesis that "long-term use of cocaine is inevitably associated with an escalating dependency marked by more frequent patterns of use is not supported by these findings" (Siegel, 1984, pp. 105, 106). If the drug were less expensive, however, it is possible that it would be used with considerably greater frequency. One study of 111 Canadian users (Erickson et al., 1987, p. 86) found that they mentioned the drug's cost as its least appealing aspect, even before the risk of addiction, negative social consequences, or adverse physical or psychological effects. In contrast to the nonabusive social-recreational user, the minority of subjects whose use did escalate and whose use became compulsive were invariably smokers. They became incapable of controlling their use, became dependent on cocaine, and experienced a wide range of physical and psychological reactions, some of which were life-threatening and required treatment. Extreme paranoia and depression were extremely common in this minority (Siegel, 1984).

Another study (Murphy, Reinarman, and Waldorf, 1986) interviewed nineteen cocaine users in 1975 and again eleven years later, in 1986. (The original study included twenty-seven users, but not all of them could be located for the follow-up.) They had been using the drug for an average of three years when the original study began; all were social-recreational—or, in the words of the researchers, "controlled"—users at that time. What happened to their use of cocaine in the intervening eleven years? All of them began by snorting cocaine and, for the most part, stuck with this route of administration. Five injected cocaine less than a half-dozen times, and three freebased, but they returned to snorting because they recognized that they could fall into compulsive, uncontrolled use patterns. Of the nineteen, six were "controlled" users throughout the 1975–1986 period. Seven were "heavy" users during most of the time between the two interviews, but they had eased into a "controlled" pattern by 1986. Two were "controlled" users through most of that time but ended up as abstainers, and three were heavy users who also became abstainers. Only one was a heavy user throughout.

This study is not representative of cocaine users in general. While the proportions of users among the public at large in these different categories is likely to be quite different from those in this study, it does point out the inescapable fact that cocaine use does not always or inevitably lead to addiction. "Despite what the popular press would have us believe, there is not *one* inevitable result of beginning to use cocaine—that of eventual 'addiction' or dependence. . . . Continued and uncontrolled cocaine use is, however, a possible outcome, but so is controlled use" (Murphy et al., 1986, p. 17). The authors use the findings of their study to question what they call "pharmaco-economic determinism," or the assumption that "users become powerless before or lose control over their use of consciousness-altering substances, and hence will do 'anything' to obtain a supply of their drug" (Murphy et al., 1986, p. 27). For instance, research based on treatment populations or callers to hotlines (Gold, 1984; Chatlos, 1987) include mainly people who are experiencing or have experienced difficulty as a result of their drug use. Consequently, they are unlikely to be typical of users in general. This type of study supports the "inevitability" model these authors are arguing against. Rather than claiming that drug use creates a kind of inevitable progression in which all experimenters become regular users, who, in turn, become heavy, chronic, and dependent abusers what makes more sense, the authors argue, is to see the process as a *tendency*; for some, there is a tendency to escalate to heavier use, more dangerous modes of use, and more dangerous drugs. For most, this tendency does not exist. Seeing addiction as an inevitable outcome of use, they add, denies the existence of the power of human free will.

CRACK

Part of the reason for the increase in the heavy use of cocaine in recent years is the substantial rise in the use of crack, which emerged on a widespread scale only since the second half of 1985. Like freebase cocaine, crack is a crystalline form of cocaine. Like freebase, crack is smoked. However, there are differences as well. What is sold on the street as cocaine is actually powdered cocaine hydrochloride (mixed with impurities, of course). Prior to the mid-1980s, cocaine powder was soaked in ether, out of which purified cocaine base was crystallized. This substance was called *freebase.* Freebase crystals were crushed and smoked. It is possible that roughly between 1970 and 1985, one out of ten regular users of cocaine were freebasing. Beginning in the middle 1980s, crack made its appearance on the street in great quantity. In contrast to freebase, crack is made by soaking cocaine hydrochloride and baking soda in water, then applying heat. The crystals that are precipitated out of this solution are what is called crack. (Baking soda causes a crackling sound when smoked, presumably the origin of the name.) Unlike freebase, which (without adulterants) is pure cocaine, crack is impure by its very nature, containing only 30 to 40 percent cocaine. Most of what's in crack is baking soda, or sodium bicarbonate.

A $75 gram of powdered cocaine will yield enough crystals for fifteen vials, which are sold for $20 each—a huge incentive for the dealer to sell crack instead of powdered cocaine. Crack is smoked; more accurately, the crystals are not combusted, but heated, and their vapors are inhaled. As reinforcing as powdered cocaine is, crack is considerably more so. Taking powdered cocaine nasally produces a high that takes roughly three minutes to occur and lasts perhaps a half hour. There is no real rush. Injected, the high will take only twelve to fifteen seconds to appear, and the rush is a major attraction of IV administration. However, when cocaine is smoked, in the form of either freebase or crack, the onset of the drug's impact is even faster, a matter of six to eight seconds, and the intense, orgasmlike high or rush lasts for perhaps two minutes, followed by a kind of afterglow that lasts ten to twenty minutes. The euphoria achieved in this rush is extreme, and it impels the user to want to use the drug over and over again.

Although crack has been used on the West Coast since the early 1980s, and freebase has been smoked since the early 1970s, the large-scale use of crack is recent. As of mid-1985, its use was still practically nonexistent. The national telephone hotline for cocaine information and help (1-800-CO-CAINE) received no mentions whatsoever of crack from its founding until mid-1985—a total of a million calls. A year later, *half* of all its calls dealt with crack (Chatlos, 1987, p. 12)!

In spite of the drug's recent explosion in use, the extent of its use has nonetheless been greatly exaggerated by the media. Newspaper headlines and TV news programs imply that all teenagers in the country have either used crack or are in imminent danger of doing so, that every community in the country has been saturated by the drug. This is pure sensationalistic overstatement. While crack is indeed a frightening drug, the facts on the scope of its use are considerably less unsettling than the news would have us believe.

In a survey of high-school seniors conducted every year since 1975, which included questions on crack for the first time in 1986 (Johnston et al., 1987, pp. 16–17, 38), only 4 percent of those questioned said that they had used crack at least once during the previous year. Crack was more likely to be used by non–college-bound seniors (5.2 percent) than by those who planned to attend college (2.8 percent). It was significantly more prevalent in large urban communities (5.9 percent) than in smaller ones (3.5 percent). And it was used more in the Northeast (6.0 percent) and the West (7.5 percent) than in the Midwest (3.1 percent) or the South (1.6 percent). Males were slightly more likely to have used it (4.2 percent) than females (3.6 percent). Approximately half of the high schools in the study showed some crack use, while half showed none. College students were considerably less likely to have used crack (1.3 percent) than were their noncollege peers (4.3 percent). No questions were asked about crack use before 1986 in part because the drug burst onto the American drug scene only toward the end of 1985. Thus these figures are impressive if we consider the fact that they grew from next to no crack use at all for the previous year. Still, only a small minority of American youth has even tried the drug.

Nonetheless, in a drug scene, small minorities can cause extremely large problems, as we know from heroin addicts. Some experts believe that fewer young people are falling into heroin use, abuse, and addiction; the heroin-addict population is gradually aging and is not being replaced. The young people that would have used heroin two to five years ago are now using cocaine, especially crack. In emergency rooms around the country in 1981, more than 50 percent of heroin users seeking treatment were in their twenties, and 35 percent were in their thirties. In 1985, less than 40 percent were in their twenties, and just under 45 percent were in their thirties (Kerr, 1986b). In 1981, 48 percent of all drug abusers seeking treatment listed heroin as their drug of choice; only 11 percent listed cocaine. In 1986, only 13 percent listed heroin, and a majority, 52 percent, named cocaine or crack (Kerr, 1987a). The long-run implications of this trend remain to be seen. However, many experts believe that the switch from heroin to crack among the drug scene's younger and more compulsive abusers has led to an increase in paranoia and aggression on the street and a rise in violent crimes. (The FBI notes that reported crime in all categories, which declined between 1975 and 1981, is now very much on the rise; however, the role of drugs in this increase is still being debated.) It is entirely possible, however, that the same trend that was observed in the late 1960s, when a large number of speed freaks turned to heroin to bring them down after an amphetamine "run," could occur in the future with crack (Kerr, 1986b).

"Try it once and you're hooked!" "Once you start, you can't stop!" Slogans such as these are repeated about crack so often that they take on a kind of truth of their own. In fact, if we look at the actual patterns of use among crack users, these messages are immediately seen to be serious distortions of reality. One Miami study of 308 heavily involved juvenile drug users age 12 to 17 found that 96 percent had used crack once or more; 87 percent used it on a regular basis. Yet, of those that used crack, a minority, 30 percent, used it daily, and half used it once or more a week but not daily. A majority of even the daily users limited their use to one or two "hits"—"hardly an indication of compulsive and uncontrollable use. Although there were compulsive users of crack in the Miami sample, they represented an extremely small minority" (Inciardi, 1988a, p. 26). Inexpensive as crack is—$5 to $20 a vial—it is highly likely that, if the drug were more freely available, it would be used with greater frequency.

At the same time, of course, crack is far from being a totally innocuous drug. Overdoses requiring emergency room treatment as a result of crack use have become increasingly common, and fatal reactions have occurred. Chronic, compulsive use is not infrequent, and the shorter the period of time between episodes of use, the greater the chance that the users will move toward uncontrollable use. And as we saw, with the more immediate, intense, and reinforcing effect of the drug from smoking, there is a substantially increased likelihood of behavioral dependence. Moreover, many of the same medical, psychiatric, and social consequences of the heavy use of powdered cocaine also result from crack use: paranoia, violence, heart problems, blackouts, dizziness, impotence, insomnia, tremors, convulsions, and depression (Chatlos, 1987, p. 55). At the same time, the majority of crack users remain (so far) once-in-a-while users, avoid compulsive abuse, and do not experience these undesirable medical complications. To say, as *Newsweek* did (June 16, 1986, p. 18), that using crack immediately impels the user into "an inferno of craving and despair" is the kind of hysterical sensationalism that can only contribute to the drug problem.

TOBACCO

> Smoking-related diseases are such important causes of disability and premature death in developed countries that the control of cigarette smoking could do more to improve health and prolong life in these countries than any single action in the whole field of preventative medicine (World Health Organization).

The use of tobacco is interesting to any student of psychoactive drug use for a number of reasons. To begin with, very few people—whether they are smokers or not—think of ordinary cigarettes as containing a potent drug, and practically no one thinks of smokers as drug users. However, in sufficient doses, nicotine is as psychoactive as any current illicit drug. Second, as we'll see, tobacco creates a powerful dependence, and making cigarettes unavailable to committed smokers leads to a powerful craving not unlike the one that truly addicting drugs foster. Third, as we saw earlier, cigarette smoking is implicated in illegal drug use, in that adolescent smokers are more likely to go on to use marijuana, cocaine, and heroin than are nonsmokers. And fourth, governments have attempted to control or eliminate the use of tobacco in the past—with dismally unsuccessful results.

The tobacco plant is indigenous to the New World; when Christopher Columbus arrived here, Native Americans used its cured leaf for smoking, chewing, and snuff. By the sixteenth century, the plant had made its way to the European continent and the British Isles. The colonies—first Virginia, later Delaware, Maryland, and the Carolinas, and in time, the Tennessee and Kentucky territories, grew tobacco and exported it to England. Within a matter of a few decades, the use of tobacco, mainly in the form of snuff and pipe tobacco, became popular all over Europe and even in parts of Asia.

Attendant upon this development was public and official condemnation. Edicts and laws were passed, some invoking the death penalty for use, possession, and sale of the "stinking weede." In 1604, King James I of England issued a "Counterblaste" condemning tobacco. Ten years later, the English decided to live with it. In 1623, the sultan of Turkey ordered that smokers be put to death; by 1655, these efforts were abandoned, and tobacco became officially accepted in Turkey. In 1634, the czar of Russia ordered the noses of tobacco smokers slit as punishment. In China in 1638, decapitation was declared the penalty for tobacco use. In 1614 in Japan, 150 individuals were apprehended for buying and selling tobacco against the emperor's commands (Blum et al., 1969, pp. 87–97). The mogul emperor of Hindustan declared, "As the smoking of tobacco has taken a very bad effect in the health and mind of so many persons, I order that no person shall practice the habit" (Home Office, 1968, p. 16). The penalty was to have one's lips slit. Naturally, these campaigns were a failure everywhere.

Between 1615 and 1620, the export of tobacco leaf from Virginia grew from 2,300 to 40,000 pounds a year. By 1790, factories in the newly independent United States were turning out close to 30 million pounds annually. Cigarettes had been available since the mid-1800s, but during the second half of the nineteenth, and even into the early twentieth century, most tobacco was consumed in the form of cigars, pipe tobacco, chewing tobacco, and snuff. In fact, as late as the 1920s, 3 out of 4 pounds of the tobacco grown in the United States were used for these products. Today, only 1 pound out of 7 is so used. Historically, then, the shift in tobacco usage has been away from pipes and cigars to cigarettes. Even in the relatively brief period between 1960 and 1985, the yearly adult per capita consumption of pipe tobacco dropped nearly 75 percent, from more than half a pound to about 2.5 ounces. Cigar consumption, too, declined drastically during this period. As late as the 1960s, adult Americans were smoking an average of more than fifty cigars a year per capita; in 1985, this had fallen to only fifteen. (However, snuff and chewing tobacco products did not decrease in popularity during this time.)

Cigarette smoking is such an overwhelmingly favorite means of consuming tobacco nowadays that it is difficult to imagine that, just a bit more than a century ago, cigarettes were hardly smoked at all. The total American production of cigarettes in 1880 was only half a billion; on a per population basis, consumption was *one–three hundredth* as great then as it is today. A major development for the cigarette industry took place in 1881: the cigarette-making machine was invented. It could manufacture 120,000 cigarettes a day—the work of forty hand-rollers. By 1900, roughly 2.5 billion cigarettes were sold in the United States, an average of fifty-four cigarettes per adult for that year. By 1908, the latter figure had nearly doubled, to 105 cigarettes, and four years later, by 1912, it doubled again, to 223—for a total of 15.8 billion cigarettes sold. Clearly, the industry was on a roll.

Table 8.2   U.S. Cigarette Consumption, 1900–1986

Year	Billions Sold	Per Capita, 18 and Over
1900	2.5	54
1908	5.7	105
1912	13.2	223
1914	16.5	267
1918	45.6	697
1929	118.6	1,504
1935	134.4	1,564
1941	208.9	2,236
1945	340.6	3,449
1963	523.9	4,345
1975	607.2	4,123
1980	631.5	3,851
1986	584.0	3,275

SOURCE: Economic Research Service, U.S. Department of Agriculture; distributed by The Tobacco Institute.

In 1913, another development bolstered the industry: A blended, sweetened, "flue-cured" cigarette was put on the market at 10 cents for a pack of twenty. It proved to be an instant success. World War I (1914–1918) witnessed more than a doubling in cigarette consumption, to an average of 697 per American adult per annum, and by the close of the 1920s, this had more than doubled again, to more than 1,500 cigarettes per year per American adult—a total production of more than 118 billion cigarettes. During the Depression, cigarette smoking plateaued, but by the late 1930s, it was on the rise again. The World War II period (for the United States, 1941–1945) witnessed another spurt in cigarette consumption, and by the war's close, Americans were smoking nearly 3,500 cigarettes per year on a per capita basis, or 340 billion cigarettes. Consumption grew more gradually after that, and the peak was reached in 1963, when Americans smoked 4,345 cigarettes per adult. (The first and most famous Surgeon General's report on smoking was published in 1964.) A consistent decline did not begin immediately after that; even in the late 1970s, Americans were smoking an average of 4,000 cigarettes a year. But by the early 1980s, it became clear that a significant drop in cigarette consumption was taking place. In 1986, the adult per capita consumption was 3,275 cigarettes. However, because of the increase in the population, more cigarettes were sold in 1986 (584 billion) than in the 1963 peak-use year, 524 billion.[2]

Cigarette smoking is not only declining on a per capita basis; it is also less likely to be taken up nowadays by the young. In 1976, 29 percent of high-school seniors smoked daily; in 1986, this figure was 19 percent, a

[2]Much of the above historical material was adapted from *Tobacco: Deeply Rooted in America's Heritage*, Washington: The Tobacco Institute, n.d.; and *Smoking, Tobacco, and Health: A Fact Book*, Washington: Department of Health and Human Services, 1987b.

Table 8.3 Daily Cigarette Smoking in the United States, 1974–1986

	Age 12–17	Age 18–25	Age 26+
1974	25	49	39
1986	16	37	33

SOURCE: Miller et al., 1983; NIDA, 1986.

sharp drop in only a decade (Johnston et al., 1987, p. 50). At the same time, as I pointed out earlier, high-school girls are now slightly more likely to smoke than boys; 20 percent smoke daily versus 17 percent for boys, and 11 versus 12 percent average half a pack a day over the past month (Johnston et al., 1987, p. 41). The national survey of the entire population, too, shows a decline in cigarette use. In 1974, 25 percent of youth age 12 to 17 were current smokers; in 1985, this had declined to 16 percent. In 1974, 49 percent of young adults age 18 to 25 were current smokers; in 1985, this had dropped to 37 percent. And in 1974, 39 percent of older adults age 26 and over were current smokers; in 1985, this had dipped to 33 percent (Miller et al., 1983, p. 80; NIDA, 1986). By all accounts, then, cigarette smoking is very much on the decline in the United States.

There are several significant and interesting patterns in smoking by social and demographic characteristics. Socioeconomic status (SES), as measured by income, education, and occupation, is significantly related to smoking. Income is correlated negatively or inversely with smoking: 39 percent of low-income males and 33 percent of low-income females smoke; 31 percent of high-income males and 27 percent of high-income females do so. Education, too, bears a negative relationship to smoking: 37 percent of males with no high-school education, and 46 percent with some high school, smoke; for females, the respective figures are 22 and 39 percent. But 24 percent of male college graduates, and only 16 percent of those with some graduate education, smoke; for women, the figures are 18 and 17 percent respectively. In addition, smoking is correlated with the education and future education of high-school students: Among seniors who plan to complete a full college education, only 6 percent smoke half a pack a day or more, while among those with no college plans, or with plans to complete less than four years of college, 19 percent smoke this much (Johnston et al., 1987, p. 41).

For occupation, more or less the same inverse pattern prevails: Workers in higher-status occupations are least likely to smoke, while those in lower-status jobs are most likely to do so. Only 22 percent of professional men and 20 percent of professional women smoke. But 43 percent of male, and 38 percent of female, blue-collar workers, and 41 percent of male, and 37 percent of female, service workers smoke. In addition, smoking is significantly, though not overwhelmingly, related to race: Blacks are a bit more likely to smoke than whites. Exactly a third of white males smoke (33 percent), while four Black males in ten (39 percent) smoke; for white women, the figure is 29 percent, and for Black women, 32 percent. (These data come from the National Center for Health Statistics and were published in U.S. Department of Health and Human Services, *Smoking, Tobacco, and Health: A Fact Book,* 1987, p. 5.)

Tobacco exemplifies a major point in the drug controversy: society's attitudes toward a given drug and its use do not bear any necessary relationship to the drug's actual properties. Nicotine is a powerful and toxic agent. Typically it is not used for psychoactive purposes—that is, to become high. However, if it were smoked in a more efficient manner to allow greater absorption into the body, say, in the way that marijuana is smoked—deep puffs inhaled, along with a great deal of air, the breath held, and the smoke very slowly exhaled—extreme intoxication would ensue, and possibly unconsciousness as well. In fact, this was precisely the manner in which tobacco was smoked in the seventeenth century in Russia, and precisely these effects occurred. In the marijuana experiments conducted by Andrew Weil and Norman Zinberg, tobacco was used as the control placebo, but it turned out to be *even more psychotoxic than marijuana.* Five subjects smoking it experienced "acute nicotine poisoning: pale, sweaty skin, nausea and vomiting, and rapid pulse. There is . . . a marked psychic component, . . . [a] feeling of wanting to crawl under a rock and die" (Andrew Weil, August 15, 1969: personal communication). Joel Fort, a physician specializing in drug use, writes of nicotine:

> Nicotine strongly stimulates the central nervous system, with excessive doses producing tremors, convulsions, and vomiting. . . . Nicotine is one of the most toxic drugs known and is usually thought of as a poison, being used as such in insecticide sprays. . . . Cigarette tobacco contains between 1.5 and 3 percent nicotine, with each cigarette containing between 20 to 30 milligrams of the drug. As little as 4 milligrams has produced serious symptoms in nonhabituated individuals, although the fatal dose for an adult is about 60 milligrams. The smoke of an ordinary cigar may contain between 15 and 40 milligrams of nicotine. Heavy doses produce nausea, vomiting, diarrhea, headaches, disturbed vision and hearing, confusion, weakness, a sharp drop in blood pressure, convulsions, and ultimately death from paralysis of the respiratory muscles. . . . Irritation of the mouth, throat, and bronchi result from the heat, nicotine, and the many constituents of tobacco smoke. . . . Tolerance develops to the drug when taken regularly . . . and usually [there is] a "withdrawal"-like syndrome when cigarette smoking is discontinued (Fort, 1969, pp. 154–155).

The tobacco industry denies that smoking causes disease or premature death. More specifically, its spokespersons argue that the evidence linking smoking to a specific pathogenic mechanism or action is completely lacking. The Tobacco Institute publishes and distributes a pamphlet entitled "About Tobacco Smoke" (1982). It states: "What many of us haven't recognized is the consistent failure of scientists to establish any ingredient—or group of ingredients—in . . . tobacco smoke as the cause of any human disease." What ingredients in tobacco smoke have government officials and scientists pointed to as the cause of disease and premature death? asks The Tobacco

Institute. Well, nicotine, tar, and carbon monoxide. The pamphlet claims that the nicotine present in cigarettes is not sufficiently great as to represent a danger to human health; that tar ("as such") does not exist in tobacco smoke; and that carbon monoxide, present in cigarettes, is also present in "natural sources" as well as in air pollution. Hence, cigarettes do not represent a threat to human life.

Whether or not it is true that the exact mechanisms causing the higher disease and death rates of smokers have been located, the likelihood that smokers will die of a number of diseases is strikingly higher than it is for nonsmokers. Moreover, the more one smokes, the higher the chance of contracting and dying of these diseases. Smokers have nearly three times the likelihood of dying before reaching the age of 65 as do nonsmokers—28 versus 10 percent. And smokers have twice the chance of dying before the age of 75—50 versus 25 percent. A nonsmoker has a better chance of reaching the age of 75 than a smoker has of reaching the age of 65! Current smokers of half a pack a day have 3.9 times the likelihood of dying of lung cancer than nonsmokers do; smokers of ten to twenty cigarettes a day have 9.6 times the likelihood; smokers of more than a pack but less than two packs have 16.7 times the likelihood; and smokers of two or more packs have *more than twenty-three times* the likelihood. For bronchitis or emphysema, these respective mortality ratios are 4.8, 11.2, 17.5, and 22. (*Smoking, Tobacco, and Health: A Fact Book,* Health and Human Services, 1987b, pp. 7–14). It is almost inconceivable that differences on this order of magnitude could not be directly causal in nature.

In 1985, the federal Office of Technology Assessment released the report *Smoking-Related Deaths and Financial Costs.* It estimated that between $12 and $35 billion will be spent each year in the United States to treat smoking-related diseases, and that smoking-related diseases result in a yearly loss in productivity of $27 to $61 billion. The purchase of cigarettes yields about $4.6 billion per year in taxes to the federal government (Molotsky, 1985b). The American Cancer Society estimates that smoking is responsible for some 320,000 premature deaths in the United States each year, 170,000 from coronary heart disease, 130,000 from cancer, and 50,000 from noncancerous lung diseases. In 1980, the Surgeon General of the United States said that cigarette smoking is "the single most important preventable cause of death and disease." Next to these figures, the number of deaths from the use of illicit drugs pales into near-insignificance.

In addition to the direct and strictly medical hazards of smoking, cigarettes cause a large number of deaths from an ignored and publicly almost unacknowledged source: death by accidental fire. Of all the fire-related deaths in the United States each year, 2,300, or more than a quarter, are caused by smoking. The irony of these figures is that the cigarette industry refuses to manufacture self-extinguishing cigarettes, which could eliminate most of these deaths. Chemicals put in cigarette paper allow the tobacco to continue burning twenty to forty-five minutes without being puffed. This means that a cigarette, if dropped on a couch or a bed, or any other flammable household article, can smolder and start a fire. Obviously, cigarettes that continue burning will be sold in greater numbers than cigarettes that must be relit if left unpuffed for a few minutes, and consequently, it is to the disadvantage of the tobacco industry to sell self-extinguishing cigarettes. (However, once a smoker has been burned up in a fire, he or she cannot purchase any more cigarettes!) As a result, the industry has resisted legislation forcing the manufacture of cigarettes without self-burning chemicals (Dunlap, 1982). Unlike the deaths from cancer and other medical maladies, the majority of the fire deaths from burning cigarettes can easily be prevented.

In short, it is clear that cigarettes can, by any conceivable definition, be called a "dangerous drug." The chief medical officer of health for Britain summed it up by saying: *"The abolition of cigarette smoking would be the greatest contribution to public health now open to us."* Needless to say, most Americans (and most Britishers) do not see cigarette smoking as much of a problem. Rather it is regarded as a nasty habit, much like biting one's nails. We are stuck with it, the arguments run. It is here to stay; there is nothing that can be done about it; it is a socially and culturally established habit; and so on. While most of the public attention is focused on the use of illegal recreational street drugs, especially heroin and marijuana, most of the deaths continue to be caused by drugs that are legally manufactured and sold.

The reaction of the tobacco industry to the evidence that has accumulated on this drug's health hazards is as interesting as the evidence itself. Responding to reports that cigarettes cause lung cancer and heart disease, the tobacco industry financed a $10-million study conducted by the American Medical Association; that organization's study verified these early reports and found cigarettes to be a major cause of disease. The tobacco industry found the report not at all to its liking, denounced the AMA study as "unscientific," and faulted it for being epidemiological (or studying statistical correlation of diseases in different sectors of the population) rather than etiological, or tracing detailed, concrete causal sequences (Kilborn, 1979). Reacting to the 1982 surgeon general's report, a spokesperson for the Tobacco Institute issued a statement that claimed that the data presented in the report "are not new"; "the question is still open" whether smoking causes cancer, or any other diseases, the institute argued. And meanwhile, smokers' risk of death is far greater than that of nonsmokers. It is unlikely that this situation will change in the near future.

Just as medical ravages from the use of cocaine are not as serious as they would be were the drug freely available, in something of a reverse fashion, the addictive properties of tobacco are masked by the drug's ready availability. Nicotine gives tobacco its addictive quality. The majority of smokers use this drug not only daily, but hourly. "No other substance known," state the editors of *Consumer Reports,* "is used with such remarkable frequency" (Brecher et al., 1972, p. 223). The craving for nicotine is in all likelihood a physiological withdrawal symptom. When smokers attempt to quit, they experience irritability, anxiety, headaches, fatigue, energy loss, insomnia, dizziness, sweating, and other symptoms associated with drug abstention.

During World War II, when the supply of cigarettes was disrupted in Europe, German civilians were far more likely to purchase cigarettes on the black market than food; a large number of women prostituted themselves to obtain cigarettes; and the overwhelming majority of those questioned said that it felt worse to do without cigarettes than alcohol. The relapse rate of smokers who quit and then return to cigarettes is almost identical to the relapse rate of heroin addicts who "kick" their habit and become readdicted. In a summary of a number of studies, it was found that at the end of four years, 80 percent of smokers who had successfully stopped were smoking again (Brecher et al., 1972, pp. 226–228). It seems unarguable that tobacco is a drug that produces a literal physical dependence.

In 1988, the Surgeon General of the United States, C. Everett Koop, released his annual report on the health consequences of smoking. The report summarized the research of more than fifty scientists published in some 2,000 scientific articles. In its conclusions, the report warned that nicotine is every bit as addicting as heroin and cocaine. Dr. Koop, adding precision to this generalization, stated that all of the criteria used to define addiction "are met by tobacco," including the fact that users are "helpless victims" of "irresistible urges." Drug use "may persist despite adverse physical, psychological or social consequences. . . . After quitting episodes, resumption of drug use, or relapse, often occurs. Urges of cravings to use the drug may be recurrent and persistent, especially during drug abstinence." In addition, Dr. Koop said, withdrawal symptoms "often occur after cessation of drug intake." These conclusions represent a reversal of the first Surgeon General's report, published in 1964, which concluded that smoking is a habit, but not addicting. A spokesperson for the Tobacco Institute said that the claim of tobacco's addictive properties "contradicts common sense" (Martin Tolchin, "Surgeon General Asserts Smoking Is an Addiction," *The New York Times*, May 17, 1988, pp. A1, C4).

ACCOUNT: COCAINE USE

The contributor of the following account is a 35-year old writer.

> This deal kind of materialized out of nowhere, really. A mutual friend, a guy I know through another guy, copped a pretty large quantity of coke, like, a key [kilogram, or 2.2 pounds], and my friend said I could acquire an ounce at a reasonable price—it was $1,800, I think, or a shade less. This dealer was a very respectable guy—he later went on to medical school and became a doctor—and he was very tight with my friend, whom I was very tight with, so I wasn't afraid of getting ripped off or burned or anything. I went over to his place, and examined the merchandise; I snorted a line. It was cut maybe fifty-fifty, which is terrific, you hardly ever get coke that pure, at least, I don't seem to be running into it. So I gave him the bread and took it home. Now, my plan was this. I'd divide the Z [ounce] into grams—twenty-seven of 'em, cause I gave my friend a little taste for being so helpful. Then I'd sell the grams at a very reasonable price (eighty dollars per was what I decided), and keep maybe five Gs for myself,

and I'd get them for free, in effect. No real profit, just some coke for myself. That was my plan.

I have maybe six close friends who do coke on a semiregular basis, and so I called 'em, one by one, and asked if they wanted to purchase a few grams at a very reasonable price. Well, the funny thing was, each one had a different reason for saying no. One was coked up to his eyeballs and decided, that week, to lay off the stuff for a while, he was getting into it something fierce and spending a fortune and doing nothing but doing coke. A second friend had just copped, like, six Gs. A third didn't like the looks of the stuff. (Turns out he was mistaken, but he learned some dumb rule about how it's supposed to look.) And so on. Anyway, the upshot was, I had twenty-seven grams of pretty good coke just lying around the house, and no buyers.

Now, I wasn't gonna contact any of my more casual friends to try to sell to them, 'cause that's the way you get busted—you eventually bump into a nark if you do business with people you don't know too well. OK, so I figured I'd use some myself and let the rest sit around for a few weeks, and I'd keep my eyes open for respectable customers. You can guess what happened.

Coke is like candy, it's so delicious, you can't stop. Some nights I'd be alone, and some nights I'd be with friends, usually just one of my lady friends. And I'd start out with a taste, you know, a line for each nostril, and I'd feel good, *real* good. So I didn't stop there, I'd hit another line, and then another, and within a week, I'd be snorting a *whole gram* in one evening—sometimes all by myself, or with just one friend, or sometimes with another couple. Now, I'm a writer, and I like to get some work done at night, but I'd end up having dinner, watching the six o'clock news, and then I'd get wired up every night, devote myself totally to pleasure, getting high, getting laid, sipping a little wine, smoking dope, lying around, listening to music—and I'd do this for maybe eight, ten hours, you know, and I'd go to sleep at four, five o'clock.

And the women I was with would have a wonderful time, with me, with the coke, you know. And I'd act like such a *big shot* when I went out and visited friends, I'd go over to their house, we'd hit a few lines, and everybody'd be feeling very cool, and my lady friend would whisper in my ear, let's go home and make love, and I'd get this sheepish grin on my face, and I'd say to my friends, time to go, you know, and I'd leave the rest of the gram *there*; I'd say, with a big flourish, keep the rest—and it might be *half a gram*! I acted as if I had an unlimited supply and I got it practically for free. Can you imagine being so profligate? Then we'd go home, like I said, and devote ourselves to hedonism.

And I'd wake up sometime in the afternoon the next day and say to myself, hey, what happened to last night? I've got work to do, I've got a deadline—and I ended up getting coked out the whole evening! Do you understand? I had absolutely no control over myself! Getting high would feel so good I'd want to do it again and again, I didn't want to stop, and all the things I had to do went down the tubes. I could see myself snorting up the whole Z, $1,800 down the drain, and nothing to show for it. Finally, I gathered up what was left of the ounce—I think it was six, eight grams, something like that—and gave it back to my friend and I said, look, man, sell this to somebody and we'll split what you get. I just can't trust myself around this stuff. I can't spend $75 a night just to get high; pretty soon, coke'll totally dominate my life. Take it out of my hands and sell it, man, 'cause I shouldn't be anywhere *near* cocaine. [From the author's files.]

CHAPTER 9

Sedatives and Tranquilizers

Sedatives are general depressants; they retard signals passing through the central nervous system. They also inhibit or slow down a number of functions and the action of a wide range of organs of the body, as well as general activity, or "behavioral output." Sedatives also decrease anxiety. At higher doses, sedatives are also *hypnotics,* that is, they induce sleep. The term "sedative-hypnotic" can be regarded as synonymous with "general depressant"; I'll simply use the term "sedative" to cover drugs that act as general depressants. Alcohol is the most widely used of all sedatives; it was discussed in Chapter 5. Barbiturates are another type of sedative; so is methaqualone. Others include chloral hydrate and the bromides—drugs that are hardly used at all today.

The principal function of the tranquilizers is treatment of neuroses and psychoses. The "minor" tranquilizers are used for "minor" mental illness, or neuroses; the "major" tranquilizers are used for "major" mental illnesses, or psychoses. "Minor" tranquilizers produce a reduction in the user's level of anxiety. The characteristics that presumably set tranquilizers apart from sedatives, and made them superior to sedatives as therapeutic agents, were that they were nonaddicting and produced no mental clouding or drowsiness in the user. Later experience with all of the "minor" tranquilizers has shown that they are, in fact, addicting, and do produce mental clouding. Actually, the differences between the "minor" tranquilizers and the sedatives are fewer and much less significant than the similarities. "Major" tranquilizers suppress the symptoms of psychosis. They do not produce intoxication or a high, and are rarely used illegally for recreational purposes.

SEDATIVES

Aside from alcohol, the most widely used sedatives are the barbiturates and methaqualone. Barbiturates are defined as central nervous system depressants that are derived from barbituric acid. The first barbiturate, Veronal, was marketed commercially in 1903. Since then some 2,500 different derivatives have been synthesized, but only a dozen of these are widely sold and used in the United States. Barbiturates are classified according to the speed of their action. The *short-acting* barbiturates include Amytal ("ammies," in street parlance), Tuinal ("tooies," or "Christmas trees"), Seconal ("sekkies," "seggies," "reds," or "red devils"), and Nembutal ("yellow jackets," "nimmies," or "nimbies"); they all produce an intoxication or high if taken in sufficient doses, and they are used recreationally on the street. *Long-acting* barbiturates include phenobarbital and Fiorinal; they do not produce a high, and are rarely used on the street, and need not be discussed here. Methaqualone is marketed under a number of different trade names, including Quaalude ("ludes"), Sopor ("soaps"), Parest, and Optimil. At one time, methaqualone was regarded by the medical profession as safe and nonaddicting. Today, it is regarded as capable of producing death by overdose, extreme mental clouding, drowsiness, discoordination, disorientation, and a true physical dependence.

Barbiturates are, in many ways, even more dangerous than heroin. The barbiturate withdrawal is even more severe and life-threatening than withdrawal from heroin—that is, it is much more likely to result in death. The classic withdrawal syndrome appears upon the discontinuation of "chronic" use of barbiturates: nausea, muscular twitching, aches and pains about the head and body, anxiety and nervousness, trembling, profuse sweating, dizziness, cramps, a feeling of feebleness, and finally, in the later stages, convulsions and sometimes coma, occasionally resulting in death. Naturally, the heavier the dependence, the more extreme the reactions. Severe dependence is induced as a result of taking roughly 800 to 1,000 milligrams daily for a month to six weeks. A moderate physical dependence can be induced with half that amount. Tolerance builds, although more slowly than with the opiates. There seems to be a kind of leveling off in tolerance level; the plateau seems to stabilize at between 1 and 2.5 grams a day. As with heroin addiction, babies born of barbiturate-dependent mothers are themselves addicted and must be withdrawn, a painful and sometimes lethal process.

Death from an overdose of a barbiturate can occur at ten times the therapeutic dose (one Amytal tablet contains 100 milligrams, for example). Death is typically caused by respiratory failure, an inhibition of the breathing mechanism. Barbiturates demonstrate something of a cross-tolerance with alcohol, the two being remarkably similar in their actions; the effects of the two taken together are synergistic—that is, more toxic than the sum of their separate effects. Since the two are commonly taken in conjunction, this synergistic function is especially problematic.

The prescription use of the short-acting barbiturates, as well as methaqualone, has been dropping throughout the 1970s and 1980s, as we saw in Chapter 4. In the decade and a half from the early 1970s to the late 1980s, the number of prescriptions written for most sedatives and tranquilizers has been cut by 90 percent; this development is probably the most remarkable change that has taken place in patterns of drug use and abuse in America during this period. Has this decline in the legal prescription use of the general depressants translated into less abuse and misuse of these drugs? Are they associated with fewer medical maladies?

The evidence is consistent enough to discern a trend. Judging by the data provided by the Drug Abuse Warning Network (DAWN), the implication of barbiturates in both lethal and nonlethal overdoses diminished significantly from the late 1970s and early 1980s to the mid- to late 1980s. The number of yearly emergency-room episodes associated with barbiturates dropped by 65 percent from October 1979–September 1980 to 1986; the number of deaths by overdose in which the drug was implicated declined by 46 percent. The decline in the number of emergency room episodes and medical examiner's reports in which methaqualone was implicated during the same period was even more precipitous. (Methaqualone was not prescribed by physicians in the United States in 1985 and 1986.) ER episodes and lethal overdoses in which methaqualone was reported present declined by 90 percent between 1979–1980 and 1986. Thus the trend for these two sedatives, barbiturates and methaqualone, is unambiguously down; for the latter, it is down spectacularly. A continuation of this downward trend seems likely, at least for the foreseeable future.

The same cannot be said for PCP (also known as Serinyl, phencyclidine, or "angel dust"). PCP is usually classified as a hallucinogen, but it is in fact a powerful animal tranquilizer, sedative, and anesthetic with often inconsistent and contradictory effects. (The reason why it is mistakenly classified as a hallucinogen by most observers is that some users occasionally experience hallucinations, mainly of a delusional character. These experiences are, of course, totally uncharacteristic of those typical or common with the psychedelics or hallucinogens: There are no colors, for example, no synesthesia, no eidetic imagery, none of the same feelings of timelessness or "oneness" with the universe, no sense of the fluidity of things in the physical world, and so on. In fact, PCP shares next to no typical effects in common with the true hallucinogens. Why it is placed in this category is a mystery to me.) The number of mentions of PCP in emergency-room data fluctuates somewhat from year to year, without apparent temporal pattern, while the medical examiner's reports implicating PCP in deaths by overdose rose from 91 in 1979–1980 to 245 in 1986. Table 9.1 details the trends in overdoses for the three sedatives barbiturates, methaqualone, and PCP.

In the 1960s, barbiturates were heavily overprescribed, and the number of estimated addicts ran in the hundreds of thousands (Weinswig and Doerr, 1968, p. 149); the syndrome of the heavy use of prescription drugs was dubbed "the hidden addiction" (Moffett and Chambers, 1970). Such misusers tended to be older, more respectable, better educated and more middle-class than the heroin addict. They began their heavy drug use much later in their lives, almost always (except for alcohol and cigarette consumption) in some sort of medical or quasitherapeutic context—to ease tension, anxiety, or sleeplessness. Few had anything to do with crime in the conventional sense. They were able to secure their "fix" without having to steal or prostitute themselves; they got their drug supply legally. Society did not frown severely on such drug use; addiction was hidden from the public and often from the addicts themselves. With the sharp cutback in prescribing barbiturates, such misuse and overuse have declined, as has the number of patients dependent on the drug.

Beginning on a small scale in the 1950s, and on a large scale in the 1960s,

Table 9.1   **Drug-Abuse Indicators for Barbiturates, Methaqualone, and PCP, 1979–1986**

	Emergency-Room Episodes (nonlethal)	Medical Examiner's Reports (lethal)
BARBITURATES		
1979–1980	8,717	845
1981–1982	7,112	648
1985	3,562	424
1986	2,994	459
METHAQUALONE		
1979–1980	5,492	91
1981–1982	3,921	121
1985	517	8
1986	306	4
PCP		
1979–1980	7,024	95
1981–1982	6,024	113
1985	5,677	195
1986	6,421	245

SOURCE: DAWN, 1983, 1986, 1987.

barbiturates came to be used recreationally to get high. Adolescents and young adults took barbiturates at first only if they stole them from their parents. Later, they became available on the underground market. The illegal use of barbiturates increased significantly in the late 1960s and early 1970s; in one study of a university campus, barbiturates were used four times as frequently in the six months prior to May 1971 as prior to February 1970 (Goode, 1972b). This campus is probably not reflective of the nation as a whole, but there appears to be no doubt that the recreational use of barbiturates increased dramatically between the late 1960s and the early 1970s.

The barbiturate intoxication would seem to have little to recommend it aside from an obliteration of one's surroundings and the creation of a hazy, dreamlike state. A reporter describes what heavy users of "downs" look like to the outside observer:

> . . . look at their eyes. Chances are they'll be heavy, sleepy-looking, blinking in slow motion stop and go. There won't be much conversation. Most of the kids in the group you watch will probably have taken some combination of barbiturates and amphetamines. If they're lucky, they'll feel balanced on the kind of thin edge of consciousness you experience just before dropping off to sleep. If not, they'll be genuinely drowsy, depressed, and in ill temper. Strangely, despite their general depression, they'll be jittery, easily excitable, slightly paranoid. If any of the kids are really strung out on pills . . . they'll look and act like maniacs. They'll be confused, argumentative, and violent (Truscott, 1971, p. 9).

The acute effects of barbiturates are not uniformly sedating. In a study of criminal assaults by adolescents in California, it was found that, after alcohol, the drug the assailant most often identified himself as being under the influence of at the time of his offense was Seconal. In addition, a sizable proportion of the assaults were carried out while the offender was under the influence of alcohol and Seconal simultaneously. When asked what drug or drug type was most likely to "enhance assaultiveness," more than three-fourths of these violent offenders, 78 percent, chose Seconal; 11 percent chose alcohol. A matched group of nonassaultive juvenile offenders was asked the same question. More than half (56 percent) chose Seconal and 8 percent chose alcohol (Tinklenberg, 1973; Tinklenberg et al., 1974). (The selection of Seconal over the other barbiturates reflects the illicit distribution patterns in the area in which the study was done, California, and not its special effects in contrast with the other barbiturates.) Barbiturates do not literally and directly cause criminal or violent behavior. But they may very well potentiate it or make it more likely.

As we saw in Chapter 4, since the 1970s, the recreational use of barbiturates, like their pharmaceutical use, has been dropping, although considerably more gradually. In the study of high-school seniors that has been cited previously, the proportion who had tried a barbiturate drug dropped from 17 percent in 1975 to 8 percent in 1986; in 1975, 5 percent had used a barbiturate within the past thirty days, but by 1986, this figure had shrunk to 2 percent. (The other study that I have cited, a nationally representative survey of the entire population, did not ask about barbiturates specifically, but inquired about its sample's "sedative" use generally, so that it is impossible to determine from it separate trends in barbiturate and methaqualone use.)

The decline in the recreational use of methaqualone lagged a few years behind its spectacular decline in prescription use. In 1972, one of the trade names of methaqualone, Quaalude, ranked 112th among the nation's most commonly prescribed drugs (up from 153rd in 1971). In 1973, the federal government reclassified it as a Schedule II drug, and in a few short years, it dropped out of the circle of the top 200 drugs, never to return. As we saw in Chapter 4, more than ten times as many prescriptions for the methaqualone drugs were written in 1971 and 1976 as in 1966; in 1981, only one-third as many were written as in these 1970s peak years. By 1986, no prescriptions were written for methaqualones in the United States at all. Its heyday of popularity on the street as a recreational drug was the early 1980s. Among high-school students, its use in the mid- to late 1980s dropped by half from its peak years, and now, it is at its lowest point ever since the national surveys on high-school students were begun in 1975. Table 9.2 tells the story of methaqualone's rise and fall among America's high-school seniors. However, while methaqualone's decline in prescription use was precipitous, even spectacular, the decline in street recreational use has been much more gradual.

Methaqualone became popular as a recreational drug in the early 1970s. One of its appeals was its alleged aphrodisiac properties. It is not a literal aphrodisiac, but it is a muscle relaxant in addition to being a tranquilizer; for some uptight people, it might make sex more enjoyable. Originally

Table 9.2   Use of Barbiturates, Methaqualone, and PCP by High School Seniors, 1975–1986

	1975	1981	1986
BARBITURATES			
Lifetime Prevalence	16.9	11.3	8.4
Annual Prevalence	10.7	6.6	4.2
30-day Prevalence	4.7	2.6	1.8
METHAQUALONE			
Lifetime Prevalence	8.1	10.6	5.2
Annual Prevalence	5.1	7.6	2.1
30-Day Prevalence	2.1	3.1	0.8
PCP			
Lifetime Prevalence	*	7.8	4.8
Annual Prevalence	*	3.2	2.4
30-day Prevalence	*	1.4	1.3

*Drug not asked about in 1975; figures for PCP for 1979, the first year when it was asked about, were 13, 7, and 2 percent respectively.

SOURCE: Johnston et al., 1987, pp. 47, 48, 49.

developed as an nonaddicting nonbarbiturate sedative-hypnotic, this drug escaped from strictly therapeutic use and hit the streets with enormous publicity. News of large numbers of dazed, stuporous, semiconscious "luded out" users stumbling about in a kind of numb euphoria became widespread, the subject of a number of newspaper and magazine articles (for instance, Zito, 1972; Zwerdling, 1972). The husband of a couple described an experience with Quaaludes that the two of them had had in the early 1970s to me in the following words:

We had heard an awful lot about Quaaludes and, you know, about sex. That it was supposed to be so fabulous in bed and everything. So Ellen had been bugging me for weeks about copping some. I had this really hip shrink at the time, and he said he'd write up a script, you know, for me, for the Ludes. We both figured it would be therapeutic, make my sex life better. So I asked him—why not, right? Thing is, at that time, we both worked at night, and we'd come home kind of tired. So Ellen came home one night and she starts groping me, with a crazed look on her face—"Quaaludes, Quaaludes," she was whispering in my ear. So we both dropped—I think it was two 300-milligram tablets each. Which, I know it now, it's a pretty heavy hit. I made Ellen some dinner while she took a shower. She came out of the shower, wobbling around like she was drunk. I figured she was goofing, cuz I didn't feel a thing. She sat down in front of the food I made—a cheeseburger, beans and a salad. I was watching the tube. I looked over at her, and she's just lookin' at the food. I say, Ellen, why don't you eat? I look back at the tube for a few minutes. Then I look back at Ellen. She's still just staring at the plate of food in front of her. I go over and wrap each hand around a knife and fork and say, "Eat, eat." I look back at the tube. Couple of minutes later, I look back at Ellen. She's still staring at the food. I look more closely, and her head is slowly falling down. I keep lookin' at her, and her head dropped right into the plate of food! There's ketchup and beans all over her face. Then I got scared and got up to take care of her, and *I'm* feeling like I'm drunk. I wiped the food off her face, turned off the tube, and we both hit the sack. As soon as we pulled the covers over us, we were sound asleep. That was our big sex orgy on Quaaludes!

Along with the stories of Quaalude's effects came medical reports of cases of a literal physical addiction to the drug, as well as cases of deaths from an overdose of methaqualone (Inaba et al., 1973). In 1970, recording artist Jimi Hendrix died of an overdose of a British version of methaqualone, Mandrax. (To be more precise, Hendrix took the drug, vomited, passed out, and died of asphyxiation.) Throughout this furor, the most widely used drug reference volume, the *Physician's Desk Reference,* or *PDR,* treated methaqualone with astonishing generosity: "psychological dependence has rarely been reported with Quaalude," the *PDR* declared, and "physical addiction has not been clearly demonstrated." But the *PDR*'s judgment didn't seem to sway either the federal government or physicians.

With barbiturates and methaqualone, we can see a common pattern. A drug is manufactured and distributed for profit. Aggressive advertising campaigns are launched to sell the drug and to drum up new customers for a broader and broader range of maladies and pseudomaladies. Initial claims as to its safety are made—typically with skimpy and insufficient evidence—that are later revealed to be false. The medical establishment underplays its dangers. (Remember, the bulk of revenues earned by medical journals stem from drug advertisements.) Use is initially restricted to the medical arena. Users are not deviants or criminals. As more information is gathered about the drug, increasingly, pathologies are found to be associated even with legitimate, prescription use, "as directed" by the physician. Then news of the drug's psychoactive properties leaks out. Some medical users begin to take the drug to get high. Adolescents may steal a few tablets from the family medicine chest. Eventually, the illicit use of the drug becomes sizable, not uncommonly challenging the magnitude of prescription use. A huge underground market is created; illegal distribution networks are established.

Then the scare stories begin, touching off government investigations. Controls are established on the manufacture and distribution of the drug in question—controls that may or may not stem the tide of recreational use. What began as a legal, conventional activity—medication—is converted into an illegal, deviant one. Often, the effects that are sought for both activities—an alteration of one's ordinary, everyday consciousness—are the same. Often the dangers of the legal and the illegal use of these drugs are not very different. And the original impetus for the creation and growth of illegal recreational drug use is a venerable American tradition: the quest for profit. In this case, as in so many others, crime and deviance are simply converted forms of conventional, legal behavior, with a slightly different twist and a somewhat different cast of characters.

As I've stated earlier, PCP (phencyclidine, or Serinyl) is not a true hallucinogen, and should not be classified as such. Unfortunately, most observers, including the Drug Abuse Warning Network (DAWN), the National Institute on Drug Abuse (NIDA), and the Institute for Social Research do classify it as a hallucinogen. With the exception of hallucinations, the effects of the two drug types share have next to nothing in common. I prefer to see PCP as a sedative with hallucination-like effects at high doses.

At low to moderate doses, PCP's subjective effects have been described as numbness, disorientation, "spaciness," and a kind of floating sensation. The descriptions are much like barbiturate and methaqualone highs described in the 1970s. However, in larger doses, some users experience schizophrenia like psychotic episodes, hallucinations, violence, suicidal impulses, a seeming disregard for safety, violence, convulsions, and coma. (For users' descriptions of the PCP high, see Carlson, 1979.)

PCP conforms to the medical-to-illicit use pattern discussed above, but with at least one important difference. Phencyclidine was originally developed and used as a general anesthetic for humans. However, because of the incidence of psychotic reactions observed, along with hallucinations, the medical fraternity decided that the drug was too dangerous to be used on humans. Its current legal use is entirely confined to veterinary medicine, to immobilize large animals. DAWN's data indicate a sharp increase in PCP abuse indicators between the early and the late 1970s, followed by a decline into the early 1980s, then a resurgence (Crider, 1986, p. 163). Most individuals who show up at a hospital emergency room for treatment for a PCP overdose are male (72 percent), Black (54 percent), and in their twenties (62 percent). The public image of PCP users is that they are teenagers or younger; this was true in the 1970s, but is no longer the case. In 1976–1977, users age 6 to 19 made up 51 percent of all individuals presenting themselves to a clinic for a PCP-related emergency in 1983, they comprised only 18 percent. We can surmise from this that PCP users are probably getting older. During this same period, the proportion of Blacks doubled, from 24 to 54 percent, but the proportion of males remained stable throughout (Crider, 1986, pp. 168–171).

In two-thirds of all cases of PCP-related deaths, phencyclidine was found in combination with another drug—typically, alcohol or heroin. The majority of these deaths (245 in 1986) were not drug overdoses, but came about as a result of "external" sources—homicides, suicides, or accidents. (More than half of the accidental deaths were drownings.) "The various methods of death . . . are consistent with observed symptoms of disorientation and violent aggressive behavior" (Crider, 1986, p. 171). This points to a possible link between PCP use and the commission of violent crime. Certainly, newspaper and magazine articles, and TV news stories, have emphasized the violence-inducing properties of PCP. However, one study of some 4,800 Manhattan arrestees whose urine was analyzed for the presence of drugs (Wish, 1986) found that PCP's apparent role in violence and crime was not drastically different than that of the other drugs studied. Of the four drugs tested for, cocaine was the one most likely to have been found in the urine

(42 percent); opiates were next most common (21 percent), PCP was third (12 percent), and methadone was last (8 percent). Almost exactly half of all the PCP-positive cases also included one of the other drugs. The most common charge for the PCP-positive arrestees was robbery. In short, the PCP-positive arrestee "looks much like other drug-using arrestees. Far from being charged with assaults or bizarre types of offenses," users of phencyclidine tend to be apprehended "for goal-oriented, income-generated crime." The study did not find "a preponderance of the types of offenses one might expect from persons committing the bizarre, irrational acts ascribed to PCP users" (Wish, 1986, pp. 186–187).

It is likely that most users, including those engaged in committing crimes, take PCP in fairly small doses; "emotionally stable people under the influence of low doses of PCP probably will not act in a way very different from their normal behavior" (Siegel, 1978, p. 285). While PCP is probably the most psychologically dangerous of all drugs currently in use, the vast majority of all episodes of phencyclidine use result in no serious untoward effects at all, and are described by users as mainly positive or pleasant. One estimate holds that of the roughly 20 million instances of use experienced in a given year by some 300,000 regular users, only about 5,000 or 6,000 result in such unpleasant or life-threatening effects that they require a trip to an emergency room—approximately *one-thirtieth of 1 percent* of all such episodes (Newmeyer, 1980, pp. 214–215). It is easy to see that the media have sensationalized the drug and its effects, and exaggerated the most violent and bizarre aspects of the PCP experience to the point that what is actually atypical is described as common, even routine. While one does take a certain psychological risk by ingesting PCP, and while that risk is probably higher than it is for any other illicit drug currently in use, at low doses, that risk is also extremely small. Whether that risk is worth it—common sense asks, why on earth should it be?—is not a scientific or even a medical issue, but a matter of personal values.

MINOR TRANQUILIZERS

The minor tranquilizers constitute a chemically miscellaneous group of drugs that are prescribed to allay anxiety. They include Valium (whose generic or chemical name is diazepam), Librium (chlordiazepoxide), Equanil and Miltown (meprobamate), and Placidyl (ethchlorvynol). The pharmaceutical use of the minor tranquilizers dropped sharply between the late 1970s and the early 1980s, as was explained in Chapter 4. Valium, once the most popular of all prescription drugs, lost almost half of its sales between 1975 and 1980, and its use is still declining; it now ranks eleventh in popularity among prescription drugs. Equanil ranked as the fiftieth most popular prescription drug in the United States in 1972, and ninetieth in 1976; by 1981, it had slipped off the list of the top 200 pharmaceuticals. Librium dropped during that same period from third to forty-fourth, and Placidyl

(120th in 1972) and Miltown (155th in 1972) are now not represented among the 200 most-prescribed drugs in the country. (The total number of all prescriptions written has remained stable at slightly less than 1.5 billion between 1972 and 1986.) Clearly, the prescription use of the minor tranquilizers is declining sharply. Physicians are being much more careful and conservative about writing prescriptions for these drugs as a result of their fear that these substances may do more harm than good. The DAWN data show a declining number of nonlethal overdoses associated with minor tranquilizers, but lethal overdoses have actually shown something of an increase. (The numbers for both are fairly high on an absolute basis, since this drug type is still extremely commonly used.) And the recreational tranquilizer use among America's high-school seniors seems to be inching down somewhat, as Table 9.4 indicates.

The minor tranquilizers are sold on the street (at several times the pharmacy price) and are used for both recreational (when taken in sufficiently large doses) and quasitherapeutic purposes. There is little illicit manufacture of the minor tranquilizers; nearly all of the supply stems from diversion of the legally obtained product into the black market. Often, a patient will visit a number of physicians, complain of the same symptoms, fill each prescription obtained, and then sell the surplus. Considering how many doses of the minor tranquilizers are used every day, this drug type is actually fairly safe. However, in large enough doses taken over a long enough period, all of the minor tranquilizers can produce a physical addiction or dependency. If an individual takes 300 milligrams of Librium, or 120 milligrams of Valium, daily for more than two months, he or she is probably physically dependent on the drug (Ray and Ksir, 1987, p. 135). Librium is

Table 9.3   Lethal and Nonlethal Overdoses Associated with Taking Minor Tranquilizers, 1979–1986

	Emergency-Room Episodes (nonlethal)	Medical Examiner's Reports (lethal)
1979–1980	24,395	455
1981–1982	21,413	480
1985	18,543	619
1986	18,453	750

SOURCE: DAWN, 1983, 1986, 1987.

Table 9.4   Use of Tranquilizers by High-School Seniors, 1975–1986

	1975	1982	1986
Ever Used	17	14	11
Used in Past Year	11	7	6
Used in Past Month	4	2	2

SOURCE: Johnston et al., 1987, pp. 47, 48, 49.

taken in 25-milligram capsules and Valium in 2-, 5-, or 10-milligram tablets; thus, some ten to fifteen times the therapeutic dose of tranquilizers will produce a physical dependency. With the cessation of such heavy, long-term use, the patient will experience withdrawal symptoms consisting of convulsions, tremors, cramps, and sweating. The vast majority of users take nowhere near an addicting quantity, and such reactions are therefore relatively rare.

MAJOR TRANQUILIZERS

The major tranquilizers are in most ways almost completely different from the minor tranquilizers, which actually share far more characteristics with the sedatives. Major tranquilizers are referred to as *antipsychotics,* and are used in the treatment of psychosis; they do not produce a high or intoxication, are almost never used recreationally, and are not sold on the underground market. Nearly all major tranquilizer use is legal, licit prescription use for the purpose of controlling mental illness, especially schizophrenia. The major tranquilizers are technically called phenothiazines, and include drugs that bear the brand names Thorazine, Stelazine, Compazine, and Mellaril.

The impact of the phenothiazines can be measured by an examination of the changes in the number of the resident patients in state and local mental hospitals in the United States from the 1950s onward. In 1955, there were almost 560,000 mental patients in residence on a given day; in that year, the phenothiazines were introduced to treat psychosis. The number of resident patients dropped every year after that; in 1985 there were about 130,000 resident patients, and this number continues to decline yearly. The change has not been due to a decline in new admissions to mental hospitals, because these actually rose from 178,000 in 1955 to 435,000 in 1976. Rather, the change was a result of the drastic decline in the average length of stay in mental hospitals. In 1955, the average period of hospitalization was six months; by 1975, it had dropped to twenty-six days (Ray, 1983, p. 273). The decline in the number of mental patients living in hospital facilities at a given time, and the reduction in their average length of stay in those facilities, is due in large part to the use of the major tranquilizers. About 85 percent of all patients in state, local, and federal mental hospitals receive some phenothiazine medication.

One of the phenothiazines, Thorazine (whose chemical name is chlorpromazine) is described as having the following effects on agitated, manic, and schizophrenic patients: The drug, one observer wrote, "produces marked quieting of the motor manifestations. Patients cease to be loud and profane, the tendency to hyperbolic associations is diminished, and the patients can sit still long enough to eat and to take care of normal physiological needs" (Goldman, 1955). The emotional withdrawal, hallucinations, delusions and other disturbed thinking, paranoia, belligerence, hostility, and "blunted affect" of patients are all significantly reduced (Veteran's Administration, 1970, p. 4).

As a result of the use of the antipsychotics, patients exhibit fewer symptoms of psychosis and have become more manageable, which has permitted hospitals to cut back or discontinue such ineffective or dangerous practices as hydrotherapy, electroshock therapy, and lobotomies. And, as a result of the administration of these drugs, hospitals have, in the words of one observer, been transformed from "zoo-smelling, dangerous bedlams into places fit for human beings to live and, at times, to recover from psychosis" (Callaway, 1958, p. 82). And by inducing a more "normal" psychological state in patients, it has been possible to release them into the community as outpatients, with only minimal treatment and care in aftercare facilities. Studies have shown that about three-quarters of all acute schizophrenics demonstrate significant improvement following the administration of phenothiazine drugs, and between 75 and 95 percent of all patients relapse if their medication is discontinued (Ray and Ksir, 1987, p. 238). The antipsychotic drugs are not only regarded as effective for most mental patients, but are also the least expensive of all treatment modalities. It should be added that, though these drugs do reduce the most bizarre symptoms of schizophrenia and other mental illnesses, very few mental patients are able to live what are regarded as completely "normal" lives; one estimate places this figure at only 15 percent (Veteran's Administration, 1970).

The phenothiazines are not addictive and rarely result in lethal overdoses. There are some side effects of these drugs, however, including abnormal, involuntary, and sometimes bizarre movements of the tongue, lips, and cheeks, facial tics, tremors, rigidity, and a shuffling walk. These symptoms are treated with a separate type of drug, the anti-Parkinsonian drugs. Some critics also argue that the phenothiazines reduce the mental acuity and intelligence of patients.

ACCOUNT: GIVING UP VALIUM

A personal account follows, describing the Valium use of a secretary in her early thirties. She abruptly discontinued her use of the drug. The drug can be addicting in sufficiently large doses, and it is possible to die as a consequence of taking too massive a dose. However, considering the millions of patients who take it, these experiences are fairly rare.

> For about ten years, I had been getting my Valium prescription filled by my own physician, the doctor I see when something's wrong with me. Recently, I ran out of my supply of those friendly little turquoise-colored tablets, and I called my doctor; this time, unlike the previous times, he asked me to have a check-up before he filled the prescription. When I walked into his office, he wore a long, serious face. He was holding my medical file. He said that he had calculated my Valium usage over the past year; I had averaged nearly two 10-milligram tablets per day—and this represented an increase over the year before. I was becoming

tolerant to the drug, he said, and my use was now reaching a level at which it had become a hazard to my health. He felt that I had become dependent on Valium. He said that either directly, in his own practice, or indirectly, through his medical group, he has contact with some 3,000 patients. Not one, he said, regularly uses as much Valium as I do, though a few take it as often for brief periods of time. He said that I should seek some more permanent means of dealing with my anxiety—such as psychotherapy. He agreed to fill this prescription, but he warned that it would probably be the last one. I should think very seriously about phasing out the use of Valium altogether.

I walked out of that office almost in a state of shock. I just couldn't believe it. First of all, I hadn't realized that I was using that much. It did make sense, though; there were very few days (or nights) when I didn't pop a tablet or two. Maybe no nights when I didn't; I really hadn't kept track. But the other thing was, I never thought of Valium as a real drug. I put it on the same level drug-wise as aspirin. *Everybody* takes Valium, I thought—it's the number-one prescription drug in the country, it's got to be safe! I have friends who won't walk out of the door without their little vial of Valium. In the movie *Starting Over,* Burt Reynolds has an anxiety attack on a showroom bed in a department store, as a crowd gathers around him. His brother, who's a doctor, I think, asks the crowd, "Does anybody have a Valium?" and around ten people take out their little vials. I honestly didn't think that my use of this safe, safe drug was out of line with what other people were doing. I had heard about that book, *I'm Dancing As Fast As I Can,* which was about a woman's withdrawal from Valium "addiction," and I thought the whole thing was ludicrous. In the doses I was taking it, Valium, I thought, wasn't any more addicting than milk.

What I did was, I filled the prescription, took my vial of fifty tablets home, and put it in the medicine chest. I felt a sense of security to have it there. But I wanted to see how dependent I really was, so I just stopped taking it altogether. It didn't matter if I was staring at the ceiling at four in the morning—I was going to stop taking Valium. I also wanted to make sure my drinking didn't increase to compensate for not taking the drug. What happened was—nothing. I simply discontinued taking Valium; the vial is still in the medicine chest, unopened. That was over a year ago. I do have a harder time getting to sleep at night, but at least it's a natural sleep. There are times during the day when I feel tense and anxious, but I'll just have to deal with those feelings. I decided that I didn't want to harm my body, and so I made a resolution and stuck with it. I just wonder, though, how dependent I could have been if it was so easy to stop, just like that. [From the author's files.]

CHAPTER 10

Heroin and the Narcotics

The most feared, the most dreaded, the "hardest" drug (Kaplan, 1983)—for decades, heroin has virtually defined the drug problem. In spite of being somewhat overshadowed, since the mid-1980s, by cocaine, heroin is still the substance the American public is most likely to point to as an example of a dangerous drug; disapproval of any level of use is higher for heroin than it is for any other drug; opposition to legalization is higher for heroin than it is for any other drug; and heroin addicts are the most stigmatized of all drug users. Heroin is the epitome of the illicit street drug. Its association in the public mind with street crime, even today, in spite of strong competition from crack, is stronger than for any other drug. The stereotype of the "junkie" is that he or she is by nature a lowlife, an outcast, a dweller in the underworld, an unsavory, untrustworthy character to be avoided at almost any cost. This fact alone makes heroin an immensely fascinating drug to study.

Heroin is chemically derived from morphine; in volume, five units of morphine produce one of heroin. Morphine is in turn extracted from opium, which is roughly 10 percent morphine by weight. Opium is grown in and imported mainly from Southeast Asia, Afghanistan, Pakistan, Iran, the Middle East, and Mexico. All the various alkaloid products of opium are called *opiates*, and they include, aside from opium itself, morphine, heroin, codeine, Dilaudid (a semisynthetic derivative of opium), laudanum (a 10 percent tincture of opium), and paregoric (a 4 percent tincture of opium). There are also a number of synthetic narcotics with many of the same effects as heroin, usually called *opioids*, which include Demerol (meperidine), Dolophine (methadone), Percodan, and Darvon. In addition, there are the newer "designer" narcotics, including fentanyl, whose potency in some cases, is far greater than heroin's.

The term "narcotic" is often used loosely and incorrectly to refer to any illegal drug. A newspaper headline, for instance, might read, "Police Nab Suspect, Confiscate Narcotics Stash" to refer to cocaine, marijuana, or illegal prescription drugs. Properly speaking, however, narcotics are painkillers or *analgesics*. (It could be that one feels pain under the influence, but is unconcerned about it.) These drugs tend, in fact, to reduce sensory feeling and sensitivity of all kinds—to pleasure as well as pain. A second characteristic of narcotics is that they tend to be *soporific*—that is, in sufficiently large doses, they induce drowsiness, mental clouding, lethargy, even sleep. (Morphine is named after Morpheus, the Greek god of dreams, and the scientific name for the opium poppy is *Papaver somniferum,* named for its quality of inducing somnolence.) As analgesics, narcotics are without peer, and are therefore of immense therapeutic value.

But they are also, without exception, *physically addicting*—a third characteristic of the narcotics. In the terms we introduced in Chapter 2, they generate a *physical* dependence. They are also highly reinforcing—that is, they generate a very strong psychic or *psychological* dependence, possibly second only to that of the stimulants. And they are capable of generating an overwhelming *behavioral* dependence. (However, the belief "One shot and you're hooked for life" is completely false; of the total universe of all people who have tried heroin, most are or were experimenters, and there are far more sporadic or infrequent heroin users than addicts.)

And fourth, narcotics generate *euphoria*—after the IV injection of a narcotic, the user feels a "flash," a "rush," an intense voluptuous, orgasmlike sensation. Following this is the feeling of well-being, tranquility, ease, and calm, the sensation that everything in the user's life is just fine. Tensions, worries, problems, the rough edges of life, seem simply to melt away. Few drugs or drug types generate this feeling of well-being as effectively as narcotics, and of the more commonly used narcotics, heroin seems to do the job best of all.

There are a number of painkillers that are not classified as narcotics—aspirin is the best-known; they do not produce mental clouding or dependence, and are far safer in terms of overdosing. Still, as we saw in Chapter 4, thousands of Americans overdose on aspirin each year; in 1986, there were 5,500 nonlethal emergency-room episodes in the United States associated with aspirin. At the same time, on a user-for-user, dose-for-dose basis, the non-narcotic analgesics are relatively safe; the narcotics, clearly dangerous.

One thing that makes heroin and the other narcotics dangerous is that the range between their effective dose (ED) and lethal dose (LD) is fairly narrow; the quantity that can kill a user is only ten to fifteen times the amount that can get him or her high. Thus it is extremely easy to die of an overdose of any of the narcotics, especially heroin. Although the mechanism of death by narcotics overdose is not completely understood (Inciardi, 1986, pp. 64–67)—the adulterants mixed with heroin and/or the other drugs used in conjunction with it, possibly alcohol, may contribute—still, taking huge doses of a narcotic is an almost certain way to kill oneself. As with alcohol and barbiturates, an overdose of heroin causes respiratory paralysis, resulting in oxygen starvation of the brain.

It is remarkable that heroin is such a well-known and almost universally dreaded drug, since it attracts far fewer users than almost any other illegal drug or drug type. The small number of heavy heroin users that we do have inflict a great deal of damage on the rest of society—and, in turn, the rest of society inflicts a great deal of damage on them.

In the high-school survey I've so often cited, heroin ranks dead last in popularity among all drugs asked about, with the next least-used drug (PCP) used by *four times* as many individuals as heroin. In this survey, marijuana was used by almost *fifty times* as many high-school seniors as heroin was. In 1986, only 1.1 percent of these high-school seniors had even tried heroin; 0.5 percent had used it at least once in the past year; and 0.2 percent used it within the past month. These numbers represent a decline from 1975, when the comparable figures were 2.2, 1.0, and 0.4 percent respectively. The figures for college students were significantly *below* those for the high-school seniors (Johnston et al., 1987, pp. 47–49, 179, 180, 206, 207).

In the national survey, about 1 percent of all Americans had tried heroin at least once in their lives—less than 0.5 percent for youths age 12 to 17; 1.2 percent for young adults age 18 to 25; and 1.1 percent for adults age 26 and over. Less than 0.5 of youth and older adults had used it in the past year; 0.6 percent of 18- to 25-year-olds had done so. Of all individuals who had used at least one illegal drug once or more in their lives, fewer than 3 percent had tried or used heroin (NIDA, 1986). A fraction of 1 percent of all episodes of illegal drug use involved heroin. Clearly, then, heroin is one of the least widely used of all the well-known drugs or drug types.

At the same time, heroin shows up with remarkable frequency in the available abuse statistics. According to the Drug Awareness Warning Network (DAWN) statistics, in 1986, nearly 18 percent of all emergency-room episodes entailed the use of heroin, and, in a whopping 30 percent of all lethal drug overdoses, heroin was involved (DAWN, 1987, pp. 30, 54). As we saw, not every time a drug is mentioned or reported in DAWN's figures is it the causal mechanism in the overdose. Nonetheless, when a given drug shows up frequently in overdose episodes, it can be presumed to play a significant role in lethal or life-threatening reactions. Given how infrequently heroin is used in comparison with all other drugs, its contribution to nonlethal and especially lethal overdoses is nothing short of spectacular.

Heroin is not the only narcotic that is used for recreational or nonmedical purposes. In the survey of high-school seniors cited above, all the other narcotics, added together, were used by *ten times* as many respondents as heroin was. In its national survey, the National Institute on Drug Abuse (NIDA) estimated that, while 1.9 million Americans had used heroin at least once during their life, 12.6 million had used one or more of the "analgesics" for nonmedical purposes. Thus the narcotics aside from heroin—Darvon, Percodan, methadone, Dilaudid, codeine, and Demerol—make up a major type of illicit drug, used outside a medical context by roughly as many Americans as are stimulants (not counting cocaine), tranquilizers, sedatives, hallucinogens, or inhalants. (Opium, a major narcotic, is not widely used in the United States; and DAWN counts another narcotic, morphine, as belonging to the same category as heroin, since heroin breaks down to morphine once it enters the body.) At the same time, among users of narcotics, heroin is the drug of choice. Street addicts will ingest any narcotic that is available at a particular time; while heroin is preferred, at some times, in some of the nation's smaller cities, or in certain neighborhoods, or in some social circles, it may not be as readily available as some of the other narcotics, such as codeine, Dilaudid, Percodan, or Darvon. Consequently, these drugs will be used until heroin becomes available.

In 1986, there were about 25,000 mentions of narcotics in nonlethal emergency-room overdoses; more than 15,000 of these involved heroin or morphine. There were roughly 2,500 lethal drug overdoses with one or more narcotics implicated reported by medical examiners; more than 1,500 of these entailed heroin or morphine. Thus, while all the narcotics other than heroin attract 90 percent of the users of narcotics, and heroin only 10 percent, heroin contributes to more than 60 percent of the lethal and nonlethal narcotics overdoses. Once again, we must be impressed with heroin's massive contribution to harmful drug effects, even among the narcotics.

Heroin's role in the number of both nonlethal and lethal overdoses is growing over time. In fact, from 1979–1980 to 1986, the number of emergency-room episodes involving heroin doubled (from 7,784 to 15,832) and the number of medical examiner's reports more than tripled (474 to 1,549). As we know from our discussion of DAWN data in Chapter 4, an increase in overdoses over time could involve a number of factors—an increase in the purity of the drug, an increase in the frequency of use among the same number of users, a greater tendency for users to take that drug in combination with other drugs, and its use by means of more potentially lethal routes of administration (injecting, for instance, instead of snorting). It is entirely possible that, as both lethal and nonlethal heroin overdoses increase, the number of heroin users is actually declining. There are three indications that this might in fact be the case.

To begin with, none of the indicators in the available national surveys has demonstrated an increase in heroin use in the past few years; if anything, most of these indicators are down. Second, as we noted in the discussion on cocaine (in Chapter 8), recruitment of young heroin addicts seems to be slowing down, at least in New York City, possibly as a result of their use of crack instead of heroin.

And third, the potency of street heroin has been increasing dramatically. For decades, the heroin available at the retail or user level has been 3 to 5 percent pure, with the rest made up of adulterants and fillers, such as mannitol, lactose, and quinine. In 1986, though, the New York City police were confiscating heroin with a purity of 30 to 70 percent. Much of this is "China White" heroin—derived from opium grown in Southeast Asia, and imported from Hong Kong by ethnic Chinese. Chinese gangs have been getting into heroin importation in a big way, at least on the East coast, only in the last few years. (In fact, heroin is now being smuggled into the United States by gangs with a wide variety of national and ethnic backgrounds; they include—aside from Chinese—Thais, Pakistanis, Indians, Iranians, Afghans, Nigerians, Lebanese, and Israelis; see Kessler, 1985; Kerr, 1987b.) Inciardi (1986, p. 69) says that a substance found on the streets of Miami in 1980 called China White was not in fact this "mythical strain of heroin." However, the New York City police claim that what they are seeing invading the streets of New York in the late 1980s is, in fact, remarkably pure heroin from Hong Kong. In 1983, only 3 percent of the heroin confiscated on the streets of New York was "China White"; in 1986, 40 percent of it was; and in 1987, police estimate, this had reached 70 percent. In addition, between 1983 and 1986, a new strain of Mexican heroin, called "black tar," with a purity of 60 to 70 percent, showed up with great frequency across the country (Brinkley, 1986). And third, a synthetic "designer drug," a narcotic called *fentanyl*, with a potency of twenty to forty times that of heroin, began to appear on the street all over the country, especially California; it is especially frequently used by physicians (Gallagher, 1986a).[1] Many observers believe that the purity of today's street heroin is as high as it is in part to attract a dwindling clientele who are moving away from heroin to other drugs, especially cocaine.

NARCOTICS: A HISTORICAL PERSPECTIVE

Self-administering narcotics has a long history in the United States and elsewhere. In the nineteenth century, opium and morphine (as well as cocaine) were contained in thousands of over-the-counter preparations. They were called "patent medicines," and were used to cure headaches, toothaches, teething pains, menstrual cramps, insomnia, nervousness, depression, rheumatism, athlete's foot, diarrhea, dysentery, consumption, the common cold, and even baldness and cancer; they were panaceas, or ineffective cure-alls, and they were sold under names such as Ayer's Cherry Pectoral, Mrs. Winslow's Soothing Syrup, McMunn's Elixir of Opium, Dover's Powder, Godfrey's Cordial, and Hamlin's Wizard Oil (Inciardi, 1986, pp. 2–3; Brecher et al., 1972, pp. 3–16; Berridge and Edwards, 1987, pp. 62–72). During the nineteenth century, no restrictions whatsoever existed on what was put into these potions or what claims the manufacturer was allowed to make as to their medical effectiveness; indeed, the contents of these concoctions did not even have to be listed on the package or the bottle. They were sold to anyone, without benefit of a prescription, in pharmacies, grocery stores, general stores, through mail-order catalogues (the 1897 edition of the Sears Roebuck catalogue offered hypodermic kits for sale), and at traveling medicine shows. Patent medicines containing narcotics were as easily obtainable as aspirin is today (Brecher, 1986, p. 1). Nineteenth-century America was truly a "dope fiend's paradise" (Brecher et al., 1972, p. 3). In 1898, heroin was synthesized, and it quickly joined the

---

[1]To make things confusing, the drug called "China White" that Inciardi mentions (1986, p. 69) turned out to be fentanyl. However, the New York City police claim that they are now seeing a new strain of heroin from Southeast Asia, which they call China White. To confound the issue even further, there are a number of chemical analogues or variants of fentanyl, ranging in potency from roughly the same as heroin to 3,000 times as potent. Of the latter, one authority said, "You could kill fifty people with the amount that fits on the head of a pin" (Blakeslee, 1985).

ranks of the ingredients in the pseudomedicines freely available to the American public.

It is necessary to stress three crucial points about nineteenth- and early twentieth-century over-the-counter patent medicines containing narcotics. First, they were taken for medical (or pseudomedical) reasons, not for the purpose of attaining a high or euphoria. They were used by people with medical ailments who did not consult a physician to determine the most effective cure, and by people whose physicians were quacks. The reason why these concoctions often appeared to be effective was that, since they contained opiates, they dulled the pain of the disease; eventually, the body overcomes most diseases, and thus the potion appeared to be the curative agent. Often, however, after the disease passed, the user of the patent medicine was left with a physical dependence.

Second, a very large number of individuals were taking these patent medicines. It is impossible to estimate with any degree of precision just how many addicts the freely available over-the-counter narcotic preparations created. Figures at the time were notoriously unreliable; in fact, the concept of physical addiction was not yet clearly understood. Estimates as to the total number of addicts at the turn of the century range from a low of 100,000 to a high of several million. In 1919, the Treasury Department issued a report claiming that approximately a million individuals were addicted to narcotics at the turn of the century. Other estimates, based on extrapolations from several local surveys, range from less than a quarter of a million (Terry and Pellens, 1928) to just under half a million (Kolb and DuMez, 1924).

And third, narcotics users and addicts at, just before, and just after the turn of the century were, for the most part, respectable folk. The heavy users of patent medicines were disproportionately drawn from the middle and upper-middle-classes. Said one article published in 1881, "opium eating" is an "aristocratic vice and prevails more extensively among the wealthy and educated classes than among those of inferior social positions" (Brecher et al., 1972, p. 18). While some criminals did use narcotics—mostly they smoked opium—the vast majority of narcotics users were users for medical reasons, and were not involved in a life of crime. There was no necessary connection between the heavy, chronic use of narcotics and criminal behavior, as there is today. The addict was seen as an unfortunate, sick person in need of medical attention, a helpless victim but not a criminal (Terry and Pellens, 1928; Lindesmith, 1965, 1968; Duster, 1970).

Four additional facts are of interest here. First, the late nineteenth-century, early twentieth-century addict was more likely to be a woman than a man—in several surveys conducted at the time, roughly two-thirds of heavy opiate users were women. Second, users tended to be middle-aged rather than young. In a Chicago survey, the average age of male users of opiates was 41, and of females, 39; in Iowa, the average age was 46; and in Tennessee, it was 50 (Brecher et al., 1972, p. 18). Third, some indications point to the fact that Blacks were underrepresented among the users of opiates eighty to a hundred years ago. And fourth, it is likely that users were drawn from the entire rural-urban spectrum; use, in other words, did not appear to be heavily concentrated in large cities. Users were as likely to come from Iowa farms as from New York City, on a per population basis.

By the 1920s, the public image of the narcotics addict had become totally transformed into that of a criminal, a willful degenerate who was immoral and depraved, a hedonistic thrill-seeker in need of a stiff prison sentence. Moreover, the actual social composition of narcotic addicts also underwent a transformation so that by the 1930s, they bore no resemblance whatsoever to the turn-of-the-century addict. For roughly half a century, users and abusers—and especially addicts—of heroin and the other narcotics have been predominantly or overwhelmingly in search of euphoria or a high rather than a medical cure for a disease; of relatively low rather than relatively high socioeconomic status; criminals rather than respectable folk; males rather than females; Black rather than white; young rather than middle-aged; and from large cities rather than less heavily populated areas.

What accounts for this transformation? Why did the image of the addict change? And what brought about the total turnaround in the socioeconomic portrait of addiction?

In December 1914, Congress passed the Harrison Act, which outlawed the sale of over-the-counter narcotic preparations and placed the addict in the hands of the physician. Whatever the intent of the law, it is clear that most addicts simply continued to receive drugs from their physicians, on prescription, instead of directly from their local pharmacists. If a physician construed the administration of morphine to a patient to be within the scope of legitimate medical practice, he had the right, within the law, to maintain that addict on morphine. On the face of it, then, the law did not change anything. It was the Supreme Court that drew a restrictive interpretation of the Harrison Act and that decided what was to constitute "legitimate" medical practice; in a series of decisions from 1919 to 1922 the Court declared maintenance of an addict to be outside the scope of medical practice and therefore illegal. However, in 1925, in the famous *Linder* case, the Supreme Court overturned its earlier decisions, declaring addiction per se not to be a crime and paving the way for the legality of maintenance. The Court affirmed the decision in 1962, in *Robinson* v. *California*. Thus the present punitive policies are a consequence of decisions made by the Supreme Court between 1919 and 1922, decisions that were superseded and reversed by later rulings. A good case could therefore be made for the unconstitutionality of present legal policies.

Because of police harrassment of physicians following the passage of the Harrison Act and the wave of arrests of doctors following the Supreme Court's decisions, most physicians became unwilling to shoulder the legal risks attendant upon treating the addict and eventually discontinued administering narcotic drugs. One study estimated that in the two dozen years after the Harrison Act—and primarily after 1919—25,000 physicians were arraigned on narcotics-selling charges, and 3,000 actually served prison sentences (New York Academy of Medicine, 1963). Thousands more had their licenses revoked. The authorities could not have encouraged the emergence of an underworld traffic in narcotic drugs better even by design. The arrest of physicians during this period took the following form: selling drugs was declared illegal, thus driving most physicians out of the practice of treating addicts; the few who continued to do so, whether for idealistic or mercenary reasons, naturally attracted a sizable clientele—and just as naturally were charged with "trafficking" in narcotics.

Apparently, the dilemma was at least dimly perceived by some officials, since in 1919 and 1920, forty-four ambulatory clinics were opened with a view toward the rehabilitation and eventual cure of addicts. The programs were highly variable in method and effectiveness. In the New York clinic, which received the most attention and publicity, drugs were handed out more or less indiscriminately to anyone who claimed to need drugs; moreover, through various tricks many addicts were able to obtain much more than their share and to sell what they did not use to other addicts. The New York clinic was investigated by the Bureau of Internal Revenue, and a highly critical report of its operations was written. Muckraking journalists attacked the program; several reporters posed as addicts and discovered that they could receive addicting drugs almost upon demand. There was a public outcry; campaigns were launched to close the clinics. All but one of the forty-four clinics had been shut down by 1921, and the project was entirely abandoned by 1923. The program was branded a disastrous failure. Actually, the New York clinic, the object of the most vigorous criticism, was the least well run and most clearly unsuccessful. The clinics in New Orleans and Shreveport, Louisiana, appeared to have been successful in their stated goals: (1) relieving the addict's suffering; (2) offsetting the illegal drug trade; (3) curtailing the spread of addiction; and (4) reducing the criminal activity of addicts. These efforts, however, received little public attention.

The demise of the public clinics, engineered by prohibitionistic officials, was then used by them to galvanize popular sentiment against the strictly medical approach to addiction. The public came to support the view that the addict had to be dealt with punitively, that addiction was a matter for the police and not the physician. Actually, the medical approach was not tried in most clinics; rather simple maintenance, or handing out drugs without any medical treatment whatsoever, was the rule. The more carefully run, medically oriented programs did not convince those in power that a true medical approach could in fact work. Addiction came to be seen as inherently untreatable—and inherently criminal. A shift in enforcement came about at almost the same time as the demise of the public clinics. In 1919, the first year of their operation, there were only 1,000 federal arrests on narcotics charges. In 1921, when all but one of the public clinics had closed, there were 4,000 federal arrests. And by 1925 there were more than 10,000 arrests (Lindesmith, 1965, p. 143).

Clearly, then, what happened as a result of the Harrison Act and subsequent Supreme Court rulings was not simply the diminution of a once-large population but the appearance of a totally different population. Far from simply reducing the problem of drug addiction, legislation and enforcement practices appear to have created some problems.

It is obvious, then, that the first half of the 1920s witnessed the dramatic emergence of a criminal class of addicts—*a criminal class that had not existed previously.* The link between addiction and crime—the view that the addict was by definition a criminal—was forged. The law itself created a new class of criminals.

Probably the most important contribution that law enforcement has made to the problem of addiction is *the creation of an addict subculture.* It is important to emphasize that prior to 1914 no addict subculture of any significance existed in the United States, and there was no inevitable link between narcotics and crime. There was a small population of opium smokers, consisting primarily of Chinese immigrants and of bohemian, literary, underworld, and demimonde figures who learned the habit from the Chinese. Addicts did not display any special cohesion or loyalty as a group; they possessed no lore concerned with the acquisition and administration of drugs, no ideology elaborating the qualities of various drug highs, no justification for using drugs, no status ranking unique to the world of addiction, no rejection of the nonaddict world.

During the formative 1920s, these elements of an addict subculture began to emerge. Alfred Lindesmith has said that by 1935, when he was studying addicts in Chicago, "there already was a subculture without doubt" (Alfred Lindesmith, 1971, personal communication). *It was the criminalization of addiction that created addicts as a special and distinctive group, and it is the subcultural aspect of addicts that gives them their recruiting power.* Up until the past few years, external factors have played a more important role in curtailing the spread of addiction than anything the police have done. Alcohol prohibition (1920–1933) focused the activities of organized crime on the distribution of liquor rather than narcotics—in fact, got organized crime started on a big-business scale. The Depression of the 1930s also had a delaying effect on the growth of the addict subculture. And the disruption of drug supply lines during World War II slowed down to a considerable degree the recruitment of new addicts. By the end of the war some experts thought that addiction to narcotics had ceased to be a problem of any magnitude; at that time there were only 20,000 known narcotic addicts in the United States. But starting in 1945, and especially in the late 1960s, addiction began to rise dramatically. It is entirely reasonable to view this rise as largely due to the recruitment powers of a gradually developing subculture of intensely committed addicts. And it was through the efforts of the police and the courts that this subculture came into being in the first place.

A second major consequence of the punitive police approach to drugs was the rise in *the criminal activity of addicts.* The view that addicts are "inherently" criminal is totally without foundation. The Harrison Act and the legal decisions that followed in its wake created a class of criminal addicts. Beginning in the 1920s, every narcotic addict was by definition a criminal. Soon thereafter, nearly all narcotic addicts, except the very wealthy and members of the medical profession, were also criminals in a second sense as well: most engaged in money-making criminal behavior. Before the turn of the century, it did not cost a great deal of money to maintain an opium or morphine habit. But the process of criminalization changed that; narcotics became expensive and difficult to obtain. Moreover, it became profitable to sell narcotics, products that were both expensive and highly valued. Addicts wanted it, and criminal gangs were eager to sell it. Thus one of the consequences of criminalizing addiction was that it served to forge a strong link between using narcotics and engaging in criminal behavior.

It cannot be doubted that criminalizing narcotics early in the twentieth century had the short-term impact of reducing the number of addicts in the population. It is almost certain that the less heavily involved users of the medicinal narcotics discontinued their habit without a great deal of difficulty following the Harrison Act. Some users may have turned to other drugs, such as the newly marketed barbiturates, as a substitute. But it is also true that there were a number of unanticipated and undesired long-range consequences of the punitive approach to the narcotics problem; clearly several of these consequences included the generation and growth of the criminal addict subculture, the intensification of the involvement of its members in money-making crimes, and the strengthening of the recruiting powers of this subculture. Today, of course, we have far more addicts than existed at the turn of the century, although possibly the same percentage, taking size of population into account.

If nineteenth-century America was a "dope fiend's paradise," what is late twentieth-century America?

ADDICTION AND CRIME

It is no surprise that today's narcotics user, abuser, or addict is deeply involved in a life of crime. As we saw in Chapter 3, drug users generally, and users of narcotics especially, tend to be recruited from social circles in which deviance, delinquency, and crime are more acceptable and more common than average. We also know, commonsensically, that heroin users have extremely high rates of criminal behavior, especially with respect to money-making crimes. Some observers have concluded from the narcotics-crime connection that it is the criminal who turns to narcotics. Narcotics do not cause criminal behavior, they reason; the reverse is true—heroin users are indeed criminals and should be treated as such. In contrast, other observers have advocated the "enslavement" theory of addiction: otherwise law-abiding citizens are forced into a life of crime to support a prohibitively expensive drug habit. The solution? Legalize heroin. (Inciardi, 1979, 1986, p. 140, discusses these two positions.) Which of these two views is correct?

Studies show that the heroin user, abuser, or addict commits a massive quantity of crime; no observer of the drug scene doubts this. But is it the heroin or the user that is the main criminogenic factor here? One study traced 354 male heroin addicts living in the Baltimore area from the very beginning of their use of opiates throughout periods of addiction, abstinence, and relapse (Ball, Shaffer, and Nurco, 1983). It compared addiction periods with nonaddiction periods and found striking differences in the rates of crime during the two types of period. During the individuals' very first "on" period of addiction, compared with the first "off" or nonaddicted period that followed it, individuals committed crimes of theft on four times as many days (34 versus 9 percent of all days, on a yearly basis), crimes of violence on twenty times as many days (2 versus 0.1 percent of all days), and fraud or confidence games on fifteen times as many days (7 versus 0.5 percent of all days). As we might expect, drug-dealing crime days were considerably more common (23 versus 6 percent). And days on which all other crimes were committed were three and a half times more frequent (28 versus 8 percent).

This same pattern prevailed over the addicts' second, third, and subsequent "on" and "off" periods, except that during the later "on" periods, they committed crime on more days, and during the later "off" periods, they committed crime on fewer days, than during the first period. Overall, there were *four times* as many crime days during addicted periods as during nonaddicted periods; even more significant, there were *fifteen times* as many multiple crime days (Ball, Shaffer, and Nurco, 1983). Since, obviously, these men were the same individuals during days when they were "on" heroin as "off," the theory that they are simply criminals who use heroin—and would engage in a life of crime whether they use the drug or not—cannot be the whole explanation. At the same time, even on their "off" days, these men did commit a great deal of criminal behavior.

Inciardi (1979, 1986, pp. 122–132) found that the amount of crime that heroin users committed was "astronomical"—far greater than most experts had imagined before systematic studies were conducted. Miami narcotic users committed an average of 375 crimes per individual per year—more than 200,000 offenses for a one-year period for 573 users. Even discounting drug offenses, there were more than 230 offenses per year per user. The range or diversity of crimes the sample engaged in was enormous—from procuring and prostitution to armed robbery and assault. At the same time, the likelihood of arrest was extremely low—only one arrest for every 353 crimes committed! Only 0.3 percent of all offenses led to arrest. When the criminal behavior of a sample of narcotic users was compared with that of a sample of users of non-narcotic drugs, it was found that "the narcotics-using group were more criminally involved. They committed more crimes, engaged in a greater diversity of offenses, and significantly larger proportions committed the more serious offenses" (Inciardi, 1986, p. 129). What clearly emerged from these data is the conclusion that *"narcotics drive crime"*; the use of or addiction to narcotic drugs seems to *intensify* a tendency to be involved in a life of crime (Inciardi, 1986, pp. 130, 140).

Going back to the two theories of the narcotics-crime connection mentioned above—the "criminals turn to narcotics" theory and the "enslavement" theory—it seems that both are clearly so flawed as to be misleading. They posit what is a false dichotomy, an either-or proposition, neither alternative of which fits the data. While it is true that most individuals who become users of narcotics engage in delinquent behavior even before they try or use drugs, their use of and involvement in narcotics does significantly *accelerate* the frequency with which they engage in criminal activity, as well as the seriousness of these crimes. Thus the "enslavement" view is not wholly correct, since narcotics users are not innocent of crime at the point of their initial use. And the "criminals turn to narcotics" view is not wholly correct either, since users' patterns of criminal behavior are strikingly different during periods when they are using narcotics as compared with times when they are not. Thus a third view is necessary to explain the narcotics-crime connection: the intensification model.

"TAKING CARE OF BUSINESS": THE ECONOMIC LIFE OF THE HEROIN ABUSER

Heroin use, abuse, and addiction are among those subjects about which most people are long on opinion and short on fact. A number of myths abound on the topic. Recently, a careful and detailed study of 201 New York heroin abusers was conducted (Johnson et al., 1985); the book that reports its findings is called *Taking Care of Business*—that is, doing what one has to do to survive, a common theme in narcotic addicts' lives. Instead of conducting a one-shot interview with the addicts, this research team rented a storefront in a neighborhood noted for its high level of heroin addiction and remained in the community, collecting interviews over a period of time and obtaining users' detailed day-to-day reports of use and criminal activities. This technique turned out to be far more accurate and valid than one based on a single interview. Some surprising findings emerged from this study, findings that belie a number of common myths about addiction.

First, *most "addicts" are not really addicted in the physical sense*! They are psychologically and behaviorally dependent on heroin—they use it as much as they can, week after week, and their lives pretty much revolve around procuring money to pay for it, getting hold of the drug itself, and using it. But most regular users of heroin may not be addicted in the strictly physiological sense—that is, they would not suffer painful withdrawal symptoms if they were to discontinue use. Most regular users of heroin take their drug often, but not necessarily several times a day, day in and day out, in classic junkie fashion. Instead, they use twice one day, once the next, not at all for three days, four times the day after that, and so on. The vast majority of the study's sample displayed an extremely complicated pattern of heroin consumption. Even more common than the regular user was the occasional user, taking heroin once a month, once a week, from time to time. Roughly a third of the study's sample was made up of "irregular" (up to twice a week) users, a third of "regular" (three to five times a week) users, and a third of "daily" (six or more times a week) users. The issue of the literal physical addiction of the study's respondents was never raised.

Some observers will object, claiming that the study's respondents "aren't really addicted"; they merely represent the lower end of the heroin-use spectrum. But the Johnson study suggests that the "classic" junkie may be relatively rare compared with nonaddicted heroin abusers. It is entirely likely that the figures commonly quoted for the number of addicts—half a million in the United States, half of them in New York City—refer to heroin abusers like the ones in this study, and not addicts who are literally physically dependent on heroin. Moreover, this study suggests that this distinction is really not very important: The differences in criminal behavior among the daily user, the regular user, and the irregular user are linear—a question of degree—and not an either-or proposition. At the same time, the extent of a heroin user's habit is a crucial dimension, influencing other aspects of his or her life.

Of course, many heroin abusers are addicted, just as it is likely that a proportion of those in this study were. (Though, again, physical dependence was not explored by the Johnson team.) Certainly the abusers at the upper end of the use spectrum were physically addicted to heroin. However, the important point is this: There is a spectrum of physical dependence; there is a spectrum of psychological dependence; and there is a spectrum of behavioral dependence. A common myth is that it is not possible to use heroin on an occasional or recreational basis; one is either an addict or an abstainer. But clearly one can have a small "jones" or a habit without being addicted in the classic sense. Clearly, addiction and dependence are far more complicated phenomena than has been thought in the past. Were heroin freely available, however, most of Johnson's sample would clearly have become physically dependent on the drug; they did not simply because it is so expensive and so difficult to raise the money to pay for it day after day, week after week, year after year. We'll meet the *controlled* heroin user shortly; most of Johnson's sample was not made up of controlled users.

Second, *most "addicts" are not driven by the need to avoid withdrawal.* A major implication of the finding that "most addicts aren't literally addicted" is that the popular image of the addict being impelled by the physiological drive to avoid withdrawal symptoms ("I need a fix") is highly likely to be a myth. As we saw in Chapter 3, psychological dependence is every bit as powerful a drive as—and in fact, may be a more powerful drive than—physiological dependence. These heroin abusers are driven to continue taking heroin; in their scheme of things, they *do* "need a fix." But most do not need it to avoid withdrawal, since the majority of individuals who are referred to as addicts are not taking heroin or any other narcotic sufficiently frequently, or in large enough doses, to be literally physically dependent.

Third, *most regular heroin users do not become physically dependent on the drug.* The erratic and complicated pattern of heroin use displayed by these "addicts" calls into question the belief that once someone begins using heroin at all, and especially regularly, then a literal addiction is an inevitability. The majority of the Johnson study's sample had been taking heroin regularly for years, and yet most continued to take it in quantities that would not produce physical dependency. It is also likely that, were heroin freely available, they would become true-blue addicts; it is only because raising the cash to "cop" heroin two, three, or four times a day is such a difficult, risky, dangerous proposition that most are not using with that frequency.

Fourth, *addicts and abusers spend much less on heroin than most people think.* A major myth that the Johnson study explodes has to do with the dollar value of the heroin consumed by abusers. Commonly cited figures for how much addicts spend per day to maintain their habit fall in the $100–$150 range—and sometimes as high as $300. The image projected of the addict, with respect to money-making crimes, is much like that of a voracious blast furnace that requires feeding several times a day, consuming everything hurled into its maw. The Johnson team finds such an addict to be highly atypical. The "total criminal income" of the study's respondents is substantial, averaging nearly $12,000 annually ($38 a day) for the whole sample, and $19,000 ($52 a day) for the daily users. It is, however, nowhere near the commonly cited $100 to $150 per day that the heroin costs. What accounts for the discrepancy?

The dollar value of the heroin consumed by addicts and heroin abusers—and, along with it, their rate of criminal activity—is almost always calculated in an extremely slipshod fashion. One way is to assume that a certain number of shots are necessary to remain addicted, and then to calculate the cost of these doses. Another way is to ask users to estimate the size and the cost of their habit. As the Johnson team discovered, neither of these methods produces an even remotely accurate estimate of heroin abusers' habit size or cost. When asked on an "off-the-cuff" basis, irregular users estimated their habit at $25 per day. And yet, when they were asked to note how much they bought and used on a careful day-by-day basis, the total actually came to an astoundingly low total of $4 per day—one-sixth of their initial estimate! The higher their actual use, the more accurate their estimates were of their heroin use. Still, even the daily users were off by 50 percent—$53 per day estimated, $36 actually spent. The sample as a whole estimated the dollar value of what they used to be more than twice what they actually spent.—$43 versus $18.

It seems that these rough estimates were based on the respondents' self-image as heroin abusers; they tended to forget about days when little or no use took place. When they were asked to average out across long periods of time, such as a year, they usually recalled only those days when they successfully obtained heroin. It is easy to see how some journalists and careless researchers could have arrived at inflated $100- to $150-a-day habits for the typical heroin addict or abuser. The authors of this report warn us that researchers should regard long-term estimates of heroin habits, especially by less active users, with healthy skepticism. The only way to arrive at an accurate figure, they insist, is to calculate it in a careful, detailed, day-by-day fashion.

Fifth, *most of the money spent on narcotics is not derived from street crime.* A major myth that the Johnson team deflates is that every dollar heroin users spend on drugs is a dollar procured by means of predatory crime—in short, ripping others off. Of course, heroin users, abusers, and addicts do victimize others by committing classic street crimes. Robbery, burglary, and shoplifting made up 44 percent of the sample's total income, and nearly two-thirds of its total criminal income. But clearly, from these figures, it is also possible to see that much—indeed, *most*—of the addict's income was derived not from predatory crimes where someone is hurt or victimized, but from so-called victimless crimes, where no one is hurt or victimized, or from non-criminal activity. To begin with, heroin addicts or abusers do not use cash to purchase all of the heroin they consume. In fact, the more frequently that users consume heroin, the lower the proportion of the drug that they use is actually purchased. Daily users purchase only 58 percent of the heroin they consume with hard cash; regular users, 62 percent; and irregular users, 71 percent. Heroin abusers receive a substantial proportion of their heroin by serving as the "day laborers" in the heroin-distribution industry. They bag, cut, and sell heroin; they "steer, tout, and cop" customers on the street for a slightly higher-level seller. Most of the value they receive for these activities is in the form of heroin rather than cash.

The research team also calculated a category of drug "income" that they called "avoided drug expenditures," or mooching free drugs from others. This amounted to a whopping $2,000 annually for the whole sample, and $3,400 for the daily users. Addicts also stole drugs from other users—$1,700 worth on a yearly basis. And they sold drugs to others, but to judge from the dollar value sold (a $2,400 yearly average for the sample as a whole, $3,400 for the daily user), they are as low on the distribution chain as it is possible to get, short of their own catch-as-catch-can customers. And their revenue from prostitution and pimping accounted for more than 40 percent of the sample's total criminal income—more than half for irregular users. (For an account of the role of prostitution in the lives of female heroin addicts, see Rosenbaum, 1981, pp. 71–81.) In short, the classic image of junkies as earning all of their drug money, or even most of it, from thievery and other forms of criminal victimization is erroneous. At the same time, we must not lose sight of the fact that addicts do commit a great deal of predatory crimes, including robbery, burglary, and simple larceny.

Sixth, *most heroin abusers do not stop taking other drugs.* A sixth myth the Johnson team corrected involves the narcotic abusers' use of non-narcotic drugs. A common belief among many observers of the drug scene is that heroin users have little interest in any other drug. Once involved with heroin, users and abusers lose interest in other psychoactive substances. After all, isn't heroin the hardest of all the hard drugs? Doesn't injecting it produce the "ultimate" drug high? And aren't all other drugs rendered superfluous as a result of taking heroin? Although the recent growth in the use of cocaine in the United States, especially in the form of crack, has eaten into this stereotype, it still persists in some quarters.

The Johnson team found that the vast majority of heroin abusers used a variety of other drugs as well. Most of the heroin abusers were in fact *polydrug* users. For the two drugs most often used by the sample aside from heroin—cocaine and alcohol—use was *positively* related to involvement with heroin: The daily users consumed significantly more of these substances than the regular users who, in turn, consumed more than the irregular users. Clearly, then, the frequent, chronic, even daily, use of heroin did not rule out the use of other drugs. In fact, daily heroin users consumed alcohol on nearly two-thirds of the days under investigation; on days they used heroin, they also consumed some 6 ounces of absolute alcohol, sufficient to qualify them as alcoholics in the eyes of most experts. On well over a quarter of the days studied, respondents used cocaine at least once. In fact, the yearly dollar value of the cocaine consumed by the irregular heroin abusers ($2,500 per year) outstripped that of the heroin they consumed ($1,400). Few facts so eloquently express the generalization that the problem of the heroin abuser or addict entails far more than the consumption of heroin alone.

CONTROLLED OPIATE USE

As we saw, many heroin abusers take their drug of choice on less than a daily basis and are not literally physically dependent on it. However, most street opiate abusers would become addicted if given the opportunity. They simply cannot sustain the daily grind of raising the cash, locating the seller, dealing with the consequences, or running the risk of arrest that several-times-a-day use would entail. At the same time, a high proportion of opiate users take their drug or drugs on a *controlled* basis. Until recently, it was not realized that controlled opiate use is possible; again, one was considered either an addict or an abstainer. However, it is entirely possible that the occasional yet regular controlled user of narcotic drugs is more common than the addict. The term that is used in the world of narcotic drug use to describe this limited use is "chippying." "Chippying" means to fool around or play around with heroin, to use it once in a while or somewhat more often without getting hooked. How common is opiate "chippying"?

We all recognize that the controlled use of alcohol is not only possible;— it is in fact the majority pattern. Most drinkers are moderate in their consumption and do not become alcoholics. Yes, one might object, but narcotics are, well, *addicting*; they produce a physical dependence. Fair enough, but so does alcohol. As we saw in Chapter 5, during much of the history of the United States, alcohol was consumed at levels far greater than it is now, and in terms of quantity consumed, there were proportionally many more alcoholics than there are today. The simple fact is, patterns and styles of drug use are not a simple function of the properties of the drugs themselves. To think that they are is to fall victim to what I called the chemicalistic fallacy, discussed in Chapter 1, or what Himmelstein calls "the fetishism of drugs" (1979). It is people who take drugs, not drugs that control people; what they take, how they take them, how often, and under what circumstances, are under the control of the actor, the individual deciding to take (or not to take) a given drug or set of drugs. All drug use is surrounded by values and rules of conduct; these values and rules spell out sanctions—penalties for misuse and rewards for proper use—and these values, rules, and sanctions have an impact on how drugs are actually used.

These rules (sociologists call them *norms*) may be widely accepted and operate on the society-wide level, as with alcohol, or they may be characteristic only of small groups or subcultures, whose attitudes and values differ from those of society at large. But when the important people in one's life believe in a rule and act on it, one's own behavior will be influenced by that fact. Of course, some will follow their society's or subculture's rules on drug use and some will not. Norms set limits or establish guidelines that form the framework within which use takes place; they influence people's behavior, but they do not dictate it.

Values, rules, and sanctions promoting controlled or moderate use "function in four basic and overlapping ways." First of all, they "define moderate use and condemn complusive use." For instance, controlled opiate users "have sanctions limiting frequency of use to levels far below that required for addiction." Second, such sanctions "limit use to physical and social settings that are conducive to a positive or 'safe' drug experience." Third, sanctions "identify potentially untoward drug effects." Precautions must be taken before and during use; for instance, opiate users may "minimize the risk of overdose by using only a portion of the drug and waiting to gauge its effect before using more." And fourth, sanctions and rituals "operate to compartmentalize drug use and support the users' non–drug-related obligations and relationships." For instance, users may budget the amount of money they spend on drugs and limit use to evenings or weekends to avoid interfering with work and other obligations (Zinberg, 1984, pp. 17–18).

Is it really possible to use heroin or the other opiates on a moderate or controlled basis? One study (Zinberg, 1984) located a number of controlled opiate users and examined their patterns of use—what made them distinctive, how they accomplished this seemingly impossible feat. They had been using opiate drugs for an average of more than seven years; for four and a half years, they had been using them on a controlled basis. (Some controlled users had used opiates compulsively, and some on a marginal basis, for part of the time they had been using opiates overall.) For the year preceding the study, about a quarter (23 percent) used opiates sporadically, or less than once a month; a third (36 percent) used one to three times a month; and four in ten (41 percent) used twice a week. None used daily or more. Their pattern of use, and the length of time that they sustained this pattern, showed "without question that controlled use can be stable" (Zinberg, 1984, p. 69).

Some observers have objected that opiate users who are not yet addicted have simply not reached the stage in their drug "careers" when use inevitably becomes uncontrolled or complusive (Robins, 1979). But in fact, the length of time of opiate use in this sample was not only substantial (more than seven years), but it was not significantly different from that of compulsive users in the sample. Moreover, most compulsive users had never had a period of controlled use. And the length of time controlled users had been taking opiates on a moderate basis, four and a half, years, was ample time for them to have become compulsive users (Zinberg, 1984, pp. 69–70). Clearly, controlled use is a stable pattern for a significant proportion of narcotic users; moderate use does not necessarily or inevitably turn into compulsive use or addiction. It is a phenomenon that must be understood in its own right.

This same study compared and contrasted the patterns of use that characterized controlled users with those of the compulsive users and found interesting differences. They did not differ in type of opiate used—say, sticking with some of the "soft" narcotics, such as Darvon or codeine, versus using heroin. They did not differ in route of administration—snorting versus IV injection. They did not differ in personal acquaintance with other users who suffered extremely negative consequences as a result of opiate use—for instance, death from an overdose.

However, the controlled users *did* differ from the compulsive users in a number of crucial ways. In contrast to compulsive users, controlled users:

- Rarely used more than once a day.
- Often kept opiates on hand for a period of time without immediately using them.
- Tended to avoid using opiates in the company of known addicts.
- Tended not to use opiates to alleviate depression.
- Rarely or never used opiates on a "binge" or a "spree" basis.
- Usually knew their opiate source or dealer personally.
- Usually used opiates for recreation or for relaxation.
- Tended not to use opiates to "escape" from the difficulties of everyday life (Zinberg, 1984, pp. 69–81).

HEROIN: DRUG EFFECTS AND THE DRUG SCENE

When summarizing the effects of drugs, it is necessary to keep in mind the qualification that patterns of use bear only an oblique relationship to the pharmacological effects of the drug. This might appear to be self-evident. But we can appreciate the importance of nonpharmacological forces only when we examine the details of each specific drug scene. As an example, I submit that the question of whether heroin is a "dangerous" drug is primarily a nonpharmacological one. Roughly 1 percent of all heroin addicts die each year—an astronomical death rate for their average age group. To conclude, however, that heroin is an extremely toxic and dangerous drug is an oversimplification, a deceptive generalization. Whether heroin or any other drug is or is not dangerous depends almost entirely on the *context* in which it is used—a socially determined aspect of the drug scene. Most heroin deaths result from conditions arising from its *illegality*, not its toxicity. The medical literature on heroin use and addiction is replete with a wide range of extreme pathological sequelae, including hepatitis, tetanus, pneumonia, nutritional deficiencies, and of course overdosing, which results in coma and often death (Helpern and Rho, 1967; Louria, 1967; Cherubin, 1968). Take the issue of overdosing, which would appear to be a crude and unambiguously biophysical event, a drug reaction plain and simple. Not so. The addict is nearly always unaware of the potency of the packet or "bag" of heroin he or she purchases on the street. A kilogram of heroin bought in Europe or Hong Kong would be roughly 80 percent pure. On its way to the streets of American cities, it passes through half a dozen hands and is diluted to a fraction of this strength, usually with quinine, milk sugar (lactose), and mannitol ("mannite"); it reaches the junkie at a strength of 5 to 10 to as high as 30, 40 even 70 percent heroin nowadays. Thus a typical "dime" bag (or $10 packet, a tiny glassine envelope) may contain about 90 milligrams of relatively inert adulterants and 10 milligrams of actual heroin. However, the contents of street packets can vary considerably—they have a theoretical range from no heroin at all to 80 percent pure heroin, or 180 milligrams. Thus the addict is always injecting a drug of unknown potency into his or her system.

It is largely because of the great variability in the strength of the doses purchased and the narrow ED-LD ratio that addicts overdose. If high-potency samples are sold, a sudden rash of overdoses and even deaths will crop up in one neighborhood. (And addicts will flock to that neighborhood to purchase those strong, deadly doses, since, to the user, if they are lethal they must be good, or "righteous," dope.) An addict who is used to 5 percent heroin may one day receive a packet of 50 percent or more—which may be fatal to his or her individual system. If the samples of street heroin could be magically standardized as to strength, the problem of overdosing would be reduced dramatically.

Hepatitis and tetanus, two diseases commonly associated with heroin use, are consequences of using unsterilized needles communally rather than of injecting heroin specifically; the same diseases are frequently observed among speed freaks, or chronic amphetamine users, who also inject their drug. Were care taken to use only sterilized needles, these diseases would not crop up among addicts. In addition, inept handling of the needle may result in the injection of bubbles into the veins, which is dangerous and sometimes fatal. Or a novice may inject heroin into the arteries instead of the veins, which will result in gangrene. Other diseases, such as pneumonia, are largely a result of the frantic, scrambling, hand-to-mouth existence of the junkie, who is committed to raising the money to support a habit that would cost a few pennies a day if heroin were manufactured legally. And lastly, of course, there is the threat of AIDS, which is not an effect of heroin itself, but a consequence of sharing unsterilized needles with infected addicts. We will look at this topic in more detail later in this chapter.

This discussion should not be construed as an endorsement of the legalization of heroin, or as an endorsement of the use of heroin. But whether we support the present legal structure or oppose it, the fact remains that nearly all the features of the heroin scene that society finds repugnant (except, of course, for taking the drug itself) are artificial in the sense that they are a product of the present legal and social system surrounding addiction, and scarcely a function of the drug itself.

Drug use and dependence are extremely common among physicians, much more so than for the population at large (Vaillant et al., 1970). One study found that 59 percent of a sample of physicians and 78 percent of a sample of medical students reported that they had used illegal psychoactive drugs at least some time in their lives; for most, the preferred substance was marijuana, and most used it occasionally. Still, in the year preceding the study, fully a quarter of the physicians had "treated" themselves with a psychoactive drug, usually a tranquilizer or a narcotic. One in ten had used a psychoactive drug recreationally within the past year. Ten percent reported "regular current use" (once a month or more) of one or more drugs, and 3 percent "had histories of drug dependence" (McAuliffe et al., 1984; McAuliffe et al., 1986). Estimates have it that roughly 1 percent of currently practicing physicians, or 3,000 to 4,000 individuals, are heavily dependent on a psychoactive substance, usually a narcotic. It might be instructive to contrast the lives of doctors dependent on narcotic drugs (Winick, 1961; Modlin and Montes, 1964) with those of the street junkie. Physician addicts typically use Demerol (meperidine), an artificial narcotic, although methadone, Dilaudid, and morphine are also sometimes used. The physicians who are addicted rarely suffer any of the negative physical consequences that street junkies do, because (1) their dosage is standardized as to strength and purity; (2) their needles and other equipment are sterile; (3) they are aware of and compensate for nutritional deficiencies (narcotics depress the appetite, and junkies are typically uninterested in food); and (4) they do not have to search for drugs and money to maintain their habit and therefore do not incur the various health problems that street addicts suffer.

One of the more interesting medical facts about heroin and the other narcotics is that, aside from the danger of overdosing, they are relatively nontoxic drugs. In the controlled medical environment of the physician, addiction is experienced without apparent life-threatening consequences. Many physicians have been addicted for forty or fifty years without medical complications. Unlike alcohol, the amphetamines, and the barbiturates, which are toxic to the body over the long run with relatively heavy use, the narcotics are relatively safe. The organs are not damaged, destroyed, or even threatened by even a lifetime of narcotic addiction. There are no major malfunctions of the body, no tissue damage, no physical deterioration directly traceable to the use of any narcotic, including heroin.[2] "Opiate addiction per se causes no anatomical changes in the body," writes a physician working at the Lexington Addiction Research Center (Isbell, 1966, p. 62). Another medical expert puts it this way: "No irreversible organic damage to the nervous system or viscera is known to occur as a result of opioids per se" (Wikler, 1968, p. 292). Two Lexington drug researchers, one a sociologist, the other a physician, studied thirty-one addict patients who were an average age of 61.5 and who had been addicted to narcotics for an average of 34.5 years; these subjects were found to be in remarkably good health:

> Initially we expected that a study of the thirty-one patients who, over a thirty-two-year period, were most frequently hospitalized at Lexington for their addiction would result in the selection of a chronically ill and debilitated group. It seemed likely that the end result of extended opiate abuse would be physical and perhaps mental deterioration. This did not occur. . . . Opiate effects per se must be differentiated from the medical complications associated with the hectic way of life pursued by youthful heroin addicts. While there is ample evidence that the aberrant way of life followed by most heroin abusers has both acute and chronic medical consequences . . ., there is insufficient scientific basis for maintaining that the long-term use of opiates—in and of itself—is related to any major medical condition (Ball and Urbaitis, 1970, pp. 305–306).

Withdrawal from narcotics also appears to be relatively non–life-threatening, in contrast with barbiturate withdrawal. In an extensive survey of all the medical literature on reported cases of death during narcotic withdrawal, as well as an examination of all deaths during withdrawal among addicts at the Lexington center, Frederick Glaser, a physician, and John Ball, a sociologist, concluded that none could be attributed directly to withdrawal of opiates itself, and that in general the phenomenon is probably unknown (Glaser and Ball, 1970.)

WHY TURN ON? THE USER'S PERSPECTIVE

Given the obvious social and medical pathologies associated with addiction, the question that immediately comes to mind is: Why should anyone want to become involved with narcotics? Why should a young person—with the facts staring him or her in the face—wish to experiment with dangerous drugs? It is extremely easy for the more conventional members of society to apply their own standards of evaluation to an activity. Commonsense explanations will be offered in an attempt to verify morality by attributing a negative cause to something that is socially condemned. Thus heroin addiction—"evil" in the public mind—has to have an evil or negative cause. Yet commonsense explanations are often wide of the mark; common sense, after all, is what tells us that the world is flat. Most explanations of drug

---

[2]Actually there are two medical conditions related to addiction, a slight constipation and a lowering of the sex drive, both of which are reversible.

experimentation are little more than an effort to inform the public that it is bad, and they nearly always ignore the most important source of information—users themselves. Typically, theories about addiction are based on virtually no firsthand acquaintance with the addict, the user, or the drug experimenter. Such theories are necessarily cut off from the drug *experience*—which only the user is capable of conveying. It is an easy matter for us, removed from the drug scene, to declare what the user "should" feel, what he or she inevitably "must" experience. Yet how can we possibly know unless we go directly to the source?

In the past the great majority of the works on addiction adopted an externalistic and "objective" posture toward the addict. (There were a few outstanding exceptions to this rule, however.) Obviously, the method we select to study the addict influences what we see. Many studies relied on addicts in prison, or those who came to the attention of psychiatrists, a highly skewed segment of the addict world. But the prison is not the street, and by relying on prison addict populations researchers inevitably distort the reality of the whole drug scene. Data collected from "caught" criminals are extremely biased, as well as heavily suspect. Any reliable and valid study of drug use must utilize information secured outside an institutional context. Fortunately, a number of recent attempts to understand addicts have involved getting out into the street with them, into their world, their natural habitat.

A 22-year-old college senior wrote me a detailed account of her involvement with heroin. Naturally, her experiences are at once unique and representative; no one else has undergone quite the same experiences, yet many of the broad features of what she did and felt are shared by many middle-class college heroin users. Although she never became addicted and stopped using heroin about a month before she wrote her account, she was a weekly user for almost two years. Heroin use, especially one's initial experience, and particularly for women, is almost exclusively a group phenomenon. "I did it because my boyfriend did it," she explains. "He did it because his two closest friends did it." Coming back from a vacation with her family, my informant writes, "my boyfriend had a surprise for me. He said he had shot heroin. Suddenly, all of the conventional stereotypes were forgotten. I was more mad about not being there when the first shots were fired than anything else. Instantly, I said I wanted to try it too."

It should be reiterated that most people are first "turned on" to a drug, whether it is heroin or marijuana, by friends rather than drug sellers ("dealers"). It is precisely because drugs are initiated, used, and circulated among intimates that their spread appears almost impossible to stop. Friendship networks are far more difficult to penetrate than those of the drug peddlers.

A kind of bizarre ranking system seems to have emerged among many drug-oriented youths today. My young heroin informant writes:

> . . . there was in our group an unofficial competition, usually unverbalized, concerning who could do [take] the most drugs. . . . I was taken over to the house

of a friend who . . . was given to stating that he intended to be the most outrageous drug addict in town, no matter what the drug was. (He was one of the few who talked openly about the competition.) As an example, the best show I ever saw him put on was the night he swallowed some LSD and shot a couple of bags of dope [heroin], after which he *shot* several more LSD trips, shot at least four more bags of dope, smoked hash [hashish] all night, and took some amphetamines as a nightcap.

This case is obviously extreme, but there seems to be no question that, among a certain proportion of today's youth, experience with, and ability to handle, various types of drugs has formed a new ranking system, partially replacing athletics, schoolwork, sex, or the ability to "hold your liquor" among some young men who require affirmations of their masculinity. Thus daring and bravado play some part in the lure of many drugs, although certainly not all.

As an example of such a ranking system, in the 1960s in Haight-Ashbury in San Francisco, being the biggest freak in a subculture of freaks was not an easy task. Pride in one's ability to shoot massive doses was reflected in the following statement from a speed freak:

I know I scared an intern half to death once. He said that a person who took 500 milligrams would croak, so I shot a flat gram [1,000 milligrams] right in front of him; he turned every color of the rainbow just watching me. I fixed two spoons [slightly more than a gram] in Marin County, I'm a legend in Marin County. They're always talking about the guy who shot two spoons.

The same individual recalled a speed-shooting contest, which he frankly admitted was a self-destructive act:

This was a down to the death dope-shooting contest. One of the two of us was supposed to die when the thing was over. He'd shoot a half gram and I'd shoot a gram, and he'd shoot one and a half, and I'd shoot two grams, and he'd shoot two and a half, and I'd have to shoot three. Nobody would back out, we'd die before we'd back out (Smith, 1969, p. 82).

It is a cruel irony that many of the values of the drug subculture appear to be almost a mirror image, somewhat distorted to be sure, of some of the most sacred tenets of mainstream America. Thus the values of success and competition, evidenced by these quotations, can be poured into molds of many different shapes. A country that urges its adolescents to get ahead, to do better than their classmates, and to attend a prestigious college is going to be a country with a competitive drug subculture, with such exotic specimens as these.

Often the user will explain his use of a drug by contrasting the excitement of the drug world with the banality of the "straight" world—particularly that of his parents. My informant writes:

I tend to think that the primary target of my striving for deviance is possibly the sterility and blandness of the life I had always been exposed to. . . . My parents . . . gave me a life devoid of real, deep feeling. I wanted to feel! I wanted to play in the dirt. I wanted to transgress those lily-white norms, break those rules designed to make me a good little Doris Day. And when the first transgression was followed not by the wrath of God . . . but by feeling of being alive, and free, and different, that I had never known before, then I guess after that, all rules and norms lost their meaning and power over me. . . . I knew that there was a way for me to declare my independence from the straight, conventional, and BORING! life my mother wanted me to lead. . . . When I shot up, I felt so superior, so wicked, so unique, . . . I thought I had found the ultimate rebellion, the most deviant act possible. I was drawn to it because it set us apart from, and above, everyone—even the other drug users, the "soft" drug users. . . . I was . . . irresistibly attracted to and proud of the deviance and antisociability of the act. . . . The "badness" of shooting heroin was precisely why I did not hesitate to do it.

It has been conventional wisdom among drug experts for some time that drug effects are not inherently pleasurable, that users do not experience euphoria the first time they take a given drug, and they have to learn to enjoy the effects that they do experience. As a generalization, this is fairly sound, but it is far from universally true. It is true that many marijuana smokers do not even become high the first time they smoke. On the other hand, when novices do experience the effects of the drug for the first time, they have already been socialized to know what to expect and to define what they do experience as pleasant. Certainly alcohol's effects are not always pleasurable to all drinkers, and animals tend to avoid taking it in the laboratory setting. However, amphetamine and cocaine seem to be a different matter; without knowing what they are taking, human subjects usually enjoy the effects of these drugs and want to take them again. Animals seem to enjoy these stimulants, too, and will do almost anything to continue taking them over and over again. What about the narcotics, especially heroin? Many individuals who take heroin for the first time do not enjoy its effects. This is not, however, always the case. A summary of a number of studies of individuals' first experience with heroin found that about two-thirds of future addicts felt euphoria on their first trial; among nonaddicts, the comparable figure was 31 percent (McAuliffe, 1975, p. 379). Thus, what is often stated in the form of a universal truth should be qualified: Some individuals, including future addicts, do not experience euphoria the first time they take heroin. Not a few, in fact, will describe the experience in extremely negative terms; it will be experienced as distasteful and unappealing. But often the negative aspects will be explained away. Part of the potential addict's learning experience is an arsenal of rationalizations and justifications. My informant described to me her first shot, taken with her boyfriend, who had tried the drug before. Her boyfriend took his shot first: "The rush was so powerful that he almost fell down. He turned white and began to sweat profusely." After her injection, she writes:

I, too, began to sweat and tremble. If anyone had seen . . . us walking out of the house, he would have called an ambulance, . . . we could barely walk. For some insane reason, we had decided to drive home immediately after shooting up. . . . I had to keep pulling over to throw up on the side of the road. . . . I am truly surprised that we both didn't die that very first night. I was more physically miserable than I had ever been before. The whole night was spent vomiting. The thing that surprises me is that we didn't forget about heroin right then and there. It was horrible! *But we later decided that our dear friend had given us too much. So I decided to give it another chance.* . . . My friends were all doing it, and it had become a question of prestige within our small group [italics added].

Heroin users and addicts paint the pleasure and pain of the drug experience as the most exaggerated that life has to offer. Because of the Manichean, black-or-white, nature of the drug controversy, antidrug propagandists feel obligated to denounce what might be considered positive traits in illegal drug use; even so primrose an experience as euphoria becomes reinterpreted as something insidious, false, and artificial. As Philip Slater has pointed out, by conceding favorable characteristics, "we thereby admit their deductive appeal." With drugs, as with all phenomena about which there is considerable controversy, we wish to "devise a conceptual system in which all the things one likes fall into one category and all those things one dislikes into another. But good and bad are always orthogonal to important distinctions" (Slater, 1970, pp. 2, 154).

Extreme pleasure, then, is a self-reported feature of a large proportion of heroin experiences. My informant described her first few experiences, after the first shot, in these terms: "I can't describe the rush to you. . . . At the time, *it was better than orgasm*" (italics added). In fact, sexual imagery and analogies are prominent in the descriptions by junkies of their drug experiences. The needle being inserted into soft, yielding flesh, the wave of ecstasy flooding the body just after the injection, the feeling of calm satisfaction and well-being after the initial period of euphoria—all these have sexual overtones; indeed, for many junkies heroin becomes a substitute for sex. (Addiction to heroin produces a reduced interest in sex and often temporary impotence.) In evaluating the appeals of heroin therefore one cannot omit its hedonistic component. I have been told by heroin addicts and experimenters that the euphoria occurring upon injecting heroin into the vein is far more glorious and pleasurable than anything the nonaddict could possibly experience.

"KICKING" HEROIN

The linguistic categories used in a particular subculture to typify various forms of behavior and conditions often capture the flavor of the attitudes that participants have about them. Both heroin addicts and marijuana smokers employ the term "straight" to describe pharmacological states (as well as to describe someone who does not use drugs), but the term refers to precisely the opposite states for these two drug users. Addicts say that they are "straight" when they have just averted withdrawal sickness and are back again on an even keel, under the influence of the drug. Marijuana users say that they are straight when they are *not* under the influence of the drug. This linguistic distinction reveals the radical contrast between the use of an addicting drug, which becomes an entire way of life (the drug state being a state of "normalcy" toward which all other aspects of life are directed), and the use of a "recreational" drug, which is typically little more than a hobby, an amusement that is somewhat outside the routine of the everyday. For the heroin addict, heroin is precisely "the everyday."

Evaluations of heroin vary according to one's attitudes and social location. Addicts attribute magical powers to the drug. Far from viewing continued administration of heroin as stupid and senseless, the addict sees abstention as stupid and senseless. In abstention there is pain and misery; in taking the drug there is health and comfort. The addict's view of heroin as a "magic potion" arises both from the euphoric rush achieved upon administration and from its wondrous ability to allay withdrawal sickness. "We are in the realm of myth," Seymour Fiddle writes, "with heroin as a divine or heroic substance" (Fiddle, 1967, p. 66). This mythic attitude extends even to the nonuser, who describes the drug in quite similar terms but evaluates it in precisely opposite terms. Nonusers often credit heroin with *demoniacal* powers, with a kind of black magic hold on the addict.

It is difficult for a nonaddict to understand the almost religious quality of addiction; to someone enmeshed in the drug and the drug subcommunity, heroin is an absolute, something that transcends utilitarian calculation. Every conceivable aspect of life becomes translated into the heroin equation. It is beyond rational cost accounting. Something becomes relevant only insofar as it is related to the acquisition and use of dope. Everything else must be subordinated to it. A choice between heroin and anything else is no choice at all. A journalist quotes an addict (who is also an undercover agent working for the police) on the value of heroin versus the value of money:

> A good stash is a lot better than money. Money is phony stuff. . . . It's not a commodity. But heroin's a real commodity. Get a couple of kilos of clean, pure heroin and you've got lifetime security. Better than gold. You've got gold, you've got to spend it to get dope—if you can get it. You've got dope, you've got everything you need. Gold you can always get if you've got dope (Keating, 1970, p. 30).

Another aspect of addiction often distorted by public stereotypes and misunderstood by nonusers is the role of the heroin seller, or the "dealer." Public wrath is reserved for the peddler who profits from human misery by selling the junkie heroin. Sentences ranging up to death have been designed for the "pusher." He is, it seems, one of the most insidious characters in the current popular demonology. But the problem is that the addict does not view the dealer in this light. Far from viewing the dealer as a source of misery and pain, the junkie sees him as a kind of savior—a faith healer, a medicine man. Without his supply, the addict would undergo the agonies of withdrawal. The peddler is his lifeline. From this limited perspective, it is possible to view the dealer in positive terms.

As we have seen, not all individuals who are referred to as addicts or junkies are in fact literally physically dependent on heroin. Most find this drug so immensely psychologically reinforcing that they want and try to take it again and again. For them, discontinuing the use of the drug is painful not because it might entail withdrawal symptoms, but because they would be deprived of an experience that has been so euphoric for them in the past. At the same time, it must be remembered that the narcotic user or addict is enmeshed in a social network of other users, and "kicking" the habit is extremely difficult for that very reason. If "turning on" is a group phenomenon, so is turning off—or failing to do so. My college informant writes:

> Whenever I saw my friends, they were shooting up, too. . . . The problem with kicking heroin . . . is that all of your friends aren't kicking at the same time. . . . A three months' abstention was accomplished only by almost total isolation from friends in the drug world. . . . One guy . . . sat there praising my boyfriend for being the only one who had managed to avoid getting a habit, telling him to "keep it up." My boyfriend said something like, "We couldn't shoot up if we wanted to, we haven't got a spike." Immediately this guy gets a brand new needle and says, as he hands it to my boyfriend, "I hate to think I'm knocking down one of the barriers that keeps you away from dope." He then proceeded to offer my boyfriend a free shot.

In her autobiography, *The Fantastic Lodge,* published under the pseudonym Janet Clark, a young woman heroin addict (who died of an overdose of barbiturates) explained the pressure that others place on the user to continue taking heroin:

> . . . when you hear about them kicking, how does the junkie friend feel about his junkie friend who's kicked, supposedly, and is really cool, making some steps toward improvement in a hopeful manner? He hates his guts. For one thing, he's envious, deeply envious that the friend can get out of the morass, and not him.
>
> But for another thing, it gives him a feeling of panic; like, are they all fleeing the scene? Am I going to be left here alone? I have to have these people (Hughes, 1961, pp. 143–144).

Lest we become unduly pessimistic about the addict's chances of getting off heroin, we need only remind ourselves of the remarkable success rate of returning Vietnam veterans who were addicted to heroin. Of all the Army enlisted men who returned to the United States in September 1971, just over 1 in 10 was found to have urine that tested positive for narcotics, amphetamines, or barbiturates. Just under 9 out of 10 of the men with positive urine for narcotics were actually addicted—that is, had one or more signs of physical dependence: They designated themselves as addicted, used a narcotic regularly for more than a month, experienced withdrawal lasting two days or more, experienced two or more of the "classic" symptoms of withdrawal, and preferred injecting or sniffing narcotics to smoking them. Three out of four of the narcotic-positive men had three or more of these signs of dependence.

These men were interviewed eight to twelve months after their return to the United States. Only 2 percent of the total sample told the interviewers that they were currently using narcotics; urine samples collected at the interview were positive for narcotics for only 1 percent of the sample. Half the men who were dependent on narcotics stopped use entirely on their return, only 14 percent became readdicted, and the rest used sporadically. Entering a treatment program had nothing to do with this remarkable success rate, since only 5 percent had enrolled in such a program since their return. Clearly, a high proportion of the men who used drugs, and even became heroin addicts, did not continue their habit upon their return to the United States. Simply being an addict does not force the individual to continue using (Robins, 1973; Robins, Davis, and Goodwin, 1974; Robins, Helzer, and Davis, 1975).

For some addicts, the habit is relatively easy to discontinue. The old saw "Once an addict, always an addict" is clearly false. It is entirely possible that the low success rate for addicts in treatment programs can be accounted for by the fact that individuals who successfully kick a habit on their own do not figure into treatment statistics. Treatment programs enroll only those addicts who are failures at discontinuing their habit. There is evidence indicating that this may also be the case for other habits, including cigarette smoking, overeating and alcoholism (Brody, 1983).

HEROIN ADDICTION: MYTH AND REALITY

It is a simple matter to apply conventional judgments and evaluations to the world of the addict. Thus psychiatrists will proclaim that the addict is immature and irrational, and that he or she has a compulsion to avoid responsibility. An earlier tradition of sociologists also built an entire theoretical edifice on the assumption that addiction (this is often stretched to include all illegal drug use) is a "retreatist" adaptation to the problem of social adjustment, and that addicts are attracted to their drug because they are "double failures" (Cloward and Ohlin, 1960, pp. 178–184). These views have built into them the biased assumption that to conform to society's expectations is "normal" and that to do otherwise requires an explanation invoking a pathology or a dysfunction of some kind.

The look at the behavior of the addict from the perspective of the addict subculture is to judge the behavior radically differently. Indeed, from conventional society's point of view, addict behavior is irresponsible—because addicts generally do not do that which society has decided to define as responsible. Thus the validity of the "retreatist" conception of the addict is based on the value assumption that he "should" want the things that society (as well as the researcher) has decided are appropriate for him. However, the addict will have a different definition of what constitutes responsible behavior. From the addict's point of view, responsibility rests in being able to hustle the money necessary to maintain a hundred-dollar-a-day habit. Admiration is reserved for those addicts who are able to succeed gracefully at these demanding requirements: "Prestige in the hierarchy of a dope fiend's world is allocated by the size of a person's habit and his success as a hustler" (Sutter, 1969, p. 195). Addicts are acutely aware that they are masters of forms of behavior at which the "square" would be a hopeless failure. The public image of the addict derives in part from the Chinese opium smoker of more than half a century ago. He is seen as existing in, or "retreating into," a state of dreamy idleness, a euphoric temporary death. This state of oblivion does, indeed, typify a certain temporal slice of the addict's day and is known as "going on the nod." (Its occurrence is, however, dependent on the quality of the heroin administered.) But it is only a small portion of the addict's daily life—the climax so to speak—and the hectic hustle and bustle of the day is oriented toward this brief moment of transcendence. Far from taking the addict out of contact with the world, addiction "plunges the newly recruited addict into abrasive contact with the world" (Lindesmith and Gagnon, 1964, p. 179). Fiddle calls the kind of life the typical street addict lives a "pressure cooker universe" (Fiddle, 1967, pp. 55–63). Paraphrasing the addict's views on rejecting the "retreatist" theory of drug addiction, Fiddle writes: "Could a square survive . . . in the kind of jungle we live in? It takes brains, man, to keep up a habit that costs $35 to $40 a day—every day in the year" (Fiddle, 1967, p. 82).

A sensitive and informative account of addiction written by an anthropologist and an economist, entitled "Taking Care of Business" (Preble and Casey, 1969), neatly summarizes the aggressive, rather than retreatist, orientation of addicts' lives:

> Their behavior is anything but an escape from life. They are actively engaged in meaningful activities and relationships seven days a week. The brief moments of euphoria after each administration of a small amount of heroin constitute a small fraction of their daily lives. The rest of the time they are actively, aggressively pursuing a career that is exacting, challenging, adventurous, and rewarding. They are always on the move and must be alert, flexible, and resourceful. The surest way to identify heroin users in a slum neighborhood is to observe the way people walk. The heroin user walks with a fast purposeful stride, as if he is late for an important appointment—indeed, he is. He is hustling (robbing or stealing), trying to sell stolen goods, avoiding the police, looking for a heroin dealer with a good bag . . . , coming back from copping . . . , looking for a safe place to take the drug, or looking for someone who beat (cheated) him—among other things. He is, in short, *taking care of business* (Preble and Casey, 1969, p. 2).

HEROIN ABUSE AND AIDS

A specter is haunting the needle-using heroin community—the specter of acquired immune deficiency syndrome, or AIDS. AIDS was first recognized only in 1981 and was not widely publicized until 1983; it has since spread among heroin users like wildfire. The disease is caused by a virus that is spread through bodily fluids—mainly semen and blood. During anal intercourse, infected semen can enter the body through a break, a tear, or a sore or infection. IV injection itself represents a rupture of the skin; an infected needle transmits the virus from a fluid, the drug, into the bloodstream of the individual shooting up. Vaginal intercourse can also spread the virus, but much less effectively than anal intercourse. A given act of vaginal intercourse between an infected and a noninfected person has between a one in 100 and one in 1,000 chance of transmitting the virus. Thirty percent of those who become infected with the virus have contracted the disease within five years, and this rate rises with time. Currently, the disease, which impairs the immune system and leaves the body prey to deadly infections, is 100 percent fatal. Experts estimate that 1.5 million Americans are carrying the virus, many of whom are not aware of it. A bit more than 50,000 actual cases of the disease have been diagnosed so far.

In the early 1980s, the vast majority of all AIDS cases were homosexuals. Over time, the proportion of AIDS deaths who are homosexual has declined, while the proportion who are IV drug users has risen. (The drug of choice of the vast majority of IV drug users is heroin, and most of these people are addicts.) In fact, recent tabulations have shown that IV drug users account for a higher proportion of all AIDS cases than had previously been thought. Many narcotics-related deaths have not been recognized as AIDS-related. When addicts die of pneumonia, hepatitis, or another related by-product of addiction, the fact that they have AIDS has often been overlooked. More than half of New York City's estimated 200,000 to 250,000 addicts are infected with the AIDS virus, though most have not yet contracted the disease itself. In a recent breakdown of the AIDS-related deaths in New York City between 1981 and 1986, the majority, 53 percent, were IV drug users in no other risk category; an additional 5 percent were IV drug users who were also homosexual or bisexual. Just over a third (38 percent) were homosexual in no other risk category (Sullivan, 1987). While the national profile of AIDS cases still includes more gays and fewer IV drug users, this picture is likely to change by the 1990s.

In a sense, there are two nearly separate AIDS epidemics in the United States. Among whites, AIDS affects mainly homosexual males. Among racial minorities, especially heterosexuals, AIDS is overwhelmingly a disease of addicts, their sex partners, and their children. The majority of these cases are among the poor. Nationally, just under 60 percent of AIDS cases have been white, 25 percent have been Black, and 15 percent have been Hispanic. The incidence of AIDS among Black men is 2.6 times that of whites; for Hispanics, it is 2.5 times. Among women, these figures are 12.2 and 8.5 respectively. But among addicts, these figures are even more lopsided. For heterosexual men who are IV drug users, 21.8 times as many Blacks have AIDS as whites; for Hispanics, the figure is 20.7. Among women, the comparable figures are 18.1 and 11.3 times (Schmidt, 1987).

There are indications that the spread of the AIDS virus in the gay community has been checked, but among IV heroin users, it continues unabated. One study (Kleinman et al., 1987b) found that only 75 percent of a sample of street IV drug users had "salient knowledge" of the drug-related transmission of AIDS, and only 44 percent of those who had been injecting drugs for two years or less did so. Moreover, only 16 percent of the new injectors say that they take drugs via "safer practices" (that is, not sharing needles or cleaning needles after each injection), while nearly seven out of ten of the 11-or-more-year injectors said that they followed safer practices. In addition, it is likely that the very lifestyle of the addict encourages risk-taking. "Narcotics addicts . . . are by necessity furtive and suspicious. Their habit alone is a daily dalliance with mortality. Given a life filled with risks— overdoses, hepatitis, jail—the threat of dying from AIDS seems, to many, merely redundant." Addicts rarely seek medical help for any ailment. "They don't want to know if they're sick. And if they're sick, they want to put it off—til tomorrow comes. But tomorrow never comes." Said one addict, "I don't care if I get AIDS. I'm gonna die anyway, might as well take someone with me" (Freedman, 1987, p. B7).

ACCOUNT: USING HEROIN

The contributor of this account is 29 years old; she works for a market-research firm. She used heroin for about six years. Although she was never literally physically addicted, she used it almost daily, and had what is called a "chippy" habit. She has remained drug-free (except for cigarettes and an occasional drink) for about five years.

> I started on drugs when I was 16. That's when I was introduced to marijuana. A lot of things were involved with my starting. My brother was having problems, and there was a lot of tension at home, my parents were very upset, and this bothered me, and then I started having my own problems. My older brother was experimenting with various drugs, LSD and things like that, and he started going into therapy, and his shrink told him that his mind had been destroyed by drugs. This is not something you tell somebody who is supposed to be a patient. So he left school, and he stayed home, in his room, all the time. It was pretty bad. Plus, with me, I began having problems with my parents and with my friends. I was raised to believe that everyone is supposed to be treated equally. Only my parents really did not mean that, literally. So I happened to make some friends who were Black, and then it wasn't OK any more. When it came to bringing them home, it was another story—they disapproved. And I was really doing nothing wrong, I wasn't into drugs then or anything, so I became very rebellious about that, because I felt I was right and my parents were wrong. Also, I had my group of friends, and when I started having Black friends, my group of friends did not approve. So I ended up losing all of my previous friends, and it narrowed down to one girlfriend who I had a great friendship with—and she moved away. So there was this, on top of everything else. I was in pretty bad shape. So I started blocking everything out. I couldn't deal with it. People who use drugs don't like pain. They like to take the easy way out of everything. So I started getting high pretty frequently.
>
> It was marijuana at first. What happened was that people who were using marijuana that I knew, a good number of them, were also using other drugs, like

up and downs. A guy I met in my therapy group, ironically, said, why don't I go to a party with him. And this was a party where they were doing acid. That's when I started using that. I met a lot of people there that I ended up hanging out with, and I started tripping. And I started coming home all hours of the night, and my parents could tell something in my eyes, my face, that I was high. I never saw it myself—you never do—but people who know you very well and who love you can detect a change. I became very belligerent and short-tempered. I had been a very good student up until high school. When I started using drugs, I really didn't care very much about school. It didn't matter to me any more. And my grades went down. When I came home at 5 in the morning and I was high, my parents were rather upset. A lot of crying, a lot of screaming and yelling. And trying to get me to go for help, and they went for counseling, and we went for counseling together. It really took its toll on our family. It was very upsetting for us. I couldn't deal with it. So I wanted to be on my own, and be able to do what I wanted.

So my goal in life at that time was to move out of my house when I graduated from high school. That was the most important thing to me then. I didn't want to go to college. So I moved out and got a job driving a taxi. And while I was driving a taxi, one of the people I worked with was dealing heroin, and we developed a relationship. One day, he asked me to take a ride with him to the city to cop. I was 18 or 19 years old. So I went and I snorted some heroin. I thought I'd just try it. And I liked it. And since I had this relationship, and he was selling drugs, I was able to get drugs. And heroin was like a warmth that envelops you. It's an automatic warmth that encompasses your whole being as soon as it enters your body. It softened all of my problems, where they didn't bother me as much. I guess it must be like being in the womb. You feel warm and safe and protected. It makes you feel calm. It made me feel like I loved the whole world.

I started using heroin pretty often, maybe every day. And it wasn't long, maybe a few months, until I started shooting, because everyone tells you that it's much better, much quicker, and you need less. And it was true. When I got into shooting it, the first few times, I got sick. But after the sickness passed, the feeling of euphoria came over me. I never thought, in my wildest dreams—I mean, I'm a stereotype, I'm white, Jewish, middle-class, I live in the suburbs, and when I was younger, I used to yell at my mother for smoking cigarettes, I used to preach against drugs—I never in my wildest dreams thought I'd be sticking a needle in my arm. A lot of people think, oh, I could never do that. But it's *amazing* what you can do. And I ended up doing it just about every day. And I did things that I would not have done if I wasn't under the influence. I became very free with my body. If I hadn't been under the influence, I wouldn't have been as free as I was. When you're high, you are not completely yourself. Because all drugs alter the way you think. You do things you wouldn't ordinarily do. So what happens is, after using whatever drugs, you lose touch with yourself—how bad it is, what it really does to you.

The way I began to live my life was, I'd wake up—there were many times I'd be awakened by somebody who would come to my house because I had a car and the other people I was hanging around with didn't have cars, and they would want to go either to cop, or go hit one of the stores and get some money from there. So maybe we'd go and hit a few stores, try and steal something, and then try and get the money for it by selling the merchandise. And this all takes a while.

Then, if nobody in town had any drugs or anything that was good, we'd go to the city to a shooting gallery, which are not very nice places. Sometimes, in the shooting galleries, you could cop right away. Other times, you might be there for hours, waiting. It's probably one of the dirtiest places in existence. You can purchase hypodermic equipment there, which also isn't that sanitary. Of course, we'd try and cop locally before going to the city. There was an area nearby—there still is—where people would hang out on the street and we'd cop, if dope was in town. Most of the time, though, we'd cop in somebody's house. There were a few times when I tried dealing, but I wasn't very good at it, because I liked heroin too much, and I also was generous to other people, so I didn't do very well with that. If we copped someplace and brought it back, sometimes we would pull over on the side of the road on the way back, and stop somewhere to shoot up right in the car. One or two times I came close to having accidents because I started nodding out while I was driving. We'd come home, shoot some more, use just about all we could until we had a nice high, and then maybe I would have sex, listen to music, hang out on the street—and that was really about the whole day.

I was never physically addicted. I had what they called a "chippy" habit, where I had the sniffles if I stopped—that was the extent of what I had. I had more of a *mental* addiction, which is just as bad as a physical one. I tried methadone for a while. When I got the methadone, I wasn't serious about kicking. It was just a free high. That's why a lot of people go to the methadone clinics. This one nearby, they're paid by the federal government for each person they have on the program, and it seems, from my experience there, that they actually try and keep people on the program. First, I went into a live-in program for a couple months. And then I left. You're supposed to "graduate" from these places, but I didn't graduate. I just left and ended up getting high again. Then I thought I would try to help myself. I thought at least, with methadone, I wouldn't be involved in copping and the needles and all the illegal aspects of it. And so I tried that for a while. What I did was, before I went to the clinic, I shot a lot of heroin and I went there, and I had a blood test or a urine test they take to see what's in your system, and they found what I had put into my system, and I lied to them about my habit—and that was it. They let me in. They gave me a very high dosage in the beginning, which sometimes put me into a kind of daze, it was so strong. And the funny thing is, withdrawal from methadone is worse than with heroin. When they were cutting me down and I stopped, I felt achy in my bones. I was on the methadone program for two or three months—not all that long. I went on a detox program. They offered me, if I wanted to go on maintenance, and I didn't, I chose detox. Because through all my experiences, I never made a good dope fiend. Through it all, my goals in life came through. Being a dope fiend wasn't enough for me, it wasn't the kind of life I wanted to live. Luckily, I came through it.

The way I was supporting myself during these years was several things. At one point, I was on welfare, which I got on very easily. Also, I had a few friends, one or two, who were very generous with both money and dope, which is unusual to find in dope fiends. And I was working part of the time during this period. But I never lasted at a job, because I always wanted to get high. I used to shoot up at work in the bathroom sometimes. I also resorted to stealing. I had a few friends and we used to go to the store and steal things and bring the merchandise back in and get a refund. I wasn't very good at that either, but I managed to do it a number of times. And maybe I would turn a trick sometimes. I sold myself to men. I rationalized it in my own mind that it wasn't really prostitution because I knew these people somewhat, and it was that we were doing each other a favor. That's how I looked at it. So I did that a few times.

You think that the people you're dealing with are your friends, but they're not. They really couldn't give a damn about you. I didn't find this out until I stopped getting high. I was arrested because I was set up by two of these so-called friends. It was a federal offense—forging a money order or a check or something. I signed the check and went into a bank and my friends took off in my car when they saw the police, and I got busted, my second arrest. I was threatened by these people about saying anything about their involvement in it, but I ratted them out anyway, because they did the same thing to me. After I was arrested and taken to the police station, I wanted to call home. I wanted to tell my parents that I'd be late—I was between apartments and living at home—that I was delayed somewhere. I didn't want them to know what had happened. So the police officer who was questioning me picked up the phone and dialed my parents' house, and my mother answered and he said, hello, this is officer so-and-so, your daughter is under arrest, and he handed me the phone. Which they're really not supposed to do. It's good that he did it, because my parents came down to the police station. When I was there by myself, I was being very rebellious and hard-headed and stupid. Because my parents came there, I ended up telling them everything that had happened. And because my mother went to court with me, and I didn't have a previous record, and I was white, and middle-class—all that had to have something to do with it, I feel—and I wasn't belligerent in court, and I really did want help, they gave me probation.

I got a very easy probation officer. When I was on probation, I was getting high again. And it finally got to the point where she told me, I'd have to do something, because she couldn't keep allowing me to go on like this. So I didn't want to, but I went into a second live-in program, a therapeutic community, like Phoenix House, one of those. They helped me a lot. They also hurt me. Because the therapy that they give there is *very* harsh. I didn't graduate from there, either. I was there nine months, and then I left. I committed an infraction—someone told me about a staff member who had marijuana on his breath, and I didn't report it right away. I was given some kind of therapeutic action—it's not punishment, exactly, it's what they call a "work contract." I wasn't allowed to go to group sessions. There were various other reprisals. I became PO'ed at what they did to me. I felt it was not justified and I got angry. So I left. I was there nine months, and when I came out, I had to try heroin again.

I went to this local bar. I really didn't know where I was going or what I was doing. I wanted to get high, but I didn't know anybody. And someone from this bar, one of the locals, ended up taking me to the city to cop some heroin. And I ended up staying with him that night and going to bed with him. It wasn't that good an experience. The morning after, he was getting a little forceful with me, and I didn't care for it. Plus, the dope we got wasn't that good, either. I had been in the program for nine months, and it was not easy shooting up, after all the therapy I had gone through, and so it wasn't a good experience. So I was depressed, and I was lonely and I needed the caring of the people in the program for me. I was still screwed up. I wanted to go back because that was my family and my home. I was down and out and I needed them. When I went back into the program they cut off all my hair. And these two residents made me stand there and they called me all kinds of names—that I was a whore, that I was trash, that I was trying to kill myself by taking heroin again. I stayed on work contract maybe for two more weeks. I felt, well, I've built up such walls in my life, that it was to the point where they're yelling at me and everything, and I was starting to just block that out and it wasn't doing anything. So I felt that I wasn't going to get any more help there. I had gotten what I could and I was just wasting my time at that point. So I left. That was five years ago. I haven't touched heroin since.

I knew a lot of people who got high with me who had a lot of potential and their lives were ruined by dope. They're never going to go anywhere. I'm 29 years old. I wish that, by now, my career was all settled for me. That I had friends. You don't learn how to be a friend or what a relationship is when you're just getting high. And when you stop getting high, it's like being a baby and starting all over again from the beginning. When you're high, it's like being a robot. It's euphoric, but you could be anybody. All the people that are out there using drugs, the faces change, but they're all the same, they're all nobodies, because they're never going anywhere, they're never going to make anything of themselves.

My veins will never be the same again. From constantly shooting heroin in the same vein, it gets calloused and it collapses. And I guess that's what happened to my veins. And that's something that will never come back. I also have scars on my hands and a few on my feet from shooting in those places. I also got hepatitis. That means that I can never donate blood. The main thing that bothers me is that the years that I lost while I was taking dope I will never get back. And you lose a lot of self-pride because of the things you end up doing, and it takes a long time to get that back. What I should have been doing all that time in my life was going to college, pursuing a career, and going out and doing the so-called normal things. What I was doing was hanging out on the street corner and getting high. And that was my whole life. You don't see a lot of things when you get high. I had various relationships during that time which were all worth nothing. They were mostly physical, and when that's all over, it doesn't leave you feeling too good about yourself. Also, I was almost raped twice by my supposed friends because of the kind of people I used to hang out with. All of this takes its toll. If I hadn't gotten involved with drugs, maybe I would have had a career. Maybe I would have had more confidence in myself at this point in my life, because I don't have it now. I'd have some friends today, which I don't have now because after all those years, I really didn't have any friends left. Maybe I would have been married. That's another thing. I have a record, a past. So that will always be there. And if I do fall in love with somebody, this part of my life, my past, it's not something that I can just forget about and pretend it never happened. It's something that some people won't be able to accept.

I'm able to function in the world now. I have more confidence and pride in myself than I used to. It's not a hell of a lot, but at least it's more than I had. I'm still afraid of people, I really am. There are times I think about getting high. Not as often as I used to—it's less and less now. But I don't feel I could do it again, because if I did, I could never live with myself. I'd have to really go downhill to do that, and I wouldn't be able to deal with that. I'm still trying to learn how to get in touch with my feelings so that I can have relationships with people, and to build up my confidence. Because after everything I've been through, I guess I still think pretty lowly of myself. I'll be 30 soon, and it'll take a while before I can get my act together. [From the author's files.]

Epilogue: Fighting the Drug War

By any conceivable criterion, American society has a major drug problem on its hands. Drug use is a social condition with real-life consequences that most of us agree are undesirable, and this book has detailed many of them. In addition, it is a condition that generates social concern: Much of the public is deeply disturbed by it, laws are proposed and passed to control it, and organizations have sprung up to deal with it. This public concern exhibits two features: One, a feeling that the condition is undesirable; and two, a belief that something can be done to make things better. Clearly, the reasoning goes, if things are bad, they must have gotten that way because of existing policies. Ergo, these policies must be changed and new programs instituted.

Of proposals and programs for fighting drug abuse there is no end. Everyone seems to have a solution; everyone thinks his or her proposal will solve the drug problem—or at least improve matters considerably. All of these programs are based on certain assumptions about the nature of drug use, abuse, and addiction. More generally, drug programs are based on assumptions about how the world works—that is, on human motivation, how people usually act under certain concrete circumstances. Any program based on myth, misconception, or fallacy is extremely likely to fail when it is instituted. Indeed, programs hopelessly out of touch with reality are likely to do more harm than good.

What is the solution to the drug problem? Indeed, *is* there a solution to the drug problem? How should the drug war be fought?

Three models have been proposed: the *decriminalization* model, the *maintenance* model, and the *punitive* model. The first two overlap somewhat, and many individuals advocate both of them at the same time. Still, there are key differences, and some experts urge decriminalization for some drugs and not others, while nearly all who advocate maintenance do so only for certain drugs. The punitive model stands somewhat apart from the other two.

The decriminalization model suggests that we remove criminal penalties on the possession of one or more drugs. The problem, this model theorizes, is that, if criminalized, drugs are hard to obtain and users are stigmatized. Restrictions on availability drive up the price of drugs and encourage users' criminal involvement in drug distribution and other illegal activities; ready availability would take away the drug-crime connection and enable users to lead healthy, productive lives. Stigmatization forces users to band together into their own subculture, which limits conventional society's control over them and reinforces the strength of the drug subculture (Trebach, 1987). Decriminalization makes a major assumption concerning motives for drug use: Far from discouraging use, making drugs legally unavailable only stimulates it. Some observers have proposed the decriminalization model for some drugs but not others, while some have proposed it for all currently illegal drugs.

The maintenance model applies only to individuals who are physically dependent on a specific drug or drug type—almost always narcotics. It adopts a medical solution to narcotic addiction, and sees the addict as a sick person rather than as a criminal. It suggests that addicts, and only addicts, be supplied narcotics, and only narcotics, because their lives will thereby be healthier than if they sought drugs on the black market. In this way, addicts obtain drugs to maintain their habit cheaply, without the need to resort to crime, and the rest of society is not victimized in the addict's quest for a drug supply (Zion, 1985). "Crime would drop, and the mob would lose income. . . . Addicts could get their fix at federal clinics," explains one distinguished lawyer who advocates the maintenance model (Nizer, 1986). Legal heroin, says another commentator, is a "good idea sixty years overdue" (Levinson, 1982). The maintenance model suggests that narcotic addicts are "enslaved" by their habit, are satisfied mainly by maintaining themselves on narcotics, and do not seek euphoria as their prime motivation for use.

The punitive model suggests that drug use and abuse are widespread because American society is not tough enough on users and, especially, dealers. What we need is a "crackdown": Arrest the sellers of illegal drugs; confiscate their money, property, and drugs; send them to prison for long terms; make it impossible for them to do their dirty business; impose the death penalty for certain drug-selling crimes; set examples of imprisoned dealers so that anyone tempted to enter the drug trade is completely discouraged from doing so (Williams, 1986). The punitive model makes the assumption that harsher laws and penalties, and more rigorous enforcement of those laws, more or less automatically bring about a decline in drug dealing and use. What America needs, says Robert DuPont, president of the American Council for Drug Education, is to establish a "zero-tolerance" policy for illicit drug use. "That means no drug use in the schools, none in the workplace, none on the highways and none in the families. Sanctions need to be swift, effective, and broadly supported by all segments of our society" (1984).

The United States has relied mainly on a punitive model since the 1920s—less Draconian than some would wish, but a punitive model nonetheless. Until the 1980s, it looked like we were moving toward a modified form of maintenance for heroin addicts, and a modified form of decriminalization for marijuana, but the conservative mood that gripped the country when Ronald Reagan was elected president in 1980 seems to have curtailed these developments. Our policy is mainly punitive, with two small exceptions: maintenance-oriented for perhaps 100,000 or so heroin addicts, and decriminalization-oriented in eleven states for small-quantity marijuana possession. I'd like to explore these exceptions a bit later on.

It is my contention that, as across-the-board programs, all three of these models will inevitably fail—and, indeed, have already failed wherever they have been instituted—because they are based on a number of misconceptions. None of them is based on an accurate notion of how the world works—how and why drugs are used and abused, how the criminal justice system works, or even what motivates human behavior generally. As we'll see, they all share the same mistake—a *static* view of human behavior with respect to drug use. They assume that one or another aspect of society can be changed without major alterations in the others. But in fact, human societies are dynamic, and tinkering with one social institution often brings about unanticipated and usually undesired changes in a number of others. Most proposals to fight the drug war are extremely naive with regard to just how illicit drug sale and use hinge on and influence practice and custom in countless aspects of social life. Once we understand how, it becomes impossible to support any of these three models as a general policy to control the use of currently illicit drugs. At the same time, all three of the models are partially effective for certain drugs under certain circumstances and according to certain criteria, as we'll see.

Each drug is unique, yet it also possesses features in common with some other drugs. Each has special characteristics that make it appealing to users and difficult to eradicate. The persistence of the recreational use of each of our more popular drugs can be explained partly by its special characteristics. Each is appealing and is bought, sold, and distributed for somewhat different reasons. Consequently, any attempt to stamp out its use must be based on a thorough understanding of its special qualities. What works with one drug may not work with another; what influences the users of one drug in one way may have a very different impact on the users of another drug. At the same time, certain drugs have features in common. If a drug is smuggled into the country, its suppliers face logistical problems of how to get it from its point of origin—a foreign country—past U.S. customs officials, to its ultimate consumer. And, of course, law enforcement faces the problem of how to interrupt that flow of traffic at various points along the way. But if a drug is manufactured in a local lab, a different set of problems for both suppliers and law enforcement applies; if it is grown or manufactured domestically, another different set of problems is involved; and so on.

As we've seen, heroin is the least widely used of some ten or so drugs or drug types that are taken for euphoric purposes in the United States. At the same time, there are several features that make it "a most inconvenient substance" to public health officials and to the general public. The drug seems "almost to have been designed to give trouble to a pluralistic democratic society which lacks massive police resources, maintains a strong traditional of individualism, and values the search for personal pleasure and fulfillment" (Kaplan, 1983, p. 238).[1]

---

[1]Much of the next few pages is based on my review of John Kaplan, *The Hardest Drug: Heroin and Public Policy* (Chicago: University of Chicago Press, 1983), published in *Society,* July/August 1985, pp. 93–96. A substantial portion of the following discussion owes a great deal to Kaplan's book, from which I have borrowed freely.

The social definition of heroin in the drug subculture is such that the user is reckless and brave, an outlaw. The pharmacology of the drug conspires to compound the heroin problem. It is highly pleasurable ("reinforcing" to the behavioral psychologist), especially when injected intravenously. The drug builds tolerance swiftly, maximizing the likelihood of a physical dependence. Heroin is metabolized in the body fairly quickly so that, roughly four hours after administering a satisfying shot, the addict will want to inject it again. Heroin is an antianxiety agent so that when users are under the influence, they will more readily take certain risks to secure the drug or the necessary cash to purchase it. It is also potent, which means that substantial doses can be easily concealed.

Although their numbers are small relative to the number of alcoholics and compulsive users of marijuana or cocaine, the half-million or so heroin addicts, and the much larger number of regular but nonaddicted heroin users, wreak considerable havoc on the American public. When addicts use heroin daily, they commit six times as many nondrug crimes as when they use sporadically or not at all. A community of a few dozen addicts can easily double the crime rate of a small city. While it is not the entire picture, the addict's impact on our rate of property crime is sufficient to warrant the search for a solution to the heroin problem.

Most of these points also apply to cocaine. While not addicting in the classic sense, as we saw in Chapters 2 and 8, cocaine is highly reinforcing, and a substantial proportion of users become behaviorally dependent on it—they will do almost anything to continue taking it. Cocaine use has risen dramatically in the United States in the 1980s, and current users are taking it more often, and in larger, purer doses, than in the past. There are between five and ten times as many compulsive users of cocaine as heroin, and in the late 1980s, the police seized many times the quantity of cocaine as heroin. Huge and immensely tempting profits can be made by selling the drug, and sellers have become increasingly violent in their struggle for those profits. In Miami, a major staging area for cocaine in the United States, a quarter of all murders are a result of drug transactions. Cocaine is even more reinforcing and is metabolized even more quickly than heroin, making repetitive use even more likely. Cocaine, like heroin, is potent, which means that only small quantities are necessary to achieve its full effects; this, in turn, means that it is easily concealable and highly transportable. Compulsive use often leads to paranoia and reckless behavior, and heavy users typically become a danger to themselves and to others. If heroin is a major nightmare to law enforcement, cocaine may represent an even more frightening threat.

In many ways, our current policy of criminalizing heroin possession has been a disaster. The Harrison Act of 1914 (which included cocaine as a "narcotic") probably caused more problems than it solved. It helped transform the typical addict from a middle-class, middle-aged woman in a small town or rural area—a woman who took drugs for medical reasons and who was regarded as neither a criminal nor a deviant—to a young, urban-dwelling, lower-class, minority male who takes heroin for pleasure and routinely commits money-making property crimes. Because access to opiates was restricted by our laws, the price of using opiates at an addicting level increased beyond the reach of almost anyone working at a legal job; a life of crime became a prerequisite for the vast majority of American addicts. A cohesive, addict-based subculture was encouraged by the Harrison Act and its aftermath, making the recruitment of new addicts all the more likely. While the short-term reduction in the number of addicts may have been one by-product of the Harrison Act, its long-term impact in terms of the number of addicts is less clear. Even if the proportion of addicts in the U.S. population is smaller today than it was in 1914—actually, it looks like the proportions are about equal—"addiction was then so much less personally and socially costly that the balance is clear. . . . It is hard to deny that opiates have become a far greater social problem since the passage of the Harrison Act" (Kaplan, 1983, p. 65).

There are at least two assumptions made by the decriminalization model. One is that people will *not* use drugs more if they are not criminalized, and the second is that they *will* use them more if they are criminalized. Both are fallacious. The national prohibition of alcohol (1919–1933) is often pointed to as an example of the failure to control the use of a substance through the law, but, as we saw in Chapter 5, actually, the use of alcohol did decline—and drastically—during Prohibition. If anything, Prohibition provides evidence for a punitive policy of drug control. Of course, there are other effects of criminalization, but that is another matter altogether. In addition, although not precisely comparable, it is clear that the likelihood increases that many individuals who would not have used drugs under more restricted circumstances do so when they are readily available. For instance, about 14 percent of American servicemen returning from Vietnam, where the drug was cheap and widely available, were dependent on heroin. The vast majority of these men discontinued their use of the drug here, where it was far less readily accessible (Robins, 1973; Robins et al., 1974). While many circumstances of the Vietnam experience were unique, the point cannot be denied that many people use certain drugs when they are available but do not do so when they are more difficult to obtain. And decriminalization makes some of these drugs more available.

In fact, I believe that the decriminalization and the easier availability of heroin, and most drugs generally, would be an unmitigated disaster. The use of and addiction to narcotics are clearly functions of various factors, one of which is availability. As the examples of narcotic use among American soldiers in Vietnam, among physicians, and among individuals who live in countries that supply narcotics, a large proportion of individuals who are disinclined to use a drug if it is difficult to obtain will do so if it is readily available. Today, under a more or less punitive policy, for the majority of American youth, heroin is simply not easily obtainable; a certain proportion of those who are now prevented from using heroin would do so if it were more readily available; and a proportion of them would begin using the drug

regularly and become addicted to it. A large number of heroin experimenters in the United States will not become addicted, and many addicts will give
up heroin, because of "the trouble and expense of maintaining a large habit;
fear of involvement with the legal system because of the demands of their
habits; and the inability to 'score' enough good heroin" (Kaplan, 1983, p.
125). Restricted availability and the chances of arrest can be regarded as
"hassle factors," and they do have an inhibitory impact on the heroin use
of potential and actual users. In short, "one would have to be an incurable
optimist to believe that heroin could be made freely available [in the United
States] without a considerable degree of social dislocation" (Kaplan, 1983,
p. 146). At the same time, the lives of current addicts are made miserable
and unhealthy in part because of what they have to do to obtain the drug,
as we saw in Chapter 10. Criminalization is responsible for an enormous
amount of death and disease, not to mention predatory crime, among addicts. Still, it is foolish to assume that one policy will result in nothing but
benefits, and another in nothing but detriments. Today, under our present
punitive policy, we have half a million sick, criminal addicts; under a policy
of decriminalization, it is highly likely that we would have 5 million comparatively healthy, relatively law-abiding addicts.

These comments apply even more forcefully to cocaine. It seems inconceivable to me that anyone would suggest removing all criminal penalties
for the possession of this drug. Although many observers (including myself)
regarded the drug as relatively benign in the 1970s, more recent research
has shown that a substantial proportion of individuals who use the drug
simply cannot handle it. In fact, most people who use cocaine do so practically without untoward effect. Taking the drug occasionally—once a week
or less—in powdered form, intranasally, in small quantities, is no more
harmful than the recreational use of marijuana or alcohol (Van Dyke and
Byck, 1982). However, as we've seen, roughly one user in ten becomes
totally consumed by the drug, cannot control his or her use, and takes it in
dangerous ways and in large, often-repeated doses, wrecking lives in the
process. While using cocaine is not as dangerous as putting a gun up your
nose and pulling the trigger, as one ad campaign (sponsored by the Partner-
ship for a Drug-Free America) has suggested, it is a high-risk activity. And
it is clear to me that decriminalization will substantially increase the likelihood of use generally, and compulsive, damaging use specifically. It is not
a wise policy to follow.

Heroin maintenance has been suggested by a number of experts as a
feasible treatment option; in fact, I once suggested that an experiment be
conducted to determine the program's viability (Goode, 1973b). Today, the
evidence suggests that instituting such a program would be extremely un-
sound. Some might point to the British system of narcotics control as a
positive example of heroin maintenance. In fact, the British have been
phasing heroin out of their maintenance program for some time, to the
point where fewer than 1 percent of the addicted patients in it receive the
drug. In addition, it hardly can be said that the British system of mainte-

nance has worked, since the government estimates that the number of unregistered narcotic addicts there has *quadrupled* in the 1980s, and now stands at roughly 50,000.

In any system, there is some leakage. Under a system of heroin maintenance, a number of addicts who receive heroin will keep some to sell to nonaddicts for more than the price they will pay for heroin on the street, thus creating more users and, in the long run, more addicts. In spite of screening, some nonaddicted users will fake addiction in order to be enrolled in a heroin-maintenance program. Heroin, unlike methadone, is an extremely difficult drug on which to stabilize addicts on fixed doses. It is a rapidly metabolized drug, necessitating injection roughly four times a day—creating an administrative and logistical nightmare. If heroin is overprescribed, addicts will use the drug to get high and sell what they do not need to others; if it is underprescribed, they will try to obtain more on the street (Kaplan, 1983, p. 169). If the addict is to be given a prescription for heroin, the likelihood of diversion increases massively. Using the administration of heroin as a "hook" to induce addicts to enroll in the program and then switch the maintenance drug to the less problematic methadone inevitably results in the abandonment of the program by a high proportion of the program's enrollees and the leakage of negative evaluations of such a program onto the street. Heroin maintenance is simply not a viable program at all.

Perhaps the grandest fallacy on which the heroin-maintenance scheme is based is the notion that most users of heroin are taking the drug to avoid withdrawal. This is completely false. As we saw, even many addicts—who are physically dependent on the drug—seek the euphoria of a heroin "rush." They are not simply trying to maintain themselves on the drug—they want to get high. Even most maintainers would get high if they could obtain enough heroin, or if they could deal with the hassle or the risk of arrest. The "maintenance-not-euphoria" fallacy leads to three related misconceptions: (1) that all addicts will enroll in a maintenance program; (2) that all of their heroin will be provided by the program; and (3) that only addicts use heroin (Kaplan, 1983, p. 168). All three of these assumptions are false. Many, indeed, most street addicts do not enroll in maintenance programs. Many, indeed, most addicts seek euphoria, and not merely maintenance. In Britain, there are ten to twenty times more unregistered than officially registered addicts, and the reasons they are not enrolled in a maintenance program are that they want to get high, they want to inject their drug, and they want heroin—none of which is allowed under the British system. And the number of day-in-and-day out heroin abusers both here and in Britain is relatively small in comparison with the number of users who take the drug several times a week, but who are not physically dependent on it. And, as we speculated, much of the heroin that would be supplied by maintenance programs would find its way into their hands.

The current U.S. policy toward heroin—and toward most of the recreational drugs discussed in the book—is, of course, punitive. It's clearly not working in the sense that drug abuse is a resilient feature of the American social landscape. Advocates of the punitive policy, however, feel that the reason why there are so many drug users, abusers, and addicts is that our punitive policies just don't go far enough. We are too timid; we should strengthen our law enforcement policy against drug users and, especially, dealers. Some of the more humane proponents of this policy advocate treatment for the addict and prison for the seller, but their main emphasis remains on punishment through law enforcement. "Lock 'em up" is the motto of the advocates of the punitive model. Some of the more ambitious supporters of this approach believe in marching up the supply ladder: arrest the street-level sellers; arrest the middle- and higher-level dealers; arrest smugglers at the border; eradicate drugs at the source. What do we know about the world of drugs that bears on the validity of the punitive model?

Eliminating heroin and other drugs at the source seems attractive at first glance. What hardly anyone who proposes this suggestion seems to realize is how deeply entrenched drug cultivation and exportation are in certain countries, how profitable they are, and how easily other areas can step in to fill a void left when a crackdown or a substitution has taken place in one nation. In the early 1970s, President Richard Nixon attempted to institute this strategy by convincing the Turkish government to induce farmers to substitute wheat and barley for their opium crop. This policy appeared to work for a while, but over the long haul, it was a failure. Why? No crop can be as profitable to those farmers as opium; much of their land is not fertile enough to grow anything else; the drug is a culturally crucial crop to them; the markets for other crops are too distant to make their production worthwhile. Even if a temporary halt in opium production were to take place in one country, other areas are ready, willing, and able to step in and supply the shortfall—which is precisely what happened when Turkish farmers temporarily ceased opium production: Southeast Asia and Afghanistan became major sources of heroin instead.

The same took place with Mexico: When a U.S.-sponsored program eradicated vast fields of marijuana in Mexico, Colombia and Jamaica stepped in to take up the slack. One observer (DuPont, 1984) suggests that the Turkish and Mexican examples demonstrate the efficacy of eliminating drugs at the source, but the facts suggest precisely the opposite. With some drugs, a shutdown in drug production in one country has even stimulated domestic cultivation. Today, between 10 and 15 percent of the marijuana consumed in the United States is grown domestically. It is possible that the same could happen, on a smaller scale, with the opium and coca plants. Immense areas of the world have not even been considered for drug cultivation, and could be used if necessary. Brazil contains the largest tract of thinly populated, almost totally unpatrolled territory on the face of the earth; its potential for marijuana cultivation and cocaine processing is almost unlimited. Moreover, in many areas of the world (much of Burma and Afghanistan, for instance), the government does not control major territories, and thus cannot even monitor, let alone eliminate, cultivated drugs within its borders.

In some countries, drug cultivation is a huge business, and it is protected tenaciously and mercilessly by those who profit from it. Half of Bolivia's foreign exchange derives from the cocaine trade. The Drug Enforcement Administration estimates that Jamaicans earn well over $1 billion a year from exporting marijuana, more revenue than for all other exports combined. Jamaica is a poor country compared with the United States; do the advocates of a punitive policy toward drug cultivation have a suggestion as to how this sum might be earned in some other way? Colombia earns more revenue from exporting drugs to the United States than it does from selling coffee. In 1983, a plantation was discovered in Mexico with about 10,000 tons of marijuana growing on it, *eight times* as much as American and Mexican officials believed to grow in all of Mexico each year. Prior to that time, the Drug Enforcement Agency estimated that Americans consumed a total of only 14,000 tons of pot annually. For years, Ecuador was thought to produce no significant quantities of drugs. Police began discovering enormous and plentiful cultivated coca bushes, and officials now concede that Ecuador is probably the fourth-largest cocaine-producing nation in the world. Until recently, the State Department was unaware that marijuana is being grown in Belize; that nation is now listed as the fourth-largest exporter of marijuana to the United States.

Some successful drug smugglers earn more than the entire federal budget of the Drug Enforcement Agency (DEA). One Colombian dealer is reputed to earn $20 million a *month,* and he has his own personal army of several thousand men—a larger force than the total personnel of the DEA, which employs only 2,000 agents. Some powerful drug sellers are personally worth billions of dollars and control entire towns and even territories with an iron fist. In Colombia, even honest judges let arrested drug traffickers go free because they know that they and their families will be murdered if they do not; they are given a choice: "a big payoff or a bullet" (Riding, 1988). Corruption is not even the issue here; in some countries from which illegal drugs are imported, law enforcement has simply ceased to function. Drug dealers are even more powerful than the government; they have more money and command larger armed forces, with superior weapons. Moreover, it is not simply a small number of very rich growers and cultivators who earn money from the illegal drug trade: Their employees also stand to lose money by the shift to a legal economy. In Colombia, agricultural workers earn $3.50 a day harvesting traditional crops, and $25 a day picking coca leaves, to be processed into cocaine. They have every intention of defending their economic interests, and do so when a threat arises (Gonzales, 1985; McBee, 1985).

Moreover, both opium and coca are viable legal crops; roughly 3,000 tons of opium are produced annually worldwide, most of it for legitimate purposes. Of this production, only *one-twentieth* is necessary to supply the American street market for heroin—a shade over 100 tons of opium, which produces some 10 tons of heroin. The entire illicit American heroin market can be satisfied by opium cultivation on a mere 25 square miles of land (Kaplan, 1983, p. 71). Since cultivation is scattered over the globe in more than a dozen countries, shutting down or even curtailing production would seem to be little short of impossible. Moreover, as we saw in Chapter 10, artificial narcotics (one of a large category of "designer drugs") are becoming available on the black market. After the three presidential administrations since Richard Nixon's effort to eliminate heroin at the source, the heroin on the streets of America's cities is purer and easier to obtain than it ever has been. The same can be said of cocaine. Coca leaves are legal in Peru and Bolivia, and are chewed by the Indian population to inhibit fatigue and hunger; a substantial proportion of coca leaves are grown for domestic consumption. Moreover, the coca plant is extremely tenacious, and cannot be eradicated simply by pulling it up by the roots. The American government has poured millions of dollars into cutting cocaine off at its source and, as with heroin, cocaine is purer, cheaper, and more readily available today than it has been since the Harrison Act was passed in 1914.

Once drugs enter the United States, many of the same problems apply to any and all drugs, from marijuana to heroin. Closing the American borders to incoming illegal narcotics has produced marginally more encouraging results than eradicating these substances at the source. President Ronald Reagan, photographed from time to time behind huge piles of cash and a cache of heroin or cocaine confiscated from dealers, proclaims that the government is winning the war on drugs. Consider the enormity of the problem, however. Locating the 10 tons of heroin and the 120 tons of cocaine that come into the United States each year among the annual incoming flow of more than 100 million tons of legal freight makes finding the proverbial needle in the haystack seem a relatively simple task. In addition, there are some quarter-billion border crossings into the United States each year: Who's smuggling in the drugs? Weary customs officials admit that not much more than 5 and certainly less than 10 percent of the illicit drugs entering the country are seized at the border. Doubling or tripling this figure might have a serious impact on the street supply of narcotics, but it would represent a tactical horror story for law-enforcement officials and an intolerable inconvenience for people entering the country for legitimate reasons. Moreover, individuals crossing the border with drugs are nearly always couriers, "mules" paid to deliver the goods. Very few possess any useful information about the overall operation of the enterprise for which they work.

State police in Florida, Georgia, and other states near points of embarcation for smuggled-in drugs have had some success with patrolling the interstate highways and identifying drivers who are transporting drugs to other areas to be sold. Exactly how many such drivers slip through their net is not clear, but a substantial number are caught. How? State police have a "profile" of typical transporters of illegal drugs. They tend, the police say, to drive a rented car, have Texas, California, or, especially, Florida license plates, to belong to a racial or ethnic minority (especially Black or Hispanic), to be male, in their twenties, and to drive scrupulously, at exactly the speed limit. Still, doesn't stopping someone who has given the police no cause to do so and searching his or her car for contraband raise some extremely difficult civil liberties issues? And doesn't this practice verge dangerously on racial discrimination? And how many innocent drivers have to be stopped, inconvenienced, and hassled before one with a trunkful of heroin or cocaine is located? In any case, the profile that the state police use to find drug transporters is now well known to high-level dealers, who are now more likely to use drivers with a different profile in order to avoid detection.

Attempting to arrest high-level dealers within our borders has proven to be little more effective. The removal of one dealer by arrest results not only in another one stepping in as a replacement, but it also increases the financial rewards for anyone else entering the business. The immense profits—the possibility of instantly earning hundreds of thousands of dollars from a single suitcase full of heroin or cocaine—will always attract enough daring, enterprising traffickers to ensure an uninterrupted flow of illicit drugs. There is, in the words of John Kaplan, more than enough talent to go around to keep the upper ranks of drug dealing well supplied with personnel. The risk is simply too low and the profits too huge to expect that there will be a serious interruption in the flow of heroin or cocaine following a few dramatic, well-publicized busts. As we saw in Chapter 10, the potency of the heroin sold on the streets of New York rose between the early and the mid-1980s; in 1982, only 3 percent of New York's heroin was imported from Southeast Asia ("China White"), but by 1987, this figure was 70 percent. These shifts have come about partly as a result of police attention to Mafia figures of Italian extraction. These arrests left a vacuum in the drug trade that has been filled by distributors of Chinese background, with their connections to the previously untapped territories in Southeast Asia (Kerr, 1987b, 1987c). In short, busting one group has not resulted in a slowdown in the drug trade, only in a shift in its personnel.

Recall that more profits are to be made in the illegal drug trade than in practically any industry on earth. Some high-level drug dealers earn so much money that they do not bother to count it to determine how much they have—they *weigh* it. It's possible that as much as $100 billion are earned at the retail level in the United States annually from selling illicit drugs. In New York City alone, a quarter of a million people—from the high-level importer to the low-level street dealer—earn their primary livelihood marketing, transporting, processing, and distributing street drugs. Does anyone seriously imagine that almost any number of arrests will shut down this immensely lucrative business? Selling illegal drugs is a remarkably resilient industry. Consider the following facts. In 1983, the DEA seized 7,000 kilograms of cocaine, less than 8 tons. In 1986, this figure was well over 26,000 kilos—and it continues to rise. Cocaine use, as we saw, has been increasing along with cocaine seizures. Ronald Reagan has been as enthusiastic an advocate of the punitive policy as any American president in recent memory. In 1981, the year he took office, about 25 tons of cocaine entered the country. In 1985, the first year of his second term, this figure had risen to 85 tons. During his last year in office, 1988, it reached more than 120 tons.

The punitive policy toward drugs—indeed, the punitive policy of criminalizing any activity at all—stumbles over a most stubborn feature of law enforcement: It is called the *law of criminal justice thermodynamics* (Walker, 1985, pp. 33–35). This principle is really quite simple; it is remarkable that anyone proposing more severe penalties for a given offense is unaware of it. The law goes as follows: *"An increase in the severity of the penalty will result in less frequent application of the penalty"* (Walker, 1985, p. 34). When the penalty for a given offense rises arrests decline, dismissals rise, indictments decline, the proportion of defendants demanding trial rises, convictions decline, and appeals rise. Even mandatory sentencing is circumvented through a series of legal loopholes. In the end, because of harsher penalties, the same number or even fewer individuals actually go to prison—although those that are incarcerated spend a longer period of time behind bars.

In 1973, New York state passed "the nation's toughest drug law," sponsored by Governor Nelson Rockefeller. It called for mandatory and long prison terms for heroin dealers. It had a number of extremely Draconian provisions—for instance, a prison term of fifteen years to life for the sale of 1 ounce or the possession of 2 ounces of heroin. What kind of an impact did this law have? In an evaluation of the program, sponsored by the U.S. Department of Justice, entitled *The Nation's Toughest Drug Law: Evaluating the New York Experience,* the legal fate of defendants in 1972–1973, before the law took effect, was compared with the situation in 1976, after the law had been in effect for several years.

In 1972, 39 percent of drug arrests led to an indictment; in 1976, only 25 percent did. In 1972, 86 percent of indictments led to a conviction; in 1976, 80 percent did. Thus a total of 34 percent of arrests led to conviction in 1972; in 1976, only 20 percent did. But of those convicted, in 1972, 33 percent went to prison; in 1976, this was true of 55 percent. And the percentage of convicted offenders receiving a sentence of three years or longer rose from 3 percent in 1972 to 22 percent in 1976. And the percentage of defendants demanding trial rose from 6 to 15 percent. (A tried case takes about fifteen times as long to process as a nontried case.) Overall, 11 percent of the individuals arrested for heroin sale or possession went to prison in 1972; in 1976, it was also 11 percent (Walker, 1985, pp. 67–69).

As a result of adjustments at each point in the criminal justice system, the intended impact of the law was neutralized. In fact, it is fair to say that the Rockefeller drug law had no effect at all on drug use or sale in New York state between 1973, when it was passed, and 1979, when, because of its failure, its provisions were abolished. In fact, through no fault of the law, drug use actually rose in New York state during this period—as it did nearly everywhere in the country. And the reason why the law failed is the same as the reason why any sudden increase in penalties for a given crime will fail to have an impact on criminal behavior in a criminal justice system operating in a formally democratic society: the law of criminal justice thermodynamics.

The point is, the criminal justice system is not infinitely expandable. Something has to give. If we prosecute more drug dealers and users, where are the resources going to come from? Where are the extra police, prosecutors, public defenders, and judges going to come from? If we convict and imprison more drug offenders, where are they going to be imprisoned? And who is going to pay for all this? Which other crimes are going to be neglected as a result of this extra effort? Drug arrests have increased during the 1980s, and so have convictions—but at what cost to society? Which crimes have to be under-investigated and under-prosecuted as a result? Murder? Rape? Armed robbery? Law enforcement campaigns do not generate resources out of thin air; they have to be extracted from the flesh and bones of the present system, and that always means making painful choices. Real results very rarely come from mere words.

There is another reason why fighting the drug war by cracking down on drug dealers will not eliminate illicit drug use here: it must inevitably result in law-enforcement practices that are unacceptable to the majority of the American public. Most people who advocate punitive action against behavior they do not like envision arrest and imprisonment as acting much like a "silver bullet," cleanly hitting the target, and nothing but the target, each time the weapon is aimed. Law enforcement is much more like a net than a silver bullet. Police work is most effective when the crime entails a perpetrator and a victim who complains to the police about having been victimized. While drug-related behavior may involve victims—users may victimize themselves, and neighborhoods and entire societies in which drug use and sale take place may experience a decline in the quality of life in a number of ways—it does not typically entail someone who is either *directly* victimized by a specific act or who witnesses that act. As a result, drug activities do not usually generate a *complainant* who goes to the police with a tale of victimization. Since the vast majority of investigations leading to arrest are initiated by a citizen complaint, offender activity that is less likely to lead to such citizen complaints is also far less likely to lead to arrest. If the police are to become more vigilant at the local level, they will be forced to step up their undercover operations and investigate what few citizen complaints they do have on the basis of even flimsier evidence than is the case today.

The police rarely have complete knowledge of the illegal behavior of a suspect before they act; more typically, they have incomplete and often partly erroneous knowledge of a crime. Still, act they must, and the more vigorous and vigilant they are in their action, the more likely it is that they will ensnare innocent suspects in their net. Anyone can be a suspect, including you—the reader of this book. Most of us have done something that could become the basis of a police investigation into drug selling. Don't we know a few people who use cocaine? Didn't we say just the other day that marijuana doesn't seem as bad as heroin? Weren't we seen reading a book on drugs? Most sellers of illicit drugs do not look or act like movie or TV versions of dealers. They can be—and have been—doctors, Wall Street lawyers, successful business executives, grandparents, clean-cut, middle-class suburbanites, the couple next door. Would you be willing to be stopped and frisked on the street? To have your front door broken down and entered by a narcotics squad who may have heard a rumor from a disgruntled acquaintance of yours? To be the target of an intense police investigation, no matter how incomplete or misleading the evidence? While polls show that much of the public say that they are willing to "sacrifice" in the war against drugs (Clymer, 1986), most Americans have little or no idea just how sharply a truly concerted effort would curtail their legal rights and civil liberties. Vigorous law enforcement is far from infallible, and it won't simply be drug dealers who are caught in a wider law-enforcement net.

Is it contradictory to say that a more punitive policy will not help to stamp out or drastically reduce the illicit drug supply and drug use in the United States, and to say at the same time that decriminalization will greatly increase drug use in this country? In my view, it is not. Our current punitive policy has been a failure in that it has not stemmed the flow of illegal drugs: Street drug use is massive, and it has fluctuated almost irrespective of law enforcement. Our punitive policy has also been a failure in that law enforcement has actually stimulated some extremely undesirable features of the drug scene, as we saw in Chapter 10. If we were to adopt an idealistic or utopian view of the matter, some of the more undesirable consequences of the punitive model of drug control would have to be regarded as unacceptable. Would matters be better in a socialist state? The Soviet Union, as nearly everyone knows, has a more serious alcoholism problem than exists in the West. Moveover, both the Soviet Union and Poland have a serious problem with narcotic addiction (Inciardi, 1987, 1988b). Three things are remarkable about this fact. First, the socialist nations of Eastern Europe have a more equalitarian income distribution than we do in the United States, suggesting that drug addiction is probably not a simple by-product of inequality. Second, in a more authoritarian regime, with even more punitive sanctions at their disposal, officials in the East have not been able to stamp out drug addiction. And third, in many ways, their addicts look remarkably like ours.

On the other hand, if we apply a different criterion—containment—the punitive policy toward drug use has been successful. Law enforcement has, to a modest extent, restricted the use of street drugs. Arresting users and sellers has not been an absolute barrier against drug experimentation, use, or abuse—but it has discouraged a substantial proportion of the American population who would otherwise have used drugs from using them. William Pollin, director of the National Institute on Drug Abuse, believes that drug use would be "endemic" in this country without law enforcement. Cocaine, he points out, "is by far the most self-reinforcing drug we know," far more pleasurable than the currently legal drugs alcohol and tobacco. Does it not make sense, he reasons, that more pleasure would equal at least as much use? "If there were no law enforcement, then the number of cocaine users would be right up there in the same numbers with smokers and drinkers. . . . We'd have 60 to 100 million cocaine users" instead of the 6 to 10 million current users we now have. Viewed in this light, he says, our current law-enforcement strategy "is 90 percent effective" (Brinkley, 1984a, p. A12).

Drug enforcement is little more than a "holding action"; year after year, huge seizures "appear to leave supplies unaffected" (Brinkley, 1984b). The Rand Corporation, in a comprehensive eighteen-month study of drug-control strategies, concluded: "From the analysis we have conducted, the most basic point is that the supply of [illicit] drugs can never be eliminated" (Brinkley, 1984a). It seems difficult to argue with this conclusion. Stated in this way, the punitive model can be seen only as a failure—if its goal is to eliminate or to seriously curtail use. More realistically, however, if its goal is containment, it must be seen as successful. Containment is no mean feat, but to propose that law enforcement accomplish more than this is unrealistic—or dishonest.

In the past, observers tended either to be critics of the punitive policy, in which case they saw maintenance or decriminalization as the ideal solution to the problem, or to be critics of maintenance and decriminalization, in which case they defended the punitive model. In other words, observers of the drug scene were forced into an "either-or" position—completely for or completely against one model or another. The approach of the earlier editions of this book (1972a, 1984) followed that tradition, criticizing the punitive model without considering the consequences of decriminalization or maintenance in detail. It is clear now there is no ideal solution and that all conceivable models have undesirable consequences (Kaplan, 1983; Inciardi, 1986). If the defenders of law enforcement and the antidrug campaigners tend to be naive about the subject, so, too, are many of their critics. The fact is, in the United States, the recreational use of drugs is probably an intractable problem, regardless of the model that is instituted. It is important to pursue policies that will be, if not good, then at least not disastrous.

"What is the solution to the drug problem?" the anxious public asks. Officials repeat the question and fund research projects that hint at an answer. Actually, the deeper and more specific meaning of this question is: *How can we get people to stop using certain drugs with a minimum of economic cost, and without disrupting existing social institutions and arrangements?* The answer to this question is that there is at present no possible solution to the drug problem. There is no program in effect or under discussion that offers any hope whatsoever of a "solution." Asking for the solution to the drug problem is a little like asking for the solution to the accident problem, the problem of crime and violence, the problems created by the economy. To be plain about it, there will always be certain forms of behavior that will produce, or will be associated with, the use of drugs. The use of mind-altering drugs is linked to broader social forces and influences that are not going to change very much, at least during this century. There will probably always be a pool of "drug-prone" individuals. Of course, if some master visionary a hundred years ago had been able to predict future drug discoveries and use trends, it might have been possible to develop alternatives to psychoactive drugs; but history is behind us, and nothing can undo the past and present forces that have produced the existing situation.

Efforts at the social control of drugs—such as reducing the supply, increasing the social or economic cost, and instituting stiffer penalties for use—will often have some impact; they may produce a temporary reduction in the number of users. But typically they result in far more serious secondary social maladies. Efforts at social control will never be more substantial than a "finagle factor." The only impact on drug use will come about as a consequence of drastic and massive social change, on a scale that will destroy American society as we know it today. This may be positive or detrimental, depending on one's point of view. One solution on this scale would be to execute anyone suspected of using an illegal drug, without trial or evidence. This is clearly impossible and unrealistic (not to mention barbaric), but it would probably do the trick after a substantial proportion of the American population was eliminated. A second solution would be to undertake a massive program to restructure the society totally to ensure that all Americans live a life they consider meaningful. This would, at the very least, involve the total elimination of poverty, racial discrimination, warfare, a sterile and alienating educational system, boring employment, and a wretched public bureaucracy. However, this too is impossible, because much of the public, as well as those in positions of power, either does not see these issues as crushing problems, as many compulsive drug users do, or is not willing to pay the price to do anything about them. Moreover, this solution might reduce alcoholism and narcotic addiction but not the recreational use of psychoactive drugs, such as weekend marijuana smoking.

In short, I do not feel that any of the solutions that would make a meaningful dent in the addiction problem are in the ball park. *The only realistic approach to the drug problem is to develop methods not to eliminate drug use or even to reduce it drastically, but to live with it and to make sure that drug users do not seriously harm themselves and others.* Drug use is here to stay, and the only way to eliminate *illegal* drug use is to eliminate the laws outlawing the use of certain drugs. Addiction is a fact of American life. Heavy, frequent, compulsive, chronic drug use is also here to stay. Something might be done about the use of certain drugs—it might be realistic to ask, not too restrictively, which drugs will be available to the American public. Or steps might be taken to reduce the relative size of the addict population—for example, the nation's 9 or 10 million alcoholics or its half-million heroin addicts—but a drastic or even substantial reduction is not feasible. A large number of chronic users of various drugs will probably always be with us, at least for the next two or three generations. Thus the issue we should be exploring is: Given a population of heavy drug users in the society, how can we minimize the harm to everyone involved?

There is no end of commentators who offer simplistic solutions, make dogmatic assertions, put forth unsubstantiated claims. Almost all are charlatans who have not weighed the evidence very carefully. Most of us yearn for a quick fix to serious problems, and it is easy to fall victim to those who offer one. There is no such panacea; anyone who suggests that one exists should not be taken seriously.

I've said that there are two small exceptions to our at least moderately punitive policy toward street drugs: the decriminalization of small quantities of marijuana in eleven states, and methadone maintenance programs for a minority of heroin addicts. In my view, both policies are wise; their scope should be expanded.

As I see it, there is no conceivable nondrastic measure for reducing or eliminating marijuana use. The border blockage has had some modest success in restricting the quantity of cannabis entering the United States, but this success appears to be short-lived and typically produces countereffort on the part of the marijuana-using community to seek alternate means of acquiring the drug—growing one's own grass, broadening the spectrum of nations from which cannabis is imported, harvesting more "domestic" grass, exploring chemical alternatives to marijuana, and so on. Given the sheer size of the marijuana subculture, and the fact that use of the drug has become so intricately woven into a viable and rewarding lifestyle for many young people, attempting to "stamp out" marijuana use would seem to be a hopeless venture. Users do not see their activity as serious or as a cause for official concern. Marijuana smoking is not an isolated form of behavior. It is an expression of a certain kind of ideology; it takes place in conjunction with other activities; and it is reinforced by a social group, a subculture, a miniature community. These hard facts about marijuana use make it almost impossible to control on an official level.

As we saw in Chapter 6, the use of marijuana is associated with at least one medical malady, a decline in respiratory functioning, while the evidence demonstrating its causal link to several others is still conflicting. This suggests that the overwhelming majority of users do not experience serious health hazards as a result of their use of the drug. Moreover, the medical question is, in many ways, no more relevant with marijuana than it is with alcohol or cigarettes. Users of all three drugs are aware of the medical risks they take in using them. (No medical figure questions the wisdom of keeping alcohol, cigarettes, or marijuana away from children and adolescents.) However, given that marijuana is the number-one illicit drug in America, attracting between 50 and 60 million at-least-one-time users and nearly 20 million regular users, the likelihood of its use being stamped out by law enforcement is practically nonexistent. The magnitude of its use is so enormous, the degree to which the drug is woven into the lifestyle of millions of users is so great, and the networks of supply and demand are so entrenched, that a significant dent by law enforcement will never be made in its use.

So much is this the case, in fact, that the legal issue surrounding the marijuana question is no longer crucial. To argue that the laws against marijuana possession should be more rigorously enforced is a bit like arguing for the return of national alcohol prohibition, or calling for a ban on the manufacture and sale of cigarettes. Marijuana is a social fact and will remain so for the foreseeable future. The use of marijuana is here to stay regardless of the precise percentage of the population that turns on. Millions of Americans will continue to smoke marijuana regularly or sporadically for the foreseeable future regardless of the efforts of law enforcement.

In addition, it is not even clear that law enforcement, as it has been practiced, makes much of a difference in the marijuana picture. Since 1973, the number of arrests on marijuana charges per year in the United States has remained more or less stable in the 400,000 to 450,000 range. And yet use nearly doubled between the early and the late 1970s, and then declined substantially. It is just as unlikely that marijuana arrests decreased use in the 1980s as it is that they increased it in the 1970s. In studies that have been conducted in the states or areas where marijuana decriminalization has taken place, it is clear that the use of the drug has not risen more than it has in jurisdictions where possession remains a crime (Cuskey et al., 1978; Single, 1981; Johnston, 1980). In addition, arrest and incarceration have had no impact on marijuana smokers' intention to use the drug in the future (Erickson, 1976). What makes the most sense to me, then, is the decriminalization of marijuana throughout the United States—the removal of all criminal penalties for the possession of small to moderate quantities of marijuana. As I said, this has already taken place in eleven states. Although the number of arrests remains as high today as it was fifteen years ago, the likelihood that a first-time offender caught with a small quantity of marijuana will go to jail is negligible. In this sense, then, for all practical purposes, the possession of marijuana has become decriminalized in the United States. Since present trends are moving toward de facto legal acceptance of small-quantity marijuana possession, it will not make a great deal of difference whether this attitude is recognized by law or not. Consequently, the debate over decriminalization is swiftly becoming obsolete. Moreover, in today's conservative political climate, it is unlikely that any more states will decriminalize in the foreseeable future.

Why would decriminalization have a devastating impact on cocaine and heroin use (and use of most psychoactive prescription drugs as well—amphetamine, barbiturates, and sedatives such as methaqualone), while, as most observers agree, it has had little or no impact with marijuana? There are at least three reasons.

First, a condition of near-saturation has been reached with marijuana. The vast majority of Americans are one or two informal links away from a marijuana seller and could, if motivated and with small effort, locate a supply of pot for their personal use. Most people in their late teens or older who want to use already do so. The same, however, is not true of heroin or cocaine. Most young people do not know a supplier of these drugs, and the effort to locate one would represent more hassle than most moderately curious or motivated potential users are willing to risk. Law enforcement may not have been successful in stamping out these drugs, but it has succeeded in making them relatively difficult to obtain in mainstream America.

A second reason why decriminalization would be a disaster with heroin and coke, but has not been so for marijuana, relates to what I said about reinforcement and dependence in Chapter 2. Cocaine and heroin are *immensely* reinforcing drugs, and experimentation is likely to lead to compulsive use for a sizable minority of individuals—with catastrophic personal consequences for their lives. On the other hand, marijuana's effects have been described as pleasant but, for most users, not overwhelmingly reinforcing. Smoking crack or freebase cocaine, or injecting cocaine or heroin intravenously, is like delivering a jolt of electricity to the brain that leaves most users wanting more. Smoking pot for most is a soft, dreamy, comfortably, hazy, pleasant high that, to judge from current patterns of use, can be postponed until another opportunity arises. Marijuana is simply not in the same league as cocaine and heroin in its reinforcement- and dependency-producing potential.

And third, of course, we cannot discount the impact of law enforcement. Although there are, as I said, roughly 400,000 arrests on marijuana charges each year, the chances are practically nil that someone arrested for possessing a small quantity of the drug will be incarcerated. That likelihood is greater with cocaine and heroin. Moreover, the statistical probability of arrest for marijuana possession is much smaller than it is for cocaine or heroin, simply because the police are more concerned with tracking down the latter substances than the former. Decriminalization has little impact on the life of the marijuana user because the chances of arrest and imprisonment are extremely low, even where possession and sale are against the law. Getting involved in the world of heroin and cocaine escalates that likelihood, and discourages those who fear such an outcome.

Does methadone maintenance work in combating heroin addiction? Are there programs that are more effective?

Methadone is a synthetic narcotic. It is not a "cure" for addiction in that patients enrolled in a methadone program are maintained on the drug on a daily basis. They are physically dependent on methadone; they are methadone "addicts." If patients were to be withdrawn from methadone, they would undergo painful withdrawal symptoms, just as they would with heroin. Clearly, if methadone maintenance were to be evaluated on the criterion of achieving a drug-free existence for the addict, it would always be judged a failure, because the addict is still dependent on a drug. The former rationale for the program—that methadone provides a medicine that the heroin addict's body lacks because of a metabolic imbalance, in much the same way that insulin provides a medicine that the diabetic's body lacks—has almost no support whatsoever among drug experts nowadays. At the same time, it is possible that a program that is theoretically wrong works for other reasons.

Methadone is administered orally in doses that are designed to "block" the effects of heroin and the other narcotics. A methadone-maintained client or patient cannot get high by injecting heroin, the reasoning goes, because of the effects of methadone. And supposedly the user no longer craves heroin, because he or she is now taking another narcotic as a substitute. Orally and in the doses taken, the client does not feel high, euphoric, or "doped up." (He or she can, of course, get high by injecting methadone or taking a sufficiently large dose of it.) And, of all programs, it is the most cost-effective—that is, it is inexpensive to administer, given the results.

Let us be clear about the criteria on which a drug treatment program should be evaluated. Certainly they should include a diminution of the addict's rate of criminal activity, including drug crimes, an increase in his or her legal employment, a decrease in the use of heroin and other illicit drugs, the diminution of the addict's suffering and a virtual elimination of addiction as a cause of death, and a decrease in the recruitment of new addicts. How well does methadone maintenance work in light of these goals?

In its early years, methadone was hailed as the ideal solution for the problem of heroin addiction. Early studies were optimistic, many claiming success rates of more than 90 percent (Dole and Nyswander, 1965; Dole et al., 1968; Jaffe et al., 1969). Especially significant to many observers was the striking reduction in crime and arrest rates of methadone-maintained clients. As it turns out, these studies were not conducted very carefully; the success rates they claimed nearly melt away under systematic scrutiny. Clients who were enrolled in these programs but who dropped out were often not counted in the final tallies. Those who stayed in the programs were the most motivated to do well; those who dropped out tended to return to a life of crime and addiction. These early studies, to the detriment of their validity, seriously understated the "split rate"—that is, the proportion of enrollees who left the program before completing it. Furthermore, many methadone-maintenance programs selected addicts most likely to succeed and rejected high-risk addicts. Consequently, it was less the case that the programs' effectiveness was being measured than that the selectivity of their admissions procedures was being recorded. Also, there was a heavy overselection of older addicts in these early studies. Twice as many addicts over 30 were included in the original Dole-Nyswander study (two-thirds) as, proportionally speaking, exist in the general population of addicts. It is now clear that, through a process unrelated to treatment, a higher proportion of older than younger addicts discontinue their use of heroin, with or without methadone. In short, reports of success with methadone-maintenance programs appear to have been substantially exaggerated (Maddux and Bowden, 1972; Bourne, 1975; Kleinman et al., 1977).

In addition, methadone, in the doses typically administered, does not seem to block the euphoric effects of heroin completely. If enough street heroin is injected, the addict can get high; the trick is to take substantially more than the usual dose. The claim that methadone can turn the typical heroin addict into a productive, law-abiding citizen is wildly unrealistic. Many addicts, methadone or no methadone, are the drug world's equivalent of skid-row alcoholics (Preble and Miller, 1977). No feasible intervention of any kind will drastically alter such a lifestyle. Many methadone patients cheat, or continue to take drugs, including heroin, although those who do so take them significantly less frequently than they did without methadone. Many enrollees in the methadone programs continue to commit property crimes, even though, on average, their overall crime rate is roughly one-sixth of what it was when they were heroin addicts. Some programs do not even check to determine whether prospective clients are addicts to begin with. Programs are also highly variable with respect to the doses of methadone they administer. Some are surprisingly unconcerned about the diversion of methadone into the street; others clamp a tight control over its administration and disappearance. And diversion does occur; methadone was implicated in about 3 percent of DAWN's medical examiner's lethal mentions in 1986 (DAWN, 1987, p. 53).

Still, when all of these and other valid criticisms have been leveled at methadone-maintenance programs, they remain: "the most cost-effective treatment we have today for heroin addiction. The addict receiving this type of treatment is often much better off than on heroin—with respect to his well-being and ours. That is not to say that this treatment permanently helps all or even a majority of addicts. Probably the figure is closer to 40 percent. Considering all the costs and benefits of the other treatments and punishments at our disposal, this seems to be about as well as we can do" (Kaplan, 1983, p. 222).

Therapeutic communities (nicknamed "TCs") operate under the assumption that a drug-free existence for ex-addicts is a realistic and necessary goal. (Their advocates exclude cigarettes from this assumption, presumably because smoking may be a tougher habit to break than heroin addiction, and cigarettes are rarely a short-term threat to life.) The view of all therapeutic communities is that the addict is an immature, emotionally disturbed individual with an inadequate, insecure, neurotic personality, who needs drugs as a crutch. In order to destroy this unhealthy reliance on getting high and "copping out" on life it becomes necessary to *resocialize* the addict (now a former or recovered addict). TCs attempt to inculcate an ideology or value system that is in many ways the antithesis of the one that prevails on the street: no violence, no drugs, no deception, no stealing or even borrowing without permission, no sex, no secrets, a repudiation of the "no-squealing" rule that (some) addicts and criminals adhere to, an emphasis on both individual and collective responsibility, honesty and openness, and a stress on relating to one another as human beings rather than as objects to be exploited (Sugarman, 1974).

TCs are live-in residences made up largely of ex-addicts (most supervisors and directors are former junkies) who hold encounter sessions stressing the negative side of narcotics use (and of users) and the necessity of facing life without such destructive dependencies. Discipline is strict, penalties for breaking house rules are severe, and peer pressure is almost unrelenting. The TC assumes the role of a benevolent dictator. At first, residents must ask permission to do almost everything, including going to the bathroom or receiving a phone call. Independence must be earned. The longer they have been living in a TC, the more responsibility they are granted. An emphasis is placed on confrontation, especially in the group encounters, in which brutal honesty is demanded. A new resident arrives and explains that he wants to "kick the filthy habit." One of the long-established residents will then shout angrily and loudly: "Knock off that shit, will you? Who do you think you are talking to? We ain't no bunch of bleeding-heart social workers. The people you see here are dope fiends themselves, see? And at one time we all came in here sniveling just like you are doing now" (Sugarman, 1974). Residents get "hit over the head with a load of reality" by staff and other residents. Deception or attempting to run a "con" on others is vigorously rebuffed and punished verbally. The addict is constantly reminded that he is a *stupid* person, a *baby* in need of a firm, authoritarian hand so that he can "get his head straight." There is something of an element of degradation in the newly admitted resident's experiences—for his or her own good, it is claimed. The severity of the discipline and the seeming hostility of the residents' encounters gradually abate as they demonstrate that they have earned the respect of others, as they show others that they are responsible and mature. However, brutal honesty and directness and strong discipline remain standard features of all TCs for all residents.

Therapeutic communities administer to a much smaller number of addicts than methadone-maintenance programs do—fewer than 10,000 in the United States. And data on their effectiveness are even more difficult to come by. TCs maintain an ideology of insularity and even of contempt in the face of "experts" who meddle in their business; their view is that only a reformed addict is in a position to decide what is right on the subject of reforming another addict. Consequently record-keeping is not merely not stressed; it is actively discouraged. Even TC advocates admit, however, that the defection rate is extremely high. Leaving against the advice of the staff before one is ready for re-entry into society is characteristic of well over two-thirds of the residents. Were systematic data available, this figure might be almost nine-tenths. After living the kind of selfish, reckless, amoral existence most junkies live, dealing with a program and an ideology such as characterize all TCs is bound to be a shock. Sticking with the program requires enormous dedication; motivation plays a crucial role in the success of an addict in a TC program. There are indications that TCs work better for some types of addicts than for others. The less the addict was involved with drugs before entry—the shorter the length of addiction, the smaller the habit, and the fewer the different types of drugs used—the more successful the TC is in the rehabilitation. The younger the resident, the fewer the number of arrests, and the higher the social-class background of the resident, the greater the chances of success. Thus the addict for whom the therapeutic community approach works represents a limited segment of the addict population. Consequently, the approach cannot be considered a satisfactory across-the-board method of treatment.

It must be stressed that TCs and methadone-maintenance programs operate on opposed principles; therefore the advocates of each are hostile and denunciatory toward the advocates of the other. Proponents of the therapeutic community believe that, by definition, methadone programs are a failure, since they keep the addict on drugs; everyone, they believe, should live a drug-free existence. No change in personality is even attempted; methadone "patients" are still as sick and as immature as they were prior to using methadone. Methadone advocates point to the high defection rate of the TCs, their tiny number of "cures," the fact that they cater to a limited segment of the addict population; and they criticize the TCs' contempt for facts and figures, their antiscientific stance, and the much higher cost of maintaining ex-addicts in residences than of allowing them to live unconfined lives in their communities while receiving methadone from a clinic. It is unlikely that any reconciliation between the two approaches is possible.

The issue of drug testing erupted into the public arena with great force in the 1980s. It has become a battleground of debate and controversy: Some commentators favor drug testing, while others are opposed. Two main axes distinguish pro-testers from anti-testers. The first is ideological and political: Conservatives are more likely to favor testing, while liberals are more likely to oppose it. Conservatives feel that society has the right to protect itself from the harmful consequences of drug abuse, and that it has the right to make use of any legal means at its disposal to bring a halt to the use of illicit psychoactive substances. On the other hand, liberals argue that even individuals who engage in illegal activities are protected by certain rights, called civil liberties, which are guaranteed by the Constitution; one of them is the protection from an invasion of their right of privacy. Drug testing, many liberals argue, represents precisely such an invasion.

The second axis distinguishing pro-testers from anti-testers is the manager-worker axis—that is, the line that separates those who would have others tested from those who would themselves be tested. Managers, who are concerned about the job performance and therefore the drug use of others, tend to favor testing. Workers, who would become a target of the tests, while not exactly opposed to drug testing, nonetheless are less positive than managers are.

At the same time, most Americans are more opposed to drug use and its consequences than to testing and its implications. Since the majority of Americans do not use illicit substances, and draw a sharp boundary between legal and illegal drugs, they do not feel personally threatened by the invasion of their privacy that testing entails. Most Americans are not strong civil libertarians if they can see countervailing benefits in the violation of civil liberties (McClosky and Brill, 1983); strong drug foes are probably even less concerned about violations of civil liberties than is the general public (Marx, 1986). To many Americans, opposition to testing borders dangerously on protecting drug users and condoning the devastating consequences of abuse. The issue of drug abuse for most is seen more as a problem to be solved in a practical, utilitarian fashion than as an arena for demonstrating the validity of one or another ideological position.

Regardless of how some people might feel about drug testing, however, it is a fact of life nowadays, and it is likely to become more common in the future. Nonetheless, at least two crucial questions must be resolved before the testing dilemma is addressed. They are: *Who is to be tested?* And: *How accurate are the tests?*

Who is to be tested? An employee's work setting makes a great deal of difference as to whether he or she will be tested for drug use. In more authoritarian work settings, especially those without union representation, testing has become widespread; in work settings with less rigid rules and a more flexible hierarchy, or with strong union representation, it is almost nonexistent. In the armed forces, drug testing by means of urinanalysis is pervasive, universal, and periodic. Officials credit this practice with the sharp decline in drug use in the military—from 27 percent who said that they had used an illicit drug during the previous month in 1980, before testing began, to three percent who tested positive in 1986. In the latter year, roughly 17,000 armed forces personnel were discharged from the military for their use of illicit drugs (Halloran, 1987a). Today, all recruits into the armed forces must be tested for drugs before they enter (Halloran, 1987b).

Drug testing has been adopted with remarkable speed by private corporations. Early in 1988, a majority of the Fortune 500 corporations require drug tests (52 percent)—a doubling in only two years; this figure is likely to continue to grow. Roughly two-thirds of these firms use tests only for job applicants, while the remainder use them both for applicants and current employees (Anonymous, 1987). Drug use is regarded as serious business, even off the job, by managers and executives. In a survey conducted among personnel directors of the nation's largest corporations by the Interface Group of Washington, D.C., a major executive-search firm, suspicion of the use of marijuana was regarded as the number one job disqualifier of otherwise qualified applicants. (The use of other illicit drugs was not asked about.) While nearly half of the respondents questioned (47 percent) said that they would be very unlikely to hire an otherwise qualified applicant who uses marijuana off the job, only 2 percent said the same for alcohol.

A survey of drug testing in the workplace conducted by *The New York Times* found positive attitudes toward testing to be widespread and deeply entrenched. Said a supervisor at an aircraft factory: "Sure, they [employers] have the right to test you. Drugs are not needed in the workplace." He added that users "destroy the work and the work environment. . . . You get somebody on drugs, he'll make errors putting parts together that could cause an airplane to crash." An owner of a chemical company concurred. "If you don't have to hide, you don't have anything to worry about. The employer should have some idea how much liability they [workers] have. In this business, if someone does something stupid, it could kill a couple of hundred people." In this survey, 72 percent of full-time workers said that they would be willing to take a drug test, and 82 percent said that they would take a test if refusal to do so would result in dismissal (Serrin, 1986). There was no indication of how many would support the practice on ideological grounds. Negative views of testing were in the minority in this survey, and objections tended to revolve around issues of civil liberties, the Constitution, and rights of privacy.

In contrast to the military and private industry, testing in the civilian sector of the government has made very few inroads, with only a very few exceptions. In 1986, President Ronald Reagan called for a "drug-free workplace" and urged widespread random testing of federal employees for drug use. Within a few months, in at least thirteen courts cases, the tests were declared unconstitutional. "The courts are turning a hostile face to random testing of government employees," declared Alan F. Westin, a professor of public law at Columbia University. Legal consensus stretched from coast to coast, and from liberal to conservative. The federal cases have had repercussions at the state, county, and municipal levels, whose agencies have pulled back in their prior movement toward testing. A broad-scale, "dragnet" approach, testing without any probable cause or reasonable suspicion, experts agree, represents a violation of the individual's constitutional right to be protected against unreasonable search and seizure. On the other hand, the courts recognize that there is a payoff here. When the Government can demonstrate that a drug problem among employees represents a clear and present danger to the public—in jobs such as air traffic controllers or managers in nuclear power plants, for example—it is likely to be more lenient toward testing. "The more dangerous the situation," said Professor Abraham S. Goldstein of the Yale Law School, "the more testing may be justified" (Kerr, 1986d).

How accurate are the tests? Drug tests vary considerably in cost, quality, and accuracy. The results of a given test can be accurate, they can show a "false positive" (indicating that the person being tested has used drugs when he or she hasn't), or a "false negative" (indicating that the individual has not used drugs when he or she actually has). There are many reasons for such inaccuracies. Drug testing has become a multi-million dollar industry. Laboratories are in business, and like all other businesses, they must keep costs to a minimum to make a profit; if they do not make a profit, they cannot stay in operation. Yet, the more they minimize costs, the more corners they cut, the more inaccurate are the results of their tests. Said Bryan S. Finkle, a toxicologist at the University of Utah, there are "about a dozen competent urine testing laboratories in the country but it is hard for many to exist" because they have had to lower their fees or take short-cuts because of competitive bidding (Altman, 1986). As a general rule, the more expensive the test, the more accurate the results; urine tests cost between $15 and $250 apiece. Therefore, only one round of testing for the entire U.S. work force would cost between $1.6 and $27 billion, something to consider when contemplating such widespread testing (Cohen, 1986).

In a series of checks on the testing of a dozen laboratories conducted in the 1970s, using only 80 percent accuracy as a measure of acceptability—only one lab met the standard for barbiturates, zero for amphetamines, six for methadone, one for cocaine, two for codeine, and one for morphine. Today, it is widely conceded, testing is considerably more accurate, perhaps 90 percent accurate for one of the more widely used tests, but that still leaves enormous room for error. When someone's job is on the line, can we rely on the results of a test whose results may be only 90 percent accurate? Don H. Catlin, chief of clinical pharmacology at the University of California at Los Angeles, says that an effective safeguard against test inaccuracies would be to ask "if the laboratory director is willing to submit an unlabeled sample of his own urine to his own laboratory and then to live or die by the results" (Altman, 1986).

It would be extremely naive to believe that drug addiction will be eliminated completely. Attacking a given problem always involves balancing one value against another. A number of questions must be considered before any single problem can be dealt with. Some questions that interlock with that of effective solutions to the drug problem are: At what cost? By neglecting what other problems and values? And according to what definition of "solution"? If law-enforcement agents were given virtually unlimited powers to deal with the narcotics traffic, if laws such as a bill permitting the police to break down the doors of citizens suspected of drug possession and search their living quarters without so much as a search warrant (the so-called "no-knock" bill), were passed to make their work easier, and if drastic measures—such as the death penalty for all addicts—were effected, the illegal use of heroin could probably be brought to a virtual halt, but only after the desecration of justice and civil liberties on an unheard-of scale in this country. Thus the question is not simply how to deal with the drug problem, but under what conditions we wish to attempt to deal with the problem. As with a serious illness, the most "effective" cure might well destroy the patient.

I've suggested that attempting to curtail the supply of illegal drugs will probably not result in a serious decline in use. But products are distributed not only because they are supplied—they must be demanded as well. Fewer Americans are now using illicit drugs for recreational purposes today than was true during the peak years of the late 1970s. Clearly, law enforcement cannot take the credit for this because the consumption of *legal* drugs— alcohol, cigarettes, and psychoactive pharmaceuticals—has declined as well. If law enforcement brought down the rate of illegal drug consumption, what brought down the level of legal drug use?

American society has changed in a number of ways in the 1980s. There has been a conservative backlash on many fronts. The Equal Rights Amendment (ERA) failed to achieve ratification. The AIDS scare has forced many Americans to reconsider the virtue of casual sex, whether homosexual or heterosexual. Bills advocating equal rights for homosexuals have been defeated by popular vote everywhere they have been proposed. Government regulation of worker and product safety and pollution has been relaxed everywhere. The Supreme Court has trimmed back once-broader interpretations of the civil liberties of citizens, including police suspects. The civil rights movement, in a stagnant period, cannot seem to get back on track again. The mainstream, secularized liberal religious denominations, whose clergy and laity urge ecumenism and interfaith cooperation, have been losing members for years; the fundamentalist sects, which demand a strong, righteous, literalistic belief system and traditional practices, have experienced double-digit yearly increases in membership. Nationalism and patriotism seem to be in a resurgent period. The death penalty, once opposed by the vast majority of Americans, now finds favor with the majority. Every state except Wyoming now has a 21-year-old drinking age. The marijuana decriminalization movement ran out of steam almost precisely with the election of Ronald Reagan as president in 1980. Twice as many high-school students now believe that marijuana is harmful as was true in the late 1970s, and half as many favor the legalization of marijuana. Hedonism is no longer in vogue; many of the old-fashioned virtues have been making a comeback.

What I am suggesting is that trends as massive as the recent shifts in patterns of illicit drug use do not occur as a result of the concerted efforts of a handful of reformers. Neither law enforcement as we know it nor a few ad campaigns run on television, or published in magazines or newspapers, will be likely to have much of an impact. Young people know that taking an illegal drug does not have the same effect on one's brain as frying does on an egg, as one recent ad has suggested; they know that taking cocaine once will not damage them as much as putting a gun up their nose and pulling the trigger. No one is that ignorant or that stupid. These ads will fail to deter use because they do not resonate with people's lives as they are lived. Cultural changes are broad, they are sweeping, and they often take place as a consequence of structural factors beyond the reach of individual decisions. The sweep of history is upon us, and illicit drug use is one of its casualties.

What's in store for us in the 1990s? It is possible that present downward trend in use will continue. As we saw earlier, what may be even more likely is that middle-class recreational drug use will continue to decline, while lower- and working-class drug use will actually rise. Are we entering a period in which the social classes are becoming increasingly polarized in a number of ways? Does this also apply to the races as well? If so, what does this portend for the future?

Whatever occurs, we will continue to live, as a Chinese proverb says, in "interesting times."

References

Abel, Ernest L. 1985. "Effects of Prenatal Exposure to Cannabinoids." In T. M. Pinkert (ed.), *Current Research on Consequences of Maternal Drug Abuse.* Rockville, Md.: National Institute on Drug Abuse, pp. 20–35.

Abel, Ernest L., and Phillip Zeidenberg. 1985. "Age, Alcohol and Violent Death: A Post Mortem Study." *Journal of Studies on Alcohol,* 46 (3): 228–231.

Abelson, Herbert I., and Ronald Atkinson. 1975. *Public Experience with Psychoactive Substances.* Princeton, N.J.: Response Analysis Corporation.

Abelson, Herbert I., et al. 1973. "Drug Experience, Attitudes, and Related Behavior Among Adolescents and Adults." In National Commission on Marihuana and Drug Abuse, *Drug Use in America: Problem in Perspective,* Vol. 1. Washington, D.C.: U.S. Government Printing Office, pp. 488–861.

Adler, Jerry, et al. 1985. "Getting High on 'Ecstasy.' " *Newsweek,* April 15, p. 96.

Adler, Patricia A. 1985. *Wheeling and Dealing: An Ethnography of an Upper-Level Drug Dealing and Smuggling Community.* New York: Columbia University Press.

Akers, Ronald L., Marvin D. Kron, Lonn Lanza-Kaduce, and Marcia Radosevich. 1979. "Social Learning and Deviant Behavior: A Specific Test of a General Theory." *American Sociological Review,* 44 (August): 636–655.

Allen, David (ed.). 1987. *The Cocaine Crisis.* New York: Plenum Press.

Altman, Lawrence. 1986. "Drug Tests Gain Precision, but Can Be Inaccurate." *The New York Times,* September 16, p A17.

Andrews, George, and David Solomon (eds.). 1975. *The Coca Leaf and Cocaine Papers.* New York: Harcourt Brace Jovanovich.

Anonymous. 1985. "P.&G. Drops Logo From Its Packages." *The New York Times,* April 25, pp. D1, D8.

Anonymous. 1987. "Graduates Face Drug Tests in Joining Job Market." *The New York Times,* June 21, p 29.

Anslinger, Harry J., and Courtney Ryley Cooper. 1937. "Marihuana: Assassin of Youth." *American Magazine,* July, pp. 18–19, 150–153.

Antonil. 1978. *Mama Coca.* London: Hassle Free Press.

Armor, David J., J. Michael Polich, and Harriet B. Stambul. 1976. *Alcoholism and Treatment.* Santa Monica, Calif.: Rand Corporation.

Ashley, Richard. 1975. *Cocaine: Its History, Uses and Effects.* New York: St. Martin's Press.

Ausubel, David P. 1980. "An Interactionist Approach to Narcotic Addiction." In Dan J. Lettieri et al. (eds.), *Theories on Drug Abuse.* Rockville, Md.: National Institute on Drug Abuse, pp. 4–7.

Bachman, Jerald G., Lloyd D. Johnston, and Patrick M. O'Malley. 1981. "Smoking, Drinking, and Drug Use Among High School Students." *American Journal of Public Health,* 71 (January): 59–69.

Bachman, Jerald G., Patrick O'Malley, and Lloyd D. Johnston. 1984. "Drug Use Among Young Adults: The Impacts of Role Status and Social Environment." *Journal of Personality and Social Psychology,* 47 (3): 629–645.

Ball, John C., John W. Shaffer, and David N. Nurco. 1983. "The Day-to-Day Criminality of Heroin Addicts in Baltimore—A Study in the Continuity of Offense Rates." *Drug and Alcohol Dependence,* 12: 119–142.

Ball, John C., and John C. Urbaitis. 1970. "Absence of Major Medical Complications Among Chronic Opiate Addicts." In John C. Ball and Carl D. Chambers (eds.), *Epidemiology of Opiate Addiction in the United States.* Springfield, Ill.: Charles C Thomas, pp. 301–306.

Barber, Bernard. 1967. *Drugs and Society.* New York: Russell Sage Foundation.

Barnett, Gene, Vojtech Licko, and Travis Thompson. 1985. "Behavioral Pharmacokinetics of Marijuana." *Psychopharmacology,* 85 (1): 51–56.

Baum, Carlene, Dianne L. Kennedy, Deanne E. Knapp, and Gerald A. Faich. 1986. *Drug Utilization in the U.S.—1985, Seventh Annual Review.* Springfield, Va.: U.S. Department of Commerce, National Technical Service.

Beck, Melinda, with Gerald Lubenow and Martin Kasindorf. 1981. "Nancy: Searching for a Role." *Newsweek.* February 2, p. 54.

Becker, Howard S. 1953. "Becoming a Marijuana User." *American Journal of Sociology,* 59 (November): 235–242.

Becker, Howard S. 1955. "Marijuana Use and Social Control." *Social Problems,* 3 (July): 35–44.

Becker, Howard S. 1963. *Outsiders: Studies in the Sociology of Deivance.* New York: Free Press.

Becker, Howard S. 1967. "History, Culture and Subjective Experiences: An Exploration of the Social Bases of Drug-Induced Experiences." *Journal of Health and Social Behavior,* 8 (September): 163–176.

Becker, Howard S. 1972. "Consciousness, Power and Drug Effects." *Journal of Psychedelic Drugs,* 6 (1): 67–76.

Bejerot, Nils. 1972. *Addiction: An Artificially Induced Drive.* Springfield, Ill.: Charles C Thomas.

Bejerot, Nils. 1980. "Addiction to Pleasure: A Biological and Social-Psychological Theory of Addiction." In Dan J. Lettieri et al. (eds.), *Theories on Drug Abuse.* Rockville, Md.: National Institute on Drug Abuse, pp. 246–255.

Ben-Yehuda, Nachman. 1986. "The Sociology of Moral Panics: Toward a New Synthesis." *The Sociological Quarterly,* 27 (4): 495–513.

Bergman, Robert L. 1971. "Navajo Peyote Use: Its Apparent Safety." *American Journal of Psychiatry,* 128 (December): 695–699.

Berridge, Virginia, and Griffith Edwards. 1987. *Opium and the People: Opiate Use in Ninetheenth-Century England.* New Haven, Conn.: Yale University Press.

Blakeslee, Sandra, 1985. "California Addicts Use Legal, Synthetic Narcotics." *The New York Times,* March 24, p. 22.

Blane, Howard T., and Kenneth E. Leonard (eds.). 1987. *Psychological Theories of Drinking and Alcoholism.* New York: Guilford Press.

Blum, Richard, et al. 1969. *Society and Drugs.* San Francisco: Jossey-Bass.

Blumer, Herbert. 1971. "Social Problems as Collective Behavior." *Social Problems,* 18 (Winter): 298–306.

Boffey, Philip M. 1981. "Worldwide Use of Valium Draws New Scrutiny." *The New York Times,* October 13, pp. C1, C2.

Boffey, Philip M. 1982a. "Showdown Nears in Feud over Alcohol Studies." *The New York Times,* November 2, pp. C1, C2.

Boffey, Philip M. 1982b. "Panel Clears 2 Accused of Scientific Fraud in Alcoholism Study." *The New York Times,* November 5, p. A12.

Boffey, Philip M. 1983. "Controlled Drinking Gains as a Treatment in Europe." *The New York Times,* November 22, pp. C1, C7.

Boffey, Philip M. 1984. "Panel Finds No Fraud by Alcohol Researchers." *The New York Times,* September 11, p. C8.

Bogdanovich, Peter. 1985. *The Killing of the Unicorn: Dorothy Stratten 1960–1980.* New York: Bantam Books.

Bonner, Arthur. 1986. "For Rebels' Victory Garden: Opium." *The New York Times,* June 18, pp. A1, A8.

Bonnie, Richard J., and Charles H. Whitebread II. 1970. "The Forbidden Fruit and the Tree of Knowledge: An Inquiry Into the Legal History of American Marihuana Prohibition." *Virginia Law Review,* 56 (October): 971–1203.

Bonnie, Richard J., and Charles H. Whitebread II. 1974. *The Marihuana Conviction: A History of Marihuana Prohibition in the United States.* Charlottesville: University of Virginia Press.

Bourne, Peter G. 1975. *Methadone: Benefits and Shortcomings.* Washington, D.C.: Drug Abuse Council.

Bozarth, Michael A., and Roy A. Wise. 1985. "Toxicity Associated with Long-Term Intravenous Heroin and Cocaine Self-Administration in the Rat." *Journal of the American Medical Association,* 254 (July 5): 81–83.

Brecher, Edward M. 1986. "Drug Laws and Drug Law Enforcement: A Review and Evaluation Based on 111 Years of Experience." *Drugs and Society: A Journal of Contemporary Issues,* 1 (1): 1–27.

Brecher, Edward M., et al. 1972. *Licit and Illicit Drugs.* Boston: Little, Brown.

Brinkley, Joel. 1984a. "The War on Narcotics: Can It Be Won?" *The New York Times,* September 14, PP. A1, A12.

Brinkley, Joel 1984b. "Is Drug War Merely a Holding Action?" *The New York Times,* November 25, p. 4E.

Brinkley, Joel. 1986. "U.S. Blames New Form of Heroin for Outbreak of Overdose Deaths." *The New York Times,* March 28, pp. A1, B6.

Brodie, H. Keith. 1973. "The Effects of Ethyl Alcohol in Man." In National Commission on Marihuana and Drug Abuse, *Drug Use in America: Problem in Perspective,* Vol. 1. Washington, D.C.: U.S. Government Printing Office, pp. 6–59.

Brody, Jane E. 1981. "Though the Hazards Are Clear, 55 Million Continue to Smoke." *The New York Times,* July 8, pp. C18, C19.

Brody, Jane E. 1983. "New Therapies for the Addict Go Far Beyond Mere Abstinence." *The New York Times,* February 1, pp. C1, C4.

Bronstein, Scott. 1987. "Study Shows Sharp Rise in Cocaine Use by Suspects in Crimes." *The New York Times,* February 19, pp. B1, B4.

Brooke, James. 1986. "Drunken Driving Fatalities Declining." *The New York Times,* August 27, p. B4.

Burgess, Louise Bailey. 1973. *Alcohol and Your Health.* Los Angeles: Charles Publishing.

Burstein, Judd. 1982. "Decriminalizing Heroin." *The New York Times,* October 6, p. A27.

Byck, Robert (ed.). 1974. *Cocaine Papers by Sigmund Freud.* New York: Stonehill.

Byrd, Oliver E. (ed.). 1970. *Medical Readings on Drug Abuse.* Reading, Mass.: Addison-Wesley.

Cahalan, Don. 1970. *Problem Drinkers.* San Francisco: Jossey-Bass.

Cahalan, Don, and Robin Room. 1974. *Problem Drinking Among American Men.* New Brunswick, N.J.: Rutgers Center for Alcohol Studies.

Callaway, Enoch, III. 1958. "Institutional Use of Ataractic Drugs." *Modern Medicine,* *1958 Annual,* Part I (January 1–June 15): 26–29.

Campbell, A. M. G., et al. 1971. "Cerebral Atrophy in Young Cannabis Smokers." *The Lancet,* pp. 1219–1224.

Canadian Commission into the Non-Medical Use of Drugs. 1972. *Cannabis.* Ottawa: Information Canada.

Carlson, Katherine A. 1979. "PCP From the Other Side: Users Look at Phencyclidine." *Journal of Psychedelic Drugs,* 11 (July–September): 231–238.

Chatlos, Calvin. 1987. *Crack: What You Should Know About the Cocaine Epidemic.* New York: Perigree Books.

Cherubin, Charles. 1968. "Review of the Medical Complications of Narcotic Addiction." *International Journal of the Addictions,* 3 (Spring): 163–175.

Cisin, Ira H., Judith Droitcour Miller, and P. W. Wirtz. 1976. *Discontinuing Drug Use.* Washington, D.C.: George Washington University Social Research Group.

Claridge, Gordon. 1970. *Drugs and Human Behavior.* New York: Praeger.

Clayton, Richard R., and Harwin L. Voss. 1981. *Young Men and Drugs in Manhattan: A Causal Analysis.* Rockville, Md.: National Institute on Drug Abuse.

Clayton, Richard R., Harwin L. Voss, Cynthia Robbins, and William F. Skinner. 1986. "Gender Differences in Drug Use: An Epidemiological Perspective." In Barbara A. Ray and Monique C. Braude (eds.), *Women and Drugs: A New Era for Research.* Rockville, Md.: National Institute on Drug Abuse, pp. 80–99.

Cloward, Richard A., and Lloyd E. Ohlin. 1960. *Delinquency and Opportunity.* New York: Free Press.

Clymer, Adam. 1986. "Public Found Ready to Sacrifice in Drug Fight." *The New York Times,* September 2, pp. A1, D16.

Co, Ben T., et al. 1977. "Absence of Cerebral Atrophy in Chronic Cannabis Users." *Journal of the American Medical Association,* 237 (March 21): 1229–1230.

Cohen, Maimon M., Michelle J. Marinello, and Nathan Back. 1967. "Chromosomal Damage in Human Leukocytes Induced by Lysergic Acid Diethylamide." *Science,* 155 (17 March): 1417–1419.

Cohen, Sidney. 1985. "Reinforcement and Rapid Delivery Systems: Understanding Adverse Consequences of Cocaine." In Nicholas J. Kozel and Edgar H. Adams eds.), *Cocaine Use in America: Epidemiological and Clinical Perspectives.* Rockville, Md.: National Institute on Drug Abuse, pp. 151–157.

Cohen, Sidney. 1987. "Marijuana and the Cannabinoids." In *Drug Abuse and Drug Abuse Research,* The Second Triennial Report to Congress from the Secretary, Department of Health and Human Services. Rockville, Md.: National Institute on Drug Abuse, pp. 77–91.

Cohen, Stanley. 1980. *Folk Devils and Moral Panics.* New York: St. Martin's Press.

Cohen, Toby. 1986. "Drug-Use Testing: Costly and Corruptible." *The New York Times,* August 20, p. A23.

Combes-Orme, Terri, John R. Taylor, Ellen Bates Scott, and Sandra Holmes. 1983. "Violent Death Among Alcoholics: A Descriptive Study." *Journal of Studies on Alcohol,* 44 (6): 938–949.

Cook, Shirley J. 1970, "Social Background of Narcotics Legislation." *Addictions,* 17 (Summer): 14–29.

Crancer, Alfred, Jr., et al. 1969. "Comparison of the Effects of Marihuana and Alcohol on Simulated Driving Performance." *Science,* 164 (16 May): 851–854.

Crider, Raquel. 1986. "Phencyclidine: Changing Abuse Patterns." In Doris H.

Clouet (ed.), *Phencyclidine: An Update.* Rockville, Md.: National Institute on Drug Abuse, pp. 163–173.

Cuskey, Walter R., Lisa H. Berger, and Arthur H. Richardson. 1978. "The Effects of Marijuana Decriminalization on Drug Use Patterns." *Contemporary Drug Problems,* 7 (Winter): 491–532.

Davis, F. James. 1952. "Crime News in Colorado Newspapers." *American Journal of Sociology,* 57: 325–330.

Davison, Bill. 1967. "The Hidden Evils of LSD." *The Saturday Evening Post,* August 12, pp. 19–23.

Davison, Gerald C., and John M. Neale. 1986. *Abnormal Behavior: An Experimental Clinical Approach* (4th ed.). New York: Wiley.

DAWN, *see* Drug Awareness Warning Network.

DeLindt, Jan, and Wolfgang Schmidt. 1971. "Alcohol Use and Alcoholism." *Addictions,* 18 (Summer): 1–14.

Dishotsky, Norman I., William D. Loughman, Robert E. Mogar, and Wendell R. Lipscomb. 1971. "LSD and Genetic Damage." *Science,* 172 (30 April): 431–440.

Dole, Vincent P. 1980. "Addictive Behavior." *Scientific American,* 243 (December): 138–154.

Dole, Vincent P., and Marie E. Nyswander. 1965. "A Medical Treatment for Diacetyl-morphine (Heroin) Addiction." *Journal of the American Medical Association,* 193 (August 23): 646–650.

Dole, Vincent P., and Marie E. Nyswander. 1980. "Methadone Maintenance: A Theoretical Perspective." In Dan J. Lettieri et al. (eds.), *Theories on Drug Abuse.* Rockville, Md.: National Institute on Drug Abuse, pp. 256–261.

Dole, Vincent P., Marie E. Nyswander, and Alan Warner. 1968. "Successful Treatment of 750 Criminal Addicts." *Journal of the American Medical Association,* 206 (December 16): 646–650.

Donovan, John E., and Richard Jessor. 1985. "Structure of Problem Behavior in Adolescence and Young Adulthood." *Journal of Consulting and Clinical Psychology,* 53 (6): 890–904.

Drug Abuse Warning Network (DAWN). 1983. *Annual Data, 1982: Data from the Drug Abuse Warning Network.* Rockville, Md.: National Institute on Drug Abuse.

Drug Abuse Warning Network (DAWN). 1986. *Annual Data, 1985: Data from the Drug Abuse Warning Network.* Rockville, Md.: National Institute on Drug Abuse.

Drug Abuse Warning Network (DAWN). 1987. *Annual Data, 1986: Data from the Drug Abuse Warning Network.* Rockville, Md.: National Institute on Drug Abuse.

Dunlap, David. 1982. "Death by Cigarette Fire: A Solution Stirs Debate." *The New York Times,* April 19, p. B2.

DuPont, Robert L. 1984. "Two Prongs in a Winnable Assault on Drugs." *The New York Times,* September 26, p. A22.

Duster, Troy. 1970. *The Legislation of Morality: Law, Drug, and Moral Judgment.* New York: Free Press.

Eastland, James O. (Chairman). 1974. *Marihuana-Hashish Epidemic and Its Impact on United States Security.* Washington, D.C.: U.S. Government Printing Office.

Eckholm, Erik. 1986a. "Cocaine's Vicious Spiral: Highs, Lows, Desperation." *The New York Times,* August 17, p. 2E.

Eckholm, Eric. 1986b. "Radon: Threat Is Real, but Scientists Argue Over Its Severity." *The New York Times,* September 2, pp. C1, C7.

Eddy, Nathan B., H. Halbach, Harris Isbell, and Maurice H. Seevers. 1965. "Drug Dependence: Its Significance and Characteristics." *Bulletin of the World Health Organization,* 32: 721–733.

Efron, Daniel (ed.). 1967. *Ethnopharmacologic Search for Psychoactive Drugs*. Washington, D.C.: U.S. Government Printing Office.

Erickson, Patricia G. 1976. "Deterrence and Deviance: The Example of Cannabis Prohibition." *The Journal of Criminal Law and Criminology*, 67 (2): 222–232.

Erickson, Patricia G., Edward M. Adlaf, Glenn F. Murray, and Reginald G. Smart. 1987. *The Steel Drug: Cocaine in Perspective*. Lexington, Mass.: Lexington Books.

Federal Bureau of Investigation (FBI), Department of Justice. 1987. *Crime in the United States: Uniform Crime Reports*. Washington, D.C.: U.S. Government Printing Office.

Fiddle, Seymour. 1967. *Portraits from a Shooting Gallery*. New York: Harper & Row.

Fishburne, Patricia M., Herbert I. Abelson, and Ira Cisin. 1980. *National Survey on Drug Abuse: Main Findings: 1979*. Rockville, Md.: National Institute on Drug Abuse.

Fisher, Seymour, Allen Raskin, and E. H. Uhlenhuth (eds.). 1987. *Cocaine: Clinical and Biobehavioral Aspects*. New York: Oxford University Press.

Fishman, Mark. 1978. "Crime Waves as Ideology." *Social Problems*, 25 (June): 531–543.

Fort, Joel. 1969. *The Pleasure Seekers*. Indianapolis, Ind.: Bobbs-Merrill.

Franks, Lucinda. 1985. "A New Attack on Alcoholism." *The New York Times Magazine*, October 20, pp. 46–50, 61–65, 69.

Freedman, Samuel G. 1987. "AIDS Battlefield: Addicts' World." *The New York Times*, April 8, pp. B1, B7.

Freidson, Eliot. 1968. "Ending Campus Drug Incidents." *Trans-action*, 5 (July-August): 75, 81.

Fried, P. A. 1985. "Postnatal Consequences of Maternal Marijuana Use." In T. M. Pinkert (ed.), *Current Research on Consequences of Maternal Drug Abuse*. Rockville, Md.: National Institute on Drug Abuse, pp. 61–72.

Fuerbringer, Jonathan. 1986. "Wide Bill on Drugs Pressed in House." *The New York Times*, September 11, p. A24.

Fuller, Richard C., and Richard R. Myers. 1941. "The Natural History of a Social Problem." *American Sociological Review*, 6 (June): 320–329.

Furst, Peter T. 1976. *Hallucinations and Culture*. Novato, Calif.: Chandler & Sharp.

Gagnon, John H., and William Simon. 1973. *Sexual Conduct: The Social Sources of Human Sexuality*. Chicago: Aldine.

Gallagher, Winifred. 1986a. "The Looming Menace of Designer Drugs." *Discover*, August, pp. 24–35.

Gallagher, Winifred. 1986b. "MDMA: Is There Ever a Justifiable Reason for Getting High?" *Discover*, August, p. 34.

Galliher, John F., and Linda Basilick. 1979. "Utah's Liberal Drug Laws: Structural Foundation and Triggering Events." *Social Problems*, 26 (February): 284–297.

Galliher, John F., and John Ray Cross. 1982. "Symbolic Severity in the Land of Easy Virtue: Nevada's High Marihuana Penalty." *Social Problems*, 29 (April): 380–386.

Galliher, John F., and John Ray Cross. 1983. *Moral Legislation Without Morality: The Case of Nevada*. New Brunswick, N.J.: Rutgers University Press.

Galliher, John F., James L. McCartney, and Barbara E. Baum. 1974. "Nebraska's Marijuana Law: A Case of Unexpected Legislative Innovation." *Law and Society Review*, 8 (Spring): 441–455.

Gallup, Alec M. 1986. "The 18th Annual Gallup Poll of the Public's Attitudes Toward the Public Schools." *Phi Delta Kappan*, 68 (September): 43–59

Gallup, George, Jr. 1980. *The Gallup Poll: Public Opinion 1979*. Wilmington, Del.: Scholarly Resources.

Gallup, George, Jr. 1986. *The Gallup Poll: Public Opinion 1985.* Wilmington, Del.: Scholarly Resources.

Gallup, George, Jr. 1987. *The Gallup Poll: Public Opinion 1986.* Wilmington, Del.: Scholarly Resources.

Gay, George R. 1981. "A Lady for the '80s: Coke Time in the E.R.—Complexities of Action and Rationale for Treatment of Acute and Chronic Cocaine Toxicity." San Francisco: Haight-Asbury Free Medical Clinic, unpublished paper.

Gebhard, Paul H., John H. Gagnon, Wardell Pomeroy, and Cornelia V. Christenson. 1967. *Sex Offenders: An Analysis of Types.* New York: Bantam.

Glaser, Frederick B., and John C. Ball. 1970. "Death Due to Withdrawal from Narcotics." In John C. Ball and Carl D. Chambers (eds.), *The Epidemiology of Opiate Addiction in the United States.* Springfield, Ill.: Charles C Thomas, pp. 263–287.

Gold, Mark S. 1984. *800-COCAINE.* New York: Bantam.

Goldman, D. 1955. "Treatment of Psychotic States with Chlorpromazine." *Journal of the American Medical Association,* 157: 1274–1278.

Goldschmidt, Walter. 1968. "Foreword." In Carlos Castaneda, *The Teachings of Don Juan: A Yaqui Way of Knowledge.* Berkeley: University of California Press, pp. vii–viii.

Gonzales, Laurence. 1982. "The War on Drugs: A Special Report." *Playboy,* April, pp. 134–137, 158, 200–216.

Gonzales, Laurence. 1984. "Cocaine: A Special Report." *Playboy,* September, pp. 113–114, 148, 194ff.

Gonzales, Laurence. 1985. "Why Drug Enforcement Doesn't Work." *Playboy,* December, pp. 104–105, 238–249.

Goode, Erich. 1969. "Multiple Drug Use Among Marijuana Smokers." *Social Problems,* 17 (Summer): 48–64.

Goode, Erich. 1970. *The Marijuana Smokers.* New York: Basic Books.

Goode, Erich. 1972a. *Drugs in American Society.* New York: Knopf.

Goode, Erich. 1972b. "Drug Use and Sexual Activity on a College Campus." *American Journal of Psychiatry,* 128 (April): 1272–1276.

Goode, Erich. 1972c. "Trends in College Drug Use: Report from One Campus." In Stanley Einstein and Stephen Allen (eds.), *Student Drug Surveys.* Farmingdale, N.Y.: Baywood, pp. 123–127.

Goode, Erich. 1973a. *The Drug Phenomenon: Social Aspects of Drug Taking.* Indianapolis, Ind.: Bobbs-Merrill.

Goode, Erich. 1973b. "Foreword." In Bruce D. Johnson, *Marihuana Users and Drug Subcultures.* New York: Wiley, pp. xi–xiii.

Goode, Erich. 1973c. "Fighting Heroin with Heroin." *Newsday,* March 4, Ideas Section, pp. 1, 10.

Goode, Erich, 1974. "Marijuana Use and the Progression to Dangerous Drugs." In Loren L. Miller (ed.), *Marijuana: Effects on Human Behavior.* New York: Academic Press, pp. 303–338.

Goode, Erich. 1984. *Drugs in American Society* (2nd ed.). New York: Knopf.

Goodman, Richard A., et al. 1986. "Alcohol Use and Interpersonal Violence: Alcohol Detected in Homicide Victims." *American Journal of Public Health,* 76 (February): 144–149.

Grant, Bridget F., John Noble, and Henry Malin. 1986. "Decline in Liver Cirrhosis Mortality and Components of Change." *Alcohol Health and Research World,* 10 (Spring): 66–69.

Greeley, Andrew M., William C. McCready, and Gary Theison. 1980. *Ethnic Drinking Subcultures.* New York: Praeger.

Grinspoon, Lester. 1971, 1977. *Marihuana Reconsidered* (1st ed., 1971; rev. ed., 1977). Cambridge, Mass.: Harvard University Press.

Grinspoon, Lester, and James B. Bakalar. 1976. *Cocaine: A Drug and Social Evolution.* New York: Basic Books.

Grinspoon, Lester, and James B. Bakalar. 1979. *Psychedelic Drugs Reconsidered.* New York: Basic Books.

Grinspoon, Lester, and James B. Bakalar (eds.). 1983. *Psychedelic Reflections.* New York: Human Sciences Press.

Grinspoon, Lester, and Peter Hedblom. 1975. *The Speed Culture: Amphetamine Use and Abuse in America.* Cambridge, Mass.: Harvard University Press.

Gusfield, Joseph R. 1963. *Symbolic Crusade: Status Politics and the American Temperance Movement.* Urbana: University of Illinois Press.

Gusfield, Joseph R. 1967. "Moral Passage: The Public Process in Public Designations of Deviance." *Social Problems,* 15 (Fall): 175–188.

Guttman, Erich. 1936. "Artificial Psychosis Produced by Mescaline." *The Journal of Mental Science,* 82: 203–221.

Haberman, Paul W., and Michael M. Baden. 1974. "Alcoholism and Violent Death." *Quarterly Journal of Studies on Alcohol,* 35, Part A (March): 221–231.

Halikas, James A., Donald W. Goodwin, and Samuel B. Guze. 1971. "Marihuana Effects: A Survey of Regular Users." *Journal of the American Medical Association,* 217 (August 2): 692–694.

Halloran, Richard. 1987a. "Drug Use in Military Drops; Pervasive Testing Credited." *The New York Times,* April 23, p. A16.

Halloran, Richard. 1987b. "New Law Requires the Pentagon to Test Recruits for Drug Abuse." *The New York Times,* December 24, pp. A1, B6.

Harclerode, Jack. 1984. "Endocrine Effects of Marijuana in the Male: Preclinical Studies." In Monique C. Braude and Jacqueline P. Ludford (eds.), *Marijuana Effects on the Endocrine and Reproductive Systems.* Rockville, Md.: National Institute on Drug Abuse, pp. 46–64.

Harner, Michael J. (ed.). 1973. *Hallucinogens and Shamanism.* New York: Oxford University Press.

Health, Education, and Welfare, Department of. 1971. *First Special Report to the U.S. Congress on Alcohol and Health from the Secretary of Health, Education, and Welfare.* Washington, D.C.: Department of Health, Education, and Welfare/U.S. Government Printing Office.

Health and Human Services, Department of. 1987a. *Sixth Special Report to the U.S. Congress on Alcohol and Health from the Secretary of Health and Human Services.* Rockville, Md.: National Institute on Alcohol Abuse and Alcoholism.

Health and Human Services, Department of. 1987b. *Smoking, Tobacco, and Health: A Fact Book.* Washington, D.C.: U.S. Department of Health and Human Services.

Heather, Nick, and Ian Robertson. 1981. *Controlled Drinking.* London: Methuen.

Helpern, Milton, and Young-Myun Rho. 1967. "Deaths from Narcotism in New York City." *International Journal of the Addictions,* 2 (Spring): 53–84.

Hevesi, Dennis. 1986. "Worried Parents Hope Children Are Free of Drugs." *The New York Times,* September 2, p. D16.

Hill, Norman (ed.). 1971. *Marijuana: Teenage Killer.* New York: Popular Library.

Hills, Stuart L. 1980. *Demystifying Social Deviance.* New York: McGraw-Hill.

Himmelstein, Jerome L. 1979. "The Fetishism of Drugs." *The International Journal of the Addictions,* 14 (8): 1083–1101.

Himmelstein, Jerome L. 1983. "From Killer Weed to Drop-Out Drug: The Changing Ideology of Marihuana." *Contemporary Crisis,* 7: 13–38.

Hirschi, Travis. 1969. *Causes of Delinquency.* Berkeley: University of California Press.

Hochman, Joel Simon. 1972. *Marijuana and Social Evolution.* Englewood Cliffs, N.J.: Prentice-Hall/Spectrum.

Hochman, Joel Simon, and Norman Q. Brill. 1971. "Chronic Marihuana Usage and Liver Function." *The Lancet,* October 9, pp. 918–919.

Hochman, Joel Simon, and Norman Q. Brill. 1972. "Marijuana Usage and Psychosocial Adaptation." Unpublished manuscript.

Hochman, Joel Simon, and Norman Q. Brill. 1973. "Marijuana Use and Psychosocial Adaptation." *American Journal of Psychiatry,* 130 (February): 132–140.

Home Office. 1968. *Cannabis: Report by the Advisory Committee on Drug Dependence.* London: Her Majesty's Stationery Office.

Hughes, Helen MacGill (ed.) 1961. *The Fantastic Lodge: The Autobiography of a Girl Addict.* Boston: Houghton Mifflin.

Hughes, Richard, and Robert Brewin. 1979. *The Tranquilizing of America: Pill Popping and the American Way of Life.* New York: Harcourt Brace Jovanovich.

Huxley, Aldous. 1963. *The Doors of Perception and Heaven and Hell.* New York: Harper & Row.

Illich, Ivan. 1976. *Medical Nemesis.* New York: Bantam.

Inaba, Darryl S., et al. 1973. "Methaqualone Abuse." *Journal of the American Medical Association,* 224 (June 11):1505–1509.

Inciardi, James A. 1979. "Heroin Use and Street Crime." *Crime and Delinquency,* 25 (July): 335–346.

Inciardi, James A. 1986. *The War on Drugs: Heroin, Cocaine, Crime, and Public Policy.* Palo Alto, Calif.: Mayfield.

Inciardi, James A. 1987. "Sociology and American Drug Policy." *The American Sociologist,* 18 (Summer): 179–188.

Inciardi, James A. 1988a. "Beyond Cocaine: Basuco, Crack, and Other Coca Products." *Contemporary Drug Problems,* 17 (in press).

Inciardi, James A. 1988b. "Narcotics Use in the Georgian SSR." *Journal of Psychoactive Drugs,* 21 (in press).

Institute of Medicine, National Academy of Sciences. 1982. *Marihuana and Health.* Washington, D.C.: National Academy Press.

Irwin, Samuel. 1970. "Potential Dangers of the Hallucinogens." In J. R. Gamage and E. L. Zerkin (eds.), *Hallucinogenic Drug Research.* Beloit, Wisc.: STASH Press, pp. 24–33.

Isbell, Harris. 1966. "Medical Aspects of Opiate Addiction." In John A. O'Donnell and John C. Ball (eds.), *Narcotic Addiction.* New York: Harper & Row, pp. 62–75.

Iyer, Pick, et al. 1986. "Fighting the Cocaine Wars." *Time,* February 25, pp. 26–35.

Jaffe, Jerome H., Misha S. Zaks, and Edward N. Washington. 1969. "Experience with the Use of Methadone in a Multimodality Program for the Treatment of Narcotics Users." *International Journal of the Addictions,* 4 (September): 481–490.

Jensen, Eric L., Jurg Gerber, and Ginna M. Babcock. 1987. "Drugs as Politics: The Construction of a Social Problem." Unpublished paper presented at the annual meetings of the Society for the Study of Social Problems, Chicago, August.

Jessor, Richard. 1979. "Marihuana: A Review of Recent Psychological Research." In Robert I. Dupont et al. (eds.), *Handbook on Drug Abuse.* Washington, D.C.: U.S. Government Printing Office, pp. 337–355.

Jessor, Richard. 1983. "A Psychosocial Perspective on Adolescent Substance Abuse." In I. F. Litt (ed.), *Adolescent Substance Abuse.* Columbus, Ohio: Ross Laboratories, pp. 21–28.

Jessor, Richard. 1987. "Problem-Behavior Theory, Psychosocial Development, and Adolescent Problem Drinking." *British Journal of Addiction,* 82: 331–342.

Jessor, Richard, James A. Chase, and John E. Donovan. 1980. "Psychosocial Correlates of Marijuana Use and Problem Drinking in a National Sample of Adolescents." *American Journal of Public Health,* 70 (June): 604–613.

Jessor, Richard, Frances Costa, Lee Jessor, and John E. Donovan. 1983. "Time of First Intercourse: A Prospective Study." *Journal of Personality and Social Psychology,* 44 (3): 608–626.

Jessor, Richard, John E. Donovan, and Frances Costa. 1986. "Psychosocial Correlates of Marijuana Use in Adolescence and Young Adulthood: The Past as Prologue." *Alcohol, Drugs, and Driving,* 2 (3–4): 31–49.

Jessor, Richard, and Shirley L. Jessor. 1977. *Problem Behavior and Psychosocial Development: A Longitudinal Study of Youth.* New York: Academic Press.

Jessor, Richard, and Shirley L. Jessor. 1980. "A Social-Psychological Framework for Studying Drug Use." In Dan J. Lettieri et al. (eds.), *Theories on Drug Abuse.* Rockville, Md.: National Institute on Drug Abuse, pp. 102–109.

Jessor, Richard, Shirley L. Jessor, and John Finney. 1973. "A Social Psychology of Marijuana Use: Longitudinal Studies of High School and College Youth." *Journal of Personality and Social Psychology,* 26 (1): 1–15.

Johanson, Chris E. 1984. "Assessment of the Abuse Potential of Cocaine in Animals." In John Grabowski (ed.), *Cocaine: Pharmacology, Effects, and Treatment of Abuse.* Rockville, Md.: National Institute on Drug Abuse, pp. 54–71.

Johnson, Bruce D. 1973. *Marihuana Users and Drug Subcultures.* New York: Wiley.

Johnson, Bruce D. 1978. "Once an Addict, Seldom an Addict." *Contemporary Drug Problems,* 7 (Spring): 35–53.

Johnson, Bruce D. 1980. "Toward a Theory of Drug Subcultures." In Dan J. Lettieri et al. (eds.), *Theories on Drug Abuse.* Rockville, Md.: National Institute on Drug Abuse, pp. 110–119.

Johnson, Bruce D. 1984. "Empirical Patterns of Heroin Consumption Among Selected Street Heroin Users." In G. Serban (ed.), *The Social and Medical Aspects of Drug Abuse.* New York: Spectrum Publications, pp. 101–122.

Johnson, Bruce D., Paul J. Goldstein, Edward Preble, James Schmeidler, Douglas S. Lipton, Barry Spunt, and Thomas Miller. 1985. *Taking Care of Business: The Economics of Crime by Heroin Abusers.* Lexington, Mass.: Lexington Books.

Johnson, Diane. 1986. "Turning In Parents: A Case of Situational Ethics." *Newsday,* September 28, Ideas Section, p. 7.

Johnston, Lloyd D. 1973. *Drugs and American Youth.* Ann Arbor, Mich.: Institute for Survey Research.

Johnston, Lloyd D. 1980. "Marijuana Use and the Effects of Marijuana Decriminalization." Unpublished testimony delivered at the hearings on the effects of marijuana held by the Subcommittee on Criminal Justice, Judiciary Committee, U.S. Senate, Washington, D.C., January 6.

Johnston, Lloyd D., Patrick M. O'Malley, and Jerald G. Bachman. 1986. *Drug Use Among American High School Students, College Students, and Other Young Adults: National Trends Through 1985.* Rockville, Md.: National Institute on Drug Abuse.

Johnston, Lloyd D., Patrick M. O'Malley, and Jerald G. Bachman. 1987. *National Trends in Drug Use and Related Factors Among American High School Students and Young Adults, 1975–1986.* Rockville, Md.: National Institute on Drug Abuse.

Jones, Hardin. 1974. "Testimony of Hardin B. Jones." In *Marihuana-Hashish Epidemic and Its Impact on United States Security.* Washington, D.C.: U.S. Government Printing Office, pp. 206–250, 265ff.

Jones, Hardin, and Helen Jones. 1977. *Sensual Drugs.* Cambridge, England: Cambridge University Press.

Jones, Helen C., and Paul W. Lovinger. 1985. *The Marijuana Question and Science's Search for an Answer.* New York: Dodd, Mead.

Jones, Kenneth, Louis W. Shainberg, and Curtis O. Byer. 1969, 1973, 1979. *Drugs and Alcohol* (1st ed., 1969; 2nd ed., 1973; 3rd ed., 1979).

Julien, Robert M. 1985. *A Primer of Drug Action* (4th ed.). New York: W. H. Freeman.

Kaelber, Charles, and George Mills. 1981. "Alcohol Consumption and Cardiovascular Diseases: Introductory Remarks." *Circulation,* 64, Supplement 3 (September): 1–6.

Kandel, Denise B. 1973. "Adolescent Marijuana Use: Role of Parents and Peers." *Science,* 181 (September 14): 1067–1070.

Kandel, Denise B. 1974. "Inter- and Intragenerational Influences on Adolescent Marijuana Use." *Journal of Social Issues,* 30 (2): 107–135.

Kandel, Denise B. 1978. "Convergences in Prospective Longitudinal Surveys on Drug Use in Normal Populations." In Denise B. Kandel (ed.), *Longitudinal Research on Drug Use.* Washington, D.C.: Hemisphere, pp. 3–38.

Kandel, Denise B. 1980a. "Drug and Drinking Behavior Among Youth." *Annual Review of Sociology,* 6: 235–285.

Kandel, Denise B. 1980b. "Developmental States in Adolescent Drug Involvement." In Dan J. Lettieri et al (eds.), *Theories on Drug Abuse.* Rockville, Md.: National Institute on Drug Abuse, pp. 120–127.

Kandel, Denise B. 1984. "Marijuana Users in Young Adulthood." *Archives of General Psychiatry,* 41 (February): 200–209.

Kandel, Denise B., Ronald C. Kessler, and Rebecca Z. Margulies. 1978. "Antecedents of Adolescent Initiation Into Stages of Drug Use: A Developmental Analysis." *Journal of Youth and Adolescence,* 7 (1): 13–40.

Kandel, Denise B., Debra Murphy, and Daniel Karus. 1985. "Cocaine Use in Young Adulthood: Patterns of Use and Psychosocial Correlates." In Nicholas J. Kozel and Edgar H. Adams (eds.), *Cocaine Use in America: Epidemiologic and Clinical Perspectives.* Rockville, Md.: National Institute on Drug Abuse, pp. 76–110.

Kaplan, Howard B. 1975. *Self-Attitudes and Deviant Behavior.* Pacific Palisades, Calif.: Goodyear.

Kaplan, Howard B. 1980. "Self-Esteem and Self-Derogation Theory of Drug Abuse." In Dan J. Lettieri et al. (eds.), *Theories on Drug Abuse.* Rockville, Md.: National Institute on Drug Abuse, pp. 128–131.

Kaplan, John. 1983. *The Hardest Drug: Heroin and Public Policy.* Chicago: University of Chicago Press.

Katz, Martin M. 1970. "The Psychological State Produced by the Hallucinogens." In J. R. Gamage and E. L. Zerkin (eds.), *Hallucinogenic Drug Research.* Beloit, Wisc.: STASH Press, pp. 11–23.

Keating, Brian. 1970. "Four Junkies." *The Village Voice,* April 2, p. 30.

Kerr, Peter. 1986a. "How Drugs Destroyed an Officer." *The New York Times,* August 8, pp. B1, B16.

Kerr, Peter. 1986b. "Growth in Heroin Use Ending as City Users Turn to Crack." *The New York Times,* September 13, pp. 1, 8.

Kerr, Peter. 1986c. "Anatomy of an Issue: Drugs, the Evidence, the Reaction." *The New York Times*, November 17, pp. A1, B6.

Kerr, Peter. 1986d. "Drug Tests Losing Most Court Cases." *The New York Times*, December 11, pp A1, D35.

Kerr, Peter. 1987a. "Crack Addiction: The Tragic Impact on Women and Children." *The New York Times*, February 9, pp. B1, B2.

Kerr, Peter. 1987b. "New Breed of Ethnic Gangs Smuggling Heroin." *The New York Times*, March 21, pp. 1, 31.

Kerr, Peter. 1987c. "Chinese Now Dominate New York Heroin Trade." *The New York Times*, August 9, pp. 1, 30.

Kerr, Peter. 1987d. "Rich vs. Poor: Drug Patterns Are Diverging." *The New York Times*, August 30, pp. 1, 28.

Kessler, Robert E. 1985. "New Smugglers on the Heroin Trail." *Newsday*, January 14, pp. 7, 20.

Ketcham, Diane. 1986. "Smoking Ban Gaining Acceptance: Widespread Compliance in Suffolk." *The New York Times*, March 16, Section 11, pp. 1, 14.

Kew, M. C. et al. 1969. "Possible Hepatotoxicity of Cannabis." *The Lancet*, March 15, pp. 578–579.

Kilborn, Peter T. 1979. "Tobacco: Profit Despite Attacks." *The New York Times*, January 25, pp. D1, D14.

Klee, G. D. 1963. "Lysergic Acid Diethylamide (LSD-25) and Ego Function." *Archives of General Psychiatry*, 8: 461–474.

Klein, Joe. 1985. "The New Drug They Call 'Ecstasy.' " *New York*, May 20, pp. 38–43.

Kleinman, Paula H., et al. 1977. "The Magic Fix: A Critical Analysis of Methadone Maintenance Treatment." *Social Problems*, 25 (December): 208–214.

Kleinman, Paula H., Eric D. Wish, Shreey Deren, Gregory Rainone, and Ellen Morehouse. 1987a. "Daily Marijuana Use and Problem Behaviors Among Adolescents." *The International Journal of the Addictions*, 22 (12).

Kleinman, Paula H., Douglas S. Goldsmith, Samuel R. Friedman, Conrad E. Mauge, William Hopkins, and Don C. Des Jarlais. 1987b. "Knowledge About Behaviors Affecting the Spread of AIDS: A Street Survey of Intravenous Drug Users and Their Associates in New York City." Unpublished paper presented to the Third International Conference on AIDS, Washington, D.C., June.

Kleinman, Paula H., et al. 1977. "The Magic Fix: A Critical Analysis of Methadone Maintenance Treatment." *Social Problems*, 25 (December): 208–214.

Kolansky, Harold, and William T. Moore. 1971. "Effects of Marihuana on Adolescents and Young Adults." *Journal of the American Medical Association*, 216 (April 19): 486–492.

Kolata, Gina. 1987. "Alcoholism: Genetic Links Grow Clearer." *The New York Times*, November 10, pp. C1, C2.

Kolb, Laurence, and A. G. DuMez. 1924. "The Prevalence and Trend of Drug Addiction in the United States and Factors Influencing It." *Public Health Reports*, 39 (23 May): 1179–1204.

Kolbert, Elizabeth. 1987. "Youths' Buying of Alcohol Fell in '86." *The New York Times*, February 13, p. B2.

Kolodny, Robert C., et al. 1974. "Depression of Plasma Testosterone Levels After Chronic Intensive Marihuana Use." *The New England Journal of Medicine*, 290 (April 18): 872–874.

Kramer, John. 1969. "An Introduction to Amphetamine Abuse." *Journal of Psychedelic Drugs*, 2 (Spring): 8–13.

Krohn, Marvin D., and James L. Massey. 1980. "Social Control and Delinquent Behavior: An Examination of the Elements of the Social Bond." *The Sociological Quarterly*, 21 (Autumn): 529–544.

Kuehnle, John. 1977. "Computed Tomographic Examination of Heavy Marijuana Smokers." *Journal of the American Medical Association*, 237 (March 21): 1231–1232.

LaBarre, Weston. 1964. *The Peyote Cult*. Hamden, Conn.: Shoe String Press.

Lang, John S., with Ronald A. Taylor. 1986. "America on Drugs." *U.S. News and World Report*, July 28, pp. 48–49.

Lasagna, Louis, J. M. von Felsinger, and H. K. Beecher. 1955. "Drug-Induced Changes in Man." *Journal of the American Medical Association*, 157 (March 19): 1006–1020.

Lau, R. Jane, et al. 1976. "Phytohemagglutinin-Induced Lymphocyte Transformation in Humans Receiving Δ9-Tetrahydrocannabinol." *Science*, 192 (21 May): 805–807.

Leary, Warren E. 1988. "13,000 Deaths a Year Indicated By Science Academy Radon Study." *The New York Times*, January 6, pp. A1, B5.

Lemberger, Louis, et al. 1970. "Marihuana: Studies on the Disposition and Metabolism of Delta-9-Tetrahydrocannabinol in Man." *Science*, 170 (18 December): 1320–1322.

Lemberger, Louis, et al. 1971. "Delta-9-Tetrahydrocannabinol: Metabolism and Disposition in Long-Term Marihuana Smokers." *Science*, 173 (2 July): 72–74.

Lender, Mark Edward, and James Kirby Martin. 1987. *Drinking in America: A History* (rev. ed.). New York: Free Press.

Lettieri, Dan J., Millie Sayers, and Helen Wallenstein Pearson (eds.) 1980. *Theories on Drug Abuse: Selected Contemporary Perspectives*. Rockville, Md.: National Institute on Drug Abuse.

Levinson, Martin H. 1982. "Legal Heroin: Good Idea 60 Years Overdue." *The New York Times*, December 12, p. E17.

Lindesmith, Alfred R. 1947. *Opiate Addiction*. Bloomington, Ind.: Principia Press.

Lindesmith, Alfred R. 1965. *The Addict and the Law*. Bloomington, Ind.: Indiana University Press.

Lindesmith, Alfred R. 1968. *Addiction and Opiates*. Chicago: Aldine.

Lindesmith, Alfred R. 1980. "A General Theory of Addiction to Opiate-Type Drugs." In Dan J. Lettieri et al. (eds.), *Theories on Drug Abuse*. Rockville, Md.: National Institute on Drug Abuse, pp. 34–37.

Lindesmith, Alfred R., and John H. Gagnon. 1964. "Anomie and Drug Addiction." In Marshall B. Clinard (ed.), *Anomie and Deviant Behavior: A Discussion and Critique*. New York: Free Press, pp. 158–188.

Little, Craig B. 1983. *Understanding Deviance and Control: Theory, Research and Social Policy*. Itasca, Ill.: Peacock.

Louria, Donald R. 1967. "Medical Complications Associated with Heroin Use." *International Journal of the Addictions*, 2 (Fall): 241–251.

Loya, F., N. H. Allen, and L. A. Vargas. 1986. "Homicide: Los Angeles, 1970–1979." *Morbidity and Mortality Weekly Report*, 35: 61–65.

Lyons, Richard D. 1983. "Physical and Mental Disabilities in Newborns Doubled in 25 Years." *The New York Times*, July 18, pp. A1, A10.

MacAndrew, Craig, and Robert B. Edgerton. 1969. *Drunken Comportment*. Chicago: Aldine.

Maddux, James F., and Charles L. Bowden. 1972. "Critique of Success with Methadone Maintenance. *American Journal of Psychiatry*, 129 (October): 440–446.

Malcolm, Andrew H. 1987. "Nation Is Gaining on Drunken Driving." *The New York Times,* March 23, pp. A1, A15.

Maltby, Karin. 1982. "Review Committee Clears Sobells on Scientific Misconduct Charges." *The Journal* (Addiction Research Foundation, Toronto), December 1, p. 2.

Manis, Jerome G. 1974. "Assessing the Seriousness of Social Problems." *Social Problems,* 22 (October): 1–15.

Manis, Jerome G. 1976. *Analyzing Social Problems.* New York: Praeger.

Mann, Peggy, 1979. "Marijuana Alert I: Brain and Sex Damage." *Reader's Digest,* December, pp. 139–146.

Mann, Peggy. 1980. "Marijuana Alert II: More of the Grim Story." *Reader's Digest,* November, pp. 65–71.

Mann, Peggy. 1981. "Marijuana Alert III: The Devastation of Personality." *Reader's Digest,* December, pp. 81–85.

Mann, Peggy. 1985. *Marijuana Alert.* New York: McGraw-Hill.

Mann, Peggy. 1987. *Marijuana: The Myth of Harmlessness Goes Up in Smoke.* Indianapolis, Ind.: Medical Education and Research Foundation.

Marx, Gary T. 1986. "Drug Foes Aren't High on Civil Liberties." *The New York Times,* February 24, p. A15.

Marx, Karl. 1906. *Capital: A Critique of Political Economy* (trans. Samuel Moore and Edward Aveling). New York: Charles H. Kerr.

Mauss, Armand L. 1975. *Social Problems as Social Movements.* Philadelphia: Lippincott.

McAuliffe, William E. 1975. "A Second Look at First Effects: The Subjective Effects of Opiates on Nonaddicts." *Journal of Drug Issues,* 5 (Fall): 369–399.

McAuliffe, William E. 1983. "Recreational Opiate Addiction in a Dentist and a Nurse." In Louis S. Harris (ed.), *Problems of Drug Dependence, 1982.* Rockville, Md.: National Institute on Drug Abuse, pp. 356–362.

McAuliffe, William E., and Robert A. Gordon. 1974. "A Test of Lindesmith's Theory of Addiction: The Frequency of Euphoria Among Long-Term Addicts." *American Journal of Sociology,* 79 (January): 795–840.

McAuliffe, William E., and Robert A. Gordon. 1980. "Reinforcement and the Combination of Effects: Summary of a Theory of Opiate Addiction." In Dan J. Lettieri et al. (eds.), *Theories on Drug Abuse.* Rockville, Md.: National Institute on Drug Abuse, pp. 137–141.

McAuliffe, William E., et al. 1984. "Psychoactive Drug Use by Young and Future Physicians." *Journal of Health and Social Behavior,* 25 (March): 34–54.

McAuliffe, William E., et al. 1986. "Psychoactive Drug Use Among Practicing Physicians and Medical Students." *The New England Journal of Medicine,* 315 (September 25): 805–810.

McBee, Susanna. 1985. "Flood of Drugs—A Losing Battle." *U.S. News and World Report,* March 25, pp. 52–57.

McClosley, Herbert, and Alida Brill. 1983. *Dimensions of Tolerance: What Most Americans Believe About Civil Liberties.* New York: Russell Sage Foundation.

McFadden, Robert D. 1988. "Drug Cases Top Others in Prisons." *The New York Times,* January 5, pp. B1, B2.

McGlothlin, William H., and Louis J. West. 1968. "The Marijuana Problem: An Overview." *American Journal of Psychiatry,* 125 (September): 370–378.

McKinley, James. 1978. "The Pusher in the Gray Flannel Suit." *Playboy,* September, pp. 165–166, 178–180, 226–230.

Mendelson, Jack H., and Nancy Mello. 1985. *Alcohol Use and Abuse in America.* Boston: Little, Brown.

Mendelson, Jack H., et al. 1974. "Plasma Testosterone Levels Before, During, and After Chronic Marihuana Smoking." *The New England Journal of Medicine,* 291 (November 14): 1051–1055.

Merton, Robert K. 1938. "Social Structure and Anomie." *American Sociological Review,* 3 (October): 672–682.

Merton, Robert K. 1957. *Social Theory and Social Structure* (rev. ed.). New York: Free Press.

Merton, Robert K. 1968. *Social Theory and Social Structure* (enlarged ed.). New York: Free Press.

Mikuriya, Tod. 1969. "Historical Aspects of *Cannabis Sativa* in Western Medicine." *The New Physician,* 18 (November): 902–908.

Miller, Judith Droitcour, et al. 1983. *National Survey on Drug Abuse: Main Findings 1982.* Rockville, Md.: National Institute on Drug Abuse.

Miller, Judith Droitcour, and Ira H. Cisin. 1980. *Highlights From the National Survey on Drug Abuse: 1979.* Rockville, Md.: National Institute on Drug Abuse.

Mills, James. 1986. "The Simplest Way to Fight Drugs." *The New York Times,* September 5, p. A27.

Mills, James. 1987. *The Underground Empire: Where Crime and Governments Embrace.* New York: Dell.

Modlin, Herbert C., and Alberto Montes. 1964. "Narcotic Addiction in Physicians." *American Journal of Psychiatry,* 121 (October): 358–365.

Moffett, Arthur D., and Carl D. Chambers. 1970. "The Hidden Addiction." *Social Work,* 15 (July): 54–59.

Moise, Lionel Calhoun. 1937. "Marijuana: Sex-Crazing Drug Menace." *Physical Culture,* February, pp. 18–19, 87–89.

Molotsky, Irvin. 1985a. "Changing Patterns in Prescriptions in U.S." *The New York Times,* March 16, p. 48.

Molotsky, Irvin. 1985b. "Smokers' Ills Cost Billions, U.S. Says." *The New York Times,* September 16, p. A13.

Morishima, Akira. 1984. "Effects of Cannabis and Natural Cannabinoids on Chromosomes and Ova." In Monique C. Braude and Jacqueline P. Ludford (eds.), *Marijuana Effects on the Endocrine and Reproductive Systems.* Rockville, Md.: National Institute on Drug Abuse, pp. 25–45.

Morris, Robert R. 1985. "Human Pulmonary Histopathological Changes from Marijuana Smoking." *Journal of Forensic Sciences,* 30 (April): 345–349.

Munch, James C. 1966. "Marihuana and Crime." *Bulletin on Narcotics,* 18 (April-June): 15–22.

Murphy, Sheigla, Craig Reinarman, and Dan Waldorf. 1986. "An 11-Year Follow-Up of Twenty-Seven Cocaine Users." Unpublished paper presented at the 36th Annual Meetings of the Society for the Study of Social Problems, New York City, August.

Musto, David F. 1973. *The American Disease: Origins of Narcotic Control.* New Haven, Conn.: Yale University Press.

Nahas, Gabriel G. 1973, 1975. *Marihuana—Deceptive Weed* (1st ed., 1973; 2nd ed., 1975). New York: Raven Press.

Nahas, Gabriel G. 1976. *Keep Off the Grass.* New York: Reader's Digest Press.

Nahas, Gabriel G., et al. 1974. "Inhibition of Cellular Immunity in Marihuana Smokers." *Science,* 183 (1 February): 419–420.

National Institute on Drug Abuse (NIDA). 1982. *Marijuana and Health, Ninth Report to the U. S. Congress from the Secretary of Health and Human Services.* Washington, D.C.: U.S. Government Printing Office.

National Institute on Drug Abuse (NIDA). 1986. "Highlights of the 1985 National Household Survey on Drug Abuse." Rockville, Md.: National Institute on Drug Abuse.

National Organization for the Reform of Marijuana Laws (NORML). 1987. "Marijuana in America: NORML's 1986 Domestic Crop Report." *Common Sense for America,* 2 (Spring): pp. 11–12, 23, 26–33.

New York Academy of Medicine. 1963. "Report on Drug Addiction." *Bulletin of the New York Academy of Medicine,* 39: 417–473.

Newmeyer, John A. 1980. "The Epidemiology of PCP Use in the Late 1970s." *Journal of Psychedelic Drugs,* 12 (July–September): 211–215.

Nichols, W. W., et al. 1974. "Cytogenic Studies on Human Subjects Receiving Marijuana and Δ9-Tetrahydrocannabinol." *Mutation Research,* 26: 413–417.

NIDA, *see* National Institute on Drug Abuse.

Nizer, Louis. 1986. "How About Low-Cost Drugs for Addicts? *The New York Times,* June 8, p. E23.

NORML, *see* National Organization for the Reform of Marijuana Laws.

O'Donnell, John A., and Richard R. Clayton. 1982. "The Stepping-Stone Hypothesis—Marijuana, Heroin and Causality." *Chemical Dependencies: Behavioral and Biomedical Issues,* 4 (3): 229–241.

O'Donnell, John A., Harwin L. Voss, Richard R. Clayton, Gerald T. Slatin, and Robin G. W. Room. 1976. *Young Men and Drugs—A Nationwide Study.* Rockville, Md.: National Institute on Drug Abuse.

Palmer, Stuart, and Arnold S. Linsky (eds.). 1972. *Rebellion and Retreat: Readings in the Forms and Processes of Deviance.* Columbus, Ohio: Charles E. Merrill.

Pendery, Mary L., Irving M. Maltzman, and L. Jolyon West. 1982. "Controlled Drinking by Alcoholics? New Findings and a Reevaluation of a Major Affirmative Study." *Science,* 217 (9 July): 169–175.

Petersen, Robert C. 1979. "Statement on Cocaine." Unpublished statement delivered before the Select Committee on Narcotics Abuse and Control, House of Representatives, Washington D.C., July 24.

Petersen, Robert C. (ed.). 1980. *Marijuana Research Findings: 1980.* Rockville, Md.: National Institute on Drug Abuse.

Peyrot, Mark. 1984. "Cycles of Social Problem Development: The Case of Drug Abuse." *The Sociological Quarterly,* 25 (Winter): 83–96.

Polich, J. Michael, David J. Armor, and Harriet B. Braiker. 1980. *The Course of Alcoholism: Four Years After Treatment.* Santa Monica, Calif.: Rand Corporation.

Preble, Edward, and John J. Casey, Jr. 1969. "Taking Care of Business—The Heroin Addict's Life on the Street." *International Journal of the Addictions,* 4 (March): 145–169.

Preble, Edward, and Thomas Miller. 1977. "Methadone, Wine, and Welfare." In Robert S. Weppner (ed.), *Street Ethnography: Selected Studies of Crime and Drug Use in Natural Settings.* Beverly Hills, Calif.: Sage, pp. 229–248.

Radosevich, Marcia, Lonn Lanza-Kaduce, Ronald L. Akers, and Marvin D. Krohn. 1980. "The Sociology of Adolescent Drug and Drinking Behavior: Part II." *Deviant Behavior,* 1 (January-March): 145–169.

Ravenholt, R. T. 1984. "Addiction Mortality in the United States, 1980: Tobacco, Alcohol, and Other Substances." *Population and Developmental Review,* 10 (December): 697–724.

Ravo, Nick. 1987. "Drinking Age Is Said to Fail for Students." *The New York Times*, December 21, pp. A1, B15.

Ray, Oakley. 1983. *Drugs, Society, and Human Behavior* (3rd ed.). St. Louis: Mosby.

Ray, Oakley, and Charles Ksir. 1987. *Drugs, Society, and Human Behavior* (4th ed.). St. Louis: Times-Mirror/Mosby.

Reasons, Charles. 1974. "The Politics of Drugs: An Inquiry in the Sociology of Social Problems." *The Sociological Quarterly*, 15 (Summer): 381–404.

Reinhold, Robert. 1980. "Tranquilizer Prescriptions Drop Sharply; So Does Reported Incidence of Abuse." *The New York Times*, September 9, pp. C1, C6.

Rickert, William S., Jack Robinson, and Byron Rogers. 1982. "A Comparison of Tar, Carbon Monoxide and pH Levels in Smoke from Marihuana and Tobacco Cigarettes." *Canadian Journal of Public Health*, 73 (November/December): 386–391.

Riding, Alan. 1988. "Intimidated Colombian Courts Yield to Drug Barons." *The New York Times*, January 11, p. A3.

Roberts, Marjory. 1986. "MDMA: 'Madness, not Ecstasy.'" *Psychology Today*, June, pp. 14–15.

Robins, Lee N. 1973. *The Vietnam Veteran Returns*. Washington, D.C.: U.S. Government Printing Office.

Robins, Lee N. 1979. "Addict Careers." In Robert I. Dupont et al. (eds.), *Handbook on Drug Abuse*. Washington, D.C.: U.S. Government Printing Office, pp. 325–336.

Robins, Lee N. 1980. "The Natural History of Drug Abuse." In Dan J. Lettieri et al. (eds.), *Theories on Drug Abuse*. Rockville, Md.: National Institute on Drug Abuse, pp. 215–224.

Robins, Lee N., Darlene H. Davis, and Donald W. Goodwin. 1974. "Drug Use by U.S. Army Enlisted Men in Vietnam: A Follow-Up on Their Return Home." *American Journal of Epidemiology*, 99 (4): 235–249.

Robins, Lee N., John E. Helzer, and Darlene H. Davis. 1975. "Narcotic Use in Southeast Asia and Afterward." *Archives of General Psychiatry*, 32 (August): 955–961.

Robins, Lee N., and George E. Murphy. 1967. "Drug Use in a Normal Population of Young Negro Men." *American Journal of Public Health*, 57 (September): 1580–1596.

Robins, Lee N., and Eric Wish. 1977. "Childhood Deviance as a Developmental Process: A Study of 223 Urban Black Men From Birth to 18." *Social Forces*, 56 (December): 448–473.

Rosenbaum, Marsha. 1981. *Women on Heroin*. New Brunswick, N.J.: Rutgers University Press.

Rosenblatt, Jean. 1982. "Prescription Drug Abuse." *Editorial Research Reports*, 1 (June 11): 431–448.

Rowell, Earle, and Robert Rowell. 1939. *On the Trail of Marihuana: The Weed of Madness*. Mountain View, Calif.: Pacific Press Publishing Association.

Schmeck, Harold M., Jr. 1987. "Million Victims of AIDS Predicted by Year 2000." *The New York Times*, March 4, p. A20.

Schmidt, William E. 1987. "High AIDS Rate Spurring Efforts for Minorities." *The New York Times*, August 2, pp. 1, 26.

Schneider, Joseph W. 1985. "Social Problems Theory: The Constructionist View." *Annual Review of Sociology*, 11: 209–229.

Schrag, Peter. 1978. "Mind Control." *Playboy*, May, pp. 135–138, 175–178.

Schuckit, Marc A. 1980. "A Theory of Alcohol and Drug Abuse: A Genetic Approach." In Dan J Lettieri et al (eds.), *Theories on Drug Abuse*. Rockville, Md.: National Institute on Drug Abuse, pp. 297–302.

Schuckit, Marc A. 1984. *Drug and Alcohol Abuse: A Clinical Guide to Diagnosis and Treatment* (2nd ed.). New York: Plenum.

Schuckit, Marc A. 1985. "Overview: Epidemiology of Alcoholism." In Marc A. Schuckit (ed.), *Alcohol Patterns and Problems.* New Brunswick, N.J.: Rutgers University Press, pp. 1–42.

Schultes, Richard Evans. 1969. "Hallucinogens of Plant Origin." *Science,* 163 (17 January): 245–254.

Schultes, Richard Evans, and Albert Hofmann. 1979. *Plants of the Gods: Origins of Hallucinogenic Use.* New York: McGraw-Hill.

Schur, Edwin M. 1980. *The Politics of Deviance.* Englewood Cliffs, N.J.: Prentice-Hall/ Spectrum.

Schwartz, Conrad J. 1969. "Toward a Medical Understanding of Marijuana." *Canadian Psychiatric Association Journal,* 14 (December): 591–600.

Serrin, William. 1986. "Drug Tests Promote Safety, Many Say." *The New York Times,* September 16, p. A16.

Shupe, Lloyd M. 1954. "Alcohol and Crime." *Journal of Criminal Law, Criminology, and Police Science,* 44 (January-February): 661–664.

Siegel, Ronald K. 1978, "Phencyclidine, Criminal Behavior, and the Defense of Diminished Capacity." In Robert C. Petersen and Richard C. Stillman (eds.), *Phencyclidine (PCP) Abuse: An Appraisal.* Rockville, Md.: National Institute on Drug Abuse, pp. 272–288.

Siegel, Ronald K. 1984. "Changing Patterns of Cocaine Use: Longitudinal Observations, Consequences, and Treatment." In John Grabowski (ed.), *Cocaine: Pharmacology, Effects, and Treatment of Abuse.* Rockville, Md.: National Institute on Drug Abuse, pp. 92–110.

Single, Eric W. 1981. "The Impact of Marijuana Decriminalization." In Yedy Israel et al. (eds.), *Research Advances in Alcohol and Drug Problems,* Vol. 6. New York: Plenum, pp. 405–424.

Slater, Philip. 1970. *The Pursuit of Loneliness.* Boston: Beacon Press.

Slotkin, James S. 1956. *The Peyote Religion.* New York: Free Press.

Slovic, Paul, Baruch Fischoff, and Sarah Lichtenstein. 1980. "Risky Assumptions." *Psychology Today,* June, pp. 44–48.

Smith, David E., and Richard B. Seymour. 1982. "Clinical Perspectives on the Toxicity of Marijuana." In *Marijuana and Youth: Clinical Observations on Motivation and Learning.* Washington, D.C.: U.S. Government Printing Office, pp. 61–72.

Smith, Gene M., and Charles P. Fogg. 1977. "Psychological Antecedents of Teenage Drug Use." In Roberta G. Simmons (ed.), *Research in Community and Mental Health: An Annual Compilation of Research,* Vol. 1. Greenwich, Conn.: JAI Press, pp. 87–102.

Smith, Gene M., and Charles P. Fogg. 1978. "Psychological Predictors of Early Use, Late Use, and Nonuse of Marijuana Among Teenage Students." In Denise B. Kandel (ed.), *Longitudinal Research on Drug Use: Empirical Findings and Methodological Issues.* Washington, D.C.: Hemisphere, pp. 101–113.

Smith, Jean-Paul. 1967. "LSD: The False Illusion." *FDA Papers,* July-August.

Smith, Roger. 1969. "The World of the Haight-Ashbury Speed Freak." *Journal of Psychedelic Drugs,* 2 (Spring): 77–83.

Smith, William French. 1982. "Drug Traffic Today—Challenge and Response." *Drug Enforcement,* Summer, pp. 2–6.

Snyder, Solomon H. 1970. "Introduction." In J. R. Gamage and E. L. Zerkin (eds.), *Hallucinogenic Drug Research.* Beloit, Wisc.: STASH Press, pp. xiii–xvi.

Sobell, Mark B., and Linda C. Sobell. 1978. *Behavioral Treatment of Alcohol Problems: Individualized Therapy and Controlled Drinking.* New York: Plenum.

Sobell, Mark B., and Linda C. Sobell. 1984. "The Aftermath of Heresy: A Response to Pendery et al.'s (1982) Critique of 'Individualized Behavior Therapy for Alcoholics.' " *Behavior Research and Therapy,* 22 (4): 413–440.

Spector, Malcolm, and John I. Kitsuse. 1977. *Constructing Social Problems.* Menlo Park, Calif.: Cummings.

Stenchever, Morton A., Terry J. Kunysz, and Marjorie A. Allen. 1974. "Chromosome Breakage in Users of Marijuana." *American Journal of Obstetrics and Gynecology,* 118 (January): 106–113.

Stevens, William K. 1987. "Deaths From Drunken Driving Increase." *The New York Times,* October 29, p. A18.

Stone, Michael. 1987. "Q. and A. on AIDS." *New York,* March 23, pp. 34–43.

Straus, Robert. 1976. "Alcoholism and Problem Drinking." In Robert K. Merton and Robert Nisbet (eds.), *Contemporary Social Problems* (4th ed.). New York: Harcourt Brace Jovanovich, pp. 181–217.

Sugarman, Barry. 1974. *Daytop Village: A Therapeutic Community.* New York: Holt, Rinehart & Winston.

Sullivan, Ronald. 1987. "AIDS in New York City Killing More Drug Users." *The New York Times,* October 22, pp. B1, B4.

Sutherland, Edwin H. 1939. *Principles of Criminology* (3rd ed.). Philadelphia: Lippincott.

Sutter, Alan G. 1966. "The World of the Righteous Dope Fiend." *Issues in Criminology,* 2 (Fall): 177–222.

Sutter, Alan G. 1969. "Worlds of Drug Use on the Street Scene." In Donald R. Cressey and David A. Ward (eds.), *Delinquency, Crime, and Social Process.* New York: Harper & Row, pp. 802–829.

Talbott, John A. and James W. Teague. 1969. "Marijuana Psychosis: Acute Toxic Psychosis Associated with the Use of Cannabis Derivatives." *Journal of the American Medical Association,* 210 (October 13): 299–302.

Tart, Charles T. 1971. *On Being Stoned: A Psychological Study of Marijuana Intoxication.* Palo Alto, Calif.: Science & Behavior Books.

Tashkin, Donald P., Bertrand J. Shapiro, Y. Enoch Lee, and Charles E. Harper. 1976. "Subacute Effects of Heavy Marihuana Smoking on Pulmonary Function in Healthy Men." *The New England Journal of Medicine,* 294 (January 15): 125–129.

Tennes, K., et al. 1985. "Marijuana: Prenatal and Postnatal Exposure in the Human." In T. M. Pinkert (ed.), *Current Research on Consequences of Maternal Drug Abuse.* Rockville, Md.: National Institute on Drug Abuse, pp. 48–60.

Terry, Charles E., and Mildred Pellens. 1928. *The Opium Problem.* New York: Bureau of Social Hygiene.

Tinklenberg, Jared R. 1973. "Drugs and Crime." In National Commission on Marihuana and Drug Abuse, *Drug Use in America: Problem in Perspective,* Vol. 1. Washington, D.C.: U.S. Government Printing Office, pp. 242–299.

Tinklenberg, Jared R., et al. 1974. "Drug Involvement in Criminal Assaults by Adolescents." *Archives of General Psychiatry,* 30 (May): 685–689.

The Tobacco Institute. 1982. "About Tobacco Smoke." Washington, D.C.: The Tobacco Institute.

The Tobacco Institute. n.d. *Tobacco: Deeply Rooted in America's Heritage.* Washington, D.C.: The Tobacco Institute.

Trebach, Arnold S. 1982. *The Heroin Solution.* New Haven, Conn.: Yale University Press.

Trebach, Arnold S. 1987. *The Great Drug War: And Radical Proposals That Could Make America Safe Again.* New York: Macmillan.

Truscott, Lucian K., IV. 1971. "The Return to Cool." *The Village Voice,* June 19, p. 9.

Ungerleider, J. Thomas, George D. Lundberg, Irving Sunshine, and Clifford B. Walberg. 1980. "The Drug Abuse Warning Network (DAWN) Program." *Archives of General Psychiatry,* 37 (January): 106–109.

Ungerleider, J. Thomas, et al. 1968. "The Bad Trip: The Etiology of the Adverse LSD Reaction." *The American Journal of Psychiatry,* 124 (May): 1483–1490.

Vaillant, George E., Jane R. Bright, and Charles MacArthur. 1970. "Physicians' Use of Mood-Altering Drugs." *The New England Journal of Medicine,* 282 (February 12): 365–370.

Van Dyke, Craig, and Robert Byck. 1982. "Cocaine." *Scientific American,* March, pp. 128–141.

Veteran's Administration. 1970. *Drug Treatment in Psychiatry.* Washington, D.C.: U.S. Government Printing Office.

Voss, Harwin L., and John R. Hepburn. 1968. "Patterns in Criminal Homicide in Chicago." *Journal of Criminal Law, Criminology, and Police Science,* 59 (December): 499–508.

Voth, Harold M. 1982. "Discussion Highlights: Cohen/Halikas et al." In *Marijuana and Youth: Clinical Observations on Motivation and Learning.* Washington, D.C.: U.S. Government Printing Office, pp. 23–26.

Wald, Matthew L. 1986. "Battle Against Drunken Driving Should Focus on Alcoholics, Experts Say." *The New York Times,* January 3, p. 5.

Walker, Samuel. 1985. *Sense and Nonsense About Crime: A Policy Guide.* Monterey, Calif.: Brooks/Cole.

Weil, Andrew, and Winifred Rosen. 1983. *Chocolate to Morphine: Understanding Mind-Active Drugs.* Boston: Houghton Mifflin.

Weil, Andrew T., Norman E. Zinberg, and Judith M. Nelsen. 1968. "Clinical and Psychological Effects of Marihuana in Man." *Science,* 162 (13 December): 1234–1242.

Weiner, Norman. 1985. "Norepinephrine, Epinephrine, and the Sympathomimetic Amines." In Alfred Goodman Gilman et al. (eds.), *Goodman and Gilman's The Pharmacological Basis of Therapeutics* (7th ed.). New York: Macmillan, pp. 145–160.

Weinswig, Melvin H., and Dale W. Doerr (eds.). 1968. *Drug Abuse: A Course for Educators.* Indianapolis, Ind.: Butler College of Pharmacy.

Wesson, Donald R., and David E. Smith. 1977. "Cocaine: Its Use for Central Nervous System Stimulation Including Recreational and Medical Use." In Robert C. Petersen and Richard C. Stillman (eds.), *Cocaine 1977.* Rockville, Md.: National Institute on Drug Abuse, pp. 137–152.

White, Steven C., et al. 1975. "Mitogen-Induced Blastogenic Responses of Lymphocyctes from Marihuana Smokers." *Science,* 188 (4 April): 71–72.

Whitehead, Alfred North. 1948. *Science and the Modern World.* New York: Mentor.

Wiatrowski, Michael D., David B. Griswold, and Mary K. Roberts. 1981. "Social Control Theory and Delinquency." *American Sociological Review,* 46 (October): 525–541.

Wikler, Abraham. 1968. "Drug Addiction: Organic and Physiological Aspects." *International Encyclopedia of the Social Sciences.* New York: Macmillan, pp. 290–298.

Wikler, Abraham. 1970. "Clinical and Social Aspects of Marihuana Intoxication." *Archives of General Psychiatry,* 23 (October): 320–325.

Wikler, Abraham. 1980. "A Theory of Opioid Dependence." In Dan J. Lettieri et al.

(eds.), *Theories on Drug Abuse.* Rockville, Md.: National Institute on Drug Abuse, pp. 174–178.

Williams, A. F., M. A. Peat, and D. S. Crouch. 1985. "Drugs in Fatally Injured Young Male Drivers." *Pharm Chem Newsletter,* 14: 1–11.

Williams, Hubert. 1986. "Every Narcotics User Is a Scourge and a Bum." *Newsday,* November 9, Ideas Section, p. 11.

Willis, J. H. 1969. *Drug Dependence.* London: Faber & Faber.

Winick, Charles. 1961. "Physician Narcotic Addicts." *Social Problems,* 9 (Fall): 174–181.

Wish, Eric D. 1986. "PCP and Crime: Just Another Illicit Drug?" In Doris H. Clouet (ed.), *Phencyclidine: An Update.* Rockville, Md.: National Institute on Drug Abuse, pp. 174–189.

Wolfgang, Marvin. 1958. *Patterns in Criminal Homicide.* Philadelphia: University of Pennsylvania Press.

Wurmser, Leon. 1980. "Drug Use as a Protective System." In Dan J. Lettieri et al. (eds.), *Theories on Drug Abuse.* Rockville, Md.: National Institute on Drug Abuse, pp. 71–74.

Yamaguchi, Kazuo, and Denise B. Kandel. 1985. "On the Resolution of Role Incompatibility: A Life Event History Analysis of Family Roles and Marijuana Use." *American Journal of Sociology,* 90 (May): 1284–1325.

Yesavage, Jerome A., Von Otto Leirer, Mark Denari, and Leo Hollister. 1985. "Carry-Over Effects of Marijuana Intoxication on Aircraft Pilot Performance: A Preliminary Report." *American Journal of Psychiatry,* 142 (November): 1325–1329.

Yin, Peter P. 1980. "Fear of Crime Among the Elderly: Some Issues and Suggestions." *Social Problems,* 27 (April): 492–504.

Young, Jock. 1971. *The Drugtakers.* London: MacGibbon & Kee.

Zinberg, Norman E. 1984. *Drug, Set, and Setting: The Basis for Controlled Intoxicant Use.* New Haven, Conn.: Yale University Press.

Zion, Sidney. 1985. "Give Drugs to Junkies." *The New York Times,* September 10, p. A27.

Zito, Tom. 1972. "Sopors: Downs as a Drug Fad." *Washington Post,* May 19, pp. B1, B5.

Zwerdling, Daniel. 1972. "Methaqualone: The 'Safe' Drug That Isn't Very." *Washington Post,* November 12, p. B3.

AUTHOR INDEX

SUBJECT INDEX

About the Author

Erich Goode is Professor of Sociology at the State University of New York at Stony Brook. A graduate of Oberlin College, he received his Ph.D. from Columbia University. He has previously taught at Columbia, New York University, and the University of North Carolina at Chapel Hill. His areas of specialization are criminology, deviance, the sociology of drug use, sexual behavior, and the sociology of obesity. Dr. Goode served as a consultant to the National Commission on Marihuana and Drug Abuse in the 1970s. He is the author of *The Marijuana Smokers, The Drug Phenomenon,* and *Deviant Behavior;* the editor of *Marijuana;* and a contributor to a wide variety of both scholarly and popular journals and periodicals, such as *American Journal of Sociology, Social Problems, Nature, American Journal of Psychiatry, The New York Times, The Charlotte Observer,* and the *Chicago Sun-Times.* Dr. Goode is a recipient of the Guggenheim Fellowship.

A Note on the Type

This book was set in a digitized version of Baskerville, originally a recutting of a typeface designed by John Baskerville (1706–1775). Baskerville, a writing master in Birmingham, England, began experimenting about 1750 with type design and punch-cutting. His first book, set throughout in his new types, was a Virgil in royal quarto published in 1757, and this was followed by other famous editions from his press. Baskerville's types were a forerunner of what we know today as the "modern" group of typefaces.